# Falun Gong and the
# Future of China

# Falun Gong and the Future of China

DAVID OWNBY

UNIVERSITY PRESS

2008

# OXFORD
UNIVERSITY PRESS

Oxford University Press, Inc., publishes works that further
Oxford University's objective of excellence
in research, scholarship, and education.

Oxford   New York
Auckland   Cape Town   Dar es Salaam   Hong Kong   Karachi
Kuala Lumpur   Madrid   Melbourne   Mexico City   Nairobi
New Delhi   Shanghai   Taipei   Toronto

With offices in
Argentina   Austria   Brazil   Chile   Czech Republic   France   Greece
Guatemala   Hungary   Italy   Japan   Poland   Portugal   Singapore
South Korea   Switzerland   Thailand   Turkey   Ukraine   Vietnam

Published by Oxford University Press, Inc.
198 Madison Avenue, New York, New York 10016

www.oup.com

Oxford is a registered trademark of Oxford University Press

Library of Congress Cataloging-in-Publication Data
Ownby, David, 1958–
Falun Gong and the future of China / David Ownby.
p. cm.
Includes bibliographical references and index.
ISBN 978-0-19-532905-6
1. Falun Gong (Organization).   2. Qi gong—Political aspects—China.   I. Title.
BP605.F36O96 2008
299.5'1—dc22      2007032423

9 8 7 6 5 4 3 2 1

Printed in the United States of America
on acid-free paper

# Preface

Although this book has been too long in gestation, I will be sad to see it leave the nest, for never have I more enjoyed working on a project. Like many of my colleagues, I have long dreamed of finding a subject which would enable me to bring my training to bear on something larger, less arcane, more immediately *useful* than the academic exercise of Chinese history sometimes seems to be. For me, Falun Gong has been that subject; it has allowed me to combine historical research with social science fieldwork among Falun Gong practitioners, reflections on China's past with concerns for China's future—all in the context of a human drama of considerable contemporary import. The reader will be the final judge of the value of this work, but for my part it has been gratifying to feel that I found and sustained my voice through the years of work and hundreds of pages of writing required to bring the project to fruition.

If I allow myself this small moment of self-congratulation, it is because I know only too well that many readers will not appreciate this book at all. Falun Gong practitioners will be disappointed by my "objective" appraisal of their master and his teachings, for if my book is not harshly critical of Li Hongzhi, neither is it laudatory. They will be doubly upset by my choice not to focus my narrative on the issue of human rights, despite its obvious relevance. Chinese authorities, and others who share the Chinese authorities' views of Falun Gong, will undoubtedly find that I have been too soft on Falun Gong and too quick to dismiss out of hand the arguments of the

Chinese state concerning the supposed dangers the group represents. The casual reader who picks up this book in the hope of learning whether Falun Gong is indeed a "cult" will probably be disappointed as well, or will at least lose patience with my seemingly endless contextualizations.

At the risk of losing certain readers, I should perhaps be clear from the outset about what this book is *not*.

First, this book is not a defense of Falun Gong doctrine and practice. As a scholar, one of my primary goals has been to arrive at a sympathetic understanding of Falun Gong practitioners and their beliefs, one uncolored by prior value judgments, and over the course of my fieldwork among North American practitioners, I came to respect and even admire many of them. In addition, I believe as a matter of principle that all people have the right to their religious convictions as long as these convictions do no harm to other people, and as long as they do not foist them on me. Having been raised as a Southern Baptist fundamentalist in Bible Belt Tennessee (and later breaking with that tradition) probably prepared me in certain ways to spend time with people who are intensely passionate about their religious beliefs. On the one hand, the moralistic overtones of Falun Gong doctrine resonate with my personal experience and earliest memories of religiosity, even if a world of difference separates the Protestant rural South of the 1960s and 1970s from the post-socialist urban Chinese landscape which gave rise to qigong and Falun Gong in the 1980s and 1990s. On the other hand, I learned long ago that perfectly normal people can hold seemingly strange beliefs, and thus had little trouble with Falun Gong computer scientists who also believe in demonic possession. I think of my cousin Donna, who often prayed for "guidance" while lost at the wheel of her car; Donna was not known for her punctuality (but we loved her anyway).

But a sympathetic understanding of Falun Gong is not the same as acceptance of Falun Gong beliefs, and I am not now nor have I ever been a practitioner. I have read Li Hongzhi's writings many, many times, not because they speak to me personally—they do not—but in order to try to understand why they might be attractive to people I know and respect. I have attempted (less frequently) to do Falun Gong physical exercises, but found that while the abstract idea of meditation might be alluring, the concrete practice can be deadly dull. I once appeared as an expert witness on the side of Falun Gong in a libel case brought by local Falun Gong practitioners against a Montreal Chinese newspaper. The rather pompous lawyer for the newspaper huffily asked me, in cross-examination, if I, as an educated person, did not find some of Li Hongzhi's statements patently ridiculous. My response was that, at least in matters of religious belief, "ridiculous" is in the eye of the beholder and that, in any event, I would not choose to live in a society where people did not have the right to believe silly things. This is my response to those who may object that I am not sufficiently critical of Falun Gong beliefs and practices.

Second, this book is not an exposé, an insider account which "rips the veil" off Li Hongzhi and the inner workings of Falun Gong. I have seen Li Hongzhi in person twice and have spent considerable time with people who have worked in close collaboration with Li (such as Zhang Erping, Li's translator and spokesperson in Li's early days in America, who remains very active in Falun Gong). I have spent a good deal of time at Falun Gong experience-sharing conferences and other events. I have interviewed local Falun Gong "leaders" (I put the word in quotation marks because there is no formal leadership structure and thus no titles accorded to local organizers). But I have learned little about the upper reaches of Falun Gong organization and thus have little to say about questions of money or connections between Li and various governments around the world (I am often asked by worldly cynics whether Li is financed by the CIA).

To some extent, I would say that there is less mystery here than meets the eye, in the sense that Falun Gong is quite decentralized, and local practitioners seem to be largely autonomous and to receive little direction from above. In addition, most Falun Gong events and activities require relatively little in the way of financing and organization. It is hardly beyond the means of a group of several hundred people to pool their resources to rent, say, a banquet hall at a local hotel for a weekend meeting and charter buses to bring in practitioners from elsewhere. On the other hand, this may have become less true over time. Falun Gong Web sites have become increasingly sophisticated, and their creation, updating, and maintenance must require more than a little investment (although many Falun Gong practitioners in North America are in the computer industry and thus can presumably provide the expertise without charge). I have been unsuccessful in my efforts to find out more about the Web sites, their organization, and their financing—and this in spite of repeated inquiries and in spite of being recognized as someone who is "friendly" to Falun Gong. In 2002, a Falun Gong–affiliated television station, New Tang Dynasty, was set up in New York. It is a nonprofit enterprise, broadcasting via satellite, and one cannot but wonder where the money comes from. More recently still, such undertakings as the Falun Gong–affiliated newspaper, the *Epoch Times*, clearly require considerable financial backing and worldwide organization. To my knowledge, no newspaper has ever met a deadline by relying on decentralized local practitioners.

I have, of course, asked myself how it would change my views if I were to discover that Li Hongzhi was financed by the Central Intelligence Agency, or the government of Taiwan, or by any other anti-Communist or anti-Chinese group—none of which I suppose is beyond the realm of possibility (Chinese authorities have linked their anti–Falun Gong campaign to the war on terror, which does seem to strain credibility). My answer is, not very much. Since my research did not open doors in this direction, I spent more time with practitioners talking about their cultivation experiences and less time with television producers and newspaper publishers. To the extent that questions of financing and support probe the larger question of the political orientation of Falun Gong, there is in my mind little doubt that Li and Falun Gong had little or no political ambition at the outset, but that the movement has become very politicized since 1999, that is, since the beginning of the campaign of suppression. How could it be otherwise, given the posture of the Chinese state? Li and his followers attempted for a long time (and still do on occasion) to define "politics" so narrowly that their activities in defense of religious liberty and hence against the campaign of suppression in China might not be seen as criticisms of or challenges to the Communist leadership as such. However sincere such efforts may have been at the beginning—and I think they were very sincere—it now strains credibility *not* to see as political, for example, calls in the *Epoch Times* for Chinese Communist Party members to renounce their memberships. In any event, although my book is not an exposé of the inner sanctums of Falun Gong leadership, it stands nonetheless as an in-depth portrait of the activities and beliefs of Falun Gong practitioners, particularly in the 1999–2005 period.

Third, this book is not a judgment as to whether Falun Gong should be seen as a cult; instead, one might take the book as a demonstration that this is not the right question to ask. There exists an academic discipline of "cult studies" (or studies of "new religious movements"), a highly divided and polemicized field which seeks, alternatively, to defend "new religious movements" or to denounce and debunk "cults." I got to know this field somewhat in the course of my research, presented papers at its conferences and published articles in its journals. But as a historian and an area specialist, I could not help but feel that this field, which is dominated by specialists in the sociology of religion, spends too little time on the context and history of individual groups and too much time attempting to model the flow of group behavior and thus predict when a "good group" might "go bad" (or vice versa). As to the endless debates within this field concerning the relative importance of religious freedom versus the need to protect the weak and vulnerable from manipulative charlatans masquerading as prophets and seers, my personal inclination would be to define *legally* what behaviors might be beyond the pale instead of attempting to draw up a definitive list of "cult characteristics" that allows for the interdiction of all such groups (which simply drives them underground). In any event, no one can spend much time working in the history of religion (or in contemporary religion, for that matter) without coming to the realization that one person's cult is another person's religion; in fact, the words were largely synonymous until fairly recently. Readers of this volume will readily grasp the importance I have accorded to history, context, and nuance and will perhaps come to share my conclusion that Falun Gong should be regarded on its own terms and not compared with ready-made examples of evil drawn from other contexts, other histories. The entire issue of the supposed cultic nature of Falun Gong was a red herring from the beginning, cleverly exploited by the Chinese state to blunt the appeal of Falun Gong and the effectiveness of the group's activities outside of China.

Finally, this is not a human rights book, nor a blanket indictment of the Chinese state or its policies on Falun Gong or religious freedom in general. I fully and openly acknowledge that the Chinese government's campaign against Falun Gong has constituted and continues to constitute a grievous, tragic violation of the human rights of those practitioners who have been arrested, tortured, and killed, and various aspects of this tragedy are discussed in the pages which follow. I accept as true much of what Falun Gong publications have to say about the brutality of the Chinese state's campaign against them, even if recent claims about the harvesting of the organs of Falun Gong practitioners appear to have been exaggerated, at least on the question of the scale of such practices. I would add that the Chinese state's policies and especially practices concerning the exercise of religious freedom in China in general leave a great deal to be desired. These violations have been exposed and condemned by such well-known human rights organizations as Amnesty International and Human Rights Watch, as well as by numerous Falun Gong organizations, whose quite professional publications have been generally accepted as legitimate and trustworthy by these human rights organizations. Other than stating that I stand with Falun Gong practitioners on this issue, I am not sure what my book can add to this topic—at least not in the form of new information. I do not have access to sources other than those provided by Falun Gong, the Chinese state, and human rights organizations, and I have no particular expertise in the history of human rights discourse, in China or elsewhere. For me to write a human rights book would thus have come at the expense of the book I am qualified to write, a book which relates Falun Gong to the history of Chinese popular religion and discusses the importance of this religious revival to the future of China.

So much for what this book is *not*. The introduction, which follows shortly, is a more appropriate place than the preface to discuss what the book *is*, but the casual reader who picks up this volume and flips through the preface might well ask, "Why should I buy this book, since the author just said that he wasn't going to focus on the very aspects that make Falun Gong interesting?" One answer to this question is the obvious one, that even if the book does not provide prefabricated, sound-bite answers to the questions which made the headlines in the period when Falun Gong was much in the news, it does not ignore these questions either. The difference is that, as a professional historian, I attempt to interrogate the questions, to examine the ways in which the debates have been framed, at the same time that I provide my own answers. Another response is that China matters to us, Falun Gong matters to China, and I, as a China scholar, have for some twenty years been quietly at work on research related to these issues—which puts me in a position of having a fair bit to say. The story of qigong and Falun Gong illustrates both the resurgence of traditional popular religious culture in the vacuum created by the failure of the Maoist revolution *and* the capacity of this culture to transform itself with the evolution of broader historical and social forces. The Chinese immigrant accountant who lives in a Toronto suburb and practices Falun Gong is just as important to understanding China's past and future as the North China peasant who supported Mao Zedong and the Red Army in the 1940s. Anyone who thinks that China will modernize and democratize, becoming just like us, or anyone who thinks that China is a mounting, monolithic "yellow peril" will profit from this book.

My first debt of thanks goes to the Falun Gong practitioners in North America among whom I did my fieldwork. Gracious, intelligent, open, and engaged, practitioners made me feel welcome and allowed me to do my work, demanding little or nothing in return (although they surely hoped for a sympathetic portrayal). I wish I had had more time to spend with them. I will not name these practitioners individually, both out of respect for their privacy and because there are too many. I have changed the names of most practitioners mentioned in this book (the exception being those already mentioned in media accounts), even if most of them are surely already known to the Chinese government.

Many colleagues have listened to me speak about Falun Gong over the years and have helped me with constructive comments. Among the venues where I have held forth are the Université de Montréal, McGill University, the University of Toronto, the University of British Columbia, the University of Ottawa, Harvard University, Princeton University, the University of Chicago, Syracuse University, Leiden University, the Groupe de Sociologie des Religions et de la Laïcité in Paris, the Chinese University of Hong Kong, and Academia Sinica in Taibei, Taiwan. Among those colleagues whose comments have been most helpful are Tim Brook, Timothy Cheek, Kenneth Dean, Vincent Goossaert, John Lagerwey, Laurence Monnais, Daniel Overmyer,

David Palmer, Susan Palmer, Vivienne Shue, Michael Szonyi, Barend Ter Haar, Robert Weller, and Catherine Wessinger. Michael Szonyi, Kenneth Dean, Kimberly Manning, Daniel Overmyer, and Timothy Cheek read a near-completed version of the manuscript, and I thank them warmly for their detailed comments. It has been a pleasure to work with Cynthia Read and Meechal Hoffman at Oxford University Press. I would also like to thank Oxford's anonymous reader and advise him to work harder on hiding his identity on future occasions.

Funding for the project came from the U.S. Institute of Peace, the Fonds pour la Formation de Chercheurs et l'Aide à la Recherche of the government of Quebec, and from the Université de Montréal, and is gratefully acknowledged.

My thanks to *Nova Religio*, the *European Journal of East Asian Studies*, and the *International Journal* for permission to reprint parts of already published articles.

# Contents

# Falun Gong and the
# Future of China

# I

# Introduction

*Qigong, Falun Gong, and the*
*Crisis of the Post-Mao State*

Few people, inside China or out, would have expected the next important organized challenge to the Chinese Communist Party after the student democracy movement of 1989 to grow out of the *qigong* boom, a loosely organized and largely apolitical movement, grounded in traditional Chinese physical and spiritual exercises and practiced in public parks by tens if not hundreds of millions of Chinese in the 1980s and 1990s.[1] Yet on 25 April 1999, some 10,000 Falun Gong practitioners, including many "old ladies in tennis shoes," in the words of a Western journalistic pundit, demonstrated outside Communist Party headquarters in Beijing in a stunning silent protest against media attacks—backed up by police truncheons—on Falun Gong in the neighboring city of Tianjin.

The ensuing campaign of suppression has been reminiscent of the extremes of the Cultural Revolution (1966–1976). According to information compiled by Falun Gong—which is generally accepted as accurate by international human rights organizations—since 1999, more than 3,000 practitioners have died in police custody, and hundreds of thousands have been arrested, detained, beaten, and tortured.[2] At the height of the campaign, the entire Chinese media and public security apparatus were mobilized to denounce and suppress Falun Gong; former Chinese president Jiang Zemin even presented former American president Bill Clinton with a comic book outlining the evils of the Falun Gong "cult."[3] The campaign occurred at the same moment that China sought increasing respectability on the world stage, and China's leaders were frustrated and, one hopes, embarrassed, to have to justify the violence of their anti–Falun Gong policy at the same time as they lobbied (successfully) to hold the 2008 Olympic Games in Beijing and to gain entry into the World Trade Organization. The activities of vocal groups of Falun Gong practitioners among the Chinese diaspora in North America—and elsewhere in the world— succeeded in adding the Falun Gong cause to the long list of human rights violations of which the Chinese state is often accused.

Although the rise and suppression of Falun Gong stand out as among the noisiest and most newsworthy events in the history of post-Mao China, many basic questions remain unanswered. Just what *is* Falun Gong? There is at present no consensus about the fundamental character of the group. Falun Gong Web sites identify their practice as a "cultivation system," which to the uninitiated is meaningless. Chinese authorities have labeled Falun Gong a "heterodox cult." Journalists have wracked their brains for a simple yet accurate moniker, but more often than not have had to resort either to vague descriptions like "spiritual movement" or to wordy formulas like "a practice combining meditation and breathing exercises with a doctrine loosely rooted in Buddhist and Taoist teachings."[4] In the academy, some scholars have dubbed Falun Gong a "new religious movement," which is a way of disputing Chinese authorities' claims about the dangers inherent in the movement without necessarily telling us much about Falun Gong itself.[5]

Falun Gong's origins are as elusive as its basic character. We know that Li Hongzhi founded his cultivation system in 1992, and that Falun Gong began as a form of qigong. But since the origins and ultimate nature of qigong are poorly understood as well, the connection between Falun Gong and qigong (a connection in any case disputed both by Falun Gong and by other schools of qigong) provides little enlightenment. And lacking insight into the origins and character of Falun Gong and qigong, we are hard pressed to understand the conflict between Chinese authorities and Falun Gong—particularly the scale and intensity of this conflict.

In my view, the first step toward understanding Falun Gong is to place it in the proper context, even if it is not immediately clear what that context is, since several possibilities suggest themselves. One could group Falun Gong together with other actors in the religious revival which has marked post-Mao China, as Christians, Daoists, and practitioners of a wide variety of popular religions have all responded to the more liberal atmosphere of the reform era regime, as has Falun Gong.[6] Seen in this light, the story of Falun Gong might be read as part of the larger story of the popular response to the spiritual vacuum created by the failure of the Maoist revolution. Or one could choose the context of dissenting or contesting groups and movements within China, linking Falun Gong to rioting peasants and disgruntled workers, to rising dissatisfaction with cadre corruption and abuse of political power, perhaps even to the student demonstrations of 1989.[7] From this perspective, the story of Falun Gong might be read as part of the popular response to the looser social atmosphere of the reform era, the beginnings of the emergence, perhaps, of a Chinese civil society. Or yet again, one could group Falun Gong together with the Taipings, the late Yuan period White Lotus rebels, the Han period Yellow Turbans, and other popular religious groups that rose up over the centuries to put an end to faltering dynasties, and thus write Falun Gong (and the reform era Chinese government) into the (apparently) timeless story of China's dynastic cycle.[8] The participants in the dramatic conflict between the movement and Chinese authorities have of course chosen their own contexts: Falun Gong practitioners foreground issues of freedom of religion and freedom of speech, placing themselves in the context of the universal fight for human rights (one finds references in Falun Gong literature to Martin Luther King, Jr., and to Mahatma Gandhi), born in the discourse of the Enlightenment, and telling the story of their fight against Chinese authorities as a morality play. As part of their campaign against Falun Gong, by contrast, Chinese authorities have linked the group both to the "international cult movement" and to China's own internal history of religiously inspired peasant rebellion; the story they tell is one of ignorance, superstition, violence, and chaos.

## Falun Gong and the Modern History of Chinese Popular Religion

Some of these narratives are more plausible than others, but most have their utility. I will explore many of them in this volume, but choose to highlight yet another context, that of the modern history of Chinese popular religion, a difficult choice in some ways since this history has yet to be written. I submit that viewing Falun Gong as anything other than a religious movement, concerned with moral purpose and the ultimate meaning of life and death (and not—at least at the movement's beginning—with the organization of power in this world), is ultimately limiting; there is no other way to understand its attraction without denying the humanity of its practitioners.[9] Some may find Falun Gong unappealing or unoriginal as a religion, and others may judge that Falun Gong is more important as a social or political movement or as a broader symbol of China's search for meaning in the post-revolutionary era, but at the core of Falun Gong cultivation, we find beliefs and practices which can only be called religious (or "superstitious"—but this bespeaks a value judgment as to what a "real" religion is).

But acknowledging Falun Gong's religious roots does not necessarily define the proper context for understanding Falun Gong, because, once again, we don't really know what modern Chinese popular religion is or what its history has been. Aside from other schools of qigong, what other popular religious bodies should be grouped together with Falun Gong, and what narrative might we construct on the basis of this categorization? After all, the history of Chinese popular religion during the Maoist period (1949–1976) might seem to be largely the history of suppression; neither state-sanctioned religion nor popular religion stands out as an important theme during this period.[10] On the other hand, China has experienced an unexpected religious revival since the late 1970s. Christian churches in many cities are full to overflowing, and a "home church movement" has swept parts of rural China. Local ritual traditions, often connected to both Daoism and to local cults,[11] have revived. Ancestral temples have been rebuilt, particularly in the southeast coastal regions, often with funds from overseas relatives. The speed and intensity with which religion has returned to China suggest that Maoist authorities may have been less successful in suppressing religion than they (or we) believed, for if no one would insist that the revived practices are identical to those of the pre-revolutionary period, links to the past remain numerous, obvious, and indisputable. I will argue in chapter 2 that the context for understanding qigong and Falun Gong similarly extends beyond the temporal and historiographical boundaries of the People's Republic and that we find their antecedents in such groups as the little-known but important and influential redemptive societies of the Republican period and perhaps even in what we have heretofore called the White Lotus, or China's sectarian tradition.

Knowing what groups to lump together with qigong and Falun Gong is only half the battle. The other half is coming to terms with what "religion" has meant in modern China, a task which requires recognizing the complex history of state discourse on religion and popular religion since the turn of the twentieth century, a discourse whose application has produced considerable conceptual and terminological confusion. As one example of this confusion, neither Chinese authorities nor Falun Gong practitioners use the term "religion" or even "popular religion" to refer to Li Hongzhi's teachings. This is not, however, because Falun Gong cultivation does not contain elements that an objective Western observer would call "religious," but rather because religion has been defined in a particular way in modern China.

The social anthropologist Talal Asad has pointed out that the modern, Western use of the term "religion" is in fact historically conditioned. We have come to think of religion as describing the sphere of individual belief (and the churches or doxa which orient such beliefs) without necessarily realizing that it is the rise of disciplinary technologies associated with the modern state and the modern economy which has reduced our modern notion of religion to this circumscribed sphere. Chinese religious life prior to the twentieth century had more in common with the European Middle Ages than with modernity as experienced in the West, both for the "practitioner" for whom life practices and rituals were suffused with "religious" significance and for authorities who sought to maintain some control over what Asad calls "authoring discourses."[12]

Beginning from the late nineteenth century, the modernizing Chinese state chose to adopt a Western view of religion as part of its modernizing project. In Asad's terms, the Chinese state has sought to replace the "disciplinary regimes" associated with Chinese religion with other regimes more suitable to state goals, a project which has involved, in part, the imposition onto the Chinese religious landscape of a nineteenth-century Western vision of religion as a world historical faith possessing trained leadership, ecclesiastical organization, and a canon of scriptures. Five religions—Buddhism, Daoism, Islam, Protestantism, and Catholicism—were granted this status in China's first constitution (1912) and were told to organize themselves in such a way as to facilitate state management—in the interest of pursuing national goals defined, of course, by the state. All other forms of religious practice—ancestor worship, local cults, sectarian groups—henceforth fell into the leftover category of "feudal superstition" to be tolerated at best, actively suppressed when necessary, even if, taken together, these leftovers played a vastly more important role in the spiritual life of China's people than the five world historical faiths. It must be stressed that these decisions were made in haste, in a period of national crisis when China's continued existence as a political entity was seen to be in question, by men who conceived of religion in largely instrumental terms. To the extent that such decisions drew on extensive reflection on the role and importance of religion in Chinese life, religion was viewed primarily as an obstacle to the achievement of national power, the exception being those that conformed to the new rules.[13] Communist policy on religion (and popular religion) has largely followed its Republican predecessors. The constitution of 1954 included language on atheism not found in the constitution of 1912 (the right "not to believe" in religion received a guarantee just as strong, if not stronger, than the right to believe), but otherwise the definition of religion remained the same as in the constitution of 1912, and the officially recognized religions were organized into "three-self, patriotic"[14] Buddhist, Daoist, Christian, and Islamic federations under close state supervision, an initiative again fully consistent with Republican intentions.

To some extent, this was not new to the twentieth century. The imperial Chinese state had long maintained a regulatory posture toward religion, the emperor claiming the right to rule over Buddhist, Daoist, and other religious establishments and to define the limits of orthodoxy and heterodoxy. This posture was linked to the historical "civilizing mission" (jiaohua) of the Chinese state by which the Confucian elite sought to impose its values and rituals throughout Chinese society, but neither regulation of religion nor mission civilisatrice were ever achieved on a continuous basis because the imperial state lacked the power to do so.[15]

The regulatory posture of the twentieth-century Chinese state appears at first glance similar, but such apparent similarities conceal important differences. Imperial Chinese political culture had no word for religion and made no clear distinction between secular and nonsecular, religious and nonreligious; the modern Chinese word for religion—zongjiao—is a neologism introduced into Chinese via Japanese translations of Western works in the late nineteenth and early twentieth centuries. Prior to this, what we (and twentieth-century Chinese) call religions would have been known as "teachings" (jiao) and included Confucianism, Buddhism, Daoism, and other, lesser teachings (including those labeled as heterodox: White Lotus = Bailianjiao). Thus, although the imperial state viewed its Confucian teachings as preeminent and orthodox and sought to regulate or condemn other less-desirable teachings, the fact that orthodox and heterodox alike shared the designation of "teachings" suggests a common discursive space—a space that served as the basis for the syncretism of late imperial popular religious culture. The imperial state might well suppress the White Lotus teachings, and often viewed the Buddhist and Daoist establishments as administrative challenges (among other things), but the idea that there was a nonreligious sphere in opposition to a religious sphere was not part of imperial Chinese culture.

When the twentieth-century state came to see itself as an agent of modernization, by contrast, religion readily came to be defined as an obstacle to that goal, as "superstition," something which no longer had the right to exist and which would disappear—naturally or with "help"—as the modernizing process moved forward.[16] The logical consequence of this was that the modern Chinese state could define all religions as unhealthy objects to be eliminated, and could define itself as being above all religions. However, the twentieth-century Chinese state, like its imperial predecessor, has often lacked the power or the resources to make good on this totalistic vision. Indeed, while the Chinese state has largely succeeded in "taming" the world historical religions, it has had less success with other popular religious practices, against which it has waged sporadic and, above all, inconclusive battles. These popular religious groups, denied the label "religion" (which they might have rejected anyway since, again, the word has no roots in China's traditional culture), were forced to call themselves something else—philanthropic societies, philosophical societies, cultivation societies, healing societies, qigong groups—thus obscuring their links to China's religious history.

China's post-Mao religious revival reveals the continuing incongruity of the situation, for the religious scene in China in 2008 is in many ways almost identical to that in 1912 when China's first constitution was promulgated: religion is defined by state authorities today in very similar ways, and many popular religious groups (and even unregistered Christian churches) which have reemerged as part of the reform era religious revival are unsure of their status (as are the cadres of the Religious Affairs Offices which are expected to manage them). In other words, the confusion created by the narrow and un-realistic definition of religion chosen in the early twentieth century has not disappeared with time and has reappeared with a vengeance in the state's campaign against Falun Gong.

Falun Gong—and to a large degree the qigong movement as a whole—must be viewed as popular religious movements which were allowed to flourish by China's reform era authorities for complex reasons having to do with the reform era state's crisis of legitimacy. As a result of the tortured discourse of religion in modern Chinese history, neither qigong masters such as Li Hong-zhi, nor China's authorities who gave their thumbs-up to the development of the movement recognized the religious elements at the core of the qigong boom. "Religion is in the churches," they would have said. "Qigong is scientific cultivation, and has nothing to do with religion." From this perspective, the campaign of suppression against Falun Gong represents a return by Chinese authorities to their habitual posture after a period when, without having real-ized it, they engaged in a dangerous flirtation with a mass movement based in popular religion.

## Falun Gong, Qigong, and the Post-Mao State

If the larger context necessary to understand Falun Gong is the modern history of popular religion in China, the more immediate context is that of the qigong boom,[17] a mass popular religious movement which swept China in the 1980s and 1990s. What is qigong? It is impossible to understand Li Hongzhi and his

Falun Gong without understanding qigong, yet many journalists and even scholars writing about Falun Gong have been largely ignorant of the larger movement out of which Falun Gong emerged.

Although many qigong masters claimed that qigong had ancient roots, the term was in fact invented in the early 1950s by cadres connected to the socialist medical system.[18] As part of a nationalistic reaction against the westernization of Chinese medicine in the 1950s, some adepts of traditional healing techniques within the ruling power structure sought out masters in rural areas who had taught the methods of cultivation, with the goal of isolating the specific healing mechanisms from the "feudal" religious verbiage surrounding them, and they subsequently dubbed the new discipline "qigong." Qigong soon became part of Traditional Chinese Medicine (itself largely created as a discrete body of knowledge in the 1950s in reaction to the growing predominance of Western biomedicine) and was taught as part of the TCM curriculum and practiced in clinics and sanatoriums frequented by China's elite, some of whom had aches and pains dating back to the Long March of the 1930s, or to the trials and privations of the revolutionary period.

Qigong was severely criticized during the Cultural Revolution as a "feudal remnant," and the nascent qigong establishment largely ceased to function during the "ten-year catastrophe." Qigong returned, however, toward the end of the Cultural Revolution, although in a different form: charismatic masters began teaching qigong in public parks in Beijing to everyday people in search of relief from pain and suffering. It is not clear if the qigong taught in the parks in the 1970s was the same as that dispensed in the clinics in the 1950s and 1960s, even though certain practices and techniques were surely shared; the masters used the term qigong because, whatever its recent troubles, it was more politically correct than "cultivation" or any other available alternative. This small-scale, idiosyncratic reemergence of traditional healing techniques was given a great boost by the discovery of the supposed material existence of $qi$ by well-known Chinese scientists in the late 1970s. This discovery meant that qi, and hence qigong, could be allied to the pursuit of the Four Modernizations and China's search for development through science—an orientation that came to the forefront as Deng Xiaoping replaced Mao Zedong as China's supreme leader.

This was the basis of the qigong boom, a mass movement which involved hundreds of millions of Chinese and which lasted some two decades, from the late 1970s through the late 1990s. With support from highly placed leaders with connections to China's military-industrial complex, charismatic masters built nationwide networks and wrote and sold books and other qigong paraphernalia in what became a pan-China craze. Their teachings emphasized healing and the development of supernormal powers through a combination of moral behavior and the frequent practice of particular corporal technologies. Qigong newspapers and magazines were created to take advantage of—and to feed—the passion of the adepts; biographies of qigong masters became best-sellers (and more than one biographer went on to become a qigong master himself). The qigong boom was a major cultural moment in post-Mao Chinese history, largely overlooked by Western commentators because they didn't know what to make of it and were understandably focused on economic growth, political reform, and dissent, admittedly major stories in post-Mao China which fit more readily into persistent master narratives about economic modernization and political change.

Li Hongzhi founded his school of qigong, Falun Gong, toward the end of the two-decade-long mass movement, in 1992—although he could not have known that the movement would soon end and certainly would not have hoped for such an outcome. Li took pains to distinguish Falun Gong from what he derided as "ordinary" qigong, but the path he followed in creating and popularizing his teachings was in fact precisely that of previous qigong superstars. Between 1992 and 1995, Li made his name and that of Falun Gong in China by giving talks, publishing lectures, selling books, tapes, and other paraphernalia, and building a nationwide organization, and he and his teachings were embraced by the qigong movement. The history of Falun Gong between 1992, when Li Hongzhi "emerged from the mountains" to announce his truth to the world, and 1995, when Li left China to establish himself in the United States, belongs wholly to the history of the qigong boom. Even the coverage of the suppression of Falun Gong in the West would have been completely different if we had been following earlier qigong masters and earlier schools of qigong, some of which were larger and more popular than Falun Gong.

It is important to ask why qigong "boomed" when it did, and why the Chinese state embraced qigong when so many practices associated with it appear so clearly—in hindsight—to be religious, superstitious, or magical. Answers to these questions may be found in the particular history of post-Mao China and its ongoing search for political and cultural identity.

Less than two generations ago, China defined itself singularly and emphatically as *Mao's* China, a revolutionary society committed to the rapid construction of socialism. Admittedly, even Mao's China was vastly more complex than this simple characterization suggests, but such oversimplification possessed at least the virtue of clarity. Since Deng Xiaoping's promotion of "market socialism," however, such clarity has largely disappeared, particularly as his successors have continued along the same path; before long, China will have been "undergoing reforms" for some thirty years. Under Mao, heavy-handed social control was exercised in the name of the rapid achievement of socialist revolution, even if definitions of what this meant and how to get there differed over time and among various leaders. In the post-Mao era, China's leaders have—in general, and with significant exceptions—relaxed the social controls of the Maoist era, allowing China's people greater latitude to engage in a search for meaning (within limits), while China's authorities have undertaken their own search for a new legitimacy to shore up, if not completely replace, their historical claims to leadership based on their superior command of scientific Marxism.

Popular searches for meaning have taken many forms—material, spiritual, cultural, literary, artistic, physical—and have been the subject of considerable scholarship too rich to lend itself to easy summary here.[19] The qigong boom and the emergence of Falun Gong must in any event be understood as important moments in this popular search for meaning, a quest for health, happiness, and perhaps redemption achieved at the individual level and outside the context of party control and work-unit tyranny, surely a refreshing experience after years of calls to sacrifice for the collectivity.

The party's search for a new legitimacy has been less varied than the popular search for meaning; the principal justifications put forward for its continued monopoly over political power include frequent recourse to Chinese nationalism; a claim to competence in economic management (which obviously extends to China's diplomatic as well as economic relations with the outside world); and an assertion that only a strong government can guarantee the social stability necessary to China's continued development.[20]

At the outset, qigong was a popular search for meaning which was sanctioned by China's leadership because it seemed to accord with the leaders' own search for a renewed legitimacy. In addition to its therapeutic virtues, qigong was nationalistic in its celebration of China's rich heritage of cultivation practices and was at the same time scientific and modern, the material existence of qi having been proven and defended by some of China's best scientists. Qigong was seen as the key to the development of a new "Chinese science" which would enable China to achieve its innate capacity in a wide variety of fields (qi-enhanced seeds were to increase agricultural productivity, qi-enhanced soldiers China's military might), thus returning China to its rightful place as the most powerful and respected of nations. What better proof of the competence of China's leaders in the fields of economic and diplomatic management than to facilitate the development of qigong? Furthermore, qigong preached a thoroughly conventional morality as the basis for successful cultivation. This seemed to promise that qigong practitioners would be respectful of hierarchy as well as honest and kind in their daily lives; an improvement in

China's moral climate, China's leaders surely said to themselves, could only benefit social and even political stability. Qigong also promised to improve the global health and well-being of the Chinese people, contributing yet again to productivity, to social stability, and to the image of competence the leadership hoped to nourish (among other things because a healthier population would mean less funds tied up in health care and more available for mega-projects, or poverty relief, or both). The happy moments of the qigong movement were almost utopian in their ebullient optimism, allowing leadership, intelligentsia, and masses to embrace a common cause which rapidly became a mass movement. In some sense, qigong was what China wanted to be: ancient and cutting edge; elitist and popular/populist; happy, healthy, and whole.

## What Went Wrong?

Yet, as qigong grew in size and popularity, becoming a major cultural movement in the urban China of the 1980s and 1990s, the intersection between the leadership's search for legitimacy and the popular search for well-being through qigong came to be potentially problematic and was criticized as such by detractors. At the height of the qigong craze, the major figures were great charismatic masters like Yan Xin, Zhang Hongbao, and, later, Li Hongzhi, each of whom had millions of followers nationwide, together with lesser masters with lesser followings which might still number in the tens or even hundreds of thousands. As far as we know, few if any of these masters had explicitly political ambitions, and most took care to attune their vocabulary to the demands of the party and to maintain good relationships with individual party leaders. But qigong masters were vastly more popular than any party or government figure, and popular enthusiasm for qigong cultivation greatly exceeded that for Chinese socialism or for government performance in general. To some extent, this was natural and proper; qigong masters were pop cultural heroes, with none of the responsibilities of a government leader, and Deng Xiaoping had decided that Mao's was to be the last cult of personality among party leaders. At the same time, what was to stop an ambitious, egomaniacal qigong master from claiming that he had just as much right to the mantle of Chinese nationalism as did the Communist Party? The Communists had perhaps saved China from the Japanese (fifty long years ago), but qigong, in the eyes of enthusiasts, was what had made China China, qigong being, as they insisted, at the very origin of Chinese civilization. What was to stop a qigong practitioner from comparing the morality preached by his master and practiced by himself and his fellow cultivators with the corrupt, rent-seeking behavior of many Communist Party officials? What was to prevent the qigong boom from morphing into the base of a principled, organized opposition to Communist Party rule, as had, for example, the Soka Gakkai in Japan through its political party, the Kômeitô?

By the mid-1990s, qigong detractors among the central leadership had begun to gain the upper hand over supporters, and the overall fortunes of qigong seemed to be on the wane. Although neither Li Hongzhi nor Falun Gong seemed to be particular targets of this anti-qigong sentiment, Li's fortunes and those of his movement nonetheless suffered the consequences. Li left China in early 1995 because he had heard rumors that there might be trouble brewing, that he and his movement might become objects of criticism. As he left China and began to develop an international ministry, Li introduced subtle changes to Falun Gong practice in China which may well have unintentionally launched the movement in the direction of an eventual confrontation with the state. For example, Li decreed that henceforth, his recently published masterwork, *Zhuan falun* (the revolving dharma wheel), would be the "bible" of the movement and that practitioners were to pursue their cultivation principally by reading and rereading this one text. The physical exercises Li had earlier taught were not renounced, nor was Falun Gong's organization dismantled, but Li was quite adamant that no one except him was to teach, preach, or explain *Zhuan falun* and that practitioners were to establish a one-to-one relationship with the master, no matter where his physical body might be, through their intensive study of this scripture. We cannot know if Li's decision grew out of a particular fondness for *Zhuan falun* or instead a savvy calculation that he could best preserve his status and charisma in absentia by insisting on the binary ties between practitioner and master at the expense of the authority of his organization. In any event, this focus on scripture was something of a departure for the qigong movement, where books—technical manuals, descriptions of exercises, masters' biographies—had already played an important role but had not, as far as we know, surpassed the presence of the master, the utility of the organization (which varied enormously from group to group), or the importance of the corporal techniques. Falun Gong practitioners became what we might call "people of the book," and perhaps developed an increased devotion to the master, even if it were something of a "virtual" devotion since Li himself was no longer physically present in China.

It was also after Li's departure from China that Falun Gong practitioners developed their penchant for peaceful protest (later dubbed "civil disobedience") in reaction to perceived media slights or misrepresentations. The declining fortunes of the qigong movement over the course of the mid-1990s translated into more frequent negative reporting in the media, some of which fell on Falun Gong. Falun Gong practitioners consistently demanded either a retraction or equal time when they felt that local media had been unfair to them, engaging in some 300 such protests between 1996 and 1999. We do not know if this was a coordinated strategy conceived by Li Hongzhi and the Falun Gong leadership, or rather a product of the decentralization of Falun Gong in the wake of Li Hongzhi's departure, a decentralization which may have encouraged local militancy by removing central controls, or some combination of the two. In any event, the fact that such protests were not immediately condemned or suppressed and that most newspapers and television stations seemed to knuckle under to Falun Gong pressure may have convinced practitioners of the soundness of the practice. It bears repeating that China has become a much more openly contentious society in the post-Mao period. Falun Gong practitioners were not necessarily pioneers in this sense.

An absent master, devoted practitioners willing to engage in civil disobedience, and a central government less and less enamored of the qigong movement—such were the ingredients for a disaster, and all were in place by the late 1990s. And indeed, when a peaceful Falun Gong protest in mid-April 1999 in the northern city of Tianjin, in response to a critical article appearing in a limited-circulation journal, was met with police brutality, a decision was made—surely by Li Hongzhi, who was in Beijing en route to Australia—to employ the same strategy at the highest possible level, that of China's central leadership. Thus, on 25 April 1999, some 10,000 Falun Gong practitioners staged a peaceful demonstration outside the gates of Zhongnanhai, the guarded compound where most of China's ruling elite lives and works, a stone's throw from Tian'anmen Square.

The rest of the tragic story is better known. Unsurprisingly, China's premier leader, Jiang Zemin, took the Falun Gong demonstration as a challenge to Communist Party authority and vowed to crush Li and his followers. A series of miscalculations on both sides quickly raised the stakes to the point where no compromise was possible, and a long, costly, and useless campaign of suppression and martyrdom ensued—indeed, the campaign continues to this day. Falun Gong practitioners have clearly paid the highest price: according to Falun Gong Web sites, as of early June 2007, 3,024 practitioners have been confirmed dead as a result of the campaign, more than 100,000 have been sent to labor camps, more than 6,000 to prison, and several hundred thousand have been arrested and detained.[21] The Chinese state lost a good deal of international prestige (authorities clearly had not counted on the persistence and effectiveness of Falun Gong practitioners outside of China), perhaps some credibility in the eyes of its own population, vast sums of money spent on suppression which the state could well have used elsewhere, and perhaps a certain amount of momentum in its proclaimed desire to establish a rule of law.[22] The brutality of the campaign strengthened the worst parts of China's authoritarian heritage.


## The Organization of the Book

The goals of this book are to offer a descriptive analysis of Falun Gong as a popular religion and to place Falun Gong within the broader context of the modern history of certain strains of Chinese popular religion, a context which includes problematic relations with the Chinese state. Chapters 4 and 5 constitute the core of this volume and provide a detailed portrait of Falun Gong as a popular religious movement. Chapter 4 offers an in-depth reading and interpretation of the teachings of Li Hongzhi, based largely on his writings (which are mostly transcripts of his lectures) in Chinese and English. Chapter 5, based on fieldwork with Falun Gong practitioners in North America, most of whom are recent immigrants from China, is a necessary complement to chapter 4, for it is perilous to attempt to interpret the teachings of a religious leader, particularly the leader of a new religious movement whose origins, vocabulary, and discourse are little known, without seeing how they are understood and lived by his followers. I would have preferred to have carried out fieldwork among practitioners in China at the height of Falun Gong's popularity, before the movement's conflict with Chinese authorities became a central fact of practitioners' lives and Li's statements, but this was not possible, and as a historian I am accustomed to the limitations imposed by source availability. In any event, chapters 4 and 5, taken together, allow the reader to appreciate Falun Gong as a popular religious movement, based on the charisma of the master and on his teachings, which are grounded in moral practice and corporal transformation and offer the promise of redemption, in the form of healing, supernormal powers, and perhaps immortality.

Much of the rest of the book seeks to elaborate on the portrait of Falun Gong presented in chapters 4 and 5 by placing the teachings and the movement in the contexts which determined my reading of the group. Chapter 2 addresses broader historical questions relating to the place of qigong and Falun Gong in the *longue durée* of the history of popular religion in late imperial and modern China, as well as the question of state discourse and its influence on religious practice in China and our understanding of the modern history of Chinese religion and popular religion. Chapter 3, which draws heavily on David Palmer's path-breaking scholarship on the qigong movement, recounts the story of the invention and evolution of qigong from the early 1950s through the mid-1980s, when the qigong boom was at its height. Qigong was the larger movement from which Falun Gong emerged in the early 1990s, and without understanding the unlikely, checkered history of qigong, it is impossible to arrive at a proper evaluation of Falun Gong.

Chapter 6 examines the conflict between the Chinese state and Falun Gong. Although it is this conflict that made Falun Gong known to the world outside qigong circles and kept the drama of the practitioners' suffering at the hands of the Chinese state in the Western news for months on end, this chapter comes at the end of my book rather than at the beginning. One reason for this choice is that, for a historian of Chinese popular religion, the various contexts which produced the conflict are more interesting than the conflict itself. Or, to put it slightly differently, the conflict is much less surprising than the fact that it took so long for it to come to a head. At the same time, the arguments marshaled by Falun Gong in defense of its practice and by the Chinese state to justify its campaign are grist for the mill of a study of the continuing evolution of modern Chinese popular religion. And it is of particular interest that the existence of Falun Gong activists among the Chinese diaspora in North America, Europe, and Australia has altered the terms of the debate between popular religious practitioners and the Chinese state.


Review of the Literature

While most academic monographs begin with a literature review, situating the questions asked and the arguments put forward in the context of one or more larger fields, I have chosen to place my modest review at the end of this introductory chapter. One reason is that mine is a wide-ranging volume that treats a broad variety of subjects and draws on several literatures, without necessarily claiming to advance one discipline or another. Detailed discussions of the state of the field of White Lotus studies, the history of science and medicine in China, or the dilemmas facing the reform era Chinese state, to name but a few of the topics addressed, would slow the reading of what I hope will be a lively narrative. I prefer to address these particular literatures, either in the text or in the endnotes, over the course of the following chapters. At the same time, the scholarly literature on the major subjects addressed in this volume, qigong and Falun Gong, remains rather thin, and one of the main purposes of this study is to flesh out what we know.

Despite the importance of qigong to the history of Falun Gong, relatively little has been published on this rich and fascinating topic. Unsurprisingly, anthropologists were the first to turn their attention to qigong, and the 1980s and 1990s saw publications by Elisabeth Hsu, Nancy N. Chen, Thomas Ots, and Evelyne Micollier. Hsu examined the modes of transmission of medical knowledge in reform era China and chose as one of her subjects a minor qigong master in Kunming and his less-than-successful attempts to carry out a secret transmission of his healing arts to his brother-in-law.[23] For the purposes of this volume, Hsu reminds us that not all qigong masters were qigong superstars. Evelyne Micollier has carried out classic anthropological studies of a number of local qigong groups in Guangzhou and elsewhere, looking particularly at the question of emotional release—or control—in the interactions between masters and practitioners.[24] Chen and Ots have, in different ways, used qigong to probe the question of the body as a central site for anthropological inquiry and subjective individuation.[25] As the title of her book—*Breathing Spaces*—suggests, Chen sees qigong as a resource that allows the much put-upon urban Chinese to assert a kind of independence, perhaps even a transcendence, in the face of the indignities of life in much of reform era China. In an even more ambitious vein, Jian Xu, writing from a cultural studies perspective, relates the debate over the proper characterization of qigong (as pseudo science or as superscience) in the latter part of the 1990s to a broader struggle to decide who will be the "subject" of Chinese modernity.[26]

These studies are excellent, as far as they go, but at the same time they tell us little about the origins—ancient or contemporary—of qigong, nor about the particular contexts which gave rise to and shaped the evolution of the qigong movement. It could hardly be otherwise, given the speed with which qigong developed in the 1980s and the fact that even in China there was no authorized historian of the movement. An anthropologist working with masters and practitioners in the field could do little more than repeat what his or her research subjects said about qigong's origins; there was no work in any language which would have permitted the anthropologist to situate his qigong group in history or in any other, larger context.

David Palmer's brilliant *Qigong Fever: Body, Science, and Utopia in China* changed all that.[27] Palmer, a sociologist of religion by training, has produced a stunning macro-level study of qigong, tracing its emergence in the early 1950s as part of the creation of Traditional Chinese Medicine and following its complex evolution in subsequent decades. His work is particularly rich on the formation of the "*qigong* realm" in the late 1970s and the subsequent qigong boom. Sifting through thousands of pages of journalistic, biographical, autobiographical, and political accounts of the rise and fall of qigong, Palmer deftly illustrates how the utopian yearnings of the elites and the masses came together in the 1980s under the nationalistic banner of scientism to produce the unprecedented mass movement, for it was the belief that qi possessed material existence which convinced China's leaders to give the green light to qigong. He also shows, in part through case studies of particular schools of qigong but also through a close reading of the long-running debate between qigong proponents and qigong detractors, how the ideologies of qigong masters and of the state came to part company. Palmer thus provides a historical study of qigong origins in the early 1950s, a narrative construction of its rise and fall through the late twentieth century, and a sociopolitical analysis of the significance of the qigong boom in the context not only of reform era China, but of China since 1949.

Palmer's work does not disprove or displace the anthropological studies of qigong discussed above, which retain their value; it provides the larger contexts which would have helped the authors of those studies better frame their work. In any event, Palmer's *Qigong Fever* is hardly the last word on the topic; for all of its thoroughness, his work is agenda setting rather than definitive. One hopes that future scholars will carry out in-depth studies of the writings of qigong masters and fieldwork among practitioners (perhaps someday in China, or in Taiwan, or elsewhere in the Chinese diaspora), which will enable us to test Palmer's hypotheses and characterizations. For my part, I have relied heavily on Palmer's work in chapter 3, where I recount the pre–Falun Gong history of qigong, even if I disagree to some extent with his depiction of Falun Gong and the place he accords Falun Gong in his global narrative of the history of qigong.

The literature on Falun Gong presents its own difficulties. Prior to 25 April 1999, almost no one outside of qigong circles within China had paid much attention to Falun Gong. Yet within a few months of that date, the campaign of suppression against Falun Gong had achieved the status of a major event in the history of contemporary China. Journalists, scholars, and sundry China watchers naturally felt compelled to explain this turn of events, even if they were hard pressed to do so.

Journalists have produced thousands of articles on Falun Gong, many of which are helpfully archived at www.cesnur.org, the site of the Center for Studies on New Religions.[28] Many journalistic accounts simply attempted to follow the unfolding of events, a task which became increasingly difficult in the months and years following the crackdown as China and Falun Gong sculpted competing representations of all elements of the drama in an attempt to sway public opinion. Some journalists stressed human rights themes, linking the campaign against Falun Gong to broader problems of governance and democracy in reform era China; others sought to determine whether Falun Gong was a cult. Ian Johnson of the *Asian Wall Street Journal* won a Pulitzer Prize for his work on the group, recounting, among other things, the story of a daughter of a Falun Gong practitioner (not a practitioner herself) who was driven to political activism by the brutality of the crackdown in Shandong province.

Johnson's work, available as part 3 of his book *Wild Grass: Three Stories of Change in Modern China*, rejects the cynicism of much reporting on Falun Gong and movingly depicts practitioners' struggles for justice and dignity. Other reporters whose work I have read with interest include John Pomfret and Philip Pan of the *Washington Post* and Susan V. Lawrence of the now sadly defunct *Far Eastern Economic Review*.

Scholars faced similar problems to those of the journalists, having to explain the emergence and significance of Falun Gong and the state crackdown with little prior knowledge of Falun Gong or qigong. Some succeeded admirably. Richard Madsen offered a competent introduction.[29] Cheris Shun-Ching Chan offered a clear sociological analysis of Falun Gong, based on fieldwork in Chicago and Hong Kong, finding that Falun Gong, in the language of the sociology of religion, should be viewed not as a sect but as a "cult-like New Religious Movement."[30] James Tong dug probably as deeply as one can in an admirable effort to determine what Falun Gong's organization may have looked like in China prior to the crackdown.[31] Benjamin Penny wrote a number of articles on Falun Gong, treating such questions as Li Hongzhi's religious biography (Penny helpfully compared it to similar texts from China's past) and "Master Li's body" (again placing Li's many teachings about the body within China's long tradition of cultivation practices).[32] *Nova Religio*, a scholarly journal dedicated to the study of new religious movements, devoted its April 2003 issue to Falun Gong, publishing eight articles and an introduction touching on issues ranging from the historical background to Falun Gong's emergence, to conversion patterns and use of the Internet.[33] Falun Gong has also been a popular subject for graduate theses.[34] There have also been many articles in the literature which use the case of Falun Gong to probe larger issues: Elizabeth Perry examined repertoires of protest in reform era China;[35] Vivienne Shue placed Falun Gong within a larger narrative about the questioning of state hegemony;[36] Robin Munro looked at the issue of psychiatric abuse;[37] Ronald Keith and Zhiqiu Lin explored the significance of the Falun Gong case from a legal angle.[38] Although such articles are welcome additions to the literature, they are not about Falun Gong per se.

Much the same could be said for the only substantial book to be published on Falun Gong to date, Maria Hsia Chang's *Falun Gong: The End of Days*.[39] Chang's volume is pleasingly written and provides a serviceable narrative of the rise and demise of Falun Gong. At the same time, the author's purpose seems to be to liken the end of Communist rule in China to the final phase of traditional dynastic decline, with Li Hongzhi as the leader of the equivalent of a millenarian peasant uprising. Provocative as such a comparison may be,

Chang's study moves too quickly over too much terrain and lacks a firm grounding in Chinese history and popular religion. Chang cites little or no scholarly literature on qigong or Falun Gong, did no fieldwork with Falun Gong practitioners, and thus offers a fine essay on China at the beginning of the twenty-first century—without telling us much that we didn't already know about Falun Gong. Noah Porter's excellent "Falun Gong in the United States: An Ethnographic Study" is, by contrast, rich in information on Falun Gong, based on fieldwork carried out in Tampa, Florida, and Washington, DC, and energetic research in all available sources.[40] Although not a sinologist by training or even a professional academic (at least when he carried out his research), Porter's methodology resembles my own, and our findings accord on many points. Wong and Liu's *The Mystery of China's Falun Gong: Its Rise and Its Sociological Implications*[41] offers a basic introduction to Falun Gong and the campaign against it, but since it was published in 1999, it can only scratch the surface of many key issues. Danny Schechter's *Falun Gong's Challenge to China* and Adams, Adams, and Galati's *Power of the Wheel* provide valuable information about Falun Gong but are partisan rather than strictly objective in their approach.[42] There are many book-length partisan denunciations of Falun Gong published in Chinese on the mainland,[43] and somewhat less-partisan treatments published in Hong Kong and Taiwan.[44] I treat examples of the denunciation literature in chapter 6, arguing that these works often reveal more about the authors than about Falun Gong. Accounts published in Hong Kong and Taiwan strike me as journalistic and often gossipy. I do not know how to evaluate the reliability of the information and thus have made relatively little use of such material.

Again, it is David Palmer's work on Falun Gong which is the most substantial to date. In his books and in several articles, he underscores the dark, apocalyptic undertones of Li Hongzhi's message, which he contrasts with the brighter, more-utopian tone of other qigong masters and groups.[45] He labels Falun Gong "militant qigong" and accords Li Hongzhi's ideas and ideology a major role in the sad final chapters of the history of the qigong movement. To me, this interpretation errs in seeking out the origin of the eventual conflict between Falun Gong and the Chinese state in the character of Li's ideas and in depicting the unfolding of events between 1992 and 1999 as "inexorable." My reading of Li's teachings acknowledges the existence of apocalyptic elements, but I do not find that such themes were highlighted prior to the stresses brought about by the crackdown. In fact, even practitioners to whom I spoke after the crackdown rarely mentioned apocalyptic themes. Similarly, I accord a higher importance to contingent factors, such as

Li's decision to leave China and the effects that his departure had on the organization, and less importance to Li's ideas in the explication of the rising tensions between Falun Gong and the state.

This does not mean that Palmer is wrong and I am right; it means we have written different books. Palmer's macro-level study of the qigong movement looks at Falun Gong as one qigong group among many, and the campaign against Falun Gong as the final chapter of his story. Palmer's work on qigong has allowed me to delve deeper into Falun Gong, doing fieldwork among practitioners and developing a fuller understanding of Li's teachings. Palmer writes as a sociologist of religion; I write as a historian. In any event, both qigong and Falun Gong are rich subjects worthy of any number of studies, and I can only hope that this one will inspire others.

# 2

# A History for Falun Gong

How should one start to think about Falun Gong? Chinese authorities have branded Falun Gong a "dangerous, heterodox sect" and have likened it to such nefarious "evil cults" as the Branch Davidians, the Order of the Solar Temple, and Aum Shinri kyô. Falun Gong practitioners insist that Falun Dafa[1] is merely a "cultivation practice,"[2] a vague term which some Western commentators have linked to "new religious movements" or perhaps "new age spirituality" (themselves rather imprecise designations). Falun Gong's links to the qigong movement are obvious, but a proper characterization of qigong remains elusive as well. As will be explored more fully in chapter 3, qigong has claimed the mantle of modern science *and* that of ancient Chinese civilization, and appears to be equal parts new religion and cultural revitalization movement (the two are often linked).[3]

Qigong and Falun Gong practitioners are proud to assert their roots in China's glorious past, but are silent (mostly out of ignorance) as to the specific historical links in the chain. Since the onset of the Chinese government's campaign against Falun Gong, numerous Western commentators have noted suggestive parallels between Falun Gong and the many historical examples of peasant rebellion under the dynasties, which were fueled by popular religious sentiment, and some Chinese scholars have traced Falun Gong's roots to the supposedly millenarian White Lotus sect of the Ming-Qing period, while insisting nonetheless on Falun Gong's more immediate kinship with groups such as the Branch Davidians.[4] Yet, even if such parallels to historical groups are tantalizing, no serious historical treatment exists which might link a late twentieth-century, largely urban mass movement with its supposed rural predecessors in late imperial times.

The goal of this chapter is to begin to construct one possible history for Falun Gong, or at the least to suggest the broad outlines of a rethinking of certain aspects of the late imperial and modern history of Chinese popular religion which would situate qigong and Falun Gong in the *longue durée* of this history. In a nutshell, I would like to suggest that qigong groups and Falun Gong stand in some kinship relation to the redemptive societies of the Republican period, a little known but important popular religious movement of the 1920s, 1930s, and 1940s; that these redemptive societies in turn stand in some kinship relation to what we have called the late imperial White Lotus tradition; and that juxtaposing Falun Gong, the redemptive societies, and the White Lotus will illuminate certain aspects of the modern history of Chinese popular religion in important ways. At the same time, proving—or even testing—this hypothesis is an undertaking fraught with difficulty for a host of reasons having to do with sources, historiography, and conceptualization, a full discussion of which would be lengthy, tedious, and distracting for the reader principally interested in Falun Gong.

The historiography of the White Lotus tradition, for example, is a minefield.[5] Long depicted as a dissenting, rebellious tradition, with roots in folk Buddhism and millenarian prophecy, the White Lotus is now seen by some scholars as a product of the paranoid imagination of the late imperial state rather than a genuine vehicle of popular discontent. Barend Ter Haar, for example, convincingly argues that "White Lotus" was little more than a label employed by the Chinese state to inculpate groups whose activities they found suspect and to justify their suppression, and not an organized, coherent, self-conscious tradition; in other words, "White Lotus" has much the same status and utility as the term "cult" in contemporary American journalistic and popular usage.[6] This does not of course mean that there were no rebels, nor that the symbols and discourses associated with the White Lotus label did not exist (or that they were never connected with dissent or rebellion), but it does mean that source materials using the White Lotus label are highly suspect and cannot be taken at face value. At the same time, although scholarly work on the basis of White Lotus scriptures (as opposed to police documents) is producing new insights which link such groups more closely to popular religion and less to rebellion and dissent,[7] no new, dominant paradigm has yet emerged, and the older image of the White Lotus as apocalyptic rebels still has its partisans (particularly but not exclusively among Chinese scholars).[8] The scholarly vocabulary employed to describe what we once confidently called the "White Lotus" reflects this confusion, as terms such as White Lotus, lay Buddhist, syncretic, and sectarian are all used, not indiscriminately, but in ways that frequently overlap, even if the connotations attached to the various terms can be quite different.

The historiography of the Republican period redemptive societies is less problematic, because they are a fairly recent discovery.[9] As already suggested, they appear to be, among other things, a historical link between the late imperial White Lotus tradition and the qigong movement of the post-Mao era: many redemptive societies incorporated into their teachings and practices elements drawn from late imperial White Lotus traditions, while at the same time building nationwide city-based organizations that reached millions of followers, as did qigong groups a few decades later. The history of such groups is only beginning to be explored, in part, one assumes, because the metanarratives of this period emphasize war, party building, and national salvation through political and social revolution, and the activities of the popular religious groups during this period do not fit well into existing story lines.

Indeed, the story I would like to tell in this chapter is difficult to elucidate because once again it lies on the contested and moving frontier between religion as lived or practiced, religion as defined by state authorities, and the politics of religion—by which I mean both the role of religion as a tool of social mobilization with occasional political consequences, as well as state decisions to target or even eliminate certain forms of popular religion or popular religious practices as obstacles to orthodoxy or modernization. As already noted in the introductory chapter, the history of religion and popular religion in modern China is inextricably interwoven with and filtered through China's complex political history, and this filter inevitably distorts our vision.

Despite these difficulties, I propose that we group together, for heuristic purposes at the present state of research, qigong, Falun Gong, and the traditions from late imperial and Republican China known as White Lotus, folk Buddhist, sectarian, syncretic, and redemptive societies, on the premise that they share the following basic characteristics. At the most fundamental level, many of these groups appear to have been organized by and around charismatic masters, who generally claim independence from other recognized religions (or "cultivation systems") and from one another. These masters preach what they claim to be a unique message of salvation often experienced first and foremost through the body—almost always as renewed health, sometimes in the cultivation of paranormal powers—and grounded in traditional moral practices. Morality is a necessary but not sufficient condition for salvation; the master's message contains corporal techniques ranging from rituals to mantras to meditation to miracle cures, and the master's individual guidance, or presence, is often necessary to the success of the practitioner's efforts. The master's message is generally—but not always—consigned to scripture, and often sounds apocalyptic themes, driving home the need for repentance and moral rectitude. Although most of these groups have been peaceful, some have maintained problematic relations with authority, either because the state considers their teachings to be heterodox, or because the groups sometimes fall outside (or cut across) the orbit of such familiar authority structures as lineages and villages, or because some groups have indeed been involved in millenarian movements or rebellions. For my part, I would be pleased to call all such groups, from late imperial times forward, "redemptive societies," the descriptive, neutral title chosen by Prasenjit Duara for the Republican period groups he has studied, and to label the content of their practices "cultivation," which to my mind is clearly a form of popular religion. For the rest of this volume, I will generally use the term "redemptive societies" for purposes of consistency. Although conventional treatments of the White Lotus identify the Unborn Venerable Mother, the Maitreya Buddha, and the apocalyptic "turning of the *kalpa*" as key features of the tradition, to me these are secondary characteristics, symbols employed by some redemptive societies but not others. Although the parallel may be inexact, my impression is that we have studied the Chinese equivalents of Anabaptists, Pentecostals, and Methodists without having grasped the core meaning of the Chinese equivalent of Protestantism.

A possible disadvantage of this recategorization is that it lumps too many disparate groups together. It is true that some groups were small and localized, completely dependent on one master's charisma, while others were large and regional—even national—the founder's charisma having been routinized in a variety of ways. Some groups had very elaborate scriptures, some groups had none. Some groups were urban, others were rural; some appealed more than others to the gentry in late imperial times and to the middle class in the twentieth century. Some groups adopted the cosmology of the White Lotus tradition, others did not. "Salvation" took a variety of forms, some more or less corporal than others.

At the same time, the benefits of such a regrouping are numerous. First, I mentioned above that many scholars, Western as well as Chinese, have continued to use the term White Lotus, despite a strong argument that the "tradition" as presented in the documents of the late imperial elite never existed outside the state discourse of persecution, in part because neither a new characterization nor a new terminology has arisen to take its place. Seeing these groups as historical examples of redemptive societies is one solution to this problem. The use of the term redemptive societies serves a corrective function in other ways as well: referring to the groups as "lay Buddhist" obscures the fundamentally syncretic nature of the teachings and practices; the use of "sectarian" overemphasizes the supposedly exclusive character of membership in such groups, which Thomas Dubois has illustrated to be largely false;[10] calling the groups "syncretic" tells us next to nothing since all of Chinese popular religion has been radically syncretic.[11] Finally, labeling the groups redemptive societies begins to disengage them from politics (or, more precisely, enables us to view their politics otherwise than through the lens of state paranoia); again, White Lotus was and is a pejorative political label, and the term sectarian suggests a willed distance from orthodoxy.

My goal is *not* to present all redemptive societies as innocent or harmless. Charismatic masters represent a form of authority with which governments and more conventional elites are often ill at ease. Cultivation represents a form of power which can easily take on dimensions—symbolic, social—outside the body of the individual master or practitioner. Fundamentalist calls to return to the straight and narrow can readily morph into social and political criticism. Apocalyptic discourse may begin as moral commentary (or as a recruitment technique) but can easily slip into a prophetic mode, leading masters and followers to attempt to hasten the coming of the new millennium through direct action. In sum, claims to redemptive power, if taken seriously, become serious claims, and the power is not always easy to circumscribe. What is clear, nonetheless, is that there have been many, many examples of redemptive societies which have *not* taken dangerous paths, suggesting that the original intentions of many masters and followers were not to bring down the established political or social order. Instead, the appeal of redemptive societies appears to lie in the hope of healing and salvation, most often at the individual level, which explains why people have been drawn to them over the centuries, despite their being labeled "heterodox" by the authorities.

In calling qigong and Falun Gong redemptive societies, I in no way wish to suggest that a changeless "Chinese tradition" has reared its hoary head in the wake of the failure of Maoism. At the same time, qigong grew very quickly in reform era China. Masters do not seem to have struggled to learn the tricks of the qigong trade, and they found a willing audience of tens if not hundreds of millions of eager practitioners virtually overnight. The flat learning curve observed in the expansion of the qigong movement suggests that qigong discourse resonated with something that many Chinese already knew; the frequent references to the greatness of Chinese "cultivation traditions" in qigong literature suggest much the same thing. Modern identities are constructed on the basis of past experiences, and the rapid rise of qigong illustrates that many contemporary Chinese continue to believe that there are charismatic masters (or exceptional individuals, *gaoshou, gaoren*) who possess extraordinary powers, in part because they live morally exemplary lives, and who can share those powers with others, who in turn experience the power primarily through their bodies. This belief seems to be an enduring predisposition within Chinese culture, and the history of redemptive societies from late imperial times through the present day illustrates just how resilient and flexible this form of spirituality can be.

## The Hidden History of Redemptive Societies

Ideally, one would now turn to a historical demonstration of the affinities among these groups, citing examples of redemptive societies from late Ming times through the present in order to test the value of this heuristic regrouping. And sure enough, passing references to charismatic powers and healing are legion in the literature on the White Lotus and on redemptive societies. But even if we could somehow enter all available data concerning redemptive societies into a database, this would not necessarily bring us closer to a definitive understanding of their basic nature, as the history of one particular redemptive society will illustrate. The problem, once again, is one of sources.

The Way of the Temple of the Heavenly Immortals (Tianxian miaodaohui, hereafter, the Temple) is in many ways a typical example of a redemptive society.[12] The Temple was founded in the mid-nineteenth century by a charismatic master, Liu Tingfang, who proclaimed in 1844 in Gong country, western Henan, that he had been possessed by the spirit of Jiang Ziya, an ancient hero-general whose exploits were celebrated in the popular Ming novel *Enfeoffment of the Gods.* The society developed slowly over the following decades, remaining, so far as we can tell, relatively localized and obscure until the Republican era, when the chaos of the warlord period led to a major expansion of Temple activities. Membership grew rapidly throughout much of central and southern Henan, extending even into northern Hubei, and attained a height of some 45,000 by the 1940s. Other charismatic leaders emerged to succeed Liu Tingfang; these leaders based their power on their ability to intervene in the spirit world to cure *xiebing*—illnesses caused by immoral behavior.

The first Temple scriptures appear to have been penned in the early twentieth century; more were written to accompany a major expansion of Temple activities in the 1920s and 1930s.[13] These texts celebrate village morality and the paranormal powers of Temple leaders and present the Temple as a vehicle for the salvation of all believers in the face of a coming apocalypse. These scriptures share with other examples drawn from North China religious traditions a basic cosmology and a certain vocabulary, while remaining none-theless recognizably distinct. For example, while the Unborn Venerable Mo-ther, one of the most widespread of northern deities, does appear in Temple scriptures, she is not an object of particular devotion, nor is her role central.

These texts were recopied and circulated in post-Mao China in the same counties where the Temple had been well known during the Republican period. Temple followers were delighted to allow me and a Chinese colleague to photocopy such materials as part of fieldwork we carried out in the mid-1990s; they believed that I might spread the redemptive message to North America. During our fieldwork, we also observed that the appeal of the Temple in the 1990s appeared to be consistent with the impression conveyed by the Repub-lican period scriptures: practitioners drew on the charismatic powers of masters living and dead to cure their aches and pains; at Temple fairs (held on the birthdays of important figures in Temple history), practitioners chanted Temple scriptures which emphasized yet again village morality, the paranormal powers of Temple masters, and the coming apocalypse.

Over the course of the Republican period, the Temple, as an organized force in local rural society, became enmeshed in politics, as did many similar groups. The details are complicated and need not concern us here, but at various moments between the mid-1920s and the early 1950s, the Temple fought against the "Christian warlord" Feng Yuxiang, with and against the ruling Nationalist Party (or Kuomintang, often abbreviated KMT), with and against the Japanese invaders, and eventually against the Communists. Consequently, the Temple became one of several regional objects of the Communist campaign against reactionary *huidaomen* (a neologism coined by the Communists during this period to refer indiscriminately to "reactionary" popular religious groups and secret societies; translating *huidaomen* as "sect" neatly captures the pejo-rative intent of the authorities) in the early 1950s, and a handful of its leaders appear to have been executed. Some sources report that sporadic Temple re-bellions against the Communists continued under the People's Republic and, as already noted, the Temple was alive and well in the Henan countryside in the 1990s, part of the religious revival which marked post-Mao China.

The Temple is, to my mind, a typical example of a rural redemptive society, but it is perhaps less important for what it tells us about these societies as such than for what it tells us about how we know what we know about them. First, had I not done fieldwork during a period of religious revival, we would know next to nothing about the Temple. The few scholarly articles available on the Temple are in obscure local publications and possess little value as accurate sources of information about the society (a judgment made possible yet again by fieldwork), even if they are grist for the mill in our effort to understand elite discourse. The Temple was a largely rural phenomenon that rarely attracted media, scholarly, or even police attention except during rare moments of "political" conflict between the Temple and larger forces, such as warlords, the Nationalists, the Communists, the Japanese. Few treatments of the Temple mention Temple scriptures or the themes sounded in such scriptures— instead, the Temple is uniformly treated as an example of premodern ignorance or "feudal superstition"—and had Temple followers in the 1990s not been ready to share their scriptures with me, this crucial aspect of Temple history would simply have been lost. I hardly need add that the fieldwork, however brief and incomplete, carried out at Temple sites during the 1990s also allowed me to place the information gleaned from scriptural sources in a context of lived practice. In other words, had we stumbled on Temple scriptures in a local archive of confiscated heterodox materials from the Republican or early Communist periods, we would have had to guess which aspects of the scriptures fired the imaginations of Temple followers.

The case of the Temple, however, illustrates more than the obvious importance of doing fieldwork when the opportunity presents itself. In the course of my visits to rural Henan, I was given not only Temple scriptures, but also Public Security Bureau materials from the early 1950s that documented the suppression of the Temple at the hands of Communist authorities. To my knowledge, this is one of the few instances in the history of redemptive societies, from Ming times forward, where we possess both society-generated texts *and* documents created by a state investigation of a redemptive society *for the same case*.[14] Such police documents are one of our major sources of information about redemptive societies from late imperial times onward, and we readily acknowledge their bias, but it has proven difficult to evaluate the precise nature of the bias in the absence of other materials affording different perspectives on the same group.

In this particular case, a comparison of the state's indictment of Temple activities with a more scholarly reading made possible through interpretation of Temple scriptures and fieldwork among Temple followers reveals, among other things, a complete lack of interest on the part of Public Security Bureau investigators in questions of healing, charisma, and the supposed paranormal powers of Temple masters (except to the extent that such issues are reduced to "trickery" or "exploitation of the ignorant masses"). Similarly, fundamentalist calls for repentance and a return to morality are ignored or are depicted as part of a dangerous millenarianism, itself an excuse for rebellion. To the Public Security Bureau, the Temple represented an imperial restorationist movement, led by criminal elements who used apocalyptic rhetoric and feudal superstition to trick the unlearned peasantry into following them for material reasons. This is a hostile reading of the Temple, which Temple scriptures obviously do not support, but the point is not that Temple leaders were paragons of virtue who never took advantage of their followers. The point is rather that the reading carried out by Public Security Bureau officials is highly selective, does little to explain the appeal of the group to those who joined, and thus ignores the elements which gave the group its power.

The case of the Temple tends to confirm the argument that state condemnation of the White Lotus (or of redemptive societies) must be read as a discourse of persecution in which police inquiries, court proceedings, and even the "confessions" of those caught up in the dragnet serve less to determine guilt or innocence and more to label those presumed to be guilty in ways that accord with state fears of heterodoxy. For the purposes of the present argument, the distance between the state representation of the Temple and that found in Temple scriptures (to say nothing of Temple practices as observed in fieldwork) means that themes such as healing, morality, or calls to repentance are simply ignored by police and prosecutors, either because such practices are so common as to seem unexceptional, or because they are of little help to those trying to build a criminal case. This means that the central messages and purposes of redemptive societies as I have portrayed them in this chapter have been simply swept under the rug in official sources treating such groups. In other words, the fact that official records do not mention healing, corporal techniques, and moral messages does not mean that these did not exist. Ironically, this disconnect between the official condemnation of heterodoxy and the lived practices of the redemptive societies—which, as we will see in chapter 6, has characterized the campaign against Falun Gong as well—probably helps to explain the historical longevity of the groups: since most adepts seek personal redemption and relief from suffering, they can share state concerns with "heterodoxy," believing that it has nothing to do with them. The "evildoers" are somewhere else; *their* master is good and powerful. "Heterodoxy" has been the discourse of the elite.

## Redemptive Societies and Chinese Popular Religion

It is clearly impossible to do fieldwork on late imperial redemptive societies (e.g., the White Lotus), so we will have to devise another strategy to see past the distortions of the official records of the Ming-Qing period.[15] Recent studies of popular religion in the Republican period, although limited in number, confirm that when we manage to look past the state discourse, either through fieldwork or by using sources other than those of Chinese authorities, we find numerous examples of the kind of redemptive societies I have been discussing. Taking advantage of the increased openness of the post-Mao period, historian Thomas Dubois, for example, has studied existing redemptive societies[16] and other popular religions in contemporary North China, more specifically in the villages of Cang county in southeast Hebei, where he carried out fieldwork between 1997 and 2002 as part of his efforts to reconstruct their historical implications in village and regional life over time.

Dubois focuses on the Most Supreme (Taishang men) and the Heaven and Earth Teachings (Tiandi men), prime examples of what he calls "village sectarians." He examines as well the Way of Penetrating Unity (Yiguandao, "apocalyptic sectarians") and the Li sect (Zailijiao, "pseudomonastic sectarians"), taking care to embed all groups in their proper historical and cultural contexts. In terms of sources, Dubois did fieldwork among his groups during their reform era revival in the late twentieth century, interviewed older members of such groups who had personal memories of society history (perhaps from late Republican times, but certainly from the 1950s and 1960s), consulted Japanese ethnographies and the work of some Chinese researchers from the 1930s and 1940s, and perused a variety of sources on the late imperial predecessors of these groups under the Ming and Qing dynasties.[17]

For the purposes of this volume, Dubois makes a number of important points. First, he demonstrates conclusively that redemptive societies have been a fixture of the North China religious landscape for centuries and that they have been largely accepted, despite their formal status as heterodox. Both the Most Supreme and the Heaven and Earth Teachings trace their origins to the White Lotus tradition, but both have come to function as part of the very moral and ritual core of village religiosity; society leaders serve as village moral exemplars and officiate at important ritual occasions, such as funerals, blessings, and exorcisms, or annual festivals and ceremonies, including prayers for rain. Moreover, the theme of healing is omnipresent. Dubois begins his book with the image of an elderly woman seeking the healing power of Dong Sihai, the founder of the Heaven and Earth Teachings, in February 1998, noting, "This scene could be set in almost any village in late imperial China."[18] To the extent that Dubois's examples are representative, he makes the important point that, if redemptive societies ever were marginal outsiders, they are not now stigmatized as such by local society and have not been so for some time. Dubois himself highlights "the ability of these groups to function quietly as stable local institutions," noting that "[u]nless somehow drawn into political intrigue, such groups remained beyond the interest of most government investigators and appear only tangentially in historical records. Yet, evidence demonstrates that the practice of such groups remained very close to the needs of everyday life."[19]

A related point is that, since the redemptive societies were not closed groups of "true believers" who emphasized their separateness from nonsectarian life, the residents of villages where such societies had established an important presence were free to decide on their individual level of association with the society's morality and votive activity. Nor were redemptive society members secret or isolated from nonmembers.

The societies studied by Dubois seem to fully subscribe to the grammar of the redemptive societies as outlined above. Yang Zai (1623–1754), the founder of the Li sect, is depicted in society scriptures and legends as "a benevolent and filial Confucian scholar who was dismayed by the wars and chaos of the time and sought to ease the sufferings of the people."[20] While grieving the death of his mother, Yang wrote the basic scriptures of the Li sect (another version insists that Guanyin revealed these teachings to Yang). Subsequently, Li retired to a cave some sixty miles north of Tianjin where he meditated for ten years. The corporal technologies he developed reportedly allowed him to live to the ripe old age of 131. The Heaven and Earth Teachings were founded by Dong Sihai (1619–1650) in the late Ming period. Like Yang Zai, Dong created his teachings out of concern for the decline in popular morality. In Dubois's apt summary, "In terms of belief, the Heaven and Earth Society is characterized by the deification of Dong Sihai and...emphasis on Confucian morality. In practice, this is reflected in the strong emphasis placed on scripture and the great demands on ritual specialists to become versed in this tradition."[21] Twentieth-century leaders of redemptive societies, if perhaps lacking the full charisma of society founders, retained their status as community leaders, respected for their knowledge and their moral rectitude; from the perspective of the local society, they represent orthodoxy. This is why some of these groups survived the suppression of *huidaomen* in the early 1950s and why they have managed to reestablish themselves—if not without some difficulty due to the loss of ritual specialists—in the post–Cultural Revolution period. Smart local cadres (like smart local magistrates under the imperial order) realize that, except during moments of intense political pressure, management of rural society is much easier if carried out with the cooperation of village leaders.

If Dubois sheds much-needed light on the question of the integration of redemptive societies at the village, or micro, level from late imperial times through the present, Prasenjit Duara explores an important expansion of redemptive societies at the macro level during Republican period China; one is almost tempted to speak of a "redemptive societies boom" to stress certain parallels with the post-Mao enthusiasm for qigong.[22] Although there may not have been as many redemptive societies under the republic as there were schools of qigong in the 1980s and 1990s, there were still thousands;[23] among the most important were the Daodehui (Morality Society), the Daoyuan (Society of the Way) and its philanthropic wing, the Hongwanzihui (Red Swastika Society), the Tongshanshe (Fellowship of Goodness), the Zailijiao (the Teaching of the Abiding Principle), the Shijie Zongjiao Datonghui (Society for the Great Unity of World Religions), and the Yiguandao (Way of Penetrating Unity). There were hundreds if not thousands of smaller societies like the Way of the Temple of the Heavenly Immortals, the Most Supreme, and the Heaven and Earth Teachings. Total membership over the Republican period appears to have amounted to tens of millions, again recalling the post-Mao qigong movement. The numbers are perhaps no more reliable than those we find during the period of qigong's most rapid expasion, but the Tongshanshe claimed 30 million members in 1929, the Red Swastika Society 7–10 million in 1937, and the Daodehui 8 million in Manchukuo alone (a quarter of the total population) in 1936–1937.

What were these groups, which have passed almost completely unnoticed in textbook treatments of modern Chinese history? According to Duara, the redemptive societies

> clearly emerged out of the Chinese historical tradition of sectarianism and syncretism. While some . . . were closely associated with the sectarian tradition including the worship of Buddhist and folk deities like the Eternal Mother, they also represented the late imperial syncretic tradition . . . which combined the three religions of Confucianism, Buddhism and Daoism in a single universal faith.[24]

Furthermore, the groups "ranged from the 'morality cultivating' charitable societies to the occasionally violent, secret-society-like entities."[25] Some groups used divination and spirit writing, thus connecting them to popular religious culture, while at the same time claiming to embrace the moral concerns of Christianity and Islam, adding those faiths to the Chinese heritage of Confucianism, Daoism, and Buddhism. Many of the groups, in their universal redemptive mission, continued to sound traditional Chinese apocalyptic themes—even as they engaged in modern charitable and philanthropic work. Although our knowledge of these groups remains rudimentary,[26] most of the societies seem to have been organized around charismatic men (and, in a few cases, women) who often promised to heal the body, the soul, and/or the world.

While the redemptive societies grew out of late imperial popular religious culture, they also developed in new ways under the changing conditions of the Republican period. Many of the best known and largest were primarily urban societies, which often enjoyed the patronage of important political leaders. Like the Rotarians or Elks Clubs in North America, many Republican period redemptive societies appealed to the middle class or even the wealthy; the Hong-wanzihui and the Daodehui, among others, engaged in a wide variety of charitable or philanthropic work ranging from famine relief, to anti-opium or anti-alcohol programs, to educational work. As already mentioned, many re-demptive societies adopted a universalist posture toward religion in general, arguing that diverse faiths are simply different expressions of the same fun-damental truth; it is hard to imagine a less "sectarian" stance. At the same time, one should not underestimate the importance of religious concerns to these societies; it will not do to identify urbanization and treaty port modernization with secularization. Many society founders were charismatic preachers who penned scriptures that were printed and circulated among the faithful; many scriptures drew on traditional apocalyptic or millenarian themes. Most societies created a range of rituals and religious symbols and called upon members to live moral lives and do good works.

## State Authorities and Redemptive Societies

Duara's study also reveals another crucial aspect of the history of redemptive societies under the Chinese republic—their relationship to the state—which brings us back to the question of politics and its role in our understanding of the history of redemptive societies. Much of Duara's work focuses on Man-chukuo, the puppet state established by the Japanese in Manchuria in 1931, which remained under Japanese control—although supposedly ruled by Puyi, China's fabled "last emperor"—until the end of the Sino-Japanese War in 1945. For complex reasons having to do with Japan's vision of its place in the world, Japanese authorities in Manchukuo—and later in Japanese-occupied China—maintained a largely favorable attitude toward Chinese redemptive societies. For the Japanese, "Eastern religion" such as that embodied in these societies was part of an "Eastern civilization" which Japan intended to liberate from the shackles of Western imperialism (and, more broadly, Western civilization); emphasis on this shared heritage and these common values was part of Japa-nese propaganda meant to justify Japan's presence in China (and elsewhere in Asia) and to win popular support, in Japanese-occupied territories, for the future of the Greater East-Asian Co-Prosperity Sphere.

   For Chinese redemptive societies, such openness represented a rare op-portunity to establish a collaborative relationship with state authorities, and many societies quite rapidly overcame nationalistic distaste for the Japanese invaders to assume a larger public role than had historically been the case. Daoyuan followers in Manchuria, for example, announced that the Daoist sage Laozi, their principal god, had prophesied the Japanese victory as a sign of the apocalypse, and they subsequently came to view the occupation as a liberation. The Morality Society reacted similarly, if for somewhat different reasons,[27] and, as already noted, its membership expanded to some 8 million in Manchukuo by the late 1930s. Much of this expansion was due to the work of Wang Fengyi (1864–1937), a charismatic, self-educated intellectual from the countryside of southern Manchuria, known to his followers as the "righteous sage" (yisheng) or the "man of goodness" (shanren). Like many other leaders of redemptive societies, Wang healed the sick and preached ethical transformation through filial piety and study of the ancient sages. With the support of the rulers of Manchukuo, Wang established 312 branches of the Manchukuo Morality Society, 235 "righteous schools," 226 lecture halls, and 124 clinics—all by 1932, one year after the establishment of Manchukuo. It is clear that this society was a genuine social institution and not a puppet society of the puppet state; it is equally clear that it appealed both to commoner and elite.[28] Charles B. Jones finds similar evidence in his study of Taiwan under Japanese occupation, where authorities classified "vegetarian societies" (zhaijiao), which were viewed with suspicion by Chinese authorities as part of the White Lotus tradition, as part of Buddhism, to be managed by the South Seas Buddhist Association, "the only instance in Chinese history in which monastic Buddhism has actively cooperated with what it considered a White-Lotus form of popular Buddhism."[29]

Although the Japanese were not blind to the "superstitious" aspects of some redemptive societies—and found it difficult to work with some groups—in general they sought to co-opt and transform the societies rather than to suppress them. Chinese authorities took the opposite approach. It was clearly the weakness of the early twentieth-century Chinese state that allowed the emergence and multiplication of the redemptive societies under discussion here, just as it was the retreat of the reform era Chinese state from the front lines of micro-level social management which permitted the qigong boom and the more general expansion of religious activities later in the century. Indeed, a brief chronology of the history of the implementation of religious policy in twentieth-century China illustrates that redemptive societies flourish in inverse proportion to the strength and assertiveness of the state.

In some instances, the modernizing thrust of state policies toward religion made itself felt on the ground, in local communities, even before the fall of the imperial regime, when the Qing, after decades of foot dragging, finally embraced a package of reforms in the early twentieth century. The goal of these reforms was state building, broadly defined; Chinese reformers drew inspiration largely from the example of Meiji Japan. Among other things, the plans called for the construction of modern schools, modern police, and modern self-government—all of which were to extend to the rural areas. In this context, religious institutions—both orthodox and less orthodox—often became targets of the campaigns. Many religious institutions possessed property which could be confiscated to serve the newly redefined "public good," and in some instances, temples were simply "converted" (read: confiscated) to serve as school buildings. In one Shandong county, for instance, of the 432 temples present in 1900, only 116 remained by 1915.[30] In this instance, as later on, the pressing material needs of local reformers, combined with their ideological distaste for "ignorant superstition," resulted in a broad assault on the institutions of popular religion. Although local elites had been implicated in many local cults in imperial times, some chose to join forces with the state in its new posture, preferring climbing onto the bandwagon of state power to sharing power with locals.[31] Vincent Goossaert estimates that "it is probable that more than half of Chinese temples had been emptied of all religious activity on the eve of the Sino-Japanese war beginning in 1937."[32]

The constitution of 1912, as mentioned in the introductory chapter, was the embodiment of elite opinion on religion in the early republic. More important than this policy statement, however, was the fact that the republic was soon subverted by Yuan Shikai and, after his death in 1916, dissolved rapidly into warlordism. Until 1927, China's central government existed largely on paper only and was incapable of affording much attention to matters of religion. Some warlords were aggressive modernizers and carried forward the anti-superstition emphasis implicit in the constitution and in previous discussions of religion and modernization: the "Christian warlord" Feng Yuxiang, for example, permitted his troops to destroy images in Buddhist and folk temples as he modernized Henan province in the 1920s.[33] Other warlords were less concerned or were even open to alliances with religious groups. Indeed, this was the period when the redemptive societies studied by Duara emerged in greatest number and greatest force. Warlords often patronized such groups for both practical and symbolic reasons, as many warlord regimes lacked well-articulated, institutionalized relations with either elite or mass; offering support to a self-proclaimed redemptive society was one way for a warlord to suggest that his regime aspired to moral legitimacy (and for the leader of a religious/philanthropic society to protect himself and his followers).

When the Nationalists reestablished central power in 1927, with their capital in Nanjing, they sought to reassert the Republican policy on religion. This reassertion is most visible in renewed campaigns against local superstitions; the Northern Expedition, which unified significant parts of China militarily in 1926 and 1927, was accompanied by considerable destruction of religious icons,[34] and in 1928 and 1929, the Nationalist Party organized "anti-religion" and "anti-superstition" campaigns in Guangdong and in the lower Yangzi.[35] The Nationalists also sought to ban some redemptive societies, on the basis that they were superstitions and "incompatible with the spirit of progress."[36] Many societies, which had the support of powerful political and military figures as well as thousands if not millions of followers, fought back, and the KMT eventually relented in the case of certain groups, particularly those which could most easily present themselves as charitable or philanthropic organizations. But in many cases—the Tongshanshe is a good example—religious (or superstitious) elements were too intermingled with social welfare activities to permit easy distinctions.[37]

The Nationalists seem to have hoped that their New Life campaign, which sought to impose a new discipline on Chinese society through the revitalization of a rather muscular Confucianism inspired by military rigor, might come to satisfy the salvationist urges which filled the ranks of the redemptive societies. However well founded (or ill founded) such hopes might have been, the Japanese invasion of China beginning in 1937 robbed the KMT of its base in coastal China and put the regime on a wartime footing which robbed such concerns of much of their immediacy—even though the New Life campaign continued in Chongqing, the wartime capital. In the occupied territories, the Japanese encouraged Chinese redemptive societies much as they had in Manchukuo, and many Chinese redemptive societies responded positively, for reasons one can readily understand. Whatever such groups may have thought about Japanese claims to be revitalizing "Eastern civilization," the societies led the relief work in the wake of the Nanjing massacre in 1937 and served as a buffer between the often cruel occupation authorities and the Chinese population. Redemptive societies continued to play this role even after the defeat of Japan in 1945 and during the civil war between the Nationalists and the Communists. The Red Swastika Society served as the largest welfare organization in Shanghai in the civil war period.[38]

With the conclusion of the civil war and the establishment of the People's Republic, however, China was once again unified, this time under a strong central authority, meaning that once again, local cults and redemptive societies became the target of suppression, and part of the consolidation of the new state's power involved a campaign against feudal, reactionary *huidaomen* in the early 1950s. At the moment of liberation in October 1949, according to the estimates of Chinese historian Shao Yong, there were more than 300 "reactionary heterodox religious societies" with a total membership of more than

13 million. In Shanxi province alone, there were more than 1 million who belonged to one group or another. In Shandong province, there were 176 groups, 1,711 leaders, and 690,000 members. In the city of Tianjin, there were some 153 different groups. To the extent possible, People's Liberation Army (PLA) troops sought to suppress such groups as they liberated various parts of the country, but success was limited, and a nationwide campaign aimed solely at the sects was launched in the spring of 1953 (following smaller, more regionally focused campaigns in 1951). In the course of the 1953 campaign, Shanghai authorities clamped down on more than 50 groups, jailing nearly 4,000 important leaders, further registering an additional 9,728 leaders of secondary importance, and reeducating and releasing 320,000 practitioners. In the adjacent province of Jiangsu, 60 more groups were suppressed, more than 50,000 leaders registered, and another 470,000 followers reeducated and released.[39] Redemptive societies were once again attacked as teaching feudal superstitions and, in addition, were accused of being traitors, having collaborated with the hated Japanese. As for the charitable or philanthropic activities of the redemptive societies, the Communists intended to establish their own welfare institutions, which would make such competition for popular support unnecessary and undesirable.

Although many redemptive societies followed the KMT to Taiwan, and continue to thrive today, the 1950s were a key period for redemptive societies in China proper. The Communist authorities arrested and executed some leaders, reeducated many followers, and closed down the national organizations of the largest Republican period societies.[40] At the same time, many village-level redemptive societies to say nothing of the belief structure underlying such organizations—remained intact, at least to the extent that Thomas Dubois's work is representative. Dubois illustrates that Shandong villagers were happy to part company in the early 1950s with the Way of Penetrating Unity (Yiguandao), a redemptive society with apocalyptic overtones which had cooperated widely with the Japanese occupation authorities, but they clung to their own village-based groups, which the Way of Penetrating Unity had never managed to challenge in any significant way. These village redemptive societies continued to function largely unhindered until the mid-1960s, when the excesses of the Cultural Revolution led to a large-scale attack on all symbols of feudal culture, including religious symbols.[41] Indeed, it is important to stress, as Adam Chau has done in his work on rural Shaanxi, that with the exception of the Cultural Revolution period, local authorities in many areas of China arrived at a modus vivendi with village- and community-based popular religious groups so as to avoid constant confrontation.[42] This may well mean that even though Western observers have tended to view the People's Republic as fundamentally atheistic and anti-religious, in reality, elements of religious life survived the transition and achieved at least a marginal status.

Part of the party's effort to establish a new legitimacy in the post-Mao era has been a significant—if fluctuating over time—relaxation in the degree to which state authorities monitor and control the daily lives, activities, and thoughts of China's people. In the realm of religion, this relaxation took the form of Document 19, issued in 1982, which in the apt summary of Pitman Potter, put forth the party's basic policy as "one of respect for and protection of the freedom of religious belief, pending such future time when religion itself will disappear."[43] This document did not alter the prevailing definition of religion, nor did it surrender party authorities' power to intervene in religious matters by establishing an independent realm of religious activity, but the statement did signal a certain tolerance, a "zone of indifference,"[44] which resulted in a significant increase in the level of religious practice in China over the course of the reform period. Policy implementation has been more or less tolerant depending on particular political or regional contexts, but long-term trends have been consistent with the spirit of Document 19, and authorities appear to have moved toward the embrace of "proper" religions as contributing to social stability. As will be illustrated in the following chapter, qigong emerged not as a religion but as a medical practice, but there is little doubt that the qigong movement, organized around charismatic masters who offered miracle cures and moral teachings, was part and parcel of the post-Mao spirit of greater tolerance of religion, even if qigong and Falun Gong were allowed much greater leeway than, say, Christian groups, because they were not seen as religious organizations.

This chronology, however sketchy, reveals a number of important points. First, the history of redemptive societies extends beyond political frontiers and historiographical boundaries, and the revival of religion in reform era China suggests that the impact of China's political revolution on religious culture has been less definitive than we have tended to believe. Second, redemptive societies have expanded during periods when the Chinese state was weak. Looking only at the twentieth century, redemptive societies flourished in the late Qing/ early Republican/warlord era, suffered under the unified Nationalist regime, thrived under the Japanese, were suppressed—at least as organized groups— during the Maoist period, and returned in reform era China. Third, the construction of this chronology is the first step toward the recognition of a history which has not yet been written, a history of redemptive societies which reaches back into the late imperial era and traverses the political and military histories of twentieth-century China; it has been eclipsed at every turn by the major narratives but is a history which has nonetheless touched hundreds of millions of Chinese. This history has yet to be written because of the attitude of state authorities toward redemptive societies. As Prasenjit Duara perceptively noted:

> All the principal Chinese regimes of the twentieth century—the imperial, the KMT, and the Communists—have banned these [redemptive] societies or sought to keep very strict control over them. . . . The Chinese regimes appear to be especially threatened by the personal empowerment that allegedly emerged from tapping into cosmic forces. . . . Whether because it claimed monopoly of access to the principle of the cosmos (the imperial state) or because it sought to guard forcefully the cosmological authority of science (modern states), the state has severely restricted religiosity to state-licensed organizations. Thus even though they may have had orthodox and elitist elements within them, the redemptive societies often found themselves beyond the law.[45]

The consequences of this attitude for the hidden history of redemptive societies are multiple. First, since the organizations have been deemed illegal, or tinged with heterodoxy, official historiography has followed suit, sounding the same themes as in political discourse and ignoring themes that do not fit the politically driven narratives of national history and national historiography. Since religion in modern China has been defined as the five great world historical faiths existing on Chinese soil, which have further been given the role of contributing to China's national purpose, it is not surprising that Chinese historians hardly know what to do with such protean groups as the Tong shanshe or the Morality Society. A typical historical treatment praises, if tepidly, their philanthropic activities, but notes sadly their roots in feudal heterodoxy, a "reactionary" tendency which explains their sad attachment to the imperialistic Japanese, with whom they joined to oppose the forces of progress and enlightenment.[46] During the anti–Falun Gong campaign, Chinese historians were called upon to write Falun Gong into the history of heterodoxy, emphasizing yet again its supposed stance as an enemy of science, peace, and stability. This of course is not history, but propaganda.

Furthermore, the groups themselves have not written their own histories, as even they have had a hard time seeing past the state discourse.[47] Part of the problem is that there exists as yet no neutral, general term such as "redemptive society" in Chinese—for the reasons I have explained. How then can such a group fight back when it is accused of being a *huidaomen*? The members cannot say "we are not a *huidaomen*, we are a religion" because religion is defined as mainstream churches, clergy, and scriptures. The category of "new religious movement," which has a shaky existence outside of certain academic circles even in the West, has only recently begun to be used in China. The lack of an appropriate terminology also means that groups have difficulty making common cause against authorities: under what banner would they group themselves? The China Qigong Science Research Society (CQRS), discussed in the following chapter, is probably the first umbrella organization of redemptive societies in Chinese history.

In part because redemptive societies have long been subject to state suppression, the groups never developed the sense of historical self-consciousness we associate with mainstream religious traditions. Imagine Christianity, or any world religion for that matter, without the physical monuments, the historically conditioned corpus of texts, the ecclesiastical organization so necessary to the creation of a sense of continuous identity. Consequently, for members of these societies, history often is esoterica: masters who emerge from the mountains, clandestine transmissions of secret knowledge, all shrouded in mystery and "truth." Qigong and Falun Gong practitioners, by now highly aware of the role of the Chinese state in defining and enforcing central visions of orthodoxy, still reject out of hand any historical connection to Republican period redemptive societies, or to the late imperial White Lotus, because the only thing they know about such traditions is that they were "heterodox" and "violent." The source of this characterization is none other than the Chinese state, testimony to the success of its historical campaign to label such organizations as evil. Ironically, the societies' lack of historical self-consciousness and their inability to make common cause with other, similar societies tend to obscure the fact that redemptive societies are widespread and largely mainstream in their cultural and political orientations. State hostility serves once again as a self-fulfilling prophecy, pushing redemptive societies away from the center and toward the periphery.


Conclusion

This chapter has suggested the outlines of a possible history for Falun Gong, and I have drawn attention to similarities among Falun Gong (and other schools of qigong), the redemptive societies of the Republican period, and the White Lotus tradition of the late imperial era. The reader might well wonder if I am making the strong claim that qigong and Falun Gong are directly descended from the late imperial White Lotus tradition, or the weaker claim that there are enough shared elements that we might well imagine some genealogical connection even if we cannot identify a specific bloodline. I would like to make the strong claim, but in fact am making neither.

Any discussion of the White Lotus tradition must, once again, begin with Barend Ter Haar's demonstration that this tradition did not exist as such, that the term "White Lotus," whatever its historical origins, was employed by the late imperial state as a shorthand gloss for heterodox religious groups which the state feared might foment rebellion. The state further identified the characteristics of such groups: the worship of the Unborn Mother and the Maitreya Buddha, the role of charismatic (and evil) masters who penned their own scriptural truths, the teaching of mantras and other healing arts, and the selling of such secrets to the naïve masses. Such characterizations, however, are hardly scientific; they were put together by the late imperial equivalents of police investigators and prosecutors as tools in a protracted campaign against what they saw as a nefarious social evil. A close parallel might be the anti-cult movement in the modern West, which draws up similar lists of "cult characteristics," which are then used to vilify and prosecute certain groups. Some detainees at Guantanamo might see parallels with the George W. Bush administration's use of the label "Islamic terrorism."

This does not mean that late imperial investigators or anti-cult crusaders (or even the Bush administration) have been wrong on every occasion and that all those caught up in the dragnet were as pure as the driven snow. Charlatans have used religion to exploit the weak and foolish throughout history, and states have indeed fallen to peasant jacqueries fueled by superstitious nonsense. But just as no one today says to himself, "I'm miserable and frustrated, I think I'll join a cult," no one in late imperial China said, "My back hurts and I'm desperately poor, please direct me to the local White Lotus recruitment bureau." The White Lotus did not exist as an organized, conscious force. What existed were charismatic masters who promised relief from physical pain and perhaps eventual salvation based on a certain cosmology, expressed in original scriptures, which were recited or chanted as part of a set of corporal technologies and which were linked in turn to fundamentalist calls to return to basic moral practices in the face of social decline and perhaps a coming apocalypse. Such ideas had long been disseminated in China, and one might draw suggestive parallels with the Celestial Masters movement in early Daoist history, or with certain strains of Buddhism in medieval China.[48] There was no one source for the White Lotus tradition, and as Daniel Overmyer, Hubert Seiwert, and other scholars who have studied their scriptures have illustrated, there are important differences in the ways in which masters expressed their visions in preaching and in scripture.[49] What we have called the White Lotus tradition should properly be seen as one strain of popular religion which offered healing and the promise of salvation through the practice of morality and body technologies. This strain of popular religion, which I hope we will someday come to call "redemptive societies," was perhaps less integrated into village and familial structures than were village cults or the ancestral cult and was looked down on by some members of the elite, particularly during periods of state suppression. At the same time, we find considerable evidence of middle-brow and even elite involvement in such activities, both in the late imperial and Republican periods, which leads me to believe that the heterodox label affixed by the state did not always strike fear into the hearts of those tempted by the promise of healing and salvation. While the state insisted on the heterodox nature of such practices, the moral fundamentalism of the teachings suggested to adepts that they themselves were thoroughly orthodox, perhaps even "model citizens," if such a concept existed in late imperial times. Many White Lotus scriptures begin with a ritual embrace of the emperor, wishing him long life.

In other words, we need to reimagine the White Lotus in fundamental ways before attempting to evaluate the links among this tradition, qigong, and Falun Gong. And I wonder if it would not be more helpful to try to reimagine the White Lotus on the basis of what we know about qigong and Falun Gong than the other way around. As we will see in the following chapter, during the qigong boom, masters emerged in great profusion and millions of Chinese answered their call. True, a vast qigong media apparatus accompanied the movement and, in part, encouraged popular participation, but my impression is that qigong practitioners needed little encouragement (other than permission) before joining in wholeheartedly. Similarly, the state attempted to control popular enthusiasm by establishing the CQRS, which was empowered to certify qigong masters and to govern their activities, but it is clear that the state followed rather than led. The qigong boom was thus an organic event, fueled by popular enthusiasm for health, well-being, and cultivation, which developed rapidly in the absence of a well-defined "qigong tradition" or of recognized norms. To my mind, it is helpful to view the late imperial White Lotus tradition in a similar fashion, instead of likening it to a discrete, underground tradition unknown but to a few. The following chapter illustrates how the redemptive societies managed to survive in the inhospitable soil of the People's Republic under Mao, and then flourish in the reform era.

# 3

# The Creation and Evolution of Qigong

Our narrative shifts gears in this chapter, the focus changing from the history of Chinese popular religion and redemptive societies to that of Chinese medicine, as it was in the guise of a medical practice, or technology, that some of the practices and discourses associated with redemptive societies entered Chinese socialist culture in the form of qigong. Although this shift may appear jarring at first view, it is completely logical (although no one involved in the redemptive societies or in Chinese medicine would have foreseen such a thing in the 1940s), in part because religion and healing were closely linked in traditional Chinese culture.

Following the Communist victory in 1949, the suppression, at the hands of the police or in some cases even the army, of "reactionary" elements such as redemptive societies and sectarian networks was an important aspect of the post-revolutionary establishment of social order. The major channels for the expression of ideas and practices associated with redemptive societies were thus closed down, the leaders of these societies arrested and often executed, and to the extent that redemptive societies continued to exist in an organized fashion after the early 1950s, it was as semi-underground, village-level organizations such as those studied by Thomas Dubois, which exercised relatively little influence beyond the village. There is no reason to believe, however, that the discourses and beliefs associated with redemptive societies disappeared. As the previous chapter demonstrated, such ideas and beliefs were widespread in Chinese society, and even if a few hundred leaders were arrested and executed, hundreds of thousands of practitioners were welcomed into the "new society."

But as the redemptive societies disappeared, qigong was born. Qigong was "invented" in the late 1940s and early 1950s in an effort to modernize and "scientize" (*kexuehua*) meditative, breathing, and other practices associated with a variety of religious and spiritual traditions and cultivation so as to preserve the health benefits of these practices in the new, socialist society. Cadres associated with the PRC health care establishment sought out masters and healers in the countryside and elsewhere and procured from them the secrets of their curative powers. These secrets were then cleaned up, the "feudal" language surrounding them removed, and the practices added to the storehouse of modern Chinese medicine under construction in the 1950s. I am not suggesting that qigong as invented in the 1950s was a carbon copy of the corporal technologies of the pre-liberation redemptive societies, or even that there were direct links between redemptive societies and the creators of qigong—even if both are concerned with health, healing, and cultivation and are pursued without biomedicine. At the same time, it is clear that, in giving a positive sanction to corporal technologies like meditation, visualization, chanting, and breathing techniques, the invention of qigong kept alive, if in a very different setting, part of the appeal and the technologies of the redemptive societies. Of course, science took the place of religion, or cultivation, in the larger discursive construct within which redemptive societies had functioned to this point, with results that differed greatly over the course of qigong's brief history. In the pre–Cultural Revolution period, qigong was a relatively unimportant part of Traditional Chinese Medicine, taught and practiced as part of Chinese medical science in clinics and sanatoriums. In the post–Cultural Revolution period, the heralded discovery by well-known Chinese researchers of the scientific existence of qi gave qigong the cachet of a genuine science and allowed qigong enthusiasts to ally their efforts with those of China's modernizers. The qigong boom resulted when China's preeminent authorities joined other qigong enthusiasts and embraced qigong practice as part of China's—and perhaps the world's—salvation. The excitement of the movement obscured the fact that the qigong of the post–Cultural Revolution period, led by charismatic masters preaching morality and corporal techniques, embracing science but bringing science and spirituality together, looked as much like pre-liberation redemptive societies as it did the tame qigong of the 1950s clinics. The first part of this chapter examines the invention of qigong in the 1950s, the second the "revival" of qigong in the 1970s and 1980s.

Science: The Savior of Modern China

What motivated the creators of qigong, and why did the modernizing socialist state sanction such behavior? The answers to these questions are complex and demand an examination of the history of science and medicine in modern China.

Science has been perceived by Chinese intellectuals as directly or indirectly linked to national salvation since the nineteenth century, when China first came into protracted contact with the modern West. At the earliest stage, science and technology (science was seen almost exclusively as technology at the outset) were seen as little more than handy, if formidable, bags of tricks which had enabled Western countries to build up redoubtable armies and navies and which China could borrow in its turn. The Chinese scholar Feng Guifen, writing in the early 1860s, captured the attitude of a small, progressive minority in China during this period:

> All Western knowledge is derived from mathematics. Every Westerner of ten years of age or more studies mathematics. If we now wish to adopt Western knowledge, naturally we cannot but learn mathematics.... If we let Chinese ethics and famous [Confucian] teachings serve as an original foundation, and let them be supplemented by the methods used by the various nations for the attainment of prosperity and strength, would it not be the best of all procedures?[1]

The notion that the essence of traditional Chinese culture could be preserved by surrounding it with a hard outer shell of Western science and technology gradually came to be popular among certain intellectuals and officials over the course of the latter part of the nineteenth century and is best summed up by the high official Zhang Zhidong's famous end-of-century remark that Chinese learning should serve as the foundation and Western learning as the practical application (*zhongxue weiti, xixue weiyong*) for the future development of China.[2]

The first two decades of the twentieth century, however, witnessed the collapse of the imperial state *and* the rapid failure of the first flimsy Republican regime set up to take its place. In the vacuum created by this dual failure, science came to be seen as more than a set of magic tricks; science came to be understood as a new, modern way of looking at the world and solving problems, perhaps the only force capable of saving China from its enemies—and itself. At first, science was often paired with democracy in the minds of iconoclastic

May Fourth period intellectuals anxious to remake China's traditional culture in a more Western image. But the ghastly spectacle of the First World War, where the world's most "civilized" nations massacred one another's youth in unprecedented numbers, followed by the refusal of the Western victors gathered at Versailles to honor China's request that its territorial integrity be respected—as the Wilsonian rhetoric of self-determination demanded—combined to reduce Chinese enthusiasm for democracy. When the Western powers at Versailles chose to honor dubious Japanese territorial claims in China in the interest of the regional balance of power, democracy came to be seen by many Chinese intellectuals as a cynical manipulation, a transparent excuse draped over the naked exercise of might-makes-right. Something so unprincipled could hardly qualify as "scientific."[3]

Science itself did not suffer the same fate.[4] Marxist claims that socialism was scientific even provided part of the appeal of this Western ideology to disillusioned Chinese intellectuals in the 1920s and after, and both Nationalist and Communist governments have claimed to harness science to the needs of national construction since national reunification in 1927. Soviet science directed the construction of China's military-industrial complex in the 1950s; Maoist science inspired much of the madness of the Great Leap Forward. Science (usually without adjectives) survived the chaos of the Cultural Revolution (1966–1976) to emerge as the focus for China's modernization efforts and continues to be at the forefront of state policy in a variety of areas. Even at the popular cultural level, science retains a cachet which it has lost in a more jaded postmodern America, perhaps because many parts of China remain underdeveloped. When I watch Chinese television or read Chinese magazines, the use of the term "science" recalls that of "new and improved" in the American advertising of my youth. On a visit to Beijing in the 1990s, I saw an old lady who had set up a booth on a bridge, with a sign advertising her wares which read kexue kanxiang—"scientific fortunetelling."

The history of medicine in modern China is part of this larger history of science. Medicine of course existed in China prior to the arrival of Western medical missionaries in the early nineteenth century and prior to the emergence of biomedicine in the later nineteenth century. Like other traditional societies, however, pre-twentieth-century China had very little in the way of a medical establishment: there was little state regulation, no recognized medical curriculum or diploma, no professional monopoly on medical knowledge and practice. As Paul Unschuld, a leading scholar of the history of Chinese medicine puts it, "[T]he Chinese physician as a definable entity did not exist [in imperial times] . . . [and patients consulted] shamans, Buddhist priests, Daoist hermits, Confucian scholars, itinerant physicians, established physicians, 'laymen' with medical knowledge, . . . midwives, and many others."[5] As part of his filial duties, an educated man was expected to be familiar with basic medical texts and practices, so as to respond to the needs of his parents and monitor the care they might receive.[6] Unsurprisingly, doctors in traditional China were not viewed as part of the educated elite and enjoyed little social prestige, even if there existed a vast array of healers and healing practices which were exploited and highly valued by the population at large.

In the first decades of the twentieth century, as Chinese elites came to blame traditional Chinese culture for China's failure to modernize, traditional medical practices and knowledge came to be viewed with derision. The opinions of such seminal figures as Lu Xun and Guo Moruo are well known and representative of an attitude which condemned traditional medicine as "feudal superstition," which should be abandoned with the rest of Confucian culture, to be replaced by modern, Western biomedicine.[7] Consequently, China's Republican period witnessed the emergence of a Western-educated Chinese medical profession, some physicians having been trained in China in Western educational establishments, others having studied abroad. Many of these modern doctors added their voices to those of other intellectuals and lobbied the emerging Chinese state for the power and authority necessary to lend their expertise to the service of China's vast medical needs. And it is true that, whatever the virtues of Chinese medicine, it is relatively useless in the face of epidemics (the Manchurian plague of 1910 and its containment via the intervention of a Western-trained doctor marks, according to certain scholars, a turning point in the history of the medicalization of China),[8] has little to offer in the way of preventive medicine,[9] and does not lend itself to the needs of a modern state whose tasks include the compilation of detailed statistics and the construction of a public health establishment.

In fact, the biomedical establishment in Republican China, articulate, well organized, and well connected, was on its way to victory over the forces of traditional medicine when it overplayed its hand at a crucial moment. In 1929, Western-trained doctors formally called on the state to abolish traditional medicine and to prevent traditional medical practitioners from treating patients. Faced with the imminent loss of their livelihood, traditional practitioners began to organize and, in so doing, created the idea of "national medicine," artfully casting the defense of their practices as part of the larger Chinese nationalistic struggle against imperialism.[10] For a variety of symbolic and practical reasons, state authorities allowed themselves to be partially won over by the cause of national medicine, even as they demanded that its practitioners respect the dictates of modernity and biomedicine. Ever since, Traditional Chinese Medicine[11] has coexisted with its arrogant and powerful big brother, biomedicine, in an uneasy sibling rivalry which has produced, under the People's Republic, a pluralistic medical system dubbed by one scholar "hegemonic pluralism,"[12] since biomedicine has generally succeeded in garnering the lion's share of resources and investments and has demanded numerous and important concessions from TCM. But, for the purposes of this chapter, what is important to note is that Chinese medicine succeeded in carving out a space for itself within the modern medical establishment of the People's Republic of China, and this was the space which sheltered the invention and propagation of qigong.

## The Invention of Qigong and the Rise of Traditional Chinese Medicine

When Li Hongzhi, or any other qigong master, refers to the "ancient history" of qigong, he is referring to techniques and discourses associated with qigong and not to the term itself. True enough, the term *qi* has an ancient and noble lineage, in both the medical and philosophical traditions, and the term *gong* is no modern invention either, but the two characters taken together as a compound appear only occasionally over the course of Chinese history prior to the mid-twentieth century.[13] The history of qigong as we now understand the concept can be traced quite clearly to the late 1940s and the activities of a small group of people.

The story of qigong begins with Liu Guizhen.[14] Liu was born in 1920, joined the Communist Party in 1944, and subsequently worked in a commercial office attached to the Communist government of the liberated area of southern Hebei. He had suffered from gastric ulcers and insomnia since 1940, and at one point saw his weight drop to less than eighty pounds. In 1947, he took sick leave and returned to his home village of Dasizhuang in Wei prefecture, southern Hubei, where he was treated by his paternal uncle Liu Duzhou, who practiced the "discipline of inner cultivation" (*Neiyanggong*). Liu Duzhou claimed to be a master in a line of transmission which stretched back to the Ming-Qing transition and an original founder, Hao Xiangwu.[15] Liu Guizhen's ulcers were cured after a hundred days of cultivation, and he rapidly gained some thirty pounds.

When Liu returned to his work unit, he was understandably excited to talk about his speedy cure to friends and coworkers, including the party secretary of his unit, Cheng Yulin. Although, as noted above, many Chinese elites were proponents of science and biomedicine, Chinese medicine had retained a place of pride in the hearts of many, particularly but not exclusively in the context of the long guerrilla war which had preceded the Communist victory.

Cut off from the cities and from modern medical practices, suffering cadres and soldiers readily turned to whatever means were at hand to ease their aches and pains, including, naturally enough, Chinese medicine which, in addition to being more readily available, cost relatively little and demanded little in the way of institutional apparatus. One might note that whatever the success of the Communist revolution, China remained poor and largely rural in the late 1940s; even diehard proponents of biomedicine were forced to concede that China did not possess the means to transform its health care system overnight and thus to dispense with Chinese medicine. Cheng Yulin sent Liu Guizhen back to his home village to become Liu Duzhou's disciple and even provided him with funds to cover his costs.

Liu subsequently shared his knowledge with his colleagues and was sent to teach his methods at the cadres' sanatorium in the region. Local leaders directed that a group of doctors be assigned to him, with the goal of systematizing these experiences. The group was led by Huang Yueting, director of the Research Office of the Health Department of southern Hebei, and efforts began to extract the pure method of the discipline of inner cultivation from its religious wrappings so as to isolate its curing powers. The outcome of these efforts was what David Palmer calls the "birth of modern qigong" on 3 March 1949, when Huang Yueting, at a work meeting on health issues in southern Hebei, proclaimed the official adoption of the term qigong to describe the techniques studied for some years by the clinical team under his direction.

Although the intention was to identify (or at least to assert) the scientific basis undergirding qigong practice, the model of qigong cultivation outlined by Huang Yueting and followed by others over the course of the 1950s remained largely within the framework of Chinese medical (and, to some extent, religious or at least spiritual) traditions. Qigong emphasized the "triple discipline" of the body, of breathing, and of the mind, often achieved via the chanting of mantras. Also emphasized was the cultivation of "qi feeling" in which the mind and qi were to complement or fulfill one another. Qigong was also to be practiced at a particular time each day, in a particular place, with the body always facing a particular direction, and following a series of clearly spelled out gestures or postures—in other words, much of the traditional ritual apparatus survived the "transformation" of qigong. The difference was that adepts had become patients and masters had become health care professionals in the service of a secular, supposedly scientific, Communist state. The transformation was more one of social context than of the essence of the healing technique. True, the old mantra of the discipline of inner cultivation, "the claw of the golden dragon sitting in meditation in the Chan chamber," had been replaced by the almost laughably earnest "I practice sitting meditation for better health," but at the same time, those present at the creation of qigong debated whether to call the practice "spiritual therapy" (*jingshen liaofa*), "psychological therapy" (*xinli liaofa*), or even "incantation therapy" (*zhuyou liaofa*) before settling on qigong.

## Qigong within the Medical Establishment, 1949–1965

In the early 1950s, the newly established Communist state sought to integrate Chinese medicine and Chinese medical practitioners into the medical establishment erected in the wake of the Communist victory. In line with the compromise adopted by health care authorities under the Nationalist regime in the 1930s, the core of this new establishment was to be scientific, Western medicine, reflecting the modernist, materialist orientation of most party and government leaders, as well as the proclivities of Soviet advisors, who had considerable influence in China during this period. Chinese medicine was to be tolerated, if only because there were not enough medical practitioners trained in biomedicine for the system to be functional. There were only 12,000 doctors trained in modern biomedicine, for a population which had already reached at least 500 million.[16] By contrast, there were some 400,000 traditional practitioners. Moreover, as already mentioned, Chinese medicine remains in general less expensive, demanding less equipment and less "medicine" in the modern sense. Still, the inferior position that Chinese medicine was meant to occupy is made clear in the remarks offered by Guo Moruo at the First National Conference on Health in July 1950:

> Chinese medicine must study the scientific knowledge of Western medicine, and Western medicine must study the universal, popular spirit of Chinese medicine. . . . In this joint effort, Western medicine must assume the principal responsibility to carry out research on Chinese medicine and thereby enhance its level of performance.[17]

Over the next few years, the state sought, in a number of ways, to bring Chinese and Western practitioners together and to induce Chinese practitioners to think of themselves as part of a larger "profession" and thereby convince them to share their secrets with other practitioners, both Chinese- and Western-trained. Yet, as a measure of the extreme politicization of all aspects of life in Mao's China, Chinese and Western medicine took on different symbolic political values in the long series of debates and campaigns, beginning in 1953–1954, over the character of China's revolution, with Chinese medicine representing populism and nationalism and Western medicine representing elitism and reliance on the outside world. The fortunes of Chinese medicine rose with the tides of Maoism, which contributed to the consolidation of a secure place for Chinese medicine within the larger medical establishment of the People's Republic.

In June 1953, for example, the South-Central Department of Health held a series of regional meetings with practitioners of TCM to discuss their role in the national health care system. Chinese medical doctors took advantage of this forum to voice criticisms of the arrogance of those trained in Western medicine, who, they felt, looked down their noses at the more numerous practitioners of Chinese medicine. Shortly thereafter, similar criticisms were voiced in the *People's Daily*, in which certain elements in the Ministry of Health were accused of "despising the medical heritage of the Motherland," sending a signal to all concerned that some sort of reevaluation of the medical establishment was under way. In the summer of 1954, doctors practicing Western medicine were once again singled out for criticism in the *Enlightenment Daily* for displaying "an erroneous sectarian attitude equivalent to ... contempt ... for Chinese medicine," as a result of their having been influenced by the "bourgeois" medicine of Europe and the United States. In October 1954, the *People's Daily* published criticisms of those in the Ministry of Health who had been "empoisoned by bourgeois concepts," and confessions of such professionals followed. Ni Bao-chun, assistant director of Municipal Hospital Number Two in Shanghai, for example, admitted to having ridiculed Chinese medicine, which represented a "nonscientific" attitude resulting from his education in missionary schools and at a university in the United States.[18] As one might imagine, the publication of these debates suggests that Chinese medicine was gaining ground on Western biomedicine during this period.[19]

To some degree, the fortunes of qigong seem to have risen with those of TCM, although most of the Chinese practitioners absorbed into the state medical establishment in this early post-revolution period were acupuncturists and herbalists. Qigong, in the early 1950s, was not yet well enough known, nor well enough developed institutionally to merit much consideration, and largely continued its development on the local scene, primarily in southern Hebei.[20] In 1953, Cheng Yulin, one of the original patrons of Liu Guizhen and of qigong, became party secretary of the city of Tangshan, Hebei (best known perhaps for a serious earthquake in 1976). The following year, Cheng arranged for Liu Guizhen and his team to be transferred there so as to establish, in 1955, a rehabilitation center for qigong treatment in the Tangshan Workers' Sanatorium, where they were eventually allocated 100 beds, nominally for patients suffering from gastrointestinal disorders. The Hebei Health Department sent Liu Guizhen to Beijing three times in 1954 and 1955 to present his work on qigong to higher authorities. On 19 December 1955, the National Ministry of

Health praised Liu Guizhen and congratulated him on his report, an event chronicled in the *People's Daily*. At the ceremony marking the founding of the Institute of Research in Chinese Medicine, Health Minister Li Dequan recognized and praised the work of the Tangshan qigong center; in his letter of congratulation, Li noted that qigong merited such praise because it "protected the health of the people and spread the traditional cultural heritage of the Motherland." In 1955, Liu Guizhen was named an "advanced worker" by Mao Zedong and was subsequently summoned for personal interviews with such high party and government officials as Liu Shaoqi, Chen Yi, and Li Fuchun.[21]

These events seemed to launch qigong on a broader trajectory. In 1956, courses on qigong were given at the seaside resort of Beidaihe (frequented by China's leaders in the summer) to those who were to become the first group of professional therapists. The following year, a center was set up in Shanghai to conduct scientific experiments on qigong therapies. Liu Guizhen published the first book on modern qigong in 1957, *Applied Qigong Therapeutic Healing*, which had a considerable influence. Another dozen or so works on qigong were published between 1957 and 1965. The publication and dissemination of such works helped to spread the concept of qigong to the larger public; use of the term "qigong" was no longer reserved to the official press. In Elisabeth Hsu's apt summary:

> *Qigong* was ... taught in several rehabilitation centers all over the country. It was promoted as a breathing technique particularly effective for the cure of chronic hepatitis, high blood pressure, heart palpitations, tuberculosis, asthma, neurasthenia, diabetes, glaucoma, and toxemia. The new name *qigong* for the old meditation practices emphasized its therapeutic merits, merits that were often proved by biomedical evidence.[22]

The denigration of expertise during the Great Leap Forward also worked in a general way against the influence of Western medical practitioners and to the benefit of those in Chinese medicine, including qigong practitioners.[23] From the late 1950s through the Cultural Revolution, the Beidaihe Qigong Sanatorium, located at the Shandong beach resort frequented by high party and government officials, became the nation's preeminent qigong institution, treating some 3,000 patients before it was closed in 1965. In 1957, the National Ministry of Health gave the Beidaihe sanatorium the task of training qigong medical personnel for all of China. Through 1964, the sanatorium organized seven such year-long courses, producing 700 specialists in qigong medicine.

The foundation for the post–Cultural Revolution qigong movement was thus laid during the 1949–1965 period, and it is important to underscore the fact that qigong, the larger category of cultivation techniques and theory to which Falun Gong belongs, possessed, prior to the qigong craze of the 1980s and 1990s, a thoroughly orthodox, largely unproblematic history. This history, in which qigong served as part of a nationalistic antidote to the perceived threat of the Westernization of Chinese medical practices, goes a long way to explaining why Chinese authorities in the post-Mao period were open to the reemergence of qigong and even to qigong as a mass movement. "Qigong has nothing to do with 'feudal superstition,'" they could say. "Qigong is part of our revolutionary heritage. In the 1950s, even Liu Shaoqi supported qigong!"

Beginning in 1964, however, the tide began to turn against qigong, in rhythm with the rising conflicts which were to eventuate in the Great Proletarian Cultural Revolution.[24] Factional politics appear to have played a role in this reversal: many of the high officials identified with qigong—Liu Shaoqi being a prominent example—were enemies of Mao for other reasons, but as they fell, so did governmental patronage for qigong, which could easily be associated with feudal superstition in any event. In early 1964, Wang Juemin, party secretary of Baoding and a passionate devotee of qigong, became the object of a rumor campaign based on his interest in qigong; the rumors insisted that it was not "proper" that a party secretary be invested in qigong to the degree that Wang was. He was publicly criticized in the summer of 1965, and made an example of throughout the country. In March 1965, an article in the journal *New Physical Education* had already criticized certain "abuses" in qigong practice, such as charlatans taking advantage of the unsuspecting masses, propagating superstition and feudal culture. This attack dovetailed with the more general attack during the Cultural Revolution on all things "old" and "feudal." Qigong was attacked in the press as "corrupt feudal leftovers," "the garbage of history," "idealism," and "absurd stories."[25] As a sad symbol of the reversal of qigong fortunes, Liu Guizhen was accused of being the "creator of the poisonous weed, qigong." He was expelled from the party, lost his job, and was sent for reeducation to a farm in distant Shanhaiguan. Like all other qigong establishments, the Beidaihe Qigong Sanatorium was closed during the campaign against the "four olds," and the personnel of the Tangshan qigong clinic were ordered to sweep the streets and clean public toilets.[26]

Still, it bears repeating that, from an ideological point of view, qigong, like Chinese medicine in general, had until 1965 been seen as populist and nationalist, that is, more on the side of Mao than on that of his "enemies." And the attack on the "superstitious" side of qigong ignores the important—if perhaps cosmetic—changes brought to traditional cultivation practices in the process of (re)inventing qigong. The form of transmission of qigong knowledge, for example, was completely different; the traditional master was replaced by a

modern medical education. Moreover, the vocabulary and conceptual references related to qigong had been revamped; gone were the traditional religious concepts and symbols (with the exception of those like yin-yang and
meridians—acupuncture points—which found a place in modern scientific
Chinese medical discourse), which were replaced by psychological and other
scientific references. It is worth repeating as well that qigong, from its origins
as institutional practice in the late 1940s, through its temporary demise in the
Cultural Revolution, had been an activity largely confined to the Chinese elite; it
was, to a great degree, therapy for cadres. Qigong was not a mass movement
prior to the Cultural Revolution, and qigong was only transmitted via state-
sanctioned medical institutions.

## The End of the Cultural Revolution and the Beginnings
of the Qigong Boom

Qigong in the pre–Cultural Revolution period functioned on a modest scale,
even as it presumably generated considerable enthusiasm among the cadres
who were the primary objects of qigong treatment. Qigong in the post–Cultural
Revolution period, by contrast, was huge, probably the first genuine mass
movement in the history of the People's Republic—in the sense that it was
directed more by participants in the movement than by party or government
authorities. Beginning from roughly 1985, the main symbols of the expansion
of qigong activities were the hugely popular qigong masters, who achieved
fame and fortune through a variety of means: national and international lecture
tours, television broadcasts, books, video- and audiocassettes, and the organization of networks of practitioners. Yan Xin was the first qigong master to
achieve this status, soon to be followed by Zhang Hongbao and Zhang Xiangyu,
to name but a few. Li Hongzhi emerged later, in 1992, as a part of the same
phenomenon, and if his message came eventually to differ somewhat from that
promoted by other qigong masters, his activities after "coming out of the
mountains" (i.e., emerging from obscurity to make his teachings known) closely followed the steps taken by his predecessors.

Prior to the emergence of the qigong superstars, however, the world of
qigong was more chaotic and harder to describe, if no less fascinating. Between 1979 and 1985, a variety of elements came together to form what was
called the "qigong realm," which had not existed prior to the Cultural Revolution. These elements included qigong teachers who conveyed their message publicly, outside of the medical, institutional setting of the pre–Cultural
Revolution period; the scientific "discovery" of the existence of "external qi"

and general scientific support for experimental work on qigong; a widespread popular enthusiasm for the "supernormal powers" associated with qigong; the popularization of qigong through the media (a media significantly altered in the post-Mao era), some of which were devoted wholly to the cause of qigong; and the construction of a political framework permitting qigong to function under the "guidance" of party and government leaders. This last element points to the key to qigong's success: the acceptance of qigong and qigong masters by an important part of the governing elite of the People's Republic of China, including Politburo members.

## Out of the Clinic, into the Park: Qigong
## in the Post–Cultural Revolution Era

In the same way that the origins of modern qigong can largely be traced to the activities of a single person, Liu Guizhen, the beginnings of the post-Mao qigong boom can similarly be traced to one hardy qigong master, Guo Lin, who, in defiance of the police and her work unit, began teaching qigong in public parks in Beijing in the early 1970s. In so doing, she began the transformation of qigong from an elite practice, institutionalized in hospitals and sanatoriums frequented by high-level government and party cadres, to a popular, mass practice, available to all interested parties. This public dimension was one of the essential bases for the surge in qigong enthusiasm.[27]

Born in Guangdong in 1909, Guo Lin learned cultivation techniques as a child from her grandfather, reportedly a Daoist master. She became a renowned painter of the Lingnan school,[28] and part of the qigong technique she later developed came from breathing methods she perfected climbing many of China's famous mountains, scenes of required inspiration for China's landscape painters. In 1949, she fell victim to cancer of the uterus, and had her uterus and part of her bladder removed. The cancer returned in 1959, and Guo Lin decided to treat herself. After ten years of diligent effort, she succeeded in ridding herself of cancer and, like many true believers, subsequently dedicated her life to sharing the method she had developed (called the "wind breathing method," *feng huxi fa*) with others.

Guo Lin had been in Beijing since 1956, attached to the Beijing Academy of Painting. In 1970, she began treating Beijing residents with cancer or other chronic illnesses. Her first public efforts were in Dongdan Park in 1971. Although her devotion won her the appreciation and acclaim of numerous patients, Chinese authorities were uncomfortable with her activities; accused of superstitious practices and of defrauding the masses, she was run out of

Dongdan Park. Apparently undaunted, Guo Lin simply moved her activities to another park, Longtanhu. There, too, she met with harassment: two of her students were arrested and imprisoned for twenty days, and police raided Guo Lin's apartment and confiscated the qigong materials she had painstakingly assembled. Between 1971 and 1977, Guo was interrogated seven times by the police and criticized many times by her work unit.

Out of stubbornness and conviction, Guo Lin persisted, and in 1975 she even managed to circulate, on a limited scale, a lithographed volume describing her methods, *The New Method of Healing through Qigong*. A second edition followed in April 1976. Finally, in 1977, as her efforts gained the support of higher-level cadres, Guo was welcomed into Beijing Normal University, which subsequently became her base of operations. In the relative calm that followed Mao's death, Guo submitted a 100-page report to the Ministry of Health, claiming that qigong could cure cancer and proposing a treatment combining qigong and Western medicine. Before long, she began to give regular courses at Beijing Normal University on her qigong methods, and she was subsequently invited to give lectures at such prestigious institutions as Qinghua University, the Beijing Number Six Hospital, and the Qingdao Medical School, among others. An updated version of her book on qigong appeared in 1978.[29]

## The Emergence of the Qigong Realm

Guo Lin unwittingly created the model of the public qigong master and also, by dint of her passion and perseverance, began to restore the linkages between high officialdom and qigong practice—although these renewed links were less institutional and more personal, providing patronage and protection on an individual basis. At roughly the same moment, scientific experiments conducted by physicist Gu Hansen on the existence of "external qi" reestablished and even bolstered the scientific credibility of qigong and set the stage for the emergence of an important community of people devoted to the defense of qi and qigong as legitimate objects of scientific inquiry. The approximation of qigong to science was a second crucial element in the rise of qigong to a status it had not enjoyed in the pre–Cultural Revolution period. Of course, qigong was not seen as *un*scientific in the pre–Cultural Revolution era, although its association with feudal religious and magical practices made it suspect in the eyes of some critics. But the discovery of the scientific basis of qi and qigong in the post-Mao period clearly was transformative and, at the same time, linked it to the party's modernizing projects.[30]

Gu Hansen was a researcher at the Shanghai Institute of Atomic Research, working specifically on radio electronics. Her own account of her discovery of qi is worth quoting:

> At the end of 1977, by chance, I became acquainted with the therapeutic method of movement by *qi*. With my own eyes, I saw this therapeutic method—without medication, without needle, and without contact with the body of the patient—succeed in making a paraplegic, paralyzed in both legs, able to crouch and get up. This miraculous event opened up new horizons for me, to the extent that I could no longer remain still. I felt that I was at the entrance of a new domain: the science of life.[31]

As a scientist, Gu opened the door to this new realm by designing and performing a series of experiments to test the existence of qi, and in March 1978 broadcast her results: qi exists as a measurable physical substance. The reaction to this news was electrifying, as revealed by this quote from two qigong proponents, writing retrospectively in 1996:

> March 10, 1978, can be considered as an extraordinary day. This day marks the start of a new age in the history of *qigong* in China. In collaboration, Gu Hansen of the Center for Atomic Research of the Academy of Sciences at Shanghai, and Lin Houseng, of the Shanghai Institute of Chinese Medicine, using modern scientific devices to make preliminary measurements on the "external *qi*" displaced during *qigong* therapy, detected low-frequency, infrared ray modulations. That confirms that the practitioner of *qigong* emitted electromagnetic waves containing information. It is the first time that the physical nature of "*qi*" was proven. The publication of the results of the experiment created waves within the country, aroused interest and drew the attention of numerous scientists towards *qigong* research. Their heroic undertaking had a determining effect on the rise of *qigong* in contemporary China, allowing it to free itself once and for all of the label of "superstition" and "sorcery" so long attached to it.[32]

Gu Hansen's pioneering work allowed qigong to enter fully into the spirit of post-Mao China, both as a physical force which could be incorporated into the political discourse of dialectical materialism and, more important, as part of the scientific and technological revolutions which were to propel China toward the future. The Four Modernizations had emerged as China's watchword as early as 1975, when Premier Zhou Enlai sought a positive counterweight to the extreme politicization of the Cultural Revolution. Alongside the well-known Four Modernizations, a "patriotic health movement" was launched in late 1978, designed to raise general sanitation and health levels, through, among other things, an accelerated development of Chinese medicine. It is clear that qigong could fit well in this agenda, particularly in the "new and improved" form that Gu Hansen's imprimatur had given it.

It is difficult to overstate the importance of Gu Hansen's scientific discoveries to the subsequent history of qigong. From this point forward, the proponents of qigong (of whom there came rapidly to be an imposing number) could always point to these laboratory experiments as proof of the reality of qi and the value of qigong and qigong research. No longer did qigong have to ride the coattails of Chinese medicine and attempt to carve out a small, safe place inside the Chinese medical establishment; once qi was accorded a verifiable, material existence, qigong was immediately catapulted beyond Chinese medicine to the forefront of valued, experimental science. Probably most important to the development of qigong was the fact that Gu Hansen's discovery captured the attention of several important figures in China's political world, immediately creating a number of qigong patrons and defenders.

In July 1979, Lü Bingkui, director of the Ministry of Health's State Administration of Chinese Medicine, presided over a meeting called to review scientific reports on qigong, a meeting attended by China's health minister, State Sports Commission director, several members of the State Council, and some 200 scientists, officials, and journalists.[33] The audience heard papers on the material nature of external qi, on the relationship of qigong to paranormal abilities (see below), and on Guo Lin's success in treating cancer with qigong. Demonstrations of the powers of "hard qigong" (i.e., martial arts qigong) were also provided. A few days later, 500 participants attended a follow-up meeting, at which Tan Gaosheng of the Chinese Academy of Sciences likened the revolutionary nature of the implications of qigong research to the discoveries of Galileo. In the apt summary of David Palmer: "These meetings were a historical turning point for *qigong*. By bringing together, under high political patronage, most of the main figures involved in *qigong* training, therapy and research, they gave birth to the '*qigong* sector'—a national network which included not only masters and practitioners, but also scientists."[34]

These meetings were widely and correctly perceived as a green light for the rehabilitation and development of qigong. Many of the pre–Cultural Revolution qigong institutions, those associated with the Chinese medical establishment, were reopened during this period. In a gesture rich with symbolic value, the Beidaihe Qigong Sanatorium was reopened in late October 1980, and Liu

Guizhen, the qigong pioneer who had suffered during the Cultural Revolution, was appointed as its director.[35]

And this was just the tip of the iceberg. In September 1979, the first academic conference on qigong under the aegis of the Ministry of Health and the National Association for Science and Technology (NAST) called for rapid movement on the organization of the scientific infrastructure necessary to qigong scientific research. Gu Hansen's experiments were featured on CCTV in January 1980, and subsequently published in the influential Chinese review *Nature*. In April 1980, the State Science Commission summoned cadres of the Ministry of Health, the State Sports Commission, and the NAST to a meeting at which qigong was declared to be an integral part of China's medical establishment. In September 1981, the founding of the All-China Qigong Scientific Research Society, a branch of the All-China Society for Chinese Medicine, the first nationwide qigong association (and the first in what was to be a long line of attempts by authorities to organize and channel qigong research and activities) was announced during the first national academic conference on qigong, held in Baoding with the support of the NAST and the Ministry of Health.[36]

One should not, however, think that qigong was reserved for the elite or for scientific research; quite the contrary, by the early 1980s, qigong had already embarked on the course that was to transform it into a mass movement. One measure of this was master Guo Lin's overnight success. Once qigong in general was given the green light, several popular magazines ran stories on Guo Lin, and her book, which had circulated to this point in limited print runs, was republished by a mainstream press in the summer of 1980. Sick people subsequently flocked to Beijing to seek her out, and by the end of the year "Guo Lin qigong" was being practiced in twenty Chinese provinces and in the Chinese diaspora in East and Southeast Asia and in North America.[37]

It is worth noting at this point the crucial role played by journalism in the qigong movement, as well as the signal differences between journalism under Mao and in the post-Mao era. From 1949 through Mao's death in 1976, although political differences between rival leaders and/or factions were sometimes played out on the pages of newspapers and journals, the media as a whole remained firmly under party control. Neither readers' opinions nor market forces in a more abstract sense influenced the practice of Chinese journalism in significant ways.[38] In the post-Mao era, by contrast, newspapers, magazines, and publishing houses were expected to make their own way in the world by selling their products in a more competitive marketplace—at the same time respecting the dictates of "socialism with Chinese characteristics" and party prerogatives, however capriciously they may have been expressed.[39]

Qigong was a topic tailor-made for the new era in Chinese journalism. It was exciting, nation and culture affirming, seemingly apolitical, and full of charismatic personalities, fascinating stories of miracle cures, other startling personal transformations, and exercise regimes—think *People* magazine (or perhaps the *National Enquirer*) "with Chinese characteristics." And indeed qigong books and magazines—both serious and less serious—proliferated in the late 1970s and early 1980s. One of the issues which attracted much of the qigong press was the relationship between qigong and paranormal powers, or "extraordinary powers" (*teyi gongneng*) to use a direct translation from the Chinese.[40]

By "paranormal," I refer to a range of phenomena which would fall under our categories of extrasensory perception, maximization of human potential, and superhuman powers. Beyond the fact that certain qigong masters themselves claimed to possess paranormal powers and that they attributed these powers to their mastery of qi, the logical, scientific links between the paranormal and qigong are not always clear. What is clear, nonetheless, is that partisans of qigong were often partisans of the paranormal, and vice versa, presumably because qigong claims were viewed as legitimate and legitimating.

Stories of the paranormal began to circulate at about the same time as qigong emerged from its forced hibernation during the Cultural Revolution, in the late 1970s.[41] One of the first such stories to catch the attention of much of China was that of Tang Yu, a schoolchild able to "read with his ear." According to journalists who interviewed Tang and witnessed his feats, the young boy, a native of Dazu, Sichuan, was able to recognize the characters on a piece of paper which had been crumpled up and placed in his ear. "When the wad of paper is placed in my ear," Tang said, "I feel a tingling, and an image of the characters appears in my head like a film projected on a screen."[42] The story was reprinted in many of China's influential newspapers within days of its initial appearance in the *Sichuan Daily*, and since publication in official media—even in post-Mao China—is interpreted (generally correctly) by readers and by other newspapers and journalists as a sign of approval by governmental authorities, other media felt free to follow up similar leads. Within three weeks, papers in Beijing, Hebei, Anhui, Hubei, Heilongjiang, and Jiangsu reported having unearthed similar youths able to read not only with their ears, but also with the palms of their hands, with their armpits, or after having chewed up and swallowed the wad of paper with the characters on it. Such exploits were not universally believed or acclaimed, and I bring them up in this context to illustrate how debates generated by the claims of qigong proponents were resolved in their favor as a result of the political power possessed by qigong patrons.

Many influential scientists and policy makers dismissed such accounts as fakes or magic tricks, and such skepticism succeeded briefly in dampening journalistic enthusiasm for the paranormal. Nonetheless, other scientists, equally influential, accepted wholeheartedly the idea that human beings in their current state of development exploited only a bare minimum of their capacities, which could undoubtedly be developed further. One prominent example is Qian Xuesen, the father of China's atomic bomb and vice president of the National Association of Science and of the Scientific Commission for National Defense, who argued that a new scientific discipline—somatic science—should be created to study the advanced capacities of the human body. In June 1980, Qian, one of China's most renowned and influential scientists, met with the editors of the authoritative Chinese magazine *Nature* and openly expressed his support for the publication of articles on qigong and on super-normal powers. Later that summer, he reiterated his support in background discussions with such influential media as the *People's Daily*, the *Enlightenment Daily*, and the New China News Agency.[43]

Yet even a scientist of Qian's stature could not have delivered his message without the support of other high-level party and government officials, a fact which was lost on no one in China. The "debate" over paranormal abilities, and over the relationship of qigong to these abilities, came to be resolved in a compromise highly favorable to partisans of the paranormal and of qigong: on the logical premise that no one could predict the nature and direction of future scientific advances, it was decided that it was "unscientific" to criticize experiments in the paranormal from the point of view of current scientific knowledge. Such unwarranted criticism, it was argued, might well harm China's scientific advancement and thus the Four Modernizations. Newton, Darwin, Einstein—all had been criticized in their time by those unable to see past the reigning scientific paradigm. This decision was not necessarily carte blanche for those engaged in research on the paranormal. Outright trickery had nothing to do with the advancement of science and should be exposed for what it is. On the other hand, the compromise left the door open for credible, serious research (or for anything which *looked* credible and serious) on the paranormal and on qigong, which, given the general enthusiasm for such topics across a broad spectrum of China's population, allowed enthusiasts and journalists to continue to publicize the results of their research, as long as they respected appearances and promised (or pretended to promise) to de-nounce the obviously fraudulent. If it is not quite accurate to say that the qigong forces emerged completely victorious from this scuffle, they remained on equal footing with the forces of scientific skepticism, which meant that all but the most objectionable of qigong activities could continue.

Among the results of this victory: some 500 delegates attended the sec-ond national scientific conference on paranormal abilities held at Chongqing,

Sichuan, in May 1981 (the first such conference, organized by the Chinese magazine *Nature*, had been held in February 1980); the National Science Association set up a committee to organize the creation of a Chinese Association of Somatic Sciences; and the 1981 *Annual Encyclopedia of China* included an article on "superhuman capacities," signaling the general recognition by China's scientific and intellectual community of the existence of this field. Such "victories" were not definitive, and debates continued over specific claims of supernormal powers and over the propriety of research in this field. Still, the visible, public support of such scientists as Qian Xuesen and the existence of committees attached to recognized national scientific structures meant that those opposed to qigong and the paranormal could not easily silence proponents of qigong and the paranormal, as these proponents could always defend themselves through reference to Qian and others like him. And the compromise continued to hold. In April 1982, after several weeks of bitter public debate between critics and proponents of research on superhuman abilities (carried out largely through newspaper articles), the Propaganda Department of the party's Central Committee issued a circular to all newspapers insisting that they "neither promote nor criticize" such research.[44]

Behind this compromise was a group of powerful qigong supporters, including the already mentioned Qian Xuesen, an authority in the scientific field; Lü Bingkui, a major player in the lesser field of Chinese medicine; Wu Shaozu, an important figure in the sports field; and especially Brigadier General Zhang Zhenhuan, whose functions were chiefly military.[45] Qian, Zhang, and Wu had been members of the National Defense Science and Technology Commission and were named to the Commission of Science, Technology, and Industry for National Defense (COSTIND) when it was created in 1982. Qian and Zhang had both served as chairs of the technology commission. Qian Xuesen is identified with the development of China's atomic weapons program; Zhang and Wu were at various points vice chairs of the China Nuclear Association. Zhang's PLA rank was later granted to Wu, in 1988. Qigong's political patrons were, as David Palmer observes, "at the center of China's military-industrial complex."[46] And there were other highly placed qigong supporters who played no role in the direct management of qigong, among them Zhao Ziyang, Peng Zhen, Ye Jianying, and Wang Zhen, to name a few of the better known, but who weighed in at important moments to lend support.[47] Perhaps someday we will know what "top secret" experiments were performed to adapt qigong to the needs of China's military, but for our present purposes, it suffices to note that, like tax cuts in Reagan-Bush America, qigong was an idea whose time had come and which had earned the patronage of powerful figures who were not to be trifled with.

The Qigong Superstars

The elements were now in place for the qigong explosion: a scientific justification, popular and journalistic enthusiasm, and political support. On this basis, charismatic masters came out of the woodwork, and many of them succeeded in building the first mass, nationwide, largely independent organizations in the history of the People's Republic.[48]

Before discussing the grandmasters, or qigong superstars, who began to emerge in the mid-1980s, a few words should be said about qigong masters in general. The first point to note is their numbers: Wu Hao's 1993 biographical directory, *The Encyclopedia of Contemporary Chinese Qigong*, lists over 500 qigong masters, with organizations both large and small.[49] The second point is that few were trained in the qigong institutions of the pre–Cultural Revolution period. Only a quarter claimed direct links with a traditional school of healing or spirituality; most stated that they had learned qigong either in the early Communist period—i.e., before qigong had assumed an institutional existence—during the Cultural Revolution, when qigong was effectively banned, or since 1979. In most cases, the method of transmission was traditional— from master to disciple—even if the master may have been loath to identify himself clearly with a traditional, "feudal" practice. To me, the emergence of these masters in the 1980s and 1990s again suggests that China scholars may well have exaggerated the popular cultural divide represented by the 1949 revolution. Our collective scholarly romance with the power of the Chinese revolution led us to ignore the facts that forty or fifty years is but a drop in the bucket of historical time and that popular cultural practices are generally quite tenacious, even in the face of seemingly much stronger political and social forces.

In any event, many of the qigong masters who emerged in the 1980s were not at all shy about connecting their powers and their practices to traditional discourses, even if they did not claim to be the direct inheritor of a past master's prowess. One early example of a qigong master with at least one foot in the realm of religion is Yang Meijun[50] who, like Guo Lin, began teaching in Beijing public parks toward the end of the 1970s. Yang, born in 1903, was the self-proclaimed heir to the lineage of the greater school of Kunlun Daoism, stretching back some twenty-seven generations. She had learned the tradition through her grandfather, who had met a Kunlun master by chance while working in a pharmacy; in traditional China, as noted above, this mixture of medicine and religion would have been seen as completely unexceptional. Yang became her grandfather's disciple at the age of thirteen, at which point he led her to the White Pagoda Temple in Beijing and showed her the eight wild geese cast in bronze which she was to take as her models. This is the origin of the name of her school of qigong. Her teachings emphasized the mastery of a series of gestures and postures, similar to the better-known *taijiquan*. Significantly, Yang Meijun claimed the ability of direct healing through the application of the qi emitted from her body, an important departure from the techniques of self-mastery and self-healing taught by institutional qigong or even by the independent master Guo Lin. In China as elsewhere, faith healing belongs more to the realms of religion and magic (or superhuman powers) than to the realm of science.

At the same time, like virtually all masters, Yang Meijun was careful not to discard science. The following quote, taken from a document written by two of Yang's followers, Zhang Wenjie and Cao Jian, who were also researchers at the Chinese Academy of Sciences, illustrates the seemingly happy marriage of religion and science which marked much of the qigong movement at the beginning of the 1980s:

> On the foundation of her ancestral method, master Yang learned from reputed masters everywhere, finally reaching a high level of accomplishment.... Her method is complete; there is no technique that she does not master, be it the arts of the still body, the moving body, or swordsmanship, or even sitting, lying or walking *qigong*, light or heavy *qigong*, the emission of *qi*, diagnosing illnesses, or feeling at a distance. To speak only of the emission of *qi* at a distance, children with Extraordinary Functions and those who have a high degree of *qigong* attainment can see a profusion of colors in the *qi* flowing from her hands....
>
> Among the disciples of Yang Meijun, the great majority are scientific researchers; this is the result of the master's arduous efforts. Generally speaking, scientific researchers ... have a special difficulty in learning *qigong*. But Master Yang knows full well that for the *qigong* cause to develop, it cannot separate itself from modern scientific technology. If we don't transmit high-level *qigong* virtuosity to people who are capable of leading scientific research, they won't be able to understand the nature of *qigong* nor to accomplish research on *qigong*....
>
> *Qigong* is a precious scientific heritage which has been bequeathed to us by our ancestors. Conserving and transmitting this heritage is a glorious mission conferred on us by history. If the millennial transmission of this exalted and profound virtuosity were to be lost with our generation, such that our descendants would be

able to research *qigong* only through archaeology, we would be condemned by history. We take this opportunity to make this call:
arise, to preserve and disseminate the grand and profound virtuosity
of master Yang and other similar *qigong* figures, so that we can
contribute as we should to our country's research on the system of
somatic science.[51]

Another example of the qigong masters who emerged during this period is
Liang Shifeng, who came out of a martial arts background.[52] Although West-
erners often associate the martial arts of the Orient with Bruce Lee and ninjas,
in China the martial arts have traditionally been understood as a set of disciplines permitting the cultivation of the body in a much broader sense. As such,
the study and practice of martial arts readily overlap with certain elements of
religious and particularly popular religious practice, inasmuch as health and
healing are primary focuses of much of popular religion. Liang invented and
taught the "qigong of the spontaneous movements of the games of the five
animals," which was based on the notion that the navel, often identified in
traditional Chinese medical/philosophical/religious language as the "cinnabar
field,"[53] was the root of life and of spontaneous movement. Practitioners of
master Liang's qigong were taught to concentrate on their cinnabar field at the
same time that they pressed repeatedly on their navel with a finger while
chanting the following mantra: "I range like an immortal in the clouds. . . . I
concentrate my mind on the cinnabar field, and deep relaxation gives rise to
movement." Deep relaxation was followed by a period of trance lasting between a half hour and two hours, during which time the adept might mas-
sage himself, strike himself, carry out acupressure on various parts of his
body, or engage spontaneously in martial arts movements, taijiquan, or a variety of dances. He might even fall to the earth and roll around, or engage
in other movements which are difficult to carry out in a normal state. With
practice, these "spontaneous" movements were to come to imitate those of the
tiger, the deer, the bear, the bird, and the monkey—the five animals mentioned
in the name of the school of qigong. Of course, Liang did not *deny* the scientific
character of qigong; at the same time, it is abundantly clear to those who are not
Liang's followers that science was not his basic training.

Zhao Jinxiang, another qigong master who emerged in the early 1980s, had
actually learned the more sober qigong of the sanatorium while hospitalized in
the early 1960s for pulmonary tuberculosis, but as a master, he chose to emphasize his martial arts abilities and his healing powers.[54] Like Liang Shifeng,
Zhao emphasized the imitation of animals: his school of qigong was known as
"the posture of the flight of the crane," in which practitioners, taught to imitate

the state of mind and the movements of the crane, used the state of profound relaxation achieved through meditation to unleash a series of spontaneous movements. Yet another qigong master to emerge from the realm of martial arts was Wei Ping'an, born in 1935, who studied and taught a variety of forms of martial arts (including that of the famous school of Shaolin) over the course of his life before opening a qigong clinic in Shanghai in 1981.[55] Such pioneers blazed the trail for the emergence of the most visible and powerful symbols of the qigong boom: the great charismatic qigong masters and their millions of followers, many of whom were organized into nationwide organizations whose size in some instances exceeded that of the Chinese Communist Party.

## Yan Xin

The first great qigong master was indisputably Yan Xin, a hitherto unknown, uncelebrated practitioner of Chinese medicine from rural Sichuan who emerged from obscurity in 1985 after healing, in one miraculous session and through the direct application of his qigong powers, a man who had been struck by a truck and who was not expected to walk again.[56] As is the case with all famous qigong masters, the media first spread the word of Yan's exceptional powers and made him known to a larger public; the word passed from local newspapers to regional and then national publications, such as *Qigong and Science*. Throughout 1985 and the early part of 1986, Yan roamed widely throughout China, responding to various appeals on the part of the sick and injured to lend his assistance, which he did—without charging for his services. The miracle worker thus established that he was an honest, sincere servant of the people.

In the summer of 1986, Yan's exploits came to the attention of Zhang Zhenhuan, one of the most important promoters and defenders of qigong at the elite level of Chinese politics. At Zhang's insistence, Yan treated a number of China's aging and suffering leaders, thereby gaining an important foothold in this crucial area of the qigong realm and piquing the interest of a number of potential patrons. By the fall of 1986, Yan had made the big time and was celebrated, for instance, in the prestigious national newspaper *Guangming Ribao* for his miraculous healing powers and his ethic of service. At the end of the year, Yan was invited to Qinghua University, often described as China's MIT, to participate in a series of experiments on the power of qi in general and his qi in particular. The conclusion: the qi emitted by Yan Xin was capable of changing the molecular structure of all of the substances toward which he directed it. Later in the month, the same experiments were carried out with Yan Xin emitting his qi toward objects as far away as 1,200 miles; the results were the same. The news was announced to all of China—and indeed to all the world—in a series of newspaper articles at the end of January 1987 in the *Guangming Ribao*, the international edition of the *People's Daily*, and the *China Daily* (China's main English-language newspaper, produced largely for foreign consumption). These articles were based on six more scientific pieces penned by the Qinghua research team on the biophysical foundation of qigong therapy. Here was spectacular reconfirmation of the scientific discovery of the material existence of qi, the discovery which had given such an important boost to the formation of the qigong realm, in the person of a great master who had already cured several of China's aging rulers. The first great qigong master was well on his way to stardom.

In the wake of the sensation created by Yan Xin's sudden ascent to the summit of the qigong world, the China Qigong Science Research Society (CQRS) created a new tool to permit Yan to spread his message: the qigong-enhanced lecture (literally, "the scientific report on *qigong* which itself is enhanced by the power of *gong*": *daigong qigong kexue baogaohui*). These were lectures in which Yan Xin discoursed on the nature of qigong theory and practice, and at the same time emitted his powerful qi in the direction of his audience. In the formal language of scientific qigong, these lectures were meant to be "scientific experiments" to measure the effects of the "messages" emitted by the great master, but it was the promise of the power to be experienced, and not curiosity as to the outcome of the scientific experiments which drew the masses in unprecedented numbers.

In 1987 and 1988, Yan gave more than 200 such lectures all over China (including Hong Kong), attended by more than a million paying customers. Yan easily achieved the popularity of a rock star: in Shanghai, 23,000 tickets for two planned lectures were sold out in half a day. The lectures themselves were remarkable. Yan spoke without interruption for hours on end (fourteen hours was the apparent record) to crowds of completely absorbed listeners. The same Chinese who talk during operas and movies, who chat and knit during political discussions, sat entranced (often literally) by Yan's words and by his powers. Members of the audience did slip into trance, or fell to the earth, or experienced miraculous cures (the paralyzed rising from their wheelchairs to walk, for example).

## Zhang Hongbao

If Yan Xin appears to typify the model of the "ingénue," the talented but innocent qigong master discovered at the local five and dime by China's media machine, Zhang Hongbao appears to be the archetype of the crafty empire builder, the opportunist who parlayed his qigong talents into remarkable fame and fortune.[57]

Zhang Hongbao was in his early thirties when he emerged on the qigong scene shortly after Yan Xin, in 1986. Like Yan, there was little in his background which would have led anyone to foresee national prominence in his future (aside, perhaps, from an overweening ambition, but this is hardly unique to Zhang). Born in the northeastern city of Harbin in 1954, Zhang spent ten years during the Great Proletarian Cultural Revolution on a state farm in the Manchurian countryside with other sent-down youth and worked his way up the hierarchy of the farm, eventually becoming a teacher at the farm school. In 1977, he was sent to study at the Harbin School of Metallurgy, where he became a party member. After graduation, his first work assignment was as a physics professor at a college in a mining region, but he focused his energies on party work and on improving himself, with an eye toward enlarging his opportunities. His efforts bore fruit, and in 1985 he was sent to Beijing to pursue further studies, this time in business administration at the University of Science and Technology.

In Beijing, Zhang was not an exceptional student and hardly captured the notice of his teachers. One gets the sense that he had a great curiosity for new knowledge, but little genuine intellectual desire to master or explore his interests. He studied, in quick succession, law, Chinese and Western medicine, and eventually qigong—he was hardly alone in this in Beijing in the mid-1980s, as the qigong craze was on the verge of exploding. After studying with a number of qigong masters, Zhang created his own school of qigong: Chinese Qigong to Nourish Life and Increase Intelligence (*Zhonghua yangsheng yizhigong*, generally known under its abbreviated form, Zhonggong). Zhang clearly positioned his school of qigong among the more scientific approaches to the practice (and Zhang did have a scientific background, we might recall). He described Zhonggong with language drawn from the fields of mechanical engineering, automation, physics, relativity theory, systems theory, and bionics, among others.

Consistent with the approaches of many other qigong masters, however, Zhang employed science in a secondary role, to explain his manifest powers, which had first appeared when he inadvertently healed one of his college roommates who had the bunk beneath his: Zhang was meditating in his bunk and the power his qi emitted spilled over onto his lucky friend, who found himself suddenly cured of his stomach ache. Zhang made good use of his powers in his public appearances as well. In his first public lecture as a qigong master at the Beijing Steel Institute in the spring of 1987, he made members of the audience shake through the mere emission of his qi. On the strength of the initial enthusiasm generated by his activities, Zhang founded, in August 1987, the Institute of Research in Qigong Sciences in Haidian, the university district in the northwest part of Beijing. From this base, he set out on an extraordinary quest to win the movers and shakers of Beijing—and thus of China—to his cause. His chief tool in this undertaking was the qi-enhanced lecture.

In November 1987, Zhang was invited to China's premier institution of higher learning, Beijing University, where he gave two intensive courses over the course of a week to some 1,400 people, almost 40% of whom were professors and researchers at some of China's finest institutions (Qinghua University, People's University, the Chinese Academy of Sciences). The *People's Daily*, China's most influential newspaper and the mouthpiece of the Chinese Communist Party, reported that some 120 participants claimed significant improvement of their chronic illnesses as a result of having taken Zhang's courses, and many participants had learned themselves to emit qi. Zhang became a national celebrity on the strength of these reports.

Subsequently, Zhang gave similar courses at the Chinese Academy of Sciences, the Chinese Academy of Social Sciences, and the Chinese Academy of Agricultural Sciences, all of which are major research institutions in China. His performance at the Chinese Academy of Sciences earned him a three-minute report on the national television news, in which Zhang was filmed causing people's bodies to shake by pointing his finger at them from some distance away. Such reports increased his notoriety, but Zhang was by no means finished.

In early January 1988, Zhang gave an intensive course to members of Beijing's journalistic and cultural elite: 130 people from seventy media and cultural organizations attended the twenty-two-hour lecture series over the course of five half-days. Among the participants was Deputy Minister of Culture Gao Zhanxiang. Immediately following this success, Zhang gave yet another week-long qi-enhanced lecture series at the school of the party's Central Committee. The auditorium which he had been assigned was filled to overflowing, and 1,500 participants who were unable to fit into the venue followed Zhang's lecture via television in adjacent rooms. Zhang invited the president of the school onto the stage and had him emit qi to the audience. Members of the audience were instructed to receive the qi with one hand only—and were amazed to discover that the fingers of the hand which received the qi were now longer than those of the other (one wonders if qi worked on their gloves as well). Zhang was subsequently invited to give similar courses to members of the Public Security Bureau (the police) and the judiciary.

Between 1987 and 1990, Zhang gave some fifty intensive courses attended by some 50,000 people, many of whom were members of China's most important ministries, universities, and research centers, in the process creating a cult of personality to rival that of Yan Xin. In 1990, the journalist Ji Yi (who later himself became a qigong master) published his biography of Zhang Hongbao, entitled *The Great Qigong Master Emerges from the Mountains*. The book sold some 10 million copies.

On the basis of his fame, Zhang went on to build a qigong empire of considerable commercial, cultural, and what looks to be potentially political importance. One might note that the abbreviated name for his school of qigong, Zhonggong, shares the pronunciation of the abbreviated name for "Chinese Communist Party" (*Zhongguo gongchandang*, or Zhonggong). In the spring of 1990, Zhang established the International Institute of Life Sciences at Mount Qingcheng, in Sichuan, which Zhang chose as one of his chief bases of operations in the summer of 1990. One of the functions of the institute was to recruit young people who had already demonstrated possession of "special powers" and to give them further training, ultimately rewarding them with diplomas at the college and university levels. At the end of 1990, Zhang established the Chongqing International University of Life Sciences, whose main purpose was to train high-level cadres for the Zhonggong organization; much of the first class admitted to the university was made up of Zhang's disciples who had displayed particular devotion to him as well as talent in their work— and who already had university degrees. After one year of "Zhonggong administrative studies," these graduates oversaw the expansion of Zhonggong into Qinghai, Ningxia, Yunnan, Guangxi, Shanxi, Shaanxi, and other parts of Sichuan. In the spring of 1991, with the support of the Shaanxi provincial government, Zhang founded the University for the Perfection of Traditional Chinese Culture in Xi'an, also known as the Xi'an University of Qilin Culture. Diplomas were offered in such fields as Qilin culture, tourism, hotel management, economic management, international commerce, finance, traditional hygiene, secretarial skills, public relations, management of educational establishments, martial arts, and advertising. The more general goal of the university was to train those who would work in the commercial expansion of Zhonggong. Also in Shaanxi, Zhang established a research center on reincarnation and, somewhat later (in the fall of 1992) a research center on "special medicine."

In 1994, a national organization was set up to unite all of the Zhonggong training centers across the country. This was accomplished through a new commercial society called the Taiweike Health Services Company. In April 1995, the Zhonggong organizations headquartered at Mount Qingcheng and in Chongqing met in Tianjin to set up the Qilin Group, yet another commercial concern consolidating the three great "systems" of Zhonggong: cultivation centers, affiliated products (medicine, tea, liquor), and commercial properties devoted to practice and research. By this point, these systems included more than thirty commercial properties, 3,000 Zhonggong practice centers, 100,000 Zhonggong employees, and 100,000 cultivation groups attached to the practice centers. Zhang Hongbao stated that Zhonggong had 30 million followers as of 1995 and that its "initial period of growth" had come to an end. During the following period of readjustment, which was to last from 1995 to 1998, Zhonggong cadres at the provincial level and higher were to reach an M.B.A. level in business management by studying cases from the Harvard Business School.

The foundation of the empire these M.B.A.-bearing Zhonggong cadres were to manage was the nationwide network of practice centers, home to the nationwide network of practitioners. Practitioners were presumably drawn to Zhonggong through word of mouth and through media reports of the master's great powers, and they could attempt to educate themselves through purchases of Zhang's biography, his books (the best known of which was the *Guide to Zhang Hongbao's Qilin Philosophy*), and his audio- or videocassettes (Zhang would now be podcasting). Like most schools of qigong, Zhang Hongbao's Zhonggong taught a set of physical and mental exercises designed to secure the corporal and spiritual health of practitioners and a body of more formal, philosophical principles explaining the theoretical basis of the practice and its fields of application. In the case of Zhonggong, Zhang Hongbao had given the name Qilin culture to the philosophical and theoretical underpinnings of his practice early in the history of the movement—notably, at an address in Beijing in early November 1990.

Qilin culture, according to Zhang's address—and he elaborated on these themes in his later writings—was made up of what he called eight "systems":

A philosophical system based on the traditional "diagram of ultimate return," which explains the origin of all creatures and their functions, their final destinations, and their evolution. This might be understood as the Chinese equivalent of the creation myth as found in the Book of Genesis.

A system of life sciences based on the use of qi to penetrate the mysteries of biological life. Included in this rubric was a theory of "special" or paranormal powers to be conferred on those who properly understood and practiced qi by following Zhang's teachings.

A system of "special medicine," which was different in important ways from Western medicine, Chinese medicine, and even garden variety qigong.

A system of art and aesthetics, which produced qigong architecture, sculpture, dance, music, painting, poetry, and martial arts.

A system of education offering an accelerated method to increase intelligence and to further train people with special powers.

A system of industrial and political management, consisting principally of sciences of leadership, administration, and commercial behavior and psychology, which combined the political and strategic arts of ancient China and the *Yijing* (*The Book of Changes*, an ancient divination text) with modern business administration.

A system of everyday behavior, including a work ethic, projects for personal renewal, and even "rules" for walking, sitting, or lying down.

A system of corporal practices, i.e., qigong in its incarnation as Zhonggong, which was taught in a series of eight ascending levels.[58]

These principles were further elaborated in many of Zhang's books and other writings, where Qilin culture was described as offering a comprehensive solution to human needs on three levels: material, spiritual, and "transcendent." At the material level, Qilin culture "promised to resolve problems of material life and to transmit the concepts of the enterprise, of capital, of price, profit, market, etc." At the spiritual level, Qilin culture "claimed to create different types of 'collective forms' and 'rites' which would foster the development of ideas of family, society, and a will toward perfection which would culminate in 'faith, aesthetics, and morals.' " The transcendent level promised salvation, enlightenment, and understanding of humans' place in the universe. Zhang's writings resonate with a heavy-handed syncretism which seeks to harmonize the best in past, present, and future human experience. Zhonggong's "system of interpersonal relations," for example, was based on "the equality of friendly mutual aid of [a] primitive society, the respect for the master in the family atmosphere of lineages throughout the ages, and the idea of ritual hierarchy in literati culture."[59]

The theory and practice of Zhonggong was learned principally in practice centers found virtually throughout China. Taking the practice center visited by David Palmer in Chengdu, Sichuan, as an example, we note that the primary functions of such centers were educational, social, and therapeutic. The center was open twenty-four hours a day. Portraits of Zhang Hongbao adorned the walls, incense wafted to the ceilings, and qigong music could be heard. Apart from elderly practitioners—or perhaps just elderly locals—most of those who came to the center did so for treatment or training. The center advertised itself as being staffed by specialists in Chinese and Western medicine, as well as by other specialists endowed with the powers of X-ray vision and diagnosis of illness through the laying on of hands. The center promised potentially miraculous results in the healing of cancers, heart problems, "strange illnesses," and sexual problems. Specialists also claimed to be able to carry out divination and to predict future events through their special powers.

A major—if not *the* major—function of the Zhonggong practice centers was education and training. Courses in levels 1 and 2 (of the eight total levels) were offered in local practice centers. Level 1 included the basic techniques and postures of Zhonggong; the collection, emission, reception, and exchange of qi; and certain diagnostic techniques related to Zhonggong's "special medicine." Level 2 was clearly designed to attract potential Zhonggong activists, as those who sought instruction at this level were taught methods of organization, how to control group meetings, qigong tricks (walking on a piece of paper suspended in air, standing on a lightbulb, changing the percentage of alcohol in a bottle of liquor), the "inner secrets" of Buddhist and Daoist methods, and specific treatments for more than thirty illnesses.

The fees charged for these courses were affordable, though hardly cheap in the context of 1990s China, where an average worker might have earned 500 RMB per month. The course itself, which lasted six days, cost 72 RMB, and the cost for food and lodging for the week was also 72 RMB, for a total of 144 RMB. Higher-level courses, given only at accredited Zhonggong institutions, lasted for twelve days and cost roughly twice as much.

It was on the base of these fees that Zhang Hongbao built his Zhonggong empire. Zhang argued that his personal qi should be understood as a sort of "invisible capital" without which the various Zhonggong undertakings, be they educational or commercial, would not be profitable. According to Zhang, this invisible capital counted for 70% of the overall capital of all Zhonggong enterprises. Consequently, practice centers and all Zhonggong units below the level of the central office were in theory expected to pass along 70% of their profits to the Zhonggong head office, as a return on Zhang's "investment." In practice, this 70% was reduced to 25% or 30%, as a measure of "generosity," but the revenue streams generated by such payments remained nonetheless enormous, especially since the payments were regarded more or less as obligations. Much of Zhonggong's internal organizational culture was aimed at encouraging—or pressuring—Zhonggong practice centers and enterprises to meet their targets. Another aspect of the internal organizational culture was the punishment of those who sought to thwart regulations and keep a larger percentage of the profits for themselves.

On the basis of these fees, paid by tens of millions of practitioners, Zhang built an international empire selling, among other things, "franchises" to practice centers, a variety of health-related products, college- and university-level education and diplomas, and commercial properties.

## Conclusion

The qigong of the pre–Cultural Revolution period had only an indirect connection to the redemptive societies described in the previous chapter. The creators of qigong wanted only the healing power of China's traditional cultivation systems and wanted nothing to do with masters, charisma, teachings, and preaching. And one must admit that qigong's creators largely succeeded, grafting corporal technologies drawn from traditional discourses of healing onto the newly created body of knowledge known as Traditional Chinese Medicine. Some of the practices included in these corporal technologies may well have smacked of feudal superstition, as Cultural Revolution period criticisms suggested, but had qigong remained in the clinic or the classroom, it is hard to imagine the surge in qigong activities which occurred in the post-Mao era.

When qigong moved to the parks, however, a double transformation occurred. Qigong therapy, or discourse, was no longer defined and controlled by the medical establishment but could be developed or "advanced" as the master saw fit. Similarly, qigong patients became qigong practitioners and were free to experience qigong in ways that would not have been considered appropriate in a therapeutic setting. One wonders to what extent the versions of qigong of the pre– and post–Cultural Revolution period were genuinely continuous. As social phenomena, they were quite different, and the very nature of qigong allows for a great definitional latitude. It seems likely that the qigong masters of the post–Cultural Revolution era, beginning with Guo Lin, seized on the term qigong because it had an acceptable, "orthodox" lineage in addition to being connected with a form of healing not rooted in biomedicine. This improvisation was given a great push forward when Gu Hansen announced the discovery of the scientific existence of qi. And when China's authorities approved wholeheartedly of both qi and qigong, it was the beginning of a brave new world.

The numerous schools of qigong that emerged in the post–Cultural Revolution period recall the pre-liberation redemptive societies, transformed (or perhaps disguised) by the special features of the era. The charismatic masters, healing techniques, corporal technologies, and moral teachings are largely consistent with what we observed in the context of the redemptive societies' expansion during the Republican period, but since the history of these groups has been largely ignored in the People's Republic, the parallels were not obvious to participants in the qigong movement. The embrace of science by qigong masters replaced the religious universalism of many of the Republican period groups and had the double virtue of binding qigong cultivation to the modernizing projects of China's elite. Indeed, were one to write the history of redemptive societies in modern Chinese history, the qigong boom would be a shining moment. With elite approval, qigong masters could take advantage of a stable market economy and a well-developed mass media to bring their messages to China's millions with little fear of suppression, and qigong enthusiasts could indulge themselves, cultivating their minds and bodies in peace.

# 4

# The Life and Times of Li
# Hongzhi in China, 1952–1995

Although it is difficult to evaluate the life and career of Falun Gong
founder and master Li Hongzhi as if the conflict between Falun Gong
and Chinese authorities had never occurred, it is nonetheless crucial to make the effort for, viewed within the context of the qigong
boom described in the previous chapter, Li Hongzhi looks like just
another qigong master among the thousands who came out of the
woodwork beginning in the late 1970s. And Li deserves to be studied
in this light; our views of Li and of Falun Gong have been inevitably
biased by the fact that he came to our attention only *after* he chose
to challenge Chinese authorities by authorizing the demonstration in
Beijing in late April 1999. True, we can readily find differences in his
tone and message (especially after Falun Gong became a cause célè-
bre), but these differences can be explained as understandable efforts
on Li's part to distinguish himself from his competition, instead of
fundamental divergences from the mainstream spirit of qigong. I
might add that, to my knowledge, no one has as yet done a careful,
detailed textual analysis of the writings of other qigong masters, even
the superstars. We might well find that Li Hongzhi innovated less
than we have thought.

At the same time, it is important to bear in mind that Li Hongzhi
emerged at a moment when the qigong movement, while still a
considerable social and cultural force, was no longer in the first blush
of youth. Certain masters had been shown to be no better than
clever magicians, others were accused of making immense fortunes

by fleecing their credulous followers. Qigong detractors in high places—and there had always been such detractors—began, in the late 1980s and early 1990s, to gain the upper hand, even if qigong supporters continued to insist that *genuine* qigong was a national treasure worthy of protection and nurturing. Li Hongzhi certainly took such factors into account in crafting his message; his criticism of other masters and other schools of qigong, as well as his insistence that he was teaching qigong "at a higher level" certainly made good marketing sense in this context—whatever his genuine beliefs might have been. In addition, Li's eventual decision to leave China and to carry on with his mission from abroad was also the result of rising tensions in the qigong milieu in China, and it seems probable that Li's absence led him to introduce certain changes within the Falun Gong movement—insisting, for example, that practitioners rely on his writings rather than on personal contact with the master (who would no longer be there) or on the Falun Gong organization.

The first part of this chapter examines Li's life prior to his emergence as a qigong master, his "coming out of the mountains" in 1992, and his career in China through early 1995. The second part of the chapter is devoted to an analysis of Li's message. Here, I seek less to find the seeds of the eventual conflict with the Chinese state, and more to explain what might have made Li and his message appealing to his many followers. In other words, in this chapter, I examine Li and his message as an example of a school of qigong, or as a late twentieth-century Chinese redemptive society, even as I attempt to point out aspects of Li's teachings which might distinguish him from some of his contemporaries. Chapter 6 will reexamine Li's writings and speeches in the context of the conflict with Chinese authorities.

## Li Hongzhi before Falun Gong

Relatively little is known about Li Hongzhi prior to his emergence into the public eye in 1992. Prior to achieving stardom, Li seems to have been as ordinary and unexceptional as other qigong masters, such as Yan Xin and Zhang Hongbao. A thumbnail sketch of his pre-1992 life includes the following basic elements.[1]

Li Hongzhi was born Li Lai on 27 July 1952, in Gongzhuling, Jilin province, in the northeastern part of China often called Manchuria. Li was the oldest of three children. His parents divorced when Li was a toddler, and he remained with his mother. In 1955, Li and his mother moved to the larger city of Changchun, also in Jilin province, where Li grew up and went to school.

Li's adolescence coincided with the Great Proletarian Cultural Revolution, which meant, among other things, that like other members of his generation, Li missed out on a good deal of the formal education he might otherwise have received. Like other children in China, his education would have been interrupted between 1966 and 1969, the three years of extreme Red Guard activities, and Li left school definitively in the early 1970s without having finished lower middle school, although he apparently later obtained both his lower and upper middle school diplomas through correspondence courses.

Once out of school, Li held a series of unremarkable jobs: between 1970 and 1972, he worked on an army horse farm; between 1972 and 1978, as a trumpeter in a band attached to the Propaganda Department of the provincial forestry police. The troupe was dissolved in 1978, and Li took an office job in the Grain and Oil Procurement Company of Changchun city. Somewhere along the way, he married and had a daughter.

Li became famous at the age of forty and controversial soon thereafter. As a result, it is difficult if not impossible to dig deeper into his early life without encountering divergent versions of Li's past constructed by his supporters and by his detractors. Such "information" must be taken with several grains of salt as the details have been composed for purposes which have little to do with establishing the true record of Li Hongzhi's life.

The divergences begin with Li's date of birth. Li has insisted that he was born on 13 May 1951, instead of 27 July 1952, and that the date appearing on his household registration documents was an error produced during the chaos of the Cultural Revolution. This would seem to be an unexceptional claim except that 13 May is also the date traditionally celebrated in China as the birth of Sakyamuni, otherwise known as the Buddha. I need hardly add that, from a nonpractitioner's point of view, such a coincidence strains credulity.[2]

The biography of Li which once appeared in Falun Gong sources (it is now harder to find) continues in the same vein.[3] The biography resembles that of other qigong masters (as well as other "holy men" throughout Chinese history) in suggesting that Li was exceptional from the very beginning of his life. Li is depicted as a special, gifted child, gifts which in early childhood took the form of appropriately Confucian piety:

> Mr. Li was born into an ordinary intellectual's family in the city of Gongzhuling, Jilin Province, China, on May 13 (the eighth day of the fourth month by China's lunar calendar), 1951. Being gifted and compassionate, he was different from the other children of his age. As a child, Li Hongzhi stood apart from his peers by virtue of his natural intelligence and benevolence. Seeing how hard his mother

had to work, he took up, of his own accord, such chores as looking after the house, cooking meals, chopping firewood, and taking care of his younger brother and sister.

Most of the rest of the document recounts Li's long and arduous spiritual training. Because of his innate gifts, he was, again according to the biography, sought out by a series of Buddhist and Daoist masters, who introduced him to the secrets of physical and spiritual cultivation. At the age of four, for example, master Quan Jue (the name translates as "complete enlightenment"), a tenth-generation master of Buddhist cultivation, came to Li in order to give him "personal instruction in the highest qualities of zhen-shan-ren (truthfulness, benevolence, and forbearance)." This instruction lasted eight years. As a result:

> at the age of eight, Li Hongzhi was already highly proficient in Dafa and had acquired supernatural powers. When he played hide-and-seek with his companions, he had only to think "other people cannot see me" to make himself invisible to others, who could not see him even if they directed a flashlight at his face. With a simple flick of a finger, he could draw long, rusty, and crooked nails out of pieces of wood. When water pipes froze up in winter, he had only to tap them with his hand for the pipes to bend; even he himself did not know how he did this.

When Li was twelve years old, Daoist master Baji Zhenren (zhenren, or "true man," is the Daoist term for a perfected person, one whose cultivation is, if not completed, superior to that of most people) assumed Li's training. While the Buddhist master Quan Jue had emphasized moral cultivation which gave rise to supernormal abilities, Baji Zhenren taught Li physical skills, martial arts disciplines which were still associated with mental and moral cultivation:

> He studied bare-handed fighting methods, fighting with sword and spear, and both internal and external gong. The master would take him to places where there were no other people and practice gong with him. When practicing the mabu zhanzhuang [immobile stance with legs spread apart], [Li] would stand like that for hours on end, frequently with sweat pouring down like rain. His body became as flexible as cotton and as hard as iron.

Li's cultivation at the direction of great masters continued even as he became an adult and joined the workaday world. A second Daoist master, Zhen Daozhi, sought Li out in 1972. This master taught Li "the internal cultivation of gong," training Li's "subjective awareness" and what we might call his moral willpower. Under Zhen's tutelage, Li "reached the state where he had absolutely no regard for the multitudinous desires and personal interests of ordinary people." Most of this training occurred under the cover of night, as the political atmosphere would have made such traditional spiritual pursuits unacceptable, and Li would have been severely criticized at work. For the same reason, Zhen Daozhi did not wear "religious vestments"—as had Li's previous masters.[4] In 1974, a female Buddhist master came to instruct Li further in the "theories and methods of Buddhist *gong*." During the qigong boom which began only a few years later, Li sought out a variety of qigong masters to continue and perfect his training.

Chinese government sources paint a very different picture of Li's pre-1992 life. An important part of the Chinese government's campaign against Falun Gong involved repeated and concentrated attacks on Li Hongzhi's credibility, including an investigation into his background, childhood, and the claims put forward in the "official" Falun Gong biography of Li. The goal of their efforts was to demonstrate that Li Hongzhi was thoroughly ordinary and that his claims to exceptional abilities and experiences were fraudulent.

Chinese authorities claim, for example, to have tracked down the midwife present at Li Hongzhi's birth, who recalled that it had been a difficult delivery, requiring the use of oxytocin to induce labor,[5] that Li's mother suffered terribly, and that Li himself had been purple when he emerged from the womb. They also claim to have located and interviewed Li Hongzhi's elementary school teachers, who recalled that there was nothing extraordinary about Li Hongzhi, that his grades were somewhat below normal, and that his skills in essay composition were particularly poor.[6] The only memorable thing about Li Hongzhi, according to this teacher, was that he played the trumpet. Indefatigable in their investigations, Chinese authorities subsequently sought out other members of the musical troupes in which Li Hongzhi played during his adolescence and early adulthood, who recalled that Li was not a particularly good trumpet player, frequently going off-key during practices and performances.[7]

Authorities further claim to have interviewed Li's family members and childhood friends, and they reported that none of these ever saw Li Hongzhi practice any kind of qigong or engage in any kind of cultivation activity prior to the qigong surge of the 1980s. His mother reportedly said: "I'm the one that brought him up, and he has no *gongfa*. Don't listen to his nonsense."[8] Investigators claimed to have interviewed his dormmates, some of whom were either insomniac or had to study late at night, who averred that if Li had been sneaking out at night to cultivate his spiritual gifts, they would have known about it. The investigators also noted that none of his relatives, friends, or classmates had ever heard of the Daoist and Buddhist masters with whom Li's autobiography claims that he studied: "[a]ccording to our research, there is no Master Quan Jue, Baji zhenren, or Zhen Daozhi in Jilin or Inner Mongolia."[9]

The investigators used this evidence to illustrate that Li could not have the powers he claims for himself in his biography and elsewhere—powers of omniscience and omnipotence. Li claims at various points in his writings to have chosen to be born in China (because of China's rich cultivation tradition) and also claims to have arranged various things for himself and for practitioners. The government documents asked: if Li had such great powers, why did he, as a supposedly filial son, not "arrange" an easier birth experience for his poor mother? Why did his mother have to use drugs, given Li's repeated claims that cultivators need not employ such artificial devices? Along similar lines, authorities claimed to have dug out forty-eight medical receipts for Li Hongzhi (and seventy-three for his family) covering the period between 1982 and 1992 and reflecting treatment in nineteen different hospitals, including once for an appendectomy, which required a ten-day stay.[10]

Finally, to these proofs that Li had lived a thoroughly unexceptional childhood and possessed no special powers, the authors added the final blow: Li is an uneducated, uncultured boob. Over and over again, they reiterated that Li has only "a lower-middle school [chuzhong] cultural level" and is a product of the Cultural Revolution, to boot:

> Li Hongzhi started school at the age of eight, and attended the Zhujiang Road Elementary School in Changchun from August 1960 through July 1967. In 1966 he started at Number Four Changchun High School for his lower-middle school [chuzhong], but this was the year that the Cultural Revolution began, and school stopped so that students could "make revolution." School didn't start up again until August of 1967, after which Li continued there for two years. In August of 1969, he transferred to the Number 48 Middle School in Changchun, where he studied for half a year, graduating in January of 1970. Thus he was only in school for two years, though it should have been three and a half. Because of the chaos of the Cultural Revolution, he didn't learn much while at school either. Between September 1982 and July 1983, Li participated in a make-up class [buxiban] for lower-middle school, but didn't study well, and barely managed to get his lower-middle school diploma; between September 1985 and July 1986, Li participated in the Changchun city upper-middle school program via correspondence . . . and muddled

through yet again to get his upper-middle-school diploma. Can [someone with] such a scholarly record create...the scientific theories Li Hongzhi has claimed to create?[11]

There is more information concerning Li's life after he set his sights on becoming a qigong master, although accounts of his activities differ considerably. Between 1982 and 1992, a period which coincided with the expansion of the qigong movement in general, Li appears to have intensified his cultivation efforts and begun to evolve his own methods of qigong practice. In the mid-1980s, he studied with a number of qigong masters, including Li Weidong, who taught a variety of qigong known as the Secret Qigong of the Chan School, and Yu Guangsheng, who taught his Qigong of the Nine Palaces and Eight Trigrams.[12] By this point, Li was quite clearly preparing his own variety of qigong, and he quit his job in 1991 to pursue his qigong studies full time.

The depiction of Li's efforts during this period differs greatly depending on the source consulted. Chinese government sources emphasize the derivative, unoriginal character of Li's teachings: according to these sources, Li copied much of his material from his qigong master Li Weidong, who subsequently scorned the manner in which Li had "deformed" genuine qigong practice; the same sources insist that many of the distinctive movements taught as part of Falun Gong exercises actually were taken from Thai dance, which Li observed while visiting relatives in Bangkok. The authorities argue that Li worked together with Li Jingchao and Liu Fengchai to put together his program of cultivation, and Liu made more than seventy corrections to Li's first attempts to put his program on paper.[13] Falun Gong sources reject such accusations.

## Li Hongzhi as Qigong Master in China

According to Falun Gong sources,[14] Li Hongzhi taught Falun Gong for the first time publicly in his home town of Changchun in May 1992, offering two series of nine-day lectures from 13 May through 22 May, and then from 25 May through 3 June. He charged 30 yuan per person, earning some 10,000 yuan for his efforts.[15] Most of Li's subsequent lectures in China followed this same nine-day format, although on occasion he shortened his teachings to seven or eight days (presumably for reasons of scheduling) and gave a few single-lecture presentations as well. Shortly thereafter, Li made his way to Beijing, the center of the qigong world, where he gave two nine-day lectures, beginning on 25 June and terminating on 24 July. Although Li was sponsored by the China Qigong

Science Research Society (CQRS), some sources—perhaps apocryphal?—report that Li and his group arrived in Beijing as complete unknowns, and spent their first few nights sleeping in the Beijing train station.[16] Li subsequently returned to Changchun for a series of talks between late August and mid-September, but was back in Beijing for another lecture series from 18 September through 25 September (eight days rather than his habitual nine).

In September, Li and Falun Gong were welcomed into the CQRS, and Li began to seek other venues for his teachings, giving lectures in Taiyuan (Shanxi) in October, and in Guan county (Shandong) in November. But Beijing remained the center of Li's activities during the fall and winter of 1992–1993. Between late October 1992 and early March 1993, he gave a total of six lecture series in the capital, not including his appearance at the Oriental Health Fair in December, where he and his group scored major successes. Li Rusong, the organizer of the health fair, remarked that Falun Gong had "received the most praise [of any qigong school] at the fair, and achieved very good therapeutic results" as well.[17] The health fair apparently did much to make Li's name in the broader qigong world, as it was attended by numerous masters and practitioners and chronicled by the qigong press. As in the case of other qigong masters, Li Hongzhi was immediately hailed as a miracle worker, journalists reporting that cripples had thrown away their crutches and risen from their wheelchairs. The organizers of the fair asked Li to give a special lecture on qigong, helping to consolidate his newfound popularity.

In the spring and early summer of 1993, Li began in earnest the nationwide lecture tours which had made previous qigong masters famous. He gave two nine-day lectures in the important industrial center of Wuhan in March and April, another nine-day course in the southern metropolis of Guangzhou between 13 and 22 April, and he began to spread his message to the southwest by giving two series of lectures in Guiyang (Guizhou) in May and June. He also found time to give yet another series of lectures in Beijing (29 April–6 May) and in Linqing (Shandong) (8–17 May). For the rest of the summer of 1993, Li returned to his home base in northeast China, giving two courses in Changchun in late June and early July and a further nine-day lecture series at Qiqihar in the adjacent province of Heilongjiang between 14 and 23 July, followed by a return to Beijing for two courses in late July and early August.

From the fall of 1993 through the end of 1994, Li was constantly on the road, giving twenty-eight full-length courses and a number of shorter lectures in a wide variety of venues. In August and September 1993, Li spoke in Guiyang (Guizhou), Beijing, Chongqing (Sichuan), and Wuhan. October and November saw him in Wuhan, Guangzhou, and Hefei (Anhui). At the end of 1993, Li once again attended the Oriental Health Fair in Beijing, where he sat on the organizing committee, testimony to his celebrity, and won several prizes for the quality of his teachings. In January 1994, Li spoke in Guangzhou, Tianjin, and Ji'nan (Shandong). In February, he gave courses in Kenli county (Shandong) and Liangyuan (Liaoning). In March, he was in Shijiazhuang, Tianjin, and Dalian. In April, he visited Jinzhou (Liaoning) and revisited Hefei (Anhui) and his home town of Changchun (where he had not spoken since July 1993). Li spent much of May in Sichuan, spreading the word in Chongqing and Chengdu. In June, he spoke in Zhengzhou (Henan) and Ji'nan (Shandong). July found him in Dalian, Zhengzhou, and Guangzhou, and August in Harbin and Yanbian (Jilin). His final nine-day lecture series in China was given at Guangzhou between 21 and 29 December. As his fame increased, Li found that sales of his publications and other paraphernalia provided sufficient revenues, and he stopped charging for attendance at his lectures, a fact which practitioners mention frequently as a sign of his virtue.

In sum, between May 1992 and December 1994, Li Hongzhi followed the route already traveled by his fellow qigong masters. He became a member of the CQRS in September 1992 and founded his own research association, the Falun Dafa Research Society, in late July 1993. He gave some fifty-four lectures during this nineteen-month period, reaching an audience of more than 60,000 who came to hear his teachings.[18] Some of these lectures were strategic: in 1994, he gave two well-attended lectures at the Public Security University in Beijing and contributed the profits to a foundation devoted to police officers injured in the line of duty.[19] This may help to explain the support Li received from Public Security Bureau officials through much of his career.

Li reached an even larger number of people through sales of his book *China Falun Gong* (first published in April 1993 and revised in December 1993) and audio- and videocassettes (the Beijing Television and Art Center Publishing Company produced the *Falun Gong Exercises* instructional video in September 1994)—although my impression is that it was the publication of *Zhuan falun* which propelled Li to genuine nationwide fame. The June 1993 edition of the review *Chinese Qigong* featured a special report on Li Hongzhi and Falun Gong, testimony to the role the media played in Li's rise to fame.

It was during this period that Li and his lieutenants began to construct the Falun Gong organization, much like other qigong masters. Chinese government sources stated in July 1999 that Li had built a network consisting of 28,263 base-level practice centers (*liangongdian*), 1,900 training stations (*fudaozhan*), charged with training those who managed the practice centers, and 39 main stations (*zongzhan*), which coordinated the network under Li's orders.[20] The national headquarters of the organization was in Beijing, and Wuhan served as a secondary center, facilitating distribution of Falun Gong materials toward South China; main stations existed at the provincial, regional, and municipal levels, establishing a presence throughout most of the country. Although impressive on paper, the precise nature of Falun Gong's organization has been a subject of some controversy. Since the beginning of the campaign of suppression,[21] Chinese authorities have insisted that Falun Gong possessed a tight, well-structured organization capable of raising impressive amounts of money, distributing large amounts of training matter, and mobilizing local practitioners, who numbered in the millions, for a variety of purposes. Falun Gong spokespeople have by contrast emphasized the supposedly decentralized, voluntarist character of the organization. Political scientist James Tong has examined these competing claims and concluded that, while there are elements of distortion and exaggeration on both sides, the Falun Gong organization appears less fearsome in reality than in the accusations made by Chinese authorities. Falun Gong did make considerable sums of money, in part from the distribution and sales of large amounts of training materials, and may have aspired to the sort of well-articulated, responsive structure described in PRC sources (and seen, perhaps, in Zhang Hongbao's Zhonggong), but conditions did not permit the fleshing out of the basic Falun Gong organization. Li left China in 1995 out of fear of future conflicts with authorities and progressively dismantled his formal organization in response to the changing attitude of authorities toward qigong (see chapter 6 for more details).[22]

In any event, it is important to stress yet again, in the light of the eventual conflict between Falun Gong and the Chinese state, that Li does *not* appear to have been particularly controversial during this 1992–1995 period. As already noted, the CQRS was quick to embrace Li Hongzhi and Falun Gong, according him membership in the nationwide organization in September 1992, only a few months after Li began his career as a qigong master. Consistent with the practices of other qigong masters, Li's lectures were sponsored by local organizations which often had direct links with the CQRS: his talks in Wuhan in March 1993, for example, were sponsored by the Wuhan City Qigong Association; his January 1994 lectures in Guangzhou were sponsored by the Guangzhou Baolin Qigong School.[23] Li insists that 40% of the fees charged to attend his lectures went to these local associations, and that he and his organization lived largely via sales of his publications (although profits were apparently shared with publishers and distributors). These publications were the work of what appear to be mainstream presses, or at least presses with connections to powerful, mainstream interests in China. Both editions of *China Falun Gong* were published and distributed by the Military Affairs Friendship and Culture Publishing Company. When *Zhuan falun* appeared in December 1994, it was published and distributed by the China

Television Broadcasting Agency Publishing Company. The unveiling ceremony for the publication of *Zhuan falun* took place in January 1995 in the auditorium of the University of Public Security in Beijing.[24] Among Li Hongzhi's most important supporters were highly placed officials in the Public Security Bureau itself; in late August 1993, the CQRS received a letter from the Ministry of Public Security thanking Li Hongzhi for having ministered to some 100 police officers injured in the line of duty.[25] None of this means that Li and Falun Gong were spared the criticism leveled at the qigong world in general during this period (see chapter 6), nor that Li did not have his detractors. But the preponderance of evidence suggests that Li was not a *particular* target of criticism and that Li succeeded in carving out a safe space for himself and his movement, a space protected by the official qigong world and—in general—by Chinese authorities.

The history of Li Hongzhi and Falun Gong entered a new period beginning in January 1995 with the publication of *Zhuan falun*, the end of Li's lecture tours in China, and his subsequent departure from the country. Much of this story more properly belongs to the history of the conflict between Falun Gong and the Chinese state, and will be treated in chapter 6. Here, continuing with our present focus on Li Hongzhi and his message, I will examine Li's teachings, as I understand them via my readings of *Zhuan falun* and Li's other writings and informed by fieldwork among Falun Gong practitioners in North America.

## Making Sense of Li Hongzhi

Interpreting Li Hongzhi's teaching presents numerous challenges. The first is that Li has said many things which appear at first (or even second) glance to be somewhat puzzling. Indeed, it is too easy to make fun of Li Hongzhi. Li declared in a 1999 interview with *Time* magazine, for example, that modern science was the invention of aliens dedicated to the manipulation and eventual replacement of humankind.[26] His writings are replete with equally startling assertions: a "small fluorescent screen like a television" positioned on the forehead permits the initiated to possess the power of total recall;[27] animals, who are not "allowed" to cultivate, regularly possess human beings in order to exploit humans' greater spiritual and supernormal capacities (which means, among other things, that Falun Gong practitioners should be very careful about raising pets);[28] and the salvation of the children of interracial marriages is problematic because, in the afterlife, the paradises are divided by race.[29] Li cites the example of the magician David Copperfield as proof that high-level spiritual beings exist in the West.[30] It would not be difficult to find other examples of seemingly absurd remarks. As a nonpractitioner, I feel no need to defend Li's statements, but as a scholar I am more interested by the fact that large numbers of otherwise intelligent people either accept or overlook what appear to be Li's nonsensical statements in their embrace of his larger vision. Thus, while I will not dismiss what strike me as outlandish claims, I prefer to try to make sense of Li Hongzhi—even at the risk of leaving certain statements unchallenged.

The overall form of Li's message poses a more difficult problem than his frequent strange remarks. Although he has written a number of poems and has composed a handful of messages which have appeared on Falun Gong Web sites, Li is in general a speaker rather than a writer, and the vast majority of his oeuvre consists of transcriptions of his numerous lectures, in China and abroad. When Li was lecturing in China, between 1992 and 1994, his teachings were most often conveyed in series of nine lectures, roughly ninety minutes each in length, given over several days in a single venue; Li's masterwork, *Zhuan falun*, is in fact an edited version of one of these sets of lectures. Many if not most of Li's addresses since leaving China in 1995 have also been transcribed and are available in published versions or on Falun Gong Web sites, which are frequently updated (see the section "New Scriptures" on the site www.falundafa.org); among other things, this opportunity affords Li's handlers a chance to edit or expunge problematic statements.

The spoken word can, of course, be just as coherent and reasoned as the written word, and orators like Li certainly do their best to be persuasive (I find him to be a good, no-nonsense speaker in terms of his presentation style; this is not a comment on the content of his message). At the same time, Li is not a rigorous thinker or speaker, and the particular setting of his lectures, delivered before crowds of adoring practitioners, some of whom—at least in the early days of his ministry—had paid for the privilege of listening to him, most certainly did *not* push him to clarify difficult questions. (One wonders if this is why Li often sounds so silly when interviewed by Western journalists; they know little or nothing about qigong, and do not play the same game or write for the same audience as Chinese journalists, who often participated actively in the construction of the cult of charisma surrounding many qigong masters.) The style of Li's talks is expansive rather than studied. Li seems to speak from an outline, or on some occasions brief notes, but generally to follow his intuition in the elaboration of the subject at hand. He sets himself the task of expounding difficult questions concerning the nature of life and the universe, the meaning of modern science, the nature of physical illness, but his exposition is considerably helped along by his assurance that those who are listening to him share his basic assumptions.

Similarly, although he states on occasion that one of his goals is to save all sentient beings, in practice he only addresses those who want to be saved and thus feels little need to defend his ideas against detractors, other than by denouncing them (and even his denunciations are often rather cursory). Those who do not understand him are often dismissed as lacking the insight that comes with the kind of enlightenment Li himself has experienced, an enlightenment, for example, that allows him both to appreciate what modern science has accomplished and to recognize its limitations (a handy way to defuse criticisms that he is spreading "superstition"). Similarly, Li often notes that even his followers cannot be expected to understand him fully, because they are at a "lower level" than he, which means among other things that he is required to use human language, a "lower-level" communications tool, to try to convey the mysteries of the universe. Li also insists that life exists simultaneously in many "dimensions," most of which are unknowable to the unenlightened (or even those who have not obtained his own exalted status); thus, Li claims, for example, to have installed a rotating dharma wheel in the stomachs of his followers—in a dimension other than that containing their physical bodies. Even if doctors would *not* find a rotating wheel in the stomach of a practitioner were they to perform surgery, this does *not* mean that Li's statements are to be taken as merely symbolic or rhetorical. The wheels are real, but observable only in a parallel universe or at a higher level, even if the effects of the wheels' rotation are felt in the daily lives of practitioners. Whatever Li and his followers may believe about such claims, it is hard for the nonbeliever not to see such rhetorical strategies as sleight of hand.

The volume of Li's work is another difficulty. Some 1,500–2,000 pages of Chinese-language material are available via the main Falun Gong Web site,[31] a portion of which, amounting to some 1,000 pages, has been translated into English.[32] For the brave-hearted, sound recordings are also available for a number of lectures which have not, insofar as I have been able to determine, been translated (or even transcribed).[33] Such amounts are not insurmountable, particularly as there is considerable repetition from lecture to lecture and thus from text to text, but this very repetition (which comes at the expense, say, of logical exposition) can often be an obstacle to comprehension for the non-practitioner. Li's lectures rarely build on one another, and new departures (such as that occasioned by the need to explain the Chinese government's campaign against Falun Gong, which came in the face of rather blithe assurances by Li that he was omniscient if not omnipotent) are rarely explained with reference to past lectures.[34]

In the face of these difficulties, my strategy for understanding Li Hongzhi has been to read him repeatedly, if rather passively or inductively, by which

I mean that instead of aggressively challenging Li's underlying assumptions, or searching his works for internal contradictions (which are manifest and many), I seek out elements of coherence which seem to accord with practitioners' accounts of their cultivation experiences. Again, my goal is to explain the attraction of Li's teachings to those who have embraced them and not to "test" Li's vision against other scientific, logical, or religious standards. This is in no way intended as an apology for Li's teachings and should be taken instead as similar to an emic reading carried out by an anthropologist of his subject's cultural habits and discourse.[35]

Li's teachings can be divided into at least two chronological phases. The first lasted from the spring of 1992 through the spring of 1999, when Li introduced and honed his message, and subsequently delivered it in China and throughout the world. The second began in the fall of 2000, when Li returned to public life after a near-silence of almost a year and a half and felt compelled by the Chinese government's relentless campaign against Falun Gong to explain this disaster within the framework of his own teachings. The discussion of Li's teachings in this chapter will confine itself to the first phase, as the teachings of the second phase belong more appropriately to the history of the conflict between Falun Gong and the Chinese state.

This first phase, 1992–1999, can be more finely divided. The period between the spring of 1992 and the winter of 1994–1995 is the period when Li first articulated his vision and spread it throughout China, finding a considerable audience. Li completed his teaching in China at the end of 1994, and after that, most lectures were given outside of China. In terms of publications, Li's teachings were first made known in *China Falun Gong*, initially published in April 1993 and then in a revised edition in December of the same year. *China Falun Gong* appears to be a mixture of edited transcriptions of Li's lectures, an explanation of the basic Falun Gong physical exercises, and a question-and-answer section where followers ask questions and Li Hongzhi replies. In late 1994, Li published his masterwork, *Zhuan falun*, which remains the bible of the movement, studied by practitioners to the virtual exclusion of Li's other writings. Like *China Falun Gong*, *Zhuan falun* is an edited transcription of Li's lectures—indeed, of an entire nine-day lecture series—but unlike *China Falun Gong* there are no illustrations of proper exercise technique (because the exercises are clearly of lesser importance than the scriptures) and no question-and-answer section. I consider *China Falun Gong* and *Zhuan falun* to be largely consistent in terms of content, although important differences in nuance distinguish the two. The following interpretation builds on all of Li's writings (I consulted both the Chinese originals and the English-language translations in most cases) during this period, not just on *China Falun Gong* and *Zhuan falun*.

## Li Hongzhi's Teachings

The appeal of Li Hongzhi's Falun Dafa, I will argue, is essentially threefold. First, Li presents his vision both as a return to a lost, or neglected, spiritual tradition *and* as a major contribution to modern science. As already emphasized in the previous chapter, it was this supposed convergence between qigong and science which gave wings to the qigong boom, and if Li gives a different spin to his "scientific" vision than did some other qigong masters, he certainly does not dispense with science. Quarks and neutrinos figure in Li Hongzhi's writings as frequently as buddhas and bodhisattvas, even if Li's chief goal is to call into question certain dichotomies (such as that between matter and spirit, for example) central to the modern scientific paradigm in order to make space for his own vision, which most nonbelievers would label as more "religious" than "scientific." Be that as it may, the scientific flavor of Li's writings resonates with the romance of scientism in modern Chinese history, the idea that science—the scientific method, scientific agriculture, scientific socialism—will bring about China's national salvation from backwardness and ineffectuality. As already noted, science is universalizing in a way that recalls the embrace by Republican period redemptive societies of all major world religions. An important part of the appeal of Falun Gong—particularly to Chinese intellectuals— must lie in its promise to wed modern science to Chinese traditions in a project with nationalistic implications—even if Falun Dafa promises ultimately to transcend science as a world view.

Second, Falun Gong is profoundly *moral*. The very structure of the universe, according to Li Hongzhi, is made up of the moral qualities that cultivators are enjoined to practice in their own lives: truth, compassion, and forbearance. The goal of cultivation, and hence of life itself, is spiritual elevation, achieved through eliminating negative karma—the built-up sins of past and present lives—and accumulating virtue. As the terms "karma" and the "accumulation of virtue" suggest, much of Li's message is cast in the language of Buddhism (although one finds other, non-Buddhist elements as well). China and the world as a whole are portrayed as having gone astray. The modern world is less virtuous than in previous ages. Despite this, through cultivation, practitioners are promised personal harmony with the very substance of the universe. One finds few lists of do's and don'ts in Li's writings, nor are there sophisticated ethical discussions. Instead, followers are advised to rid themselves of unnecessary "attachments," to do what they know is right, and hence to return to "the origin," to their "original self." Interviews with practitioners in North America have confirmed over and over again that many Chinese prefer this simple injunction to "do the right thing" to the complex dictates of "so-cialism with Chinese characteristics," the post-Mao recasting of China's revo-lutionary purpose, which many Chinese find to be strikingly irrelevant to their daily lives.

Third, Falun Dafa promises practitioners supernatural powers. There is a wide range of such powers (Li notes on occasion that there are some 10,000),[36] including the opening of the heavenly eye, which may enable practitioners to see into other spatial dimensions and/or through walls and other obstructions; the capacity to remove negative karma from family members or friends; and omniscience.[37] Most commonly, practitioners are promised that cultivation will bring them consistent health and rejuvenate them—which, for practi-tioners who are elderly and/or ailing, is readily seen as a sort of supernormal power as well. In several passages, Li seems to promise that the culmination of these powers will eventuate in a sort of immortality in this world, even if he seems to deny, or qualify, this promise in other passages.[38] However, super-natural powers are developed *only as a result of moral practice and only if the practitioner does not strive to develop them.* In other words, once someone sets his sights on, say, clairvoyance or levitation, attainment of these powers becomes impossible. Abuse of the powers, once attained, is equally impossible. They disappear with the intent of wrongful use. Thus, we see embodied in Li Hon-gzhi's Falun Dafa what must be one of the oldest, most common, and most widely shared wishes in the world: that the righteous have the power.

One might add the very "Chineseness" of Falun Dafa as a fourth element, for even as it has expanded throughout the world, Falun Dafa has remained unabashedly loyal to its national heritage, which is significant because its membership—even outside of China—remains overwhelmingly Chinese. At one point, Li cites Sakyamuni, the founder of Buddhism, to the effect that "[t]his oriental land of China is a place where people of great virtues are pro-duced."[39] Elsewhere, he notes chauvinistically that "it could not be more ap-propriate for us today to have chosen Chinese as the language for teaching the Fa. This is because Chinese is the most expressive and the richest language in the world. If English or any other language was used, nothing would have been expressed."[40] At the same time, even if this Chineseness is deeply felt, it is taken for granted, by both Li and most practitioners, and is rarely defended or elaborated on. Hence, although I note it in passing here, I will not develop it in detail.[41]

The reconstruction which follows develops and illustrates these three basic points. My exposition is neither a thorough historical exegesis nor a rigorous, critical reading of Li Hongzhi. I doubt that my exposition will please most Falun Gong practitioners, but such is not my goal. My goal is to explain the attraction of Li Hongzhi's discourse, to illustrate, once again, and despite his many nonsensical remarks, why large numbers of people have been drawn to Falun Gong and have remained loyal to Li and his vision at the cost, in many instances, of their very lives. Throughout my presentation, I make extensive use of direct quotes from Li's speeches and writings. I do this both to give the flavor of Li's teachings, but also to avoid making Li seem more logical and programmatic than he is by reducing his teachings to capsule summaries.

## Li Hongzhi on Science

> I often say that if you can see, you might find many cities in a single hair, and trains and cars might be running inside them. This sounds really inconceivable. This world is just an extremely immense and complex world like this, and is entirely different from the understanding of our modern science. I often say that today's science has developed on a flawed understanding and a wrong basis since its establishment. So it is confined to that framework alone. As for true science, from what we've really learned of the universe, life, and matter, today's science can't be considered a science because the wondrousness of the universe could never be discovered by following the path of this science.[42]

One of Li Hongzhi's favorite themes is that of modern science. Again and again in his lectures, he returns to the limitations of the scientific paradigm and the blind arrogance of the world scientific community. Not that Li's vision is antiscientific or necessarily antimodern in the way that, say, some Mennonites' world views might be understood to be. On the contrary, Li claims to speak the language of modern science and seems quite content that his followers take advantage of all that modern science has to offer—indeed, without modern telecommunications, most notably the Internet, Falun Gong most certainly would not have achieved its present form. At the same time, Li teaches that Falun Gong offers the sole avenue toward genuine understanding of the true meaning of the universe, which he often labels the "Buddha Fa," or the Buddhist "way." As I will attempt to demonstrate, Li's discussions of science are both tactical and strategic: tactical in that no one in today's China can hope to present himself as a man of wisdom without having embraced the modern scientific paradigm (if only to transcend this paradigm once having mastered it); strategic in that Li genuinely hopes to call into question the ultimate value of a scientific world view as it is currently understood.

Even a cursory reading of *Zhuan falun* reveals that Li Hongzhi considers himself to have a thorough understanding of modern science. And my impression is that his interest in (if not necessarily mastery of) science is genuine. I recall attending a Falun Gong experience-sharing conference in Ottawa, Canada, in May 2001 when Li unexpectedly appeared to address practitioners. In the middle of his stump speech ("mobilize righteous thoughts to defeat the forces of evil"), he stopped quite suddenly and launched into a seemingly unrelated disquisition on a new personal understanding of the mechanisms of gravitational force which had come to him recently.[43] My distinct impression was that this discussion—which added little or nothing to his apparently more scripted remarks—was an improvisation on Li's part and reflected genuine enthusiasm for the subject. In other words, even if at some level Li Hongzhi, like other qigong masters, embraces a scientific world view out of respect for the iconic status of science in modern Chinese history (as well as its enabling, empowering role in the legitimation of qigong in post-Mao China), Li seems to wear this tactical posture quite comfortably.

Another example of this tactical positioning is Li's open discussion of the "cultivation difficulties" experienced by his more intellectual followers, particularly those in the Chinese diaspora. To quote Li directly from a March 1998 speech to followers in New York (most of whom were undoubtedly expatriate Chinese; Li does not speak English and all of his lectures are in Chinese):

> Generally speaking, everyone has an obstacle in studying the Fa. For intellectuals, the obstacle is modern science. If something conforms to this science, they can accept it; otherwise, they cannot accept it. They are severely impeded. No one knows why I incorporate modern science in my teachings of the Fa. Why do I do that? The reason is that I want to break that shell of yours which prevents you from attaining the Fa.[44]

My fieldwork, carried out among North American Falun Gong practitioners, leaves no doubt that Li's discussions of (and challenges to) science have struck a chord with many Chinese intellectuals who became Falun Gong practitioners. This fieldwork revealed that many Chinese practitioners in North America hold advanced degrees, from both Chinese and North American universities, often in fields of science and technology (see chapter 5 for details). Although I did not design my questionnaires to solicit information as to the precise fields that practitioners have studied, I found more than a few physicists among them. When asked about Li's claims regarding science, these highly trained scientists tended to respond, among other things,[45] that Li Hongzhi has made science *relevant* in a way that it was not before by explaining its relationship to larger cosmic structures and existential questions. In part, this seems to mean that such practitioners can go on with their work, continuing to write computer programs or speculate on questions in theoretical physics much as they did before—but with greater clarity and confidence concerning the ultimate importance of their work and, especially, their lives.

Of course, if we had statistical information on Falun Gong membership inside China—both before and after suppression—it would no doubt reveal that the percentage of well-educated members is considerably lower than in North America, even if considerable anecdotal evidence from China suggests that Falun Dafa membership there, before the campaign of suppression, spanned the social spectrum, including both well- and less well-educated, well-off and less well-off, party and government cadres, and the elderly and retired. The high concentration of well-educated practitioners in North America is a function of immigration policies which favor candidates with just such profiles. But there is no reason to believe that the appeal of Li Hongzhi's scientific discussion was limited to the well-educated, as the image of "scientific fortunetelling" evoked earlier suggests. In any case, it is not my contention that science constitutes the only appeal of Falun Dafa, or even the most important. My claim is rather that any teaching seeking to win over large numbers of Chinese at the turn of the twenty-first century would be wise to include appeals to scientific insight within its claims to truth. And this, Li Hongzhi's Falun Dafa most surely does.

But Li's frequent and lengthy discussions of science are not solely tactical. His ultimate goal is to illustrate the limitations of scientific knowledge so as to make space for his own vision, which transcends science and returns it to a secondary, subservient role in our understanding of cosmic and human forces. Li's demonstration of his vision follows a number of related paths. First, he invokes "evidence" from the frontiers of what one might call "parascientific research" to cast doubt on the authority of science. Although there are many examples of such arguments in Li's writings, one quote from *Zhuan falun* will suffice to convey the flavor of Li's reasoning:

> A good number of you have probably heard of the term prehistoric culture, which is also called prehistoric civilization. . . . On the earth there is Asia, Europe, South America, North America, Oceania, Africa, and Antarctica, which geologists group together as continental plates. It's been tens of millions of years since the continental plates formed, or you could say, a number of land masses rose from the ocean floor, and a lot of land masses sank to the bottom of the sea,

and it's been tens of millions of years since they stabilized as they are now. But at the bottom of a lot of oceans people have found tall and large ancient structures, the structures have elegant designs, and they aren't cultural remains from today's human race. So they must have been built before they sank to the sea bottom. Then who was it tens of millions of years ago that started those civilizations? Back then, our human race wouldn't have even been monkeys, right—how could we have created such intelligent things? Today archaeologists have discovered that there was an organism called a trilobite, and that creature was active from 600 million years ago up until 260 million years ago. It hasn't been around for 260 million years. Yet there's an American scientist who discovered a trilobite fossil, and what was on it but a human footprint, the footprint of somebody wearing shoes, and the print was unmistakable. Isn't that like playing a joke on historians? If you go by Darwin's theory of evolution, tell me, could there be human beings 260 million years ago?[46]

Obviously, Li's argument here is that there are important holes in the evidence marshaled by modern science to establish its authority and credibility; he suggests, in part, that scientific paradigms are historically and culturally bound and thus epistemologically incapable of validating their own claims to authority. But Li clearly does *not* wish to argue that the holes in the evidentiary record can be filled in and the credibility of science reestablished. No, the ultimate point of Li's argument is to *relativize* scientific truth and thereby to create a space for his own claims, which have been ridiculed by scientists and journalists—both Chinese and Western—as being outlandish.

People think that the renowned persons, scholars and other experts in human society are quite great. In fact, they are all very insignificant, for they are just ordinary people. Their knowledge is only that tiny bit understood by the modern science of human society. In the vast universe . . . [human beings] are the lowest form of existence, so their understanding of matter and mind is very limited, superficial, and pitiful. Even if one understood all of mankind's knowledge, he would remain an ordinary person.[47]

Li's argument thus is not that science is completely wrong, but that it is only valid within certain parameters; science as a mode of understanding is useful when properly applied, but limiting when it fails to acknowledge its own limitations or, more to the point from Li's personal point of view, damaging when it is used as a standard of absolute value which serves to reject alternative—indeed, superior—approaches to knowledge and understanding.

One of science's major shortcomings, from Li's point of view, is that it has failed to include his idea of "levels." Li argues that the universe—and human understanding of the universe—exists at many different levels simultaneously and that the process of enlightenment consists of passing through these levels to arrive at ever more complete understandings (in fact, the transformation is physical as well as intellectual, as will be discussed below in the section on morality). His examples of this complexity often sound like lectures in the popularization of scientific knowledge:

> The cosmos is extremely complex. . . . Earth is nothing but a speck of dust, and it is insignificant. Yet within this expanse there are innumerable and complex structures of dimensions. What are these structures of dimensions like? . . . Which level of dimension does our humankind live in? We live in the surface matter comprised of the biggest layer of molecular particles; we live in between molecules and planets—a planet is also a particle, and within the vast cosmos, it, too, is a trivial speck of dust. The Milky Way Galaxy is also a trivial speck of dust. This universe—the small universe I just described—is also but a trivial speck of dust. The largest particles that our human eyes see are planets, and the smallest particles visible to humankind are molecules. We humans exist in between the particles of molecules and planets. Being in this dimension, you think it's vast; from a different perspective, it's actually extremely narrow and tiny.[48]

Even while denying that human language possesses the tools to describe or comprehend this complexity—the universe is too large, the particles are too small, the levels are too numerous—Li returns again and again to this point, hoping to convince his reader both that each level has an independent and coherent existence (atoms are unaware of neutrinos, and humans, even if capable of understanding intellectually the existence of a molecular level, still do not begin to understand molecular life on its own terms) and that levels exist in a variety of hierarchies, are made up of different substances, and thus are qualitatively different experiences. Had Li been enamored of entomology instead of physics, his favorite metaphor might have been that of an ant farm. Those beings at higher levels are capable of understanding—in a certain sense—those at lower levels, although the inverse is not true:

Going further beyond, one finds the existence of a larger cosmic body, which is totally different from this cosmic body of ours. The cosmic body I'm talking about goes completely beyond the concept of this universe. So the Buddhas, Daos, and Gods in that larger cosmic body are especially huge. They see us just like we see the Buddhas, Daos, Gods, humans, and things in a microscopic world or a microscopic cosmic body. So they belong to yet another system, which is incredibly huge. Not to mention the way they see us humans, they look at this cosmic body of ours the way we look at unearthed relics. They find it peculiar, wondrous, quite good, and interesting. They also think that these beings are limitlessly wondrous. This tiny little cosmic body is also full of life—they also see it this way. But they don't have the concepts within the expanse of this cosmic body that are held by beings like us—not at all. In their eyes you're a microorganism and have nothing to do with them. That's why many of our cultivators often feel the same way when they see scenes in rocks, sand, or even smaller microscopic particles.[49]

Li further notes at one point: "The dimensions I talked about before are all composed of more microscopic high-energy matter, whereas the dimension I'm talking about today is composed of surface matter."[50] In other words, while Li hopes through these discussions to relativize modern scientific understanding, he is by no means satisfied with a relativistic world view in which everyone will have the tolerance to respect everyone else's "level of understanding." Quite the contrary. For Li, these levels are real, they exist objectively, and they include the levels of gods, buddhas, and Li himself, even if the limitations of human language and understanding preclude his drawing a precise map of all of the levels and their interrelations. Furthermore, he says:

[W]ithin each level of dimension there are also vertical ones, that is, dimensions of different levels. In other words, there are dimensions of different levels that are like the many layers of heavens understood by religions. In addition, in dimensions at different levels there also exist different unitary paradises. It's extremely complex.[51]

For all the space he devotes to it, Li Hongzhi's arguments with regard to science are really quite simple. He invokes apparent anomalies in the archaeological or geological record to call into question the authority of the reigning scientific consensus. On the basis of that challenge—which Li obviously considers decisive—he goes on to suggest a less human-centered view of the universe composed of hierarchically linked levels, each of which contains a version of something similar to life as we know it. Through cultivation, humans can transcend the level into which they were born and thus achieve a different and wiser perspective on that and lower levels. This is what Li himself claims to have done, which has allowed him to see the follies of human belief in modern science. Li thus speaks from personal experience; his arguments are constructed after the fact to convince those who have not yet benefited from such experiences, rather than as a chain of logical deductions.

I personally find Li's arguments unconvincing, but he presumably would not be moved by my skepticism. To my eyes, Li is too obviously looking for evidence which will decenter the reigning scientific paradigm and too quick to interpret any challenge to this paradigm as a victory. He is a preacher, not a scientist, and does not really meet scientists at their own level nor engage them in debate. Here and elsewhere in his writings and lectures, he seems relatively unconcerned about doubters and unbelievers; his concern is rather to illustrate, *to those who are attracted to such a message*, that Falun Dafa both contains within it *and* transcends the modern scientific viewpoint:

> Everything will change. And it will be completely new. People's understanding of this society, of humanity, and of everything will all be turned around. So now many of our students in Beijing know that they're different from other people and are passing around a saying: "We are the new humankind." Of course, I'm not endorsing their saying, I'm just conveying an idea. It will definitely be different from the way today's people think and understand things—that's for sure. As you continue to study this Fa in depth you will have a new understanding of everything. Those of you present here have relatively high professional titles, and many are students studying abroad. As you gradually experience it and think about it, you'll find that your understanding of everything about humankind is undergoing a change. This is because, as I said, humankind's development, humankind's understanding of its beginning and origin—the theory of evolution doesn't exist at all—and its understanding of matter, understanding of the universe, understanding of life, understanding of the world before us, and understanding of this cosmic space have all been developed on the wrong foundations.[52]

As we will see in the subsequent section, the motor behind these fundamental changes is not scientific brilliance, but rather individual moral practice paired with cultivation under the guidance of the right master. But a promise, couched in the language of modern science, that well-educated practitioners might eventually contribute to the creation of new bodies of knowledge and even a new world could not help but appeal to a group hungry for moral purpose and historically conditioned to look favorably on elite status and service to society. As Li says: "Mankind will make a leap forward if it can take a fresh look at itself and at the universe, changing its rigid way of thinking."[53] The phrase "leap forward" reminds us yet again of the siren song of science and progress, which has taken many forms over the course of China's long revolutionary history, and reminds us again of the crucial role science has played in the qigong movement as a whole. Li manages both to capitalize on the authority science gives to those who understand it and also to transcend the limitations of a narrowly scientific viewpoint.

## Falun Gong and the Moral Universe

QUESTION [DIRECTED TO LI HONGZHI]    Is it okay if, while I'm sitting in quiet meditation, I swat a mosquito which is biting me?

ANSWER [FROM LI HONGZHI]    Swat it if you want to, but it's best not to. If you swat something during cultivation it will mess up your *qi* mechanism. Actually, it's a way for devils to disrupt you, and you should pay no attention. Wouldn't it be better to pay back a little *karma* [by letting him bite you]?[54]

The ultimate point of Li Hongzhi's discussion of science, as we have seen, is to challenge the thoroughly modern idea that science is an independent, neutral, objective realm, something apart from human morality and yet endowed with enormous power, both symbolic and real. Li argues by contrast that "the Buddha Fa can unravel the mysteries of the universe, life, and science. It enables mankind to resume the correct path in science, but it is not for the guidance of mankind's science that the Buddha Fa has been brought forth."[55] Properly understood, the Buddha Fa incorporates both the material and the spiritual and goes beyond both. This is the point of Li's frequent—if unprovable—assertion that "truth, goodness, and forbearance" are the constituent parts of the universe. In one sense, we can understand Li as making the thoroughly Buddhist point that manmade distinctions between material and spiritual, moral and scientific are in fact false and mask an underlying unity which, again, he calls alternatively the Buddhist law, or *zhen-shan-ren*. On the other hand, I'm not sure that Li fully shares the Buddhist conviction that reality is an illusion (which may not be a valid statement for many Buddhists, either). Similarly, it is a partial understanding of Li's vision to note that, according to this characterization, the universe becomes a moral place—but I suspect that it is a partial understanding which has attracted many followers. Over and over again, Falun Dafa practitioners return to the simple pleasure of being and doing good. Particularly for Chinese people whose lives and memories have spanned the eras of radical Maoism and screw-thy-neighbor capitalism, the idea that there are rewards for doing and being good is immensely appealing.

At the same time, Li Hongzhi is not an ethicist in any strict sense of the word, and one would have difficulty isolating a particular set of moral teachings in his message. There are no exhaustive lists of do's and don'ts, rights and wrongs in Li's writings (an absence which strikes me as quite *un*-Buddhist, given the frequency of such lists in traditional Buddhist scriptures, particularly non-elite scriptures) and rather than saying "don't eat meat," he will say, "when you reach the appropriate level of cultivation, you will probably lose the desire to eat meat." Nor do we find sophisticated discussions of ethical dilemmas, either in Li's writings or in conversations with practitioners. The basic shape of the moral life is assumed; like Dr. Phil—or Wang Yangming—Li would say that most of us know, in our heart of hearts, what we should do in most situations, and are generally aware when we fail to live up to these commonly accepted standards—although there are some people who, for a variety of reasons, have insulated themselves from moral concerns.

Thus, the discussion of morality in Li Hongzhi's writings does not focus on defining or preaching a new moral vision, or even refurbishing a former state of morality which has now gone by the wayside, but rather on explaining the history of humankind's fall from grace—and the mechanics of humankind's redemption—at both the collective and the individual levels. To be more precise, Li's explanations of humanity's decline to its current sorry state emphasize the collective aspect of human experience and morality, while his prescriptions for redemption rely on individual moral practice.


## The Decline of Humanity and the History of the Apocalypse

Li's vision of human history is as pessimistic as his vision of the future is optimistic. Li's discussion of the past emphasizes cycles of decline (and renewal, but he talks much less about historical examples of renewal, a trait which is hardly unique to Li) punctuated by apocalyptic moments which purge the world of evil. These apocalyptic overtones can be found virtually from the beginning of Li's writings—which means virtually from the beginning of his ministry—but, in my reading, they remained in the background until after the beginning of the conflict with the Chinese state, at which point Li gave considerably more attention to end-times discourses. By contrast, the apocalypse remained a secondary consideration among the North American Falun Gong practitioners with whom I did my fieldwork, even after the onset of the crisis. For most of them, the individual moral programs described further below still occupy pride of place.

Although much has been made of the apocalyptic features of Li's teachings, these features seem to be largely derivative, based on folk Buddhist scriptures with a centuries-long history. Many strains of the White Lotus tradition, discussed in chapter 2, stressed similar cycles of decline and renewal (often defined as *kalpas*, a Sanskrit word for "great ages"), the intervention of messianic figures (Maitreya or the "future Buddha"), and the salvation of an elite, who were to rejoin the Unborn Venerable Mother in her paradise. The fact that Li's apocalyptic visions have roots in Chinese history does not necessarily make them less worrisome or dangerous. There have indeed been numerous rebellions in Chinese history justified by prophecies of the "turning of the *kalpa*." At the same time, I suspect that millions of Chinese over the centuries have reacted to such images in the same way that American Southern Baptists generally react to the singing of such hymns as "Jesus Is Coming Soon"—as an earnest but not always urgent expression of hope that a better world will make itself known at some distant—but not too distant—point in the future.

Li does not acknowledge his kinship with the White Lotus tradition. He mentions Maitreya in the context of his lectures on the history of Buddhism, but in response to a question from a practitioner as to whether Falun Dafa "surpasses" the "Maitreyan school," Li responds that Maitreya has no school and that the idea was "made up by devils to disrupt the Law."[56] And in response to a question about the Unborn Mother—the central deity in many White Lotus scriptures—Li responds angrily:

> WHAT unborn mother? There is no such god. These days ordinary people have come up with all sorts of names, which refer to things which do not exist at all. Let me tell you: there are some hetero-dox ways [*fa*]. . . . and because one level doesn't know what is going on at another level, the enlightened beings of the orthodox Law pay no attention to them.[57]

Li's particular rendering of this vision may well be his alone, as he argues that the very existence of humankind is a product of moral decline within a previous community of higher-level beings:

> There was no such human level [i.e., no humans, no human society] in the beginning. The lives created by the motion of this matter in the universe are . . . in fact created from Zhen-Shan-Ren. Then, when

the number of such lives created in high-level dimensions increases, their living environment becomes complicated, and they form their social survival framework, just like in our human society.... Then, when they have their social modes, these lives will gradually change and become complicated. Some will develop selfish thoughts and deviate from the requirements that the characteristics of the universe maintain for lives at that level. Then, they are no longer able to stay in that realm and, they can only fall to a lower level. Then, when they become even worse at the lower level, they have to drop further down again. In this way, such lives are continually becoming worse during the endless ages of history and will gradually drop downward, dimension by dimension, until they fall to this dimension of mankind. Consequently, they lead a low life, reproducing and raising their descendants by low means.[58]

In other words, humans were originally gods of some sort, who lost their status as life became "complicated" (a word with more negative connotations in Chinese than in English) and they engaged in immoral behavior. Presumably, humans can redeem themselves through cultivation and regain their divine status.

In the context of the moral dimensions of Li Hongzhi's message, his discussion of the immorality which precedes the turning of the *kalpa* is as important as the notion of the apocalypse, as it helps us to understand his ethical preoccupations and their cultural context. Some of Li's preoccupations are entirely traditional, echoing the concerns of similar religious figures throughout Chinese history, while others are more topical and contemporary. For the purposes of clarity, it may be helpful to group Li's concerns into two large categories: social manifestations of immorality and religious manifestations of immorality, even if there are passages in his writings which do not fall directly into either.

Li's discussion of the social manifestations of immorality reveals a deep sociocultural conservatism, which resonates with the fundamentalist rhetoric of many redemptive societies over the late imperial and modern periods (and with that of many Islamic fundamentalists and American evangelical Christians). Without always clearly identifying the "good" social practices that have been abandoned, Li condemns many surface manifestations of "modernity" in popular culture, music, and social mores, arguing that they represent a "reversal of values":

All human concepts are changing in the opposite direction. A pile of trash laid out there would become a master sculptor's work.... In the past, singers would have beautiful voices and were graduates

of music schools. The physique and bearing should be as elegant as
possible since music is supposed to give people a sense of beauty.
Nowadays, there are people, hard to tell whether they are men
or women, with long hair, who when screaming hysterically "Ah!"
would become singing stars with the help of TV promotion.[59]

Presumably influenced by MTV and *American Idol*, young people adopt the
values of mass popular culture, not realizing that they are under demonic
influence:

> I see the way today's high school students wear their pants, with belts
> tied on their buttocks . . . and with part of their belts hanging out.
> Their heads are shaved bald on both sides, leaving the top like the
> edge of a roof. Still others leave only one strip of hair in the middle
> like monsters, and they think it looks good. But does it really look
> good? If you evaluate it carefully, you'll find that they don't have any
> concept of what's aesthetic. Women dress in black, wear demon-like
> hairstyles, and are stone-faced just like ghosts in the underworld.
> This is because people's values have become inverted. With demons
> stirring up disorder, humankind has taken dark and gloomy things
> as beautiful.[60]

This dangerous influence extends to even younger children, once again
through the shameless practices of toy manufacturers:

> As for the toys in stores, even excrement has been made in the
> form of toys to be sold. In the past, a doll had to be made very pretty
> so that people would be willing to buy it. Now, skulls, evil-looking
> characters, goblins, devils, ghosts, and monsters have all been made
> into toys, and they are sold quite fast.[61]

Just as children are being corrupted (elsewhere in his writings, children do
not seem to be a particular concern of Li's—although he does accord them a
particular innocence which allows them to cultivate more quickly than most
adults), so are women. The problem, predictably, is women's liberation, which
has once again "reversed" healthy traditional practices. In response to a question from a practitioner who wondered whether she lost virtue when spending
her husband's money, Li responds:

> Nowadays some people advocate women's liberation, which is a
> sensitive issue. Some people say that "We women suffer too much;
> women should be liberated; men and women should be equal; we
> women should be stronger . . . " But . . . think about it, everyone: Once

women's liberation is advocated, women feel they're oppressed and that they should stand up. But then what happens? Divorce, fighting, abandoned children, and other social problems emerge. The fundamental cause isn't whether women are liberated, but the degeneration of human society's morality—isn't this the cause?[62]

In sum, "liberation" is a false issue, an "attachment" (see below) which misleads women and confuses men, blinding them to their proper, balanced relationship in which the man, although naturally stronger and more assertive than the woman, does not use this strength for improper purposes.

Many of these problems seem to exist in both China and the West, and Li is not overly concerned to identify the precise geographic context for his observations, even if some of his remarks seem to clearly target the forthright materialism of Chinese society in the post-Mao era and to criticize the grasping, competitive atmosphere which distracts the Chinese from more fundamental concerns. (This comes up even more often in discussion with Chinese Falun Gong practitioners in North America, who frequently mention the conflictual and corrupt nature of contemporary Chinese society, as do many nonpractitioners, of course.) All of these issues, moreover, are merely symptomatic of much deeper problems afflicting human society, problems which include "drug use, drug trafficking, drug making, sex changes, homosexuality, sexual freedom . . . the demon-nature that bursts forth on the soccer field. . . . Forcefully getting money, renown, and self-interest, advocating the philosophy of struggle [among people], glorifying leaders of organized crime "[63] Moreover, "many people treat dogs as their sons or their kids, feed them milk, dress them in brand name clothes, push them around in carts, and call them 'my boy.' Meanwhile many people beg for food on the streets."[64] In short, in the period leading up to the turning of the *kalpa*, there no longer exists "the restraint of the Law in people's hearts to sustain morality."[65] Li further notes that the ancient Greeks had known a similar decline (although he does not insist that society was destroyed in that instance), and he cites the homosexuality and promiscuity which characterized the decadent state of late Roman antiquity, thus reinforcing the notion of cyclic decay and renewal to which I have already referred.[66] Interestingly, Li notes on a number of occasions that governments are complicit in these examples of social decay—by which he appears to mean that laws protecting "freedom of speech" and "freedom of expression" protect the degenerate practices discussed above.[67] But Li was resolutely apolitical in his writings in the 1992–1999 period. He treated government policy as epiphenomenal and demanded a moral revival at the social and individual level to deal with the problem.

The manifestations of moral decay in the religious sphere clearly contribute to the overall decline of society, because religions no longer serve to comfort and direct humans. One important problem is that humankind, in this final era, has become disconnected from the gods:

> In the past, people worshipped Buddhas only out of respect. That is, instead of asking for something for themselves, they came to pay respect to Buddhas, to worship Buddhas, or to cultivate themselves into Buddhas. . . . But people are not like that nowadays. In the past people always had righteous thoughts when they thought of a Buddha or a Bodhisattva. . . . But today's people no longer have concepts like this. People casually open their mouths and talk about Buddhas . . . as if the words grew on their tongues. They even casually carve and draw a Buddha's image however they want, and place them anywhere they want.[68]

The gods, continues Li, have repaid the courtesy and are no longer willing to intervene to make their influence felt in human society: "People today have completely turned into degenerate people who manifest demonic furor, and this has made all Gods completely lose their confidence in man. This is one of the main reasons why Gods no longer take care of human beings."[69] As a corollary to this, religions which in the past offered genuine salvation are no longer capable of doing so. Sounding a very old theme in Chinese sectarian Buddhism, Li warns, "He [Sakyamuni, founder of Buddhism] talked about [the dharma-ending period]. Today is the *Dharma*-ending period. Modern people can't cultivate [according to] that Law anymore. In [the dharma-ending period] it's hard for monks in monasteries to save even themselves, let alone save others."[70]

This disconnect between humanity and the gods has created a pernicious vacuum into which all sorts of evil, demonic forces have entered. Such a situation is especially dangerous because, although from a higher-level perspective (like that of Li Hongzhi), it is obvious that conventional religions no longer offer salvation in this troubled age, such is not clear to those who are suffering on the eve of the turning of the *kalpa*. On the contrary, "false religions" of a bewildering variety have won many converts. "Evil religions are everywhere!" insists Li. "On the surface they also tell people to be good, but in their bones, they are not for this. They are either for fame or for money; otherwise, they are for a dark influence."[71] In the temples, instead of gods, one finds "foxes, weasels, ghosts, and snakes" (varieties of evil spirits) that "have been brought . . . by those who come to pray for wealth and profit."[72]

Many of master Li's fellow qigong masters are denounced by Li as being among the false prophets. In some instances, these sham qigong masters are driven simply by an urge for power and money, which they gain through pretending to heal others.[73] In other instances, the fake masters are themselves the victims of spirit possession, where animals hoping to gain some of the power of cultivation properly reserved for human beings occupy the masters' bodies.[74] Perhaps the worst sort of demons are those who, taking human form:

> come to learn Falun Dafa as others do, and they also say that Falun Dafa is good—they're even more excited than others in their speech, they have stronger feelings than others, or they even see some images. Then all of a sudden they die or . . . go down the opposite path, and damage Falun Dafa this way. These are the kinds of people that are most difficult to recognize. They're hard to recognize, and for this reason they can do the most damage.[75]

In sum, today's world, in Li Hongzhi's vision, is a degenerate place, dangerous because of the omnipresence of demons, many of whom pretend to be holy men. It is even a dangerous world in which to fall ill because, as Li points out, during the final days, people "inhale large amounts of karma, viruses, and poisonous gases"[76] while at the same time the effectiveness of medications has declined.[77] Li even repeats the striking image, found in medieval Buddhist apocalyptic texts, of the words fading from the pages of the scriptures in the final days, a graphic image of their lack of salvational power.[78]


Your Karma and How to Get Rid of It: Falun Gong
at the Level of the Individual


Lest one think that the end of the world is Li's major preoccupation, I should repeat that this is not my impression. At one point, in a speech to Falun Gong cadres in 1994, he tells them not to worry about the end of the world because they will be among the saved, no matter when it might occur. Alongside examples of collective moral decay, Li Hongzhi also discusses moral behavior at the individual level, although it is never entirely clear how large-scale processes such as the unfolding of the kalpas mesh with the consequences of individual moral or immoral behavior. As already noted, in my fieldwork, I found that this individual focus was much more important to practitioners than Li's apocalyptic reading of the collective history of humankind, which was acknowledged, but passed over lightly (as many Christian churches—or individual believers, to make the parallel more accurate—choose not to emphasize St. John's Revelation on a daily or weekly basis).

The cornerstone of Li Hongzhi's discussion of individual moral behavior is the thoroughly traditional Buddhist concept of karma. Karma originally meant "deed" in Sanskrit, and at one level the idea of the operation of karma is as simple as the Christian notion of "one reaps what one sows." Good deeds are repaid with good, bad deeds with evil. Unlike in Christianity, however, karma operates through a system of rebirth, or transmigration, in which each organism is the reincarnation of a previous life form, its current form having been determined by karmic calculation of the moral qualities of the previous lives lived. It requires little theological sophistication to see how karma can both explain the seeming unfairness of the manifest inequities separating rich from poor, human from beast, and at the same time encourage moral behavior despite such inequities.

Li Hongzhi's use of the term karma differs somewhat from the more classical definition I have just given. For Li, karma is not the process of reward and punishment, but rather the fruits of bad moral behavior; in other words, karma is an exclusively negative term in Falun Dafa doctrine. All beings inherit, at the moment of their birth (or creation—even the soil, for Li, contains karma, although it is not "born" in any meaningful sense),[79] a certain amount of karma, built up during previous existences. This karma is a source of suffering, such as disease. As Li says: "A person has done bad things over his many lifetimes, and for people this results in misfortune, or for cultivators it's karmic obstacles, so there's birth, aging, sickness, and death. This is ordinary karma."[80] This idea is the basis of Falun Gong's opposition to practitioners' taking medicine when ill; they are missing an opportunity to work off karma by allowing an illness to run its course (suffering depletes karma) or to fight the illness through cultivation.

Karma is, moreover, a physical material for Li Hongzhi, one which can be removed from bodies, or exchanged, or transformed. Consistent with his notion that matter and spirit are one, Li identifies karma as a black substance which must be purged in the process of cultivation. As Li says, "The human body is like the annual rings of a tree, whereby each ring contains sickness-karma. So your body must be cleaned up from the very center."[81] However, a whole variety of practices affect karma, not just cultivation. The black substance can leave one's body, for instance, in the process of daily interaction; if you mistreat someone else, you give that person virtue (de) a white substance and take on his black karmic matter. As another example, morally gifted individuals (those born with less karma) can take on some of the karmic debt of friends, relatives, or anyone they choose:

> Some people with good bases exchange their bases for other people's karma. People with health problems have lots of karma. If you

treat somebody with a serious health problem, when you go home
after treating him you'll feel awful! A lot of people who've treated
others have experienced this, where the sick person recovers, but you
go home and suffer with serious sickness. As time goes on, you'll
have a lot of karma that's exchanged and transferred over to you,
and you'll have given other people virtue for their karma. Well, no
loss, no gain.[82]

Li is in general opposed to this kind of "benevolence," as it allows "karmic
debtors" off the hook too easily. Li wants people to work for their own salvation; at this level, his "messianic" intervention is limited to starting the
process rolling and then protecting well-meaning practitioners from harm as
they cultivate. Moreover, the whole process of "faith healing" reminds Li of
the unsavory practices of many of his competing qigong masters, who perform temporary miracle cures for money.

Karma, as an evil substance, apparently possesses consciousness and is
capable of resisting its elimination by producing what Li calls "thought karma":

Eliminating karma means eradicating it and transforming it. Now
of course the karma won't go for it, so people have tribulations
and they have obstacles. But thought-karma can directly interfere
with a person's mind, and so he might silently swear at the teacher or
swear at Dafa, or maybe he'll have some evil thoughts and bad
words. When this happens, some cultivators get confused about
what's going on, and they think that those are their thoughts. And
then there are people who think it's possession, but it's not. It's
caused by the thought-karma reflecting into their brains.[83]

Nor is karma restricted to human beings:

There is karma everywhere. There is karma in matter, plants, animals and people.... Therefore, looking from a high-level dimension,
black waves are rolling in human society. Why are there epidemic
diseases? Very serious epidemic diseases are those black waves, which
are the mass of karma with very high density, rolling around. When
they roll over to this place, there will appear epidemic diseases.[84]

Karma even takes on national forms:

[T]he development of human society is driven by the evolution of the
cosmic climate. Are the wars of mankind accidental, then? A region
with a lot of karma or a region where human hearts have become
corrupt is bound to be unstable. If one nationality is truly virtuous, it

must have little karma; there absolutely will be no wars occurring against it.[85]

In sum, karma, in Li Hongzhi's writings, very nearly comes to be a material explanation for the existence of evil and suffering in the world, although for most practitioners (and in the most central parts of Li's writings), karma continues to refer to the personal debt, incurred through immoral behavior in previous (and current) lives, to be repaid in this life through moral behavior and cultivation.

In the context of individual moral practice, it is important to point out that karma is *not* limited to the debt incurred at birth. With the exception of a few unusually gifted individuals, most people add to their store of inherited karma through their own actions. In Li Hongzhi's works, the chief karma-producing mechanism in the lives of people is called "attachment" (*zhuzhuo*). Once again, this is a thoroughly Buddhist concept; Sakyamuni spoke often of the evil of *tanha* (Sanskrit), or "craving," which led people to "make the mistake of looking upon impure, impermanent, and unpleasant things as pure, permanent, and pleasant."[86] For Li Hongzhi, an attachment is literally any desire, emotion, habit, or orientation which stands between a practitioner (or any human being, for that matter) and the pursuit of truth and cultivation. As he says at the very beginning of *Zhuan falun*, "the whole process of cultivation is a process of constantly getting rid of human attachments. Out in the ordinary world, people fight each other, they deceive each other, and they harm other people just to benefit themselves a little. The thoughts behind that all have to go."[87]

Li is often much more specific in his identification of attachments, which helps us to understand the moral challenges before would-be practitioners, even if these challenges differ little from those faced by the rest of us. The most commonly mentioned attachments are those to wealth and fame. Over and over, Li Hongzhi returns to the emptiness of material pursuits (a theme which definitely strikes a chord with North American Chinese practitioners, many of whom have found their material success less rewarding than they had originally imagined it would be). Although many of his criticisms are of other qigong masters or of ambitious practitioners hoping to use cultivation to make money, the larger thrust of Li's antimaterialist message resonates with that of many other spiritual movements which condemn our modern obsession with bigger houses, shinier cars, more toys. On the other hand, wealth itself is not condemned—only attachment to wealth. Falun Dafa practitioners are not asked to give up their jobs, nor asked to make large donations to the organization (although if they *want* to make such donations, they are certainly not turned away).

Other attachments are more specific to Falun Dafa's Buddhist background. Alcohol, for instance, is roundly condemned: "[d]rinking is definitely addictive, it's a desire. Alcohol stimulates a person's addictive nerves, and the more a person drinks, the worse his addiction. You're a practitioner, so let's think about it, shouldn't you get rid of that attachment? That attachment has to go."[88] Meat eating receives a lesser condemnation:

> One morning, as I passed by the back entrance of Triumph Park in Changchun, three people came out of the entrance, talking loudly. One of them said, "What kind of qigong is that—it doesn't let you eat meat! I'd rather lose ten years off my life than give up meat!" What an intense desire. Now think about it, shouldn't that kind of desire be removed? It definitely should.[89]

Still, Li is not doctrinaire on this point, noting, "Giving up eating meat itself is not the purpose. The purpose is to not let you have this attachment. If you can give up the attachment during the time when you cannot eat meat, you might be able to eat it again later."[90] Lust receives a similar treatment. Practitioners are warned against the power of lust in no uncertain terms:

> When you're sleeping or meditating they [i.e., lustful demons] will suddenly appear. If you're a male, a beautiful woman will show up, and if you're a female, the man of your dreams will show up. But they're naked. As soon as you're excited you might . . . [ejaculate] and it'll become a reality. Now think about it, in our practice the qi of blood and essence is used to cultivate longevity   you can't just   [ejaculate] like that all the time.[91]

Li's condemnation of overt sexuality and pornography has already been mentioned. Yet Li waffles on the question of sexual desire within marriage. "In our discipline, or at least for this part that cultivates in the setting of ordinary people, you don't have to become a monk or nun," insists Li. "Young practitioners should still have families."[92] Thus, he finishes by saying that practitioners must maintain harmonious marriages even as they reduce their attachment to sexual desire: "you can't take it as seriously as an ordinary person would."[93]

Perhaps more difficult still is Li's call to reduce the attachment to "sentimentality." In Li's words:

> Why can human beings be human? It's exactly because humans have emotion. People just live for emotion. The affection among family members, the love between a man and woman, love for parents,

feelings, friendships, doing things for friendship's sake—no matter where you go you can't get out of emotion. You want to do something, you don't want to do something, you're happy, you're unhappy, you love something, you hate something—everything in society comes completely from emotion. If you don't sever emotion, you won't be able to cultivate.[94]

This is once again quite Buddhist, as it is a way out of the web of human relations which constitutes society and thus a step toward individual enlightenment. It is important to point out, nonetheless, that Li is not urging practitioners to abandon human attachments for selfishness. Quite the contrary. Practitioners are enjoined to treat others with compassion and benevolence in order to cultivate virtue and work off karma. But such compassion and benevolence should not be reserved to those with whom one had a prior attachment, nor should the goal of such behavior be to cultivate a sense of gratitude or love in the objects of a practitioner's compassion. Instead, one should be good because this conforms to the nature of the universe, not for any ulterior motive, be it as innocuous as "feeling good about oneself and others." Li insists that practitioners should not withdraw from the world, but should continue to interact with nonpractitioners and even those who are hostile to practice. His argument is that the stress practitioners will experience—before arriving at a level of cultivation which will allow them to be dispassionate in their compassion—constitutes a form of suffering which will enable them to reduce their karma.

Li's discussion of attachments extends even to the world of cultivation and to the relations between his followers and himself. He criticizes cadres in his organization who remain attached to their image of purity and power and lord it over new recruits.[95] He criticizes those who join Falun Dafa merely to save themselves as the "end" approaches without having set their moral minds on cultivation (in fact, he very nearly reproaches himself for making this possible by revealing the Way).[96] He even criticizes higher-level practitioners who abandon their earthly bodies before having completed their cultivation because their level allows them to taste the pleasures of higher states:

At present there is a very prominent problem: namely, when some practitioners' *yuanshen* [their "original selves" or souls] leave their bodies, they see or come into contact with certain dimensions at certain levels. Feeling it is so wonderful and that everything there is of genuine existence, they do not want to return. This has resulted in the death of their physical bodies. So they stayed in that realm and could not come back.... Do not get attached to any dimension in your cultivation. Only when you have completed the entire course of cultivation can you achieve completion. So when your *yuanshen* goes out, no matter how wonderful you find those places, you must return.[97]

Finally, Li criticizes practitioners who become overly attached to him, seeking his autograph or other signs of personal attention which they then use to suggest to others a close relationship to the master which might be viewed as prestigious: "Some people say, 'I heard Teacher Li say [such and such],' everyone gathers around to listen, and he's there in the middle passing on the . . . gossip, . . . [throwing] things in here and there that come from his own understanding. So what was the motive? It all comes down to showing off."[98] I might add that Li exhibits some of this same testiness in his meetings with practitioners, at least as I have been able to judge by viewing them on videotape. His demeanor on such occasions is a blend of paternal concern and otherworldly diffidence. While expressing great concern for the progress of the Way, he makes very clear that he is far above the petty preoccupations of most of his followers—and refuses to answer questions about such matters. He is not without charm, but his charisma is based as much on his distance from his followers as on his intimacy with them.

## The Pursuit of Supernormal Powers

"Cultivation is up to you, *gong* is up to the master"—if you just have that wish you're all set. When it comes to who's actually doing it, it's the master. There's no way you could do that. You've just got an ordinary human body, and you think you can evolve a higher being's body that's made of high-energy matter? Not a chance. It's a joke to even mention it.[99]

As Li Hongzhi's remark suggests, moral practice, however desirable it might be from any number of points of view, will not and cannot have the transformative effect desired by the practitioner and promised by the master in the absence of Li's intervention, which is one of the supernormal powers associated with Falun Gong. Even if Li Hongzhi repeatedly ridicules other qigong masters for their showy displays of healing abilities and for their "magic tricks," supernormal powers remain central to Li Hongzhi's teachings and to Falun Gong practice, both in the form of powers possessed by the master and powers acquired by practitioners. These are the payoff, the reward.

Moral practice is thus a *necessary* but not *sufficient* condition for cultivation, eventual enlightenment, and the attainment of special powers. Individual moral practice can burn away inherited karma and thereby reduce the suffering experienced by the moral person. This moral person, however, will forever remain at her humdrum, ordinary human level unless and until she commits herself to a regime of cultivation designed, as already mentioned, to lead her up through the various levels until she reaches enlightenment and transformation. What is required in this instance is a master, someone who has already been through the process and who has the understanding and the power to channel the moral behavior and intentions of the practitioner in the proper direction. This is the sense of the frequently repeated phrase: "Cultivation depends on one's own efforts, while the transformation of *gong* is done by one's master [*xiu zai ziji, gong zai shifu*]." This means that it is the responsibility of the practitioner to engage in moral practice and to cultivate according to the prescriptions of the school she has joined. It is the responsibility of the master to monitor these efforts and reward those who succeed.

As already noted in the previous chapter on qigong, supernormal powers were part and parcel of qigong and the surging enthusiasm for qigong in the late 1970s and 1980s. The career of virtually any qigong master illustrates that the power to heal was seen as the most basic, universal power attributed to qigong, but the range of powers and abilities linked to qigong goes well beyond the laying on of hands. To take the example of the most famous grandmaster, Yan Xin claimed to have caused rain to fall, thus stopping a major forest fire. Yan also claimed to have altered the molecular makeup of physical matter— even at a great distance.[100] Many qigong masters claimed to be able to emit rays from their bodies of a force capable of physically displacing human beings;[101] many if not all qigong masters claimed various powers of telepathy or clairvoyance. Those who practice "hard qigong"—a kind of martial arts—claimed to be able to perform a variety of physical feats reminiscent of what one might see in a Bruce Lee or Jackie Chan movie.

In Falun Dafa, intellectual and moral enlightenment occur simultaneously with a physical transformation manifested in numerous supernormal powers (return to health, the opening of the celestial eye, clairvoyance) and ultimately in the replacement of ordinary human cells by high-energy substances which reverse the aging process and convey a sort of immortality (although it is not clear that such immortality will be manifest in the physical dimension of ordinary humans). Understood in this sense, supernormal powers are thus the most important mark of successful cultivation and result, once again, *both* from the hard work of the practitioner *and* the preexisting supernormal powers of the master.

At the same time, such success is not to be lightly displayed. Pride in one's abilities, or the desire to show off, are marks of dangerous attachments, which constitute a threat to the very development of supernormal powers. Thus, the Falun Dafa practitioner, even as he cultivates and achieves a physiological transformation of his body tantamount to immortality, keeps his light very much underneath his bushel.

Li Hongzhi's Supernormal Powers

Li Hongzhi does not do parlor tricks and is often rather coy about his own powers. However, one does not have to look far in the written record of Falun Gong to find numerous examples of the master's powers in this sphere. In his official biography, for example, we find this passage:

> One day, when in the fourth grade . . . Li left school without taking along his school bag, and when he went back to get it the door of the classroom was locked and the windows had been shut. He thought that it would nice if he could get in. No sooner had the thought flashed through his mind than he found himself in the classroom. Another thought, and he was out again.

A similar passage, again from Li's biography, illustrates how Li continued to develop his natural gifts over the course of his life:

> One evening in July, 1990, [Li] and several apprentices were practicing gong in the courtyard of a government organization in Beijing. Soon, the sky became overcast. Lightning flashed and thunder rolled, seemingly just overhead, and the apprentices were becoming somewhat nervous. According to the rules of most types of fa, such weather was inappropriate for practicing gong. However, they saw their master sitting with his legs crossed on a large stone. . . . So they continued to practice gong. Strangely enough, although the clouds were very heavy and very low, and thunder shook the skies, no rain fell. When the practicing came to an end, the master calmly told his apprentices: "It will not start to rain before half an hour is up. You may leave now with your hearts at ease." One of the apprentices lived in the western part of the city, and it took him about half an hour to get home by bus. Just as he stepped through the door of his house, the rain came pouring down, as if a hole had been pierced in the sky.[102]

Li frequently claims, in addition, to exist "at a very high level" as a result of his extensive cultivation, which gives him powers approaching omniscience and omnipotence, although he is loath to provide details on this front, arguing yet again that "ordinary people" may not understand them or—worse—may attempt to pursue such powers for the wrong reasons.

Yet the most important of the many powers Li claims to possess is that of elevating the moral efforts of his practitioners into something truly transformative on both a biological and a cosmic level. Over and over again, Li insists that a practitioner's *gongzhu*, or *gong* pillar—a "feature" installed by the master which measures the success of a practitioner's cultivation—grows or diminishes in direct relation with his *xinxing*, or moral level:

> To tell how high a person's character [i.e., *xinxing*] is, there is a measuring stick you can look at. The measuring stick and the *gong* pillar don't exist in the same dimension, but they do co-exist. . . . When your character improves, your *gong* rises. However high your character is, that's how high your *gong* is. That's a Truth, and it's absolute. There used to be some people who put their heart into doing their exercises, and it didn't matter if they were at home or out in the park, they really believed in it, and they did them pretty well. But as soon as they were back out in the real world they'd be a different person, they'd go back to their old ways, and fight and compete with ordinary people for profit and to make a name for themselves. Do you think their *gong* could grow? Not even an inch. . . . Qigong is cultivation, and it's a higher thing, it's not like ordinary people's exercises. So you have to take character seriously if you're going to get well or increase your *gong*.[103]

As a practitioner cultivates, he brings his mind and body into conformity with the structure of the universe, with *zhen-shan-ren*, and as he does so, the limitations inherent in the human dimension disappear. One expression of this transformation occurs at the human molecular level: as the black matter of karma is replaced by the white matter of virtue, the body is transformed, illness is abolished, and a kind of immortality is achieved:

> In practices that cultivate both nature and longevity [or "mind and body"], a person's energy is stored in all the cells in his body. The energy that an ordinary qigong practitioner gives off, or that somebody who's just started to build up *gong* gives off, that *gong* has large particles with gaps between them and low density, and so it has little power. When a person's level rises, it's possible that the

density of his energy will be 100 times, 1,000 times, or 100 million times higher than ordinary water molecules. That's because the higher the level, the higher the density, the finer the grains, and the greater the power.... So over time the person's body is completely filled with that high-energy matter.

That high-energy matter is an intelligent entity, and it has power. When there's more of it, when its density gets high, and after it fills all the cells in a person's body, it's able to suppress his flesh cells, those least capable cells. And once they're restrained there isn't any metabolism, and at some point it will completely replace the human flesh cells....

So, what happens next? During your cultivation, although all of your molecular cells are replaced by high-energy matter, the atoms have to have a certain configuration, and the configuration of the molecules and nuclei doesn't change either. The configuration of the cells' molecules is one way, and so they're soft to the touch; the configuration of bones' molecules has a high density, and so they're hard to the touch; the density of blood's molecules is very low, and so it's liquid. Ordinary people can't tell from your surface that there were any changes. The molecular cells still keep their former structure and configuration. So their structure hasn't changed, but the energy inside has. And that's why you won't go through the natural aging process from that point on, and your cells won't die, so you'll be young forever. You will look young during your cultivation, and eventually you'll hit a point where you don't age any further.[104]

Another expression of this transformation is the accumulation of *gong* energy, the force which enables practitioners to perform supernormal acts:

When we talk about fundamental enlightenment, it's about how during his life a person, from the time he takes up cultivation, keeps rising to higher levels and keeps getting rid of his human attachments and all those desires, and his *gong* keeps growing, until at some point he reaches the last step of his cultivation. His virtue, that matter, will all have been evolved into *gong*, he'll arrive at the end of the cultivation path his master arranged, and at that split second, "Boom!" all the locks will be blasted open. His Third Eye will reach the highest point of the level he's at, and he'll see the reality of the various dimensions at his level, the forms of existence of the various beings in different space-times, the forms of existence of matter in each space-time, and he'll see the Truth of our universe.

His divine powers will be displayed in all their grandeur, and he'll be able to communicate with all kinds of beings.[105]

In other words, the culmination of the process of karma elimination through moral practice and the suppression of attachments is the restoration of practitioners to their original status as gods of a sort, who will no longer be confined to the human dimension and who will possess scores of superhuman powers. Practitioners expect this to take a very long time, and Li Hongzhi warns his followers not to be distracted by the pursuit of supernormal powers for supernormal powers' sake, but it is clear that supernormal powers are at the very core of Falun Dafa discourse, even if Li himself has no interest in bending spoons.

Although the details of Li's "supervision" are not revealed, he does claim a number of particular supernormal powers in this context. First, as already mentioned, he claims to "clear away" the diseases of those seriously desiring to cultivate Falun Dafa, so that they can move quickly to higher-level cultivation. Second, he claims to install rotating wheels in the stomachs of all practitioners, which, as they revolve, carry out much of the work of cultivation:

> It will turn forever at your lower abdomen, once it's placed in you it won't stop, and it'll turn like that year in and year out. When it's turning clockwise it automatically absorbs energy from the universe, and it can evolve energy by itself, and supply the energy that's needed to evolve every part of your body. In the same way, when it turns counterclockwise it sends out energy, and drives used material out of you, which then dissipates around your body. When it sends out energy, it shoots it out very far and brings in new energy again. And the energy it shoots out benefits everyone who's near your body.[106]

Third, Li Hongzhi promises that his "dharma bodies" (*fashen*) will follow all practitioners wherever they go throughout the universe and protect them from harm. In part, the dharma bodies are simply another manifestation of Li Hongzhi's powers, as many stories in *Zhuan falun* attest:

> Another case happened in Beijing. In winter it gets dark earlier and people go to bed a bit earlier. The streets were empty and all was quiet. One of our students was rushing home on a bike. Only a jeep was moving along ahead of him. It was moving along steadily when all of a sudden it braked. The student wasn't paying attention and kept on peddling ahead with his head down. But the jeep suddenly started to back up then, and it was backing up fast, mighty fast. Those

two forces worked together to take away his life. Right when they were about to collide, a force suddenly pulled his bike back more than half a yard, and the jeep instantly stopped against the wheel of his bike. Maybe the jeep's driver realized someone was behind him. The student wasn't scared when that happened. Nobody who runs into this type of thing gets scared, although they might get scared when they think back about it. The first thing he thought was, "Phew! Who pulled me back? I have to thank him." He turned around to say thank you, only to find the street quiet, without a person in sight. Then it hit him, "It was actually Teacher protecting me!"[107]

In part, the dharma bodies encourage practitioners to practice forbearance in the face of suffering, since Li urges all followers to remain within the world and to suffer so as to work off their karma. More generally, Li uses his powers to ensure that practitioners cultivate in the right way and channel their efforts in the direction which may eventually lead to enlightenment. He uses his supernormal powers to ensure that his followers develop their own. Supernormal powers are thus at the very core of Falun Dafa discourse, achieved when practitioners, through moral practice and with the constant magical guidance of the master, break through the limitations of science and the human dimension to become immortals and superhumans.

In addition to his own powers, Li also discusses lesser-order supernormal powers, which practitioners are likely to acquire fairly early in their cultivation and which are not, as far as I can tell, reserved necessarily for Falun Dafa followers. Examples of these, drawn from *Zhuan falun*, include the opening of the "third eye," the "ability of remote vision," and the "ability of knowing fate." As all three examples concern transcending the limited capacities of the human dimension, a discussion of all three would be rather repetitive, and I will limit myself to a brief exposition of the third eye.

The third eye refers to developing a capacity of vision beyond that with which we are familiar in the ordinary world. In Li's words:

Now that we're talking about the Third Eye, let's start with a few words about this pair of eyes that we human beings have. Nowadays some people think that this pair of eyes can see all matter, or all material things in our world. So some people have formed a rigid concept, and think that only the things they see through their eyes are tangible and real, and they don't believe in what they don't see. In the past people always took these people to have poor comprehension. Some people can't explain why that's poor comprehension. "He doesn't believe in what he doesn't see. That's perfectly reasonable."

But, when you look at it from a slightly higher level, it's not reasonable. Every space-time is made of matter, and of course, different space-times have different material structures, just as they have different beings that take on different forms.

I'll give you an example. In Buddhism they say that everything in the world is an illusion, that it's not real. But how's it an illusion? Who'd say those real, material things right there in front of you are fake, right? The form that material things exist in is one way, while the form they manifest in, it turns out, is different. And our eyes have an ability: they can fix the material things in our material dimension so that they appear to be in the state we now see. But actually, that's not their state. That's not even their state in our dimension. For example, what does a human being look like under a microscope? His whole body is loose and made up of little molecules, just like grains of sand, and they're granular and in motion, electrons are orbiting nuclei, the whole body is wriggling and in motion, and the surface of the body isn't smooth, it's irregular. The same goes for every material thing in the universe, be it steel, iron, stone, or whatever, all the molecular elements inside them are in motion. You really can't see the overall form of it, and the truth is, none of those things are static. This table is wriggling too, but your eyes can't see the reality of it. So this pair of eyes can give you a false image.[108]

The opening of the third eye thus allows people to transcend this ordinary level and begin to perceive reality at other levels. For those who cultivate on their own, without the guidance of a master, this process can be rather long and inconclusive. Under the guidance of a master, however, practitioners can arrive at truly remarkable visionary powers, at which point "a large eye develops over the whole top half of [the practitioner's] face, and there are countless small eyes in it. Some Great Enlightened Beings at really high levels have cultivated an incredible number of eyes.... They can see whatever they want to, and when they look they see all levels at once."[109]

Li's discussion of the third eye occupies a prominent place in *Zhuan falun*; it is the subject of a lengthy exposition at the beginning of the second chapter of the book. It is clear that one of the messages Li wants to send is that he understands such phenomena thoroughly—indeed, that he can explain such powers more clearly than other qigong masters. His "revelation" includes his familiar discourse on levels, or "dimensions," as we have already seen, as well as an equally familiar recourse to science. He also discusses a variety of traditional Daoist and Buddhist approaches to the opening of the third eye, once again illustrating his mastery of cultivation techniques. Still, the overall tone of Li's discussion of the third eye or of similar powers is rather matter-of-fact, cursory, almost dismissive. Above all, Li exhibits little or no enthusiasm for these powers. He does not encourage his followers to seek to develop such powers, but suggests rather that they will emerge inevitably as a part of normal cultivation practice. And he gives several examples of cases where people who single-mindedly sought to develop such powers in order to display them to others or to otherwise profit from them inevitably lost the powers for want of a solid moral basis.

## Conclusion

This chapter has examined Li Hongzhi and his teachings in the context of the qigong boom—and, more broadly, within the longer history of Chinese redemptive societies—rather than the better-known campaign of suppression, exploring his message less for the seeds of an eventual conflict with Chinese authorities and more as a set of teachings which struck a chord with a very large number of Chinese, who became Li's followers. Although no one has as yet carried out a careful textual study of the writings and teachings of other qigong masters, my impression is that Li's teachings and his persona are largely consistent with those of his predecessors in the qigong movement and with those of certain masters of redemptive societies over the course of late imperial and modern Chinese history. Li Hongzhi clearly has modeled his career on that of predecessors such as Yan Xin and Zhang Hongbao, discussed at some length in chapter 3. The earlier careers of Yang Zai, Dong Sihai, and Wang Fengyi, in which we note suggestive parallels with the life and teachings of Li Hongzhi, were briefly discussed in chapter 2. The basic message, once again, is that healing and perhaps salvation can be obtained by the individual who practices morality and corporal techniques under the guidance of an enlightened master.

In Li Hongzhi's particular rendering of this message, the practitioner who reads and rereads *Zhuan falun* and, under the master's guidance and protection, puts the principles of this work into practice in his daily life will be healed and made whole as he comes into harmony with truth, goodness, and forbearance, the constituent forces of the universe. The results of this harmonious alignment are improved health, supernormal powers, and eventually, perhaps, some form of immortality. Li's message is cast in the language of modern science both because "science" in modern China has been understood as an iconic source of power and transformation and because Li seems to truly believe that the modern scientific world view, as purveyed by unenlightened scientists, is at best partial and at worst seriously misleading. Li's message is presented in a way that looks unsophisticated—even crude, on occasion—to the scholarly eye, but it is not difficult to find an underlying logic, with its base in the idea of rewards for moral practice, which could readily appeal to anyone searching for such confirmation.

Neither Li nor other qigong masters of the late twentieth century conceived their basic message as being at odds with Chinese socialism or even with the authoritarianism of the reform era state, which continues to make occasional appeals to socialism. But there is a fundamental difference between socialist discourse and that of qigong, which to me suggests that the qigong of the qigong boom, however influenced it may have been by the particular context of late twentieth-century China, was not ultimately a product of the Communist revolution. Socialism demands individual sacrifice for the well-being of the collectivity, and no individual can be liberated until the masses have achieved liberation. By contrast, the logic of cultivation, and of qigong, is an individualistic logic. The goal is individual healing, individual redemption, individual salvation—even if the achievement of salvation requires the suppression of individual desires and ultimately individual consciousness, a paradox found in Buddhism and in many meditative traditions. This may be pursued under the guidance of a master, in a public place, surrounded by hundreds or thousands of like-minded practitioners, and the practice may even provide the basis for collective action. Nonetheless, for the qigong or Falun Gong practitioners, the test of a master's promise lies in the individual's suffering body and not in the larger collectivity; qigong and Falun Gong promise a better world, but a world remade one practitioner at a time. The fact that this fundamental divergence passed unnoticed during the qigong boom surely has to do with the crisis of legitimacy of the post-Mao Chinese state, as discussed in the introduction to this volume, and with the validating power of science. But it directs us once again to the longer history of which qigong and Falun Gong are but the most recent chapters.

# 5

# Falun Gong Outside of China

*Fieldwork among Diaspora Practitioners*

In early 1995, having announced that his mission in China had largely come to an end, Li Hongzhi packed his bags, left China, and began to spread his message throughout the world, targeting especially the diaspora of Chinese émigrés from the People's Republic of China. There are clues which suggest that Li's abrupt departure from China was the result of increasing opposition to Falun Gong from within the Chinese government, but such opposition could not have been unanimous: Li's first stop on his world tour was Paris, where he was invited by the Chinese ambassador to France to present his teachings to embassy staff.[1]

While the qigong boom was the fundamental condition that made possible the emergence of Li Hongzhi and Falun Gong, China's openness to and involvement in the international world have been equally crucial to Falun Gong's development. Between 1995 and 1999, Li cultivated an important secondary following among Chinese living in Taiwan, Southeast Asia, Australia, Europe, and—most vitally for the post-April 1999 period—North America. The majority of these new followers (with the exception of those in Taiwan and Southeast Asia) had left China in the 1980s and 1990s and had learned of Falun Gong *after* having emigrated to the West. These followers, having passed through the numerous and difficult hoops necessary to emigrate to the West, were in general well-educated, highly competent, and often reasonably well-off. To this core of expatriate Chinese practitioners came to be added a smaller number of

Western believers (proportionally more in Europe than elsewhere), as Li's multilingual Chinese followers worked hard to make Li and his message accessible to non-Chinese speakers, but outside of China as well as inside the thrust of Li's movement remained decidedly Chinese.

The importance of this secondary community of followers outside of China can hardly be overstated. First, the existence of an important following in North America played a role in helping Li to settle in the United States in 1996,[2] although the details of this episode of his life are far from clear. In any event, there is no doubt that the existence of Falun Gong practitioners among the worldwide Chinese diaspora, probably numbering in the hundreds of thousands, gave Li Hongzhi an offshore base of operations from which to continue his ministry even as the Chinese state came to have increasing doubts about Falun Gong within China. Had Falun Gong arisen at an earlier point in China's Communist history, or when China was more closed to the world, the movement would have been crushed, the leaders imprisoned, and the followers dispersed without such events making more than a temporary splash in foreign news media. By contrast, the decision by Falun Gong practitioners outside of China to fight back against the Chinese state's campaign of suppression against Falun Gong from the summer of 1999 onward caught the attention of the world's media for months on end: this drama is the subject of chapter 6. At a deeper level, it is important to note that, as the politics of these events unfolded, practitioners' pleas for relief from suppression and torture in China came to be grafted onto a Western, Enlightenment-based human rights discourse (freedom of speech, freedom of conscience, and religion) which has little or nothing to do with Li Hongzhi's original spiritual concerns. Although activists for Tibetan independence have often struck such chords, to my knowledge no Chinese popular religion had ever attempted to defend itself on such grounds.[3]

Finally—and most important for the purposes of this chapter—the existence of Falun Gong followers outside of China made fieldwork among practitioners possible, and most of this chapter will be devoted to relating the results of such fieldwork. Fieldwork allows us to go beyond Li Hongzhi's written message, beyond the representations of Falun Gong by the Chinese state, to understand how Falun Gong, as a redemptive society, is understood and lived by practitioners. No claim is made that Chinese practitioners in Canada and the United States are *identical* to Li Hongzhi's followers in China.[4] As already noted, many if not most of Li's Chinese followers in North America have responded to the exacting criteria of Canadian and American immigration authorities, which is obviously not the case for the mass of Li's following in China. On the other hand, we should not overemphasize the differences between Chinese practitioners of Falun Gong in the West and in China. As is the case with the qigong movement as a whole, the limited evidence available suggests that Falun Gong within China appealed to a broad spectrum of social groups, including university professors and students, high party and government officials, well-educated cadres and members of the comfortable middle class, and, of course, the old, the infirm, the unemployed, and the desperate. From another perspective, successful, well-educated Chinese immigrants to Canada and the United States often bring family members with them, not all of whom are always so successful and well-educated. In any event, the existence of a well-educated, materially well-off following in North America would seem to undercut claims by Chinese authorities in the period after April 1999 that most Falun Gong practitioners were ignorant old women with nothing better to do than let themselves be hoodwinked by a smooth-talking charlatan. In fact, fieldwork among practitioners provides more convincing proof than does analysis of Li Hongzhi's writings that Falun Gong is not a strange aberration, a "heterodox cult" to which lost souls unwittingly fall victim. Seen from the proper perspective, that of the history of cultivation and redemptive societies, the practice of Falun Gong is completely comprehensible.

## Li Hongzhi Leaves China

After leaving China in early 1995, Li Hongzhi embarked on a hectic schedule of international travel as he sought to extend his network of followers throughout the world. Following his talks in Paris in March 1995, organized, as already mentioned, by the Chinese embassy in France, Li gave a number of talks in Sweden (at Gothenburg, Stockholm, and Uddevalla) in April and a series of lectures in Hong Kong in May. For reasons perhaps related to his emigration to the United States, Li gave no public lectures between May 1995 and July 1996—although he published several of his writings during this period. In the summer of 1996, Li launched another lecture tour, speaking in Hong Kong in July; Sydney, Australia, in early August; and Bangkok, Thailand, in late August. Houston, Texas, was the site of Li's first American lecture in mid-October (because he had followers there), closely followed by a lecture in New York a week later. Li returned to China to speak in Beijing in late October and early November and traveled once again to Sydney, Australia, in late November 1996. Li spoke in New York in late March 1997 and in San Francisco in April. He lectured in Hong Kong in July and in Taiwan in November. His six lectures during 1998 were in New York (late March), Toronto (May), Frankfurt (late May), Changchun (late July), Singapore (late August), and Geneva (early September). He lectured in Los Angeles in late February 1999, in New York in late

March, and yet again in Sydney, Australia, in early May, having left Beijing on the eve of the 25 April Falun Gong demonstration which rocked the Chinese government and the Chinese Communist Party and marked a crucial turning point in the history of Falun Gong.[5]

When Li began his ministry in China, he rode the coattails of previous qigong masters and capitalized on the enthusiasm they had created. The specific itineraries for his lecture tours in China were determined largely by invitations he received from various qigong associations throughout the country.[6] In Hong Kong and Taiwan, and to some degree in other countries of East and Southeast Asia, Li could count on knowledge of and enthusiasm for qigong, as other qigong masters had also made region-wide tours. Outside of Asia, however, no qigong boom had occurred, and few people had heard of qigong or Falun Gong; the closest thing of which a Western sinophile might have heard would have been taijiquan, which is perhaps related to qigong but which had not been part of the movement. Under such circumstances, Li understandably "followed his followers" in planning the itineraries of his lecture tours outside of Asia, visiting countries and cities where he knew that his followers would be able to sponsor him, rent lecture halls, publicize his arrival, and take care of the many details involved in such an undertaking. Unsurprisingly, as Li speaks no language other than Chinese and was at the time a virtual unknown outside the Chinese-speaking world, Li's followers in the West were virtually all Chinese qigong enthusiasts who had emigrated to the West sometime in the 1980s or 1990s, in other words, *after* the beginning of the mass qigong activities in China. It was Li Hongzhi's great good fortune that the internationalization of his mission coincided with a major change in the quantity and quality of Chinese emigration, for without such émigrés, he would have been hard put to find an international audience.

The New Chinese Diaspora

Chinese have left the People's Republic of China in increasing numbers since Deng Xiaoping decreed in the early 1980s that "reform and opening up" were to be central to China's salvation. Deng's first priority in opening China to the world was to bring foreign capital and expertise to the Middle Kingdom, but allowing Chinese students to study abroad was another aspect of the same initiative. Over time, many of the controls which had slowed Chinese emigration to a mere trickle since the founding of the People's Republic in 1949 were relaxed; a new law, enacted in 1985, liberalized travel abroad and thus marked a definitive rupture with the Maoist period. It is hardly an exaggeration to state that, for many Chinese, it now is easier to obtain a passport than to find a country which will accept them as legal immigrants (or even as independent tourists).[7]

Accurate statistics on the number of Chinese who have left China since the end of the Maoist era are difficult to find, particularly since this is a complex phenomenon, including legal and illegal migrants, large numbers of students (many of whom have managed, in large measure because of the events of the summer of 1989, to remain in the foreign countries where they studied), as well as Chinese who return to China, often for business reasons, after having obtained a foreign passport.[8] Still, as appendix 1 illustrates, we can readily establish from American and Canadian figures that Chinese immigration in the 1980s and 1990s increased mightily in comparison to data from previous decades, or in other words, the Chinese diaspora now includes large and increasing numbers who left China in the post-Mao era. In Canada, this immigration may be of historic significance, given its weight in Canada's relatively small population and given that emigration from China was accompanied by important peaks of emigration from Hong Kong and Taiwan, occasioned by the fears associated with Hong Kong's return to Chinese sovereignty in 1997.

In the case of the United States and Canada, the hundreds of thousands of Chinese immigrants seriously altered the nature of the Chinese diaspora in the two countries. As compared to previous waves of immigrants, the post-Mao arrivals generally spoke Mandarin (instead of Cantonese or another local dialect) and were often very well educated. Among the census data which illustrate this latter point are the following: China was the number one source of business-class immigrants (admittedly a small category) to Canada in 2000–2002, number three in 1999, and number four in 1996 and 1998. China was likewise the number one source of skilled workers immigrating to Canada between 1998 and 2002. In 1999 and 2000, nearly a quarter of all skilled immigrants to Canada were Chinese.[9] Finally, as the succeeding sections will illustrate, it was precisely this body of newly arrived Chinese immigrants who make up the bulk of Li Hongzhi's followers in the United States and Canada.

## Fieldwork among Diaspora Practitioners

I can verify that last statement because, between the fall of 1999 and the time of writing of this volume (roughly 2005, although I stopped doing regular fieldwork in late 2002), I carried out fieldwork among Falun Gong practitioners in North America. I was in Paris in late April 1999, researching the history of French sinology, when Falun Gong practitioners staged their demonstration outside Communist Party headquarters in Beijing. The first time I learned of Falun Gong's existence was by reading *Le Monde* that afternoon. My first thought was: "now *there's* a great research topic for someone," and it took me roughly a half-hour to realize that it was a topic tailor-made for me, as I had already done considerable research into the history of secret societies and popular religions, the antecedents of Falun Gong, in Qing and Republican period history. I began my fieldwork in the fall of 1999 with a trip to Toronto, an important North American center of Falun Gong activities, with researcher Susan Palmer (a specialist in new religious movements at Dawson College in Montreal). Subsequently, we attended a Falun Gong experience-sharing conference in Montreal in February 2000 and a second, much larger, experience-sharing conference in Toronto in May of that same year. We circulated questionnaires at both of these conferences.[10]

These initial activities allowed me to form relationships with a number of Falun Gong practitioners in Toronto and Montreal with whom I maintained contact on a fairly regular basis. I visited practice sites in Montreal and talked with veteran and novice practitioners. I marched together with practitioners in Toronto. I exchanged frequent phone calls and e-mails with practitioners. In October 2000, I gave two lectures on Falun Gong in Houston, Texas, one at Rice University and the other at the annual meeting of the American Society of Religion, and met with Falun Gong practitioners on the same occasions. Several of these practitioners attended my talk at Rice, which was generally favorable (or at least not hostile) to Falun Gong, and they publicized my remarks on Falun Gong Web sites; the Transnational China Project of Rice University also put the transcript of my talk on its Web site,[11] and my unlikely career as a Falun Gong expert was launched. In February 2001, I published an op-ed piece on Falun Gong in the *New York Times*, which earned me large numbers of e-mail messages from around the world.[12] Subsequently, I appeared on Australian television, was interviewed on National Public Radio and on Radio Canada, and answered countless calls from journalists.

My fieldwork continued at the same time. In November 2000, I attended an international anti–Falun Gong conference in Beijing—fieldwork of a rather different sort, to which I will return in chapter 6. In May 2001, I attended a large experience-sharing conference in Ottawa—the first time I saw Li Hongzhi and heard him speak. In June, I met with Falun Gong practitioners—including well-known spokesperson Zhang Erping—in Amsterdam, where I gave a talk on Falun Gong. I continued to interview Falun Gong practitioners over the course of the summer and fall of 2001, and I attended a Falun Gong conference in New York in January 2002 (although much of the event was given over to peaceful protests, and police barriers kept me from doing much work) and another in Boston in April 2002, where I heard Li Hongzhi speak for a second time. I circulated my questionnaire yet again at the Boston conference. I met with practitioners in Washington, DC, later that month.

I slowed my fieldwork beginning in the summer of 2002, as there was simply too much for one person to handle, I needed time to digest the data I had gathered, and I had grown wary (and weary) of becoming myself a factor in the struggle between Falun Gong and the Chinese state. As one of the few credible academic authorities on Falun Gong, my writings and talks were regularly referred to on Falun Gong Web sites, and although these sites distorted my views less than did the Western journalists who sought me out (and often misquoted me), I was still somewhat displeased that the Falun Gong organization did not ask my permission before launching me into cyberspace. I turned down an invitation to host a Chinese-language talk show on the New York–based Falun Gong television network Xintangren (New Tang Dynasty), presented to me, by the practitioner who extended the invitation, as a forum for an "objective discussion of concerns related to human rights and religious freedom" whose goal was to be "the education of the Chinese community in North America." I rebuffed repeated invitations to speak at Falun Gong–organized events. I explained patiently on each occasion to my Falun Gong friends that, although I shared their point of view that the Chinese government's campaign against them was immoral and unjust, repeated public statements to that effect on my part would reduce rather than enhance the value of my work, permitting the Chinese state to paint me as a stooge of Falun Gong. Most practitioners understood this, but as media fatigue set in and it became harder for Falun Gong to get its message into print or onto the airwaves, practitioners became understandably increasingly desperate, and the invitations continued. The only solution seemed to be to distance myself from practitioners and their activities. My final episode of "fieldwork" came in February 2004, when I appeared as an expert witness in a court case in Montreal, where Falun Gong practitioners had sued a local Chinese newspaper for slander. I was happy to put my research to the service of the pursuit of justice (the Falun Gong has appealed an unfavorable judgement)[13] but was reminded nonetheless of the reasons for establishing a certain distance between myself and practitioners: at every pause in the proceedings, practitioners in the courtroom rushed forward to politely "correct" my interpretation of Li Hongzhi and his teachings ("What master Li *really* meant when he said homosexuals were bad was . . ."), and Falun Gong "journalists" took pictures of me and badgered me for interviews even as I repeatedly demurred.

Let me be clear here. I understand practitioners' conviction that their cause is more important than a single individual. One does not have to accept Falun

Gong beliefs to roundly condemn the Chinese state's campaign against Falun Gong. I would say that even if Falun Gong were guilty of all of the heinous crimes of which the Chinese state has accused it—and I do not think it is—this would in no way justify the imprisonments, torture, and deaths inflicted on Falun Gong members in China. I admire the persistence and intelligence of Falun Gong practitioners in North America who have worked tirelessly to keep the cause of their suffering brethren in China in the public eye.

At the same time, I feel that the Chinese practitioners who solicited me overestimated the impact that the words of a university professor might have. They were too new to North America to understand that my "prestige" as an academic was not the equivalent of that of Confucian literati in China. (I should have introduced them to my relatives, who never tire of congratulating me on my savvy career choice: "Boy, I'd like to be a professor, too—you get the *whole summer off!*") I can't get my dean to return my phone calls, I reasoned—how likely was it that I could convince the Chinese state to cease and desist? My conviction was and is that, while I have something to say about Falun Gong as a scholar of Chinese popular religion, I have little to say about China's human rights violations that has not been said many, many times by scholars and institutions who have devoted their lives to precisely this cause.

To those who might view this stance as cowardly, I readily admit that the thought of not being able to return to China worried me.[14] After two rather high-profile talks (one in Amsterdam in June 2001, the other at Princeton in February 2003), I received a series of what appeared to be virus-laden e-mail messages (messages from people I did not know, with strange subject headings and attachments), all of which had been routed through the Chinese embassy in Ottawa (after the Amsterdam conference) and the Chinese embassy in Paris (after the Princeton talk). This was a relatively minor skirmish in the cyberwars which have been part of the conflict between Falun Gong and the Chinese state (of which more in chapter 6), but I was incensed (crashing an academic's computer is *nasty*) and contacted colleagues at the China desk of the Ministry of Foreign Affairs in Ottawa, who subsequently referred me to the Canadian Security Intelligence Service (CSIS)—Canada's equivalent of the Federal Bureau of Investigation. When the agent visited me, I was surprised to learn that, although CSIS could do nothing for me, it was glad to take my story because it had rapped the Chinese embassy's knuckles repeatedly on Falun Gong–related matters, reminding the Chinese that they were, after all, in Canada and subject to Canadian law.[15]

I would like to have done more fieldwork. I desperately needed a research team, but none of my Canadian students spoke Chinese well enough to be of use to me, and my few Chinese-speaking graduate students were often so hostile to Falun Gong that I could not trust them to do objective research. Trying to find Chinese, even Chinese outside of China, who are "neutral" on Falun Gong is a bit like trying to find churchgoing Texans who are "neutral" about David Koresh and the Branch Davidians. I had to fire one Chinese postdoctoral student after he began his "interview" with practitioners by asking them to levitate for him. I would have loved to have attended more experience-sharing conferences, more Falun Gong events, in other parts of North America, Europe, or even Asia (there is a thriving Falun Gong movement in Taiwan, for example), but even when I was "in the loop," I rarely managed to receive information about future events with enough advance warning to be able to plan sensibly for them. Practitioners seemed to be ready to leave for Geneva, say, at the drop of a hat, but then many practitioners seemed to have considerable extra income, a product of the happy combination of a well-paying job and a religious faith which enjoins followers to shun material attachments. Practitioners were also willing to sleep on the floor of fellow practitioners' homes in the cities they were visiting. And ultimately, if the trip cost more than they wanted to spend, practitioners could tell themselves that they were making sacrifices for the cause. A professor at a Canadian university, with three children and a mortgage, makes his calculations rather differently.

Then again, how big a team would I have needed? Falun Gong in North America is extremely decentralized, with relatively large groups in some major cities and smaller groups in others. My fieldwork was largely directed at local Falun Gong practitioners in eastern Canada (Ontario and Quebec) and the northeastern United States. If I had been able to spend a year in New York or Toronto, major centers of Falun Gong activities, and had been able to carry out systematic ethnographic fieldwork on a daily or weekly basis, I would certainly have had different insights, but would this have been representative?[16]

## Falun Gong Practitioners in North America: A Profile

Ideally, a profile of Falun Gong practitioners in North America would begin with the big picture and work down to the micro level. One thing my fieldwork did *not* allow me to do, unfortunately, was to get a handle on this big picture. Falun Gong Web sites, particularly www.falundafa.org, give an idea of the geographic breadth of the movement (follow the link "Falun Dafa Web Sites throughout the World") and allow one to contact Falun Dafa practitioners in most major and many minor cities throughout the United States and Canada. Local groups do not, however, attempt to keep up with how many practitioners there are in their areas, and there are no mid- or upper-level tiers of the organization where one might go for such information. Practitioners are not "members" of an "organization" and do not fill out a form at any point in their cultivation process; no central "church registry" asks for local statistics. The only organizational expressions of Falun Gong above the local level are the movement's Web sites, which provide general direction to local branches by making available transcripts of Li Hongzhi's speeches, by making available information which helps local branches (or even individual practitioners) to participate in achieving the movement's goals (such as bringing pressure on Western political figures in the hope of easing the Chinese government's campaign against Falun Gong in China), and by creating a "virtual" Falun Gong experience (see particularly the Clear Wisdom Web site, www.clearwisdom.net, discussed in detail in chapter 6) that is available to all and sundry. But the Web sites make no attempt to provide a summary of the activities of the many local branches, and it is thus very difficult to estimate, for example, how many practitioners there might be continent-wide. My impression is that the number of committed practitioners might be less than what one would tend instinctively to believe after consulting Falun Gong literature and Web sites—probably no more than a few tens of thousands continent-wide—though considerably more have had casual contact with Falun Gong. Li Hongzhi often claims 100 million followers, but the millions are (or, rather, were) in China, and Falun Gong, like other most new religious movements in North America, seems to have made few inroads as an international mass movement.

## Falun Gong Practitioners in North America

As already mentioned, Falun Gong in North America is a product of recent Chinese immigration. Falun Gong Web sites and publications feature Western practitioners, and there are prominent non-Chinese spokespeople, such as Gail Rachlin—and others—in New York. In addition, many of the lawyers, such as Terry Marsh, who have been at the forefront of Falun Gong's effort to indict Chinese leaders on a variety of charges in American and Canadian courts are non-Chinese practitioners. There has even been a wave of demonstrations at Tian'anmen Square in Beijing by Western Falun Gong practitioners, an effort to recapture media attention by getting themselves arrested and expelled from the People's Republic. Nonetheless, the Chinese presence has dominated at all Falun Gong events in North America which I have attended. The primary language spoken is Mandarin, and there appear to be roughly 9 Chinese for every Westerner, a ratio confirmed by my survey research: only 8 of the 80 who filled out questionnaires in Montreal in January 2000 were Western (we had prepared both Chinese- and English-language versions of the survey form); 21 of the 232 who completed questionnaires at the Toronto survey in May 2000 were Western; and none of the 116 practitioners who completed the surveys in Boston in the spring of 2002 were Western. I have met no Western practitioners who speak more than a few words of Chinese, which means that while Western and Chinese practitioners march together during parades and demonstrations, they divide up by language when it is time to read Li Hongzhi's works or to plan Falun Gong activities. At experience-sharing conferences, headsets are distributed to the audience, and translations of witness statements are provided (generally from Chinese to English and English to Chinese, but in Montreal, translations to and from French are generally available as well); testimonials are prepared ahead of time so that simultaneous translation is not necessary for most proceedings.

The Western practitioners are worthy of study in their own right, but they have not been a major focus of my work. Many of them appear to be "spiritual seekers," veterans of a variety of new religious movements, often closer to a "hippie" or "nonconformist" profile than most of the Chinese, who in general seem to be the straightest of straight arrows. Some Asian new religious movements, such as the Japanese Soka Gakkai, have managed to recruit significant numbers of non-Asians in North America and Europe; in many countries, the Japanese presence in Soka Gakkai has come to be secondary to that of native-born followers.[17] Falun Gong might possibly develop in such a direction, but given that emigration from China to North America continues at a rapid pace, it seems more likely that such migrants may serve as the major source of new recruits for the foreseeable future.

To return to my major focus, most of the Chinese practitioners with whom I came into contact or who responded to my surveys were fairly recent immigrants from the People's Republic. More than three out of four of the Chinese responding to my survey in Montreal reported having come to North America since 1989, as did more than four out of five of those responding to the Toronto survey, and nine out of ten of those responding to the Boston survey.[18] The surveys did not address the question of the reasons for wanting to leave China; in interviews, individual practitioners mentioned a variety of factors, all of which are fairly predictable and common to many if not most Chinese migrants: frustration with the slow pace of political change; anger with ongoing corruption; frustration with the lack of opportunity coupled with a desire to get ahead; frustration with the lack of idealism in contemporary

Chinese society; and/or a desire to live in a less "complicated" society. Although practitioners have developed sympathy for the student movement of 1989 over the course of their battle with the Chinese state since 1999, no one I interviewed between 1999 and 2002 emphasized such concerns.

More than 90% of the Chinese practitioners surveyed began cultivation between the years 1995 and 1999, and most practitioners—slightly more than three out of five, taking the results of the three surveys together—began practicing Falun Gong in North America. Surveys also revealed that Chinese practitioners come from all regions of China, which is not surprising, given that most of these Chinese practitioners discovered Falun Gong after emigrating to North America.

Most practitioners were relatively young: the average age was around 40 (41.88 for the Montreal survey, 40.75 for the Toronto survey, 39.47 for the Boston survey), and my impression is that the median age would be even lower, as younger practitioners quite clearly outnumber older ones (at least at events such as experience-sharing conferences).[19]

Chinese practitioners are in general well-educated and reasonably materially well-off. Of Chinese practitioners responding to the survey in Montreal, 23.8% had finished their undergraduate degrees, 33.8% had master's degrees, and 8.8% had Ph.D.'s. At the Toronto conference, 41.7% had bachelor's degrees, 18.2% had M.A.'s, 7.3% had Ph.D.'s, and 9.4% had medical degrees. Among Chinese respondents at the Boston conference, 26.5% had completed bachelor's degrees, 29.9% had M.A.'s, 22.2% had Ph.D.'s, and 4.3% had degrees in medicine.[20] Taking the three surveys together, roughly 77% of those responding had completed at least a university-level degree. By way of comparison, only 25.9% of Americans had a similar level of education (in 2002)[21] and only 15.43% of Canadians (in 2001).[22] Of course, if we had such figures for China as a whole, the numbers would be well below the 15.43% of Canadians with a university diploma, but the point once again is, first, that those Chinese who came to North America met the very tough demands of immigration authorities and, second, that Chinese Falun Gong practitioners in North America are *not* exceptions to this general rule.

The survey data reveal as well that many Chinese Falun Gong practitioners in North America have already succeeded quite well financially, despite their status as new immigrants. Chinese practitioners include many engineers, scientists, computer programmers, accountants, and professors. Of Chinese practitioners responding to the Montreal survey, 14.9% reported household incomes higher than $60,000 (Canadian dollars), and another 13.5% reported household incomes between $40,000 and $60,000. The data from the Toronto and Boston surveys are more precise. According to the Toronto survey, 18.7% of Chinese respondents had a household income between $40,000 and $60,000 (Canadian dollars), 12.7% between $60,000 and $80,000, 3.6% between $80,000 and $100,000, and 9.6% exceeding $100,000. Boston respondents claimed to be even more affluent: 17.6% reported a household income of more than $100,000 (U.S. dollars), 7.4% an income between $80,000 and $100,000, 13% between $60,000 and $80,000, and 13.9% between $40,000 and $60,000. By way of comparison, the average household income in Canada in 1995, according to the 1996 census, was $48,552 (Canadian dollars),[23] and the median household income in the United States in 2002 was $42,409 (U.S. dollars).[24]

Significant numbers of Falun Gong practitioners are thus doing considerably better than the average North American. At the same time, many Falun Gong practitioners reported being considerably poorer than the Canadian and American national averages, which is to be expected for a group largely composed of recent immigrants, many of whom are still in school. Of those responding to the Montreal survey, fully 50% reported annual household income of $20,000 (Canadian dollars) or less, of whom a significant number (27% of the entire sample) reported annual household earnings of less than $10,000. Similarly, 55.8% of Chinese respondents to the Toronto survey reported annual household incomes of less than $40,000 (Canadian dollars), including 14.5% (of the total sample) who earned less than $10,000. The results from the Boston survey confirm this distribution: almost half of Chinese respondents reported annual household incomes of $40,000 (U.S. dollars) or less, and more than 10% % reported annual household incomes of $10,000 or less. As for their perceptions of their standard of living in North America, 52.4% of Chinese respondents indicated that their material lives were better in North America, 19.1% reported having enjoyed a higher standard of living in China, and 28.5% said that there was little difference between their standard of living in China and their standard of living in North America.[25] Unsurprisingly, my fieldwork revealed that most practitioners in leadership positions are among the wealthiest of the groups, and my impression is that the wealthy bear a disproportionate share of the expenses incurred in organizing Falun Gong activities as well, although they seem to give of their time and money voluntarily.

My surveys further revealed that there was nothing unusual about the marital status or family structure of Chinese practitioners. According to the combined results of the Toronto and Boston surveys: 78.1% are married and 17.3% single (the rest checked "other"), 43% live in nuclear families made up of husband, wife, and children (and another 11.5% in households made up of husband, wife, children, and parents or other relatives), 20.7% as husband and wife (without children—as yet), and 16.1% live alone (the rest again checked "other). I suspect that the percentage of Chinese practitioners living alone (particularly given that the average age of Chinese practitioners is around forty) and the number of households including grandparents or other relatives may well be somewhat higher than North American norms, but these differences can be readily explained by the facts of recent immigration and the Chinese cultural valorization of extended families.

More women than men filled out my surveys on every occasion—the overall ratio being three women to two men—which seems to confirm my general impression that there are more women than men among Chinese practitioners. This is not particularly unusual, as many researchers have found that religiosity can often be a rather feminine domain. When I did fieldwork with Christian groups in rural China in the mid-1990s, I noticed that there were considerably more women than men among the faithful. Many leadership or spokesperson positions among Chinese Falun Gong practitioners are occupied by women, despite the fact that Li Hongzhi's teachings in no way stress "women's liberation" as a goal—quite the contrary, as we have already seen. I observed no gender tensions over the course of my fieldwork; practitioners are urged to value above all their individual relationship to master Li and his teachings and to respect other practitioners without comparing levels of "cultivation ability." As noted in the previous chapter, sexuality is viewed as an attachment to be discarded, which perhaps contributes to the overall atmosphere of friendly equality.

When I attended an anti–Falun Gong international conference in Beijing in the fall of 2000, one Chinese researcher remarked that Falun Gong practitioners he had met were "weak elements" (or, more colloquially, "losers"; *ruanzhe*), by which he meant the sick, the poor, the downtrodden, those without resources to make much of their lives (those who, one might add, might reasonably wish to make claims on a socialist state). This assertion may or may not paint an accurate picture of Falun Gong practitioners in China, but it is certainly *not* true of Falun Gong practitioners in North America. The average Chinese practitioner in North America is young, urban, dynamic, a successful recent immigrant largely living the American dream, at least from the material point of view. It would hardly be an exaggeration to say that Falun Gong as practiced by Chinese in North America is a bourgeois movement; the stereotypical practitioner lives in the suburbs and drives a Ford Taurus to her job in computers or finance. Those still in school share similar orientations and aspirations to those already in the workplace.

Why Cultivate? The Texture of the Everyday Life
of a Falun Gong Practitioner

What do Falun Gong practitioners get from their cultivation, which for many
of them is the central concern of their lives? My surveys revealed that practitioners devote considerable amounts of time to their practice: 13.7 hours per
week according to the Toronto survey, and 9.8 hours a week according to the
Boston survey. What motivates these materially comfortable people, who have
busy work and family lives, as do other North Americans, to find an hour and
a half or two hours *every day* to devote to cultivation activities? Of what do
these activities consist? What is Falun Dafa life in North America like? The
following section will address these questions, drawing again on my surveys
and on my fieldwork experience.

What might the typical week of a typical Chinese Falun Gong practitioner
in North America look like? There are no "church services" or "prayer meetings" as such; Falun Dafa possesses no physical structures and borrows or rents
space as needed on a temporary basis. Consequently, Falun Dafa activities are
largely what Falun Dafa practitioners make of them. Many meet daily, in
groups of five to fifteen, in a nearby park or public space, to do Falun Gong
exercises. The Toronto Falun Dafa Web site, for example, lists eight exercise
sites in central Toronto alone (and three more sites in eastern Toronto, two in
western Toronto, one in East York, six in North York, five in the Markham,
Scarborough, area, and three in more distant suburbs of the metropolitan area);
they provide a variety of schedules—from very early every morning, to longer
sessions held only on weekends—to try to meet the needs of all practitioners.[26]
Some of the exercise sites are chosen with an eye toward visibility—keeping
Falun Gong in the public eye and perhaps making new recruits—and some are
quite clearly political statements: the group that meets from Monday to Friday
between 9:50 and 11:10 a.m. in front of the Chinese consulate presumably
chose that spot for a purpose. Politics apart, these exercise sessions, to anyone
who has been to China, are reminiscent of the many—often elderly—people
who do taijiquan or other, similar exercises, in parks and other public places
throughout China. My impression is that the daily exercise routine may be
favored by more elderly Falun Dafa practitioners in North America as well;
most practitioners have family and/or work responsibilities and find it hard to
get to the park at 6:00 a.m. or 5:00 p.m. on a regular basis.

In addition to exercise sessions, the Toronto Web site also offers "*fa
study*"—study of the "law" or, more broadly, of Falun Dafa doctrine. Fa study

generally requires longer periods of time than performing the exercises, and Fa study meetings are held less frequently: Monday evenings between 7:00 and 9:00 p.m. at Carleton and Church, for example, or Thursdays from 7:00 to 9:00 p.m. and Saturdays from 7:30 to 10:30 p.m. at Ossington and College. The Fa study sessions that I have attended often involve large amounts of group reading of Li Hongzhi's texts, although there is no set format, and practices may vary from place to place or may have changed over time. In any event, even veteran practitioners are not allowed to "preach" or to explicate Li Hongzhi's doctrine, which means that such "discussion" as does occur tends to be very tentative; practitioners invariably preface any comment with the disclaimer "this is only my personal opinion." It is not surprising that reading scripture together often takes the place of genuine exchange. My general impression, based on fieldwork at Fa study sessions and elsewhere, is that although practitioners enjoy being with fellow believers, their goal is to advance their individual cultivation and not to forge a meaningful community— which would be yet another form of attachment to be discarded on the way to enlightenment.

In addition to exercise sessions and Fa study, practitioners also engage in activities to "make known the Way" (hongfa). Hongfa could be translated by "proselytizing" as well, but most Falun Dafa practitioners believe that people are "destined" (you yuanfen) either to be saved or not, and thus usually do not actively attempt to "convert" nonpractitioners—although they are always happy to welcome a newcomer into the fold. As already mentioned, performing the exercises in a public place is one means of making known the Way, and illustrates that there is no firm distinction between cultivation and publicization. Other such activities include handing out flyers in the metro or in a mall; depositing Falun Gong literature in stores, libraries, laundries, etc.; and participating in the many activities organized by Falun Gong, such as protests, marches, parades, and celebrations of Chinese culture. Large-scale activities of this sort are often organized in conjunction with regional experience-sharing conferences. Although handing out flyers in a mall may not at first glance appear to be a deeply "spiritual" activity, it nonetheless requires a type of courage which, for example, elderly Chinese women may lack, particularly as they are often incapable of expressing themselves well in English. I have heard practitioners talk about how difficult they found such activities, how hard it was to overcome the attachment of worrying about what others might think of them. Much the same could be said for participation in marches and demonstrations; quite apart from the political worry of being identified by Chinese embassy staff, Chinese have historically been perceived as "quiet" immigrants, who keep to themselves and go about their business without making waves. Not a few Chinese seem to share this perception. It is not difficult to imagine how hard it is for a recent immigrant from China who hopes to organize a peaceful demonstration to negotiate with the police, obtain the necessary permits, and take to the streets—where the group is often met with indifference, impatience, or even hostility ("Who the hell *are* these foreigners and why are they keeping me from getting across town?").

In addition to this ongoing rhythm of activity, newcomers to Falun Dafa may also participate in a nine-day video session. Here, they view nine ninety-minute-long videos of Li Hongzhi's lectures (the same lectures that make up the core of his book *Zhuan falun*) under the guidance of veteran practitioners. And practitioners with the dedication and the means often travel internationally, either to present Falun Dafa's case at a variety of world forums (UNESCO in Paris, the United Nations in New York and Geneva, the World Court at The Hague) or to join their voices with those of other protesters who gather on the occasions of the meetings of the Group of Seven (now Eight), for example, when the leaders of the world's most powerful nations gather to exchange views, often on important economic issues.

Despite the frenzy of activity available to Falun Dafa practitioners, the portrait I have painted to this point has omitted one crucial element: individual time spent in meditation, in doing the exercising, and above all, in reading and rereading *Zhuan falun*. Chinese respondents to the Boston survey claimed, on average, to devote 45% of their cultivation time to individual cultivation; for Chinese respondents to the Toronto survey, the number was even higher: 56.3%. I was often struck during my fieldwork by the number of practitioners I observed sitting quietly in a corner, reading *Zhuan falun* or another of Li Hongzhi's texts, even as an experience-sharing conference involving several hundred fairly noisy people continued around them. The same is true of Fa study sessions. To me, this is confirmation of what Li Hongzhi and practitioners say: the goal of cultivation is individual enlightenment; everything else is secondary and instrumental.

What do Chinese practitioners mean by "individual enlightenment"? Surveys again provide some evidence: in response to a question concerning what attracted them to Falun Dafa, 28.9% of Chinese practitioners chose the "intellectual content" of the teaching, 26.6% chose the "spiritual enlightenment" they received, 20.2% chose the "health benefits" that the practice brought them, 14.7% the exercises, 7.3% master Li himself, and 2.2% the community of Falun Gong practitioners.[27] Practitioners understand the "intellectual content" of Falun Dafa doctrine to mean its value in describing the functioning of the moral and physical universe; the two are linked, as discussed in chapter 4, and indeed, as many practitioners remarked to me after filling out the questionnaire, Falun Dafa, properly understood and properly cultivated, is a comprehensive, holistic, unifying experience which defies my simplistic listing of "points of attraction."

Many practitioners were initially drawn to Falun Gong because of its claims to heal illness. This is particularly true for older practitioners, who have more aches and pains. I recall the first evening I spent with Falun Dafa practitioners in Toronto, when I joined a weekly session held in the common area of a downtown apartment building and listened to Ophelia Zhang tell how her stomach cancer had gone into remission and subsequently disappeared after she began practicing Falun Gong, the sort of story I was to hear over and over again. But it is not only the elderly who come to Falun Gong due to illness. Frank Ye, a thirty-five-year-old paralegal worker in Toronto, is diabetic and found himself, on arrival in Canada from China, temporarily uncovered by Canadian health insurance and unable to purchase the insulin he needed to stay alive. He began attending Falun Gong meetings out of desperation and was at first bitterly sarcastic, mocking what the other practitioners were doing. As he persisted, however, his symptoms improved and his need for insulin disappeared. During the months in which I was engaged in active fieldwork, I received many phone calls from practitioners who wanted to put their medical records at my disposal, so that I could "prove" that Falun Dafa's claims to curative powers are true. Many practitioners who do their exercises outside every day in cold Canadian winters are very proud of their hardiness; particularly among male practitioners, there is occasionally a sort of macho attitude which I have also observed among those who practice other forms of qigong, especially the versions of qigong which are more closely related to martial arts.

As noted previously, however, Li Hongzhi clearly presents his teachings as going beyond the "simple" healing power of "low-level" schools of qigong. He (or his "law bodies"—his presence as manifested at higher levels, allowing him to be available to any practitioner who might need his protection) cleanse practitioners' bodies so that they can begin cultivation at a higher level, and most practitioners, while delighted and proud of their improved health, emphasize that good health is a by-product of practice and not the primary objective. Practitioners expect to suffer—physically and otherwise—as suffering provides them an occasion to put into practice the discipline demanded of them by Li Hongzhi and his teachings. As already mentioned, illness is seen as the product of karma, either carried over from sins committed in previous lives or created through immoral acts in one's present life. Cultivation is seen as a long-term process; although there are many stories of the immediate physical effects brought about by an initial encounter with *Zhuan falun*, Li Hongzhi's masterwork,[28] practitioners expect to fall ill on occasion and to encounter other sorts of difficulties. After all, master Li urges them to remain in the world, part of normal human society, because the world is filled with the sort of pain and suffering necessary to hone their will and to triumph over material and sensual attachments. As a result, for many practitioners, life becomes a moral journey in which they seek to apply the teachings of Falun Dafa to their work and family lives—and since April 1999, to the larger geopolitical arena as well.

Some of the best evidence of how practitioners view their lives and struggles is to be found in the witness statements delivered at experience-sharing conferences, which are privileged moments for the fieldworker. Experience-sharing conferences are held every few months in the major cities of a particular region. If a conference is held, for example, in Toronto in January, there may be a second such conference in Ottawa in April, a third in Montreal in July, a fourth in Boston in September, and perhaps another in New York late in the year. Practitioners attempt to attend as many as possible, and organizers arrange bus travel and home stays for those traveling between Toronto and Montreal, for example. The experience-sharing conferences afford an occasion to rekindle friendships, to hear others' experiences, to participate in parades and other demonstrations (which, at least in the past, often drew media attention), and, often, to hear Li Hongzhi speak, as he shows up, unannounced, on certain of such occasions. Analysis of several of these witness statements will reveal the central narratives of Falun Dafa experience as lived by Chinese practitioners in North America.[29]

Most witness statements are variations on a common theme, that of persisting in the Way, the law, the truth that they find in Falun Gong, in the face of great adversity, overcoming that adversity through adherence to the law, and gaining new insights into the law and into themselves as a result. Though few Chinese practitioners would have read John Bunyan's *Pilgrim's Progress*, the tone and discursive structure of these "narratives of salvation" are quite similar to this Christian classic. Practitioners recount their turmoil when faced with multiple and conflicting obligations, not the least of which being Li Hongzhi's injunction that they remain squarely *within* the world and not withdraw to cultivate in isolation. Practitioners search to understand why life must be so hard, and they come to understand that their trials and tribulations are all part of their life path, arranged for them according to the dictates of the universal dictates of truth, compassion, and forbearance. They are thus grateful to master Li for the suffering they have successfully endured, humbled by the difficulties experienced in navigating these tribulations, and convinced of the value of cultivation, while sobered by the length of the journey they still have to endure.

Still, the narratives are joyful tales of achievement, where the individual practitioner comes to appreciate her role and value as part of a larger teleology and to respect the roles that others (be they fellow practitioners, hostile family members, or even Chinese police officers) play in this drama. There is nothing self-indulgent about these narratives, little or no self-congratulation; practitioners hold themselves to extremely high standards and attempt to discard attachments to anything unconnected to cultivation, even as they maintain their commitments to being good employees, good spouses, good citizens. I have often wondered, observing Falun Dafa practitioners in action, whether they might not share some common features with early adherents to the Chinese Communist Party: dedication to a cause which promises both individual fulfillment and betterment of the group, rejection of slavish obedience to hierarchy (be it Confucian or Maoist), and refusal of nihilism or "neoliberalism." In any event, I have often found practitioners to maintain a pleasing mixture of self-awareness and sensitivity to others.

If practitioners' witness statements follow fairly predictable narrative paths, the settings surrounding the unfolding of the narratives are varied, and help us to understand the world as experienced by Chinese Falun Dafa practitioners in North America. These settings include health struggles, the world of work, family struggles, and conflicts occasioned by the Chinese government's campaign against Falun Gong.

Given the importance of the body to Falun Gong practice, it is hardly surprising that health concerns figure prominently in numerous witness statements. One example is that of Li Xingkai, a college student in Montreal, whose main attachments prior to discovering Falun Gong were to the National Basketball Association[30] and to playing Go on the Internet. Cultivation allowed him to discard such "addictions" rapidly, and with his refound energy he was delighted to imagine how much he would be able to do with his life. A senior practitioner pointed out to him that "fame and fortune" were just as much attachments as the NBA and Internet Go, and Li, sobered, returned to his study of *Zhuan falun*.

Li's real "cultivation" began, however, when he injured his knee, tripping and smashing it against the sharp tread of an escalator step (he was going up a down escalator at the time, the scamp). In the face of conflicting advice— from parents, professors, and fellow practitioners—and changing moods ("Of course I should suffer so as to burn off karma, but what kind of example do I set limping all over the place?"), Li wavered, but he did not seek medical treatment. He finally realized that all of these elements were part of the cultivation test set for him by master Li.

Another health-related story comes from Rebecca Wang, a practitioner who was discovered to have second-stage tuberculosis when she underwent her medical examination prior to emigrating to Canada. As a practitioner, she faced a real dilemma: emigration to Canada was important both for herself and for her family, and second-stage tuberculosis is a contagious disease which she risked passing on to her students if it were not rapidly brought under control. Putting aside her doubts as to what she should do "as a practitioner," Rebecca began taking the prescribed drugs. On the eighth day of her treatment, however, she "accidentally" spilled a half-bottle of the medication, and when she gave herself an injection, "the needle went in straight but came out bent, with a piece of my flesh attached." She decided that the master was telling her that she could cure her illness without recourse to medication, and immediately stopped the treatment, redoubling her cultivation efforts at the same time. She was rewarded with a clean bill of health some months later when her second set of X rays came back negative.

The theme of work figures prominently in practitioners' witness statements as well, for as the results of my surveys revealed, many of them have successfully joined the North American rat race. Many Chinese practitioners appear to have been overachievers all their lives and to have had very high expectations of their transition to North America. Take, for example, the case of Anita Qiao, a Chinese woman who had worked for an international accounting firm in China before emigrating to the United States and working in the Washington, DC, office of the same company. In her own words:

Being unfamiliar with my work and also because of the language barrier, I suffered quite a bit during the first couple of months at my new job. Even though I had worked for the same company for three years in China before I came to America, I was like an elementary school student without knowledge of American accounting systems or adequate communication skills in English.

Without any on-the-job training, I was sent to a big hospital to do a preliminary audit. I did not even know what kind of accounting system the hospital had; hospitals in China are state-run, and do not need outside auditors like us. I was extremely nervous, and I cannot even remember how I spent that very long week.

My supervisor was from another office. He complained to my Human Resources manager and had him send me back to my home base two days early, just to get rid of me. I felt very hurt and thought that the company was unfair to me. My supervisor had not given me any background on the client and he was quite rude to me every day.

Later on, after I calmed down, I looked for reasons inside myself. It's true that my supervisor was not nice to me, but this was not because I was a foreigner, it was because I did not know what I was doing. His primary concern was to be responsible to the client, and since I was not qualified, he sent me back and turned the job over to someone capable. After all, my company charged the client according to the number of hours we worked, so if the project fell behind schedule because of my poor performance, the reputation of my company would be damaged.

I am a practitioner and thus must behave according to the requirements of the Law [i.e., must fulfill workaday responsibilities, in this instance, to the company]. I should do even better than others [to illustrate the value of Falun Dafa]. After this initial project, I worked very hard. I used every opportunity to learn from my coworkers. I began to learn the American accounting system, came to master my company's financial software, and worked on my English. If I had questions on [the] job, I asked them immediately [rather than pretending to know the answer]. In this way, I made rapid progress in my work.

Anita thus interpreted her difficulties at work on a spiritual level, refused to blame her circumstances for her problems, and redoubled her efforts, but she soon found herself once again frustrated. Her next assignment was to a small company in California, where she once again ran into difficulties and had to ask her manager to bail her out. The final report was two weeks late, and Anita was once again in the depths of despair:

I was very frustrated. I cried almost everyday when I went home from work. I felt that the pressure was too much. Even if I knew this was another test, I still could not get over it. It seemed that my work effort was simply not sufficient. I spent almost all my spare time on study of Falun Dafa, which left little time for work problems. I had always thought that as long as I kept reading *Zhuan falun*, I could understand the Law more, and that through my advanced understanding I could improve my energy level, even if I left out practical cultivation, which is indeed an important step. Master Li requires us to be a good person in all circumstances. This means that we should be a valuable member of our work team, and should earn our paycheck. In other words, reading *Zhuan falun* and putting the

Law into practice in everyday life are *both* important, but I had not found the proper balance between the two.

On the basis of this insight, Anita poured herself more completely into work, temporarily reducing the time devoted to further study of *Zhuan falun*. Soon thereafter, she was rewarded with a project which touched on her previous work in China and allowed her to illustrate her expertise. Her stellar performance on this project earned her the respect of her coworkers and a large financial bonus. More important, her individual success at work came to reflect well on her country and on her cultivation practice:

> A senior partner in the company told me that I was the first person from the Beijing office to be invited to work in the Virginia office, and that due to my good example the company was going to invite more Chinese from the Beijing office to work in the States. It was also during this period that I started to introduce Falun Gong to my coworkers. Although I could not explain very clearly what cultivation was and what "returning to one's true self" meant in English, I always showed them the book and illustrated the exercises. So everyone at work knew about Falun Gong and agreed that we were a peaceful group.
>
> Before I left the United States for Canada, my fellow office workers held a farewell party for me . . . and the three things they claimed to have learned from me were "Falun Gong, cultivation practice, and Chinese New Year." When the Chinese government began to crack down on Falun Gong in July 1999, all of them said that the Chinese government must be wrong, "because we can tell from Anita's example that Falun Gong is a belief system which enables people to achieve a higher morality."

Anita went on to recount other conflicts on the road to her full commitment to the law: her struggles to find the time and energy to participate in public activities which make known the Way, and her struggle not to hate the Chinese government despite its campaign against Falun Gong.

Another similar story is that of Zhang Baojun, a software engineer at a major Canadian computer firm in Ottawa. Zhang's work life was easily as stressful as Anita's, but he had the added pressure of being called on to defend Falun Gong at the same moment that a major project came his way at work, in the summer of 1999:

> My new manager said: "The schedule for this [new] project is very tight. I heard that you did great work on your last project. Hope you

can live up to your reputation!" Unfortunately, my enlightenment
quality was not sufficient to permit me to understand that the move
to a new project with a "tight schedule" was a sign from Master Li to
abandon ordinary human consciousness and to approach my cultivation with a new mentality, as "the time for cultivation is very
limited."

   Even before July 20 [an important date in the early period of the
Chinese government's campaign against Falun Gong] I was really
busy with work. I went often to the Chinese Embassy to express our
concerns about events in China, but work seemed so important that
I could not treat Falun Gong as my first priority. Once, four practitioners came from Toronto to present a letter to the Chinese Embassy
so that I could continue with my work, but this only made me
feel more guilty.

   After July 20 . . . it was if my heart was bleeding. Sometimes I
had to close my office door at work and cry alone. . . . I realized that
this was a special time and that I needed to treat Dafa as my first
priority; I would have to abandon fame, profit, and ordinary human
emotions right away.

Zhang analyzed his work situation carefully and came to the conclusion
that he had twice as much on his plate as other workers. A sympathetic superior
agreed with him, and reassigned a portion of the work to someone else, even
though Zhang had to swallow his pride in order to ask for such help. His relief
was short-lived, however, for Zhang soon discovered that another project which
should have dovetailed with his had been sloppily done, and the software code
had been written without taking Zhang's project into consideration. Zhang had
to choose between rewriting the code of the previous project, or pretending that
he had not noticed the problem and passing the buck to someone else.

   This was in the late summer and early fall of 1999, when Falun Gong
practitioners in North America began to react vigorously to China's campaign
of suppression. Zhang, whose English is good and who has a calm, soothing,
diplomatic demeanor, was much in demand, particularly since he lived in
Ottawa, a city where there are relatively few practitioners:

   What should I do? Should I do what the other programmer did and
   cut corners to make the schedule? The campaign against Falun
   Gong in China was escalating at the same time, and . . . it took a lot of
   time to explain Falun Dafa to the media, to human rights organizations, to the government, and to society at large. Rewriting the other
   programmer's code would take me two months, and the manager

of the team which had put together the inadequate program refused to rewrite it. I was in a real bind: If I rewrote the software, I would have less time to spend protecting Falun Dafa. At the same time, a practitioner must behave according to the requirements of the Law, and should not knowingly cut corners at work. After thinking long and hard about it, I decided not to rewrite the program. The situation with Falun Dafa was too critical and time was too precious. At the end of October, however, I realized that I had only been putting things off, and that I might well wind up spending even more time trying to make the two programs fit together.

Zhang then decided to bite the bullet and to rewrite the inadequate program that the other team had produced. If the only way to accomplish this was to sleep less, then he would sleep less, Zhang decided. However, a few days later, Zhang's manager informed him that the entire project would be delayed for several months due to other, unforeseen problems which had nothing to do with Zhang or with the other team. Zhang interpreted this as a cosmic reward for his decision to do well at work *and* to defend Falun Gong: "It is just like Master said: 'Once Buddha nature presents itself, it shakes the Ten Directions of the universe.' "

Still, this brief respite only allowed Zhang to devote himself all the more fully to cultivation, which at this point was evolving into a full-time public relations campaign to get the Falun Gong message into the Western media. Zhang realized that he needed his job, so as to be able to contribute financially to the media campaign, but he could not both work full time and campaign full time for Falun Gong. He decided to try to work part time, and explained his situation in full to his supervisors. His immediate supervisor warned him that shifting to part time was a risky strategy: Zhang would be vulnerable to layoffs and his benefits would be cut.[31] Zhang allowed himself to be swayed, reasoning that it was not simply a question of his material needs or those of his family, but of the material needs of the Falun Dafa cause, to which he contributed on a voluntary and regular basis. But in November, as practitioners ratcheted up their already frenzied efforts to keep the Falun Gong cause before the public eye, Zhang realized that the only way to keep up with the demands of work and of the cause was to devote less time to cultivation. This, he realized, was too great a sacrifice, so he went and talked to another supervisor, this one higher placed in the company hierarchy. This supervisor was more understanding than the first and offered Zhang a variety of possibilities, including flex time and the installation of a high-speed modem at Zhang's home—measures which would allow Zhang to continue to work the same number of hours, while granting him freer use of his time. Zhang was so moved by this kindness that he temporarily dropped the idea of working part time. He soon realized, however, that he had been blinded by "the attachment of human sentimentality" (i.e., swayed by his boss's kindness) and that this had been yet another test that the law had placed before him. He asked once again to switch to part-time status, and both of his supervisors acquiesced.

This decision helped Zhang to resolve the conflict between the demands of his work and the demands of Falun Dafa, but there are, after all, only twenty-four hours in the day and a mountain of work needed to be done in the David-and-Goliath struggle of a handful of practitioners against the Chinese government. Zhang worked so hard that, night after night, he and his wife—also a practitioner—fell into bed, too exhausted to undress. He finally realized that the only reason his family had continued to function was because his sixty-eight-year-old mother had taken charge of virtually all domestic matters. This realization came early one morning, when the sound of the garage door opening disturbed his efforts to concentrate on his Falun Gong exercises. It was his mother, who had opened the garage door to take out the garbage. Zhang thus realized that he had failed to respect his mother as a fellow practitioner—or even as a fellow human being—and had once again fallen into the trap of human sentimentality, saying to himself "that's what mothers do" instead of "I am taking undue advantage of her." There were genuine tears in Zhang's eyes at the end of his narrative as he pledged to consider his mother according to the requirements of the law—even as he continued to struggle to be a good employee and a good representative of Falun Dafa.

The theme of family is another motif which arises repeatedly in these narratives. Cultivation is a family affair for many practitioners. As already mentioned, Zhang Baojun's wife and mother are practitioners. Jennie Zhao, the wife of Frank Ye, the diabetic discussed above, is a practitioner. Children are encouraged to cultivate as well; among the witness statements at the conferences where I was present, there was one by a primary school student, who recounted that, as a result of cultivation, her marks for "cooperating with others" had risen from "good" to "excellent," and another by the mother of a seven-year-old practitioner, who praised her daughter for refusing medication despite a very nasty bout of the flu. There usually are many children present at Falun Gong events; as the father of three sometimes rowdy boys myself, I admit feeling a certain reassurance when Falun Gong parents have to shush the noisy kids playing in the hall.

But cultivation is not always a family affair, and when it is not, life can be difficult for practitioners and nonpractitioners alike. At one point during my fieldwork, I was contacted by a young woman from Toronto whose mother had immigrated to Canada from Hong Kong in the 1960s, and had taken up Falun Gong cultivation, to the consternation of her husband and children. There was talk of separation as the father was uncomfortable with his wife's activities outside the home, and the wife was equally adamant about continuing her cultivation.

Similar conflicts appear in practitioners' testimonials as well. The most striking of these was delivered by a practitioner from Ottawa named Karen Li, who attempted to hide her continued cultivation from her family because of their opposition. She had been practicing in secret for some time, but the issue came to a head when she decided to take advantage of a nine-day intensive study session being offered in the Ottawa area. Without telling her family, she took a week off from work and went to the sessions instead of to her job; on the weekend, she said that it was the Christmas rush and that her boss had asked her to work overtime. She almost got away with it, but her father-in-law noticed that her Falun Gong books were missing and called a practitioner to ask if she had seen Karen at a Falun Gong function. When the practitioner answered affirmatively, Karen's goose was cooked:

> When I walked in the door, my husband threw a shoe at me. I raised
> my hand to stop it, but . . . I knew that I had done wrong, and that
> I should endure the suffering. . . . In a little while, my husband
> told me to leave and to go live somewhere else. He pushed me out the
> door and hit me, hard, in my right eye. I felt dizzy and thought
> that my eye must have swelled up to the size of a small bowl. I bore it
> without resentment or indignation.
>
> As I left my home, I realized that the fault was mine and that
> I should not impose on others [by looking for somewhere else to
> stay]. I decided to sit in my car and wait for my family to calm down
> and let me back in. It was very cold, even though I was wearing a
> down jacket. I checked my eye in the mirror, but saw no swelling, not
> even a bruise. I believe this is because my mind was right, and the
> Great Law was manifesting its power.
>
> At two or three in the morning, my father-in-law let me back in
> the house. The following morning, I told my family the truth and
> stated my firm belief in Falun Dafa. I am now able to go to the group
> study nobly every day.

Karen thus realized that lying to her family had been a manifestation of an attachment to ordinary human sentimentality—fear of what others might think—which had "fostered the evil demon nature" and poisoned her domestic environment. In response to her honest admission of the importance of Falun Dafa to her, her family grudgingly relented, and she now practices openly at home.

Most family conflicts are less violent than that recounted by Karen. More typical is the story of Randy Ma, owner of a Chinese restaurant in a small city on the Canadian prairie. Randy learned about Falun Gong from an employee in his restaurant who had recently immigrated to Canada. He read through *Zhuan falun* and felt immediately attracted, but at the same time wondered how to reconcile his material ambitions (why else run a restaurant if not to make money?) with Li Hongzhi's call to abandon all attachments. Still, the appeal of *Zhuan falun* was too strong, and Randy decided to continue with cultivation. He was immediately rewarded, as his asthma and his heart condition were cured without further medical treatment.

Unfortunately for Randy, his enthusiasm for Falun Gong was not shared by the rest of his family:

> My first cultivation test came from my family. I have been a filial son to my parents and a responsible husband to my wife. I am also the host of the whole family [in the context of immigration to Canada]. But my decision to cultivate was opposed by my entire family, including my parents, my wife, and my in-laws. My wife said, "We have just started to earn enough money to live a good life. Why do you want to practice something that the Chinese government has banned?" My father pointed to the current situation in China and asked me to be sensitive to the consequences of my decision. When this didn't work, they started to abuse and beat me, saying "You are so selfish! All you want to do is to be a Buddha! You don't care if we live or die!" My mother, who was still in China, often called me in tears.... Finally, my father demanded that I choose between Dafa and my parents. My in-laws also threatened to break off relations with me.... My father even cursed Master Li, which made me very determined. I said sternly: "If you curse my Master again I will cut off our relationship [i.e., the father-son relationship] at once!"

Randy regretted having hurt his family's feelings, but came to realize that their opposition had been a test which helped him to "upgrade his *xinxing* [moral stature]" and to work off some of his karma. On a more practical level, he strove to do well in business and to contribute to the housework, so as to illustrate that his cultivation did not mean a loss to his family.

Another witness statement explores work and family themes from a different angle. Angela Luk is a young Chinese woman in her mid-thirties. She was born in Hong Kong and emigrated to Vancouver, Canada, at the age of nine. She is thus neither a recent immigrant nor from mainland China, which perhaps accounts for the different tone of her narrative.

Angela once worked in the computer industry and found her career very satisfying: "I used to be very attached to my job, often working long hours and taking work home, even while I was expecting my first child." Angela anticipated being able to return to work after the birth of her child, but found this very difficult. Her baby proved to be very needy, and Angela eventually decided to put off returning to work so as to be able to take care of her child, a decision she found difficult:

> I felt fortunate that I could make this choice because our family could afford to live on one income. However, as time went by, I became more and more restless and envious of other mothers who worked. I was jealous of those whose mothers or mothers-in-law were willing and able to help them look after their baby. I was also jealous of those mothers who had calm and independent babies. They did not need to nurse or be held very much, and accepted other adults easily. Now I realize the seriousness of jealousy. In *Zhuan falun* . . . Master Li said: "If jealousy is not given up during the course of cultivation practice, one will absolutely not attain the cultivation Right Fruit."

Angela decided to return to work part time when her son was eighteen months old, but her child found adaptation to a new environment difficult, and Angela found it impossible to balance her desires to perform well at work with her desires to nurture her child. When she became pregnant again, she stopped work completely, and although her boys were aged nine and seven when she gave her witness statement, she had not yet returned to the workplace. Like many mothers, Angela wonders whether she made the right choices. Had she indulged in the attachment of human sentimentality in catering to the neediness of her children? Had she hindered their attainment of independence and autonomy? Had she slighted herself by sacrificing her career to the needs of her children?

In the teachings of Falun Gong, Angela found solace for the choices she made:

> Firstly, we have to recognize that young children have innate needs and behaviors. For example, in terms of the need to play, in 1998 in New York, Master Li said: "Young children are not the same as us adults. Young children like to play. This is their nature, and cannot be regarded as an attachment. They just live like this." Similarly, my

understanding is that it is the nature of young children to be close to and dependent on their parents. This is not an attachment. Parents have a solemn obligation to respect the nature of children. This is also not an attachment, and it is not spoiling. . . .

Secondly, we have to accept that each child comes with his own predestined personality and needs. Some will be ready for independence sooner and others later; some will be easier to teach, others harder. My understanding is that parents must accept the temperament, capabilities, and developmental pace of their children, and be sensitive and responsive to their needs at different stages. In *Zhuan falun* . . . Master Li said: "Some people will lose their temper when they take care of children, and they will yell at them and make quite a scene. You do not have to be that way in disciplining children, and you should not get really angry yourselves. You should educate children with reason so that they can be really educated well."

My understanding is that parents should teach independence and goodness using Zhen-Shan-Ren. For example, if a young child has a strong need to stay close to his parents, then it is compassionate and tolerant to meet this need as much as possible.

As for her jealousies of other working women and her doubts about her own worth, Angela came to understand that the origin of such worries was an attachment to money and to status and that, as a cultivator, she should learn to discard such attachments:

I realized that when I returned to work part-time eight years ago, the real motivating reason was that I was attached to the status of having a paid job. I justified it by saying that my baby and I were too attached to each other and he needed to become more independent from me. However, it was really because, as a mother at home, I had no status and did not feel respected as a contributing member of society.

From the point of view of a Falun Dafa practitioner, however, she came to understand that "the key to cultivation advancement is to discard whatever attachments there may linger in the heart: money, status, power, sentimentality, approval by others, or something else."

Finally, as an educated, emancipated woman, Angela worried about dependence on her husband's income. Here, she found direct quotes from Li Hongzhi to the effect that "advocacy of women's liberation appears only after the degeneration of the human race. It's not limited to women being bullied by men, instead, men are also bullying men, women are also bullying women. . . . In fact, there are also women with power who bully men. This is caused by the moral decay of the whole society." In other words, women's liberation is a false issue, a distraction from the genuine concerns of cultivation. In summary, Angela found in Falun Dafa doctrinal sanction for having followed her maternal instincts, as well as a counterweight to the perceived feminist devaluation of her personal choices.[32]

Family conflicts arise more frequently in another context: the response of practitioners to the Chinese government's crackdown on Falun Gong. We have already seen evidence of this in the reaction of Randy Ma's parents and in-laws to his decision to cultivate, their fear that he would bring the wrath of the Chinese state (and its representatives in Canada) down on his head (and, sure enough, the Chinese consulate stopped holding banquets in Randy's restaurant as a result of his choice). For cultivators who were in China at the moment of the crackdown, or who chose to return to China after the crackdown to protest the government's decision, the possible consequences for family members were more severe than the loss of revenue.

One example is the witness statement of Wei Dahai, a student at a Montreal university at the moment of giving his testimony. Like many Chinese practitioners in North America, Wei was shocked by the Chinese government's full-scale assault on Falun Gong, and even though he tried to convince himself that this was a test for practitioners in China, enabling them to burn off large amounts of karma quickly, he still felt guilty "remaining on the sidelines" in Canada. Thus, he decided to return to China in early 2000. Understandably anxious at Wei's decision, his wife left Montreal with their young son when she realized that she could not change Wei's mind (another practitioner made a similar decision to return to China from Canada, and only told his wife the night before his departure, so as to preclude her making efforts to stop him). Upon arrival in Beijing, after several run-ins with authorities at the southern border city of Shenzhen, Wei was taken into detention, and his family, worried about him since his departure from Canada, eventually tracked him down through the Public Security Bureau of his home province.[33] His parents and several of his relatives rushed to Beijing, pleading with Wei to renounce his beliefs—in the form of a letter expressing "regret" for his actions and beliefs—so that he could be released and return to Canada right away. Indeed, his younger brother had already composed two such letters for him; all Wei had to do was sign. Wei refused, explaining that to do so would be to slander Falun Dafa. His family acknowledged that he was right, but insisted that their lives were at stake, too, so he finally gave in and spent some time composing a "confession" with which he could live. Naturally, most of the document was devoted to an exposition of the greatness of Falun Gong, and Wei took care to forgive the police officers who had arrested him, noting that they had no choice but to implement incorrect government policies. Wei's family, unsurprisingly, could see immediately that this "confession" would never be accepted. Wei's father collapsed in tears, his younger brother could only sigh in despair, and his older brother lost his temper and began cursing, saying that they would all be in trouble because of Wei's stubbornness. Wei remained steadfast despite his concern for his family, reasoning that pain and suffering were necessary to cultivation; his loyalty to Dafa was greater than his loyalty to his family. Telling his family "I would rather die than betray the Law," Wei refused to write the confession demanded of him, but was eventually released despite his stubbornness.

Another practitioner, who was in China in 1999 when the campaign against Falun Gong began, recounted in her witness statement the consternation of her family members in the face of the signed letters she sent to the Chinese government opposing the campaign. In one letter, the practitioner said that, although she had been a Communist Party member for twelve years, she had only pretended to be a good person as part of her social role. After beginning cultivation, however, "I became a good person from my heart because I understood the true meaning of life." Her relatives pointed out to her the many instances when the Communist Party had "failed to respect the opinions of others," but the practitioner sent her letter anyway.

Problems with China and the Chinese campaign against Falun Gong went well beyond family conflicts. One practitioner, Pei Lihua, recounted her return to Shanghai from Canada in October 1999, when the campaign was gaining momentum, to try to help her husband emigrate to Canada to be with her. This initial objective soon fell by the wayside (it was to be several years before her husband would be released from prison and able to join her), and Pei, a quiet, soft-spoken woman, had to learn how to "cultivate nobly" in the face of constant police interference in her life.

Pei returned to a Shanghai where practitioners' telephones were bugged and where many practitioners were followed whenever they left their homes. For Public Security Bureau officials, the priority was to prevent practitioners from traveling to Beijing to engage in public demonstrations and from lodging appeals; many police officers made tacit deals with certain practitioners to leave them in relative peace as long as they carried out their cultivation indoors and did not engage in public demonstrations. For Pei Lihua, it was still quite a challenge to face police surveillance on a daily basis, even if the Shanghai police were not, at this particular moment, engaged in brutality against her. In her own words:

At the end of last October, upon my return to Shanghai, the situation I faced was the following: Because my husband is a Falun Dafa practitioner, we were under surveillance for 24 hours a day, every day. The police waited at the door all day and night and they followed us whenever we were out. Also, our telephone was monitored by the police. We had no freedom of action.

Pei viewed the situation as a test of her cultivation level:

In the beginning, I felt uneasy when the police followed us, and I was afraid whenever I had to speak in their presence. Later on, I experienced a fundamental change.... For example, we told the police not to call us by phone in the morning because that's when we did our exercises. They stopped calling us in the morning. Many of the police [officers] mouthed propaganda to us, but we responded by giving them Falun Gong classes and taking every opportunity to spread the Law. We said openly that Chinese government policies on Falun Gong were entirely incorrect, and that we would not obey them. As my *xinxing* [moral level] improved [as a result of her steadfastness], I came to understand that, properly viewed, what was superficial and what was essential had been reversed. Superficially, we were under surveillance and we did not have freedom. But I could feel in my heart that on the contrary it was those doing the surveillance who did not have freedom: we could study the Law and do the exercises at home while the police stayed outside our door day and night without eating or sleeping. We were advancing in our study of the Law and improving both minds and bodies every day.... the police were playing cards all day long just to kill time.... I finally understood the role that the cultivation environment could play [in the reconstruction of social reality]. Whenever I thought about those police in the hallway eliminating karma for us, I felt blessed.

Eventually, the twenty-four-hour surveillance was canceled, which Pei attributed to her having "passed the test" of cultivating in a difficult environment.

For a practitioner, however, one test leads to another. Pei and her husband realized that the cancellation of the surveillance meant that, practically speaking, they were now free to go to Beijing to demonstrate and to lodge an appeal with the authorities. This is what they decided to do, although Pei remained anxious and unsure of the wisdom of their decision. She had returned to China, after all, to help speed her husband's emigration to Canada; arrest and detention were unlikely to prove helpful.

Their trip to Beijing was a comedy of errors. They couldn't find the appeals office. They wandered around Tian'anmen Square without finding other practitioners. They finally decided to return to Shanghai, and the night before their departure they finally met other practitioners who were registered in the same hotel as Pei and her husband. These new friends were arrested in the night, and Pei was unable to find where they had been taken. She and her husband returned to Shanghai convinced that their cultivation level had not been high enough to pass the tests associated with the battles being waged in China's capital.

After several days of rereading *Zhuan falun*, Pei and her husband departed once again for Beijing, this time in the company of a number of other practitioners. Pei had set aside her worries about her personal safety and her husband's immigration file, and had set her sights on contributing selflessly to the cause of righting the Chinese government's slander of Falun Dafa. Thus, when they arrived in Beijing, they went directly to the appeals office, where they were detained (since no public security official from Shanghai was available for the moment). The police shouted at Pei for having written that Falun Gong was the "orthodox Law" and not a "heterodox religion." She and her group thus had an occasion to practice passive resistance. Later that day, they were transferred to the care of the representatives of the Shanghai Public Security Bureau, and were thus able to witness to yet another group of police officers. They were returned to Shanghai on the following day, under the supervision of yet another group of police. Pei came to realize that the police, despite their role as representatives of an authority which had committed a fundamental error, were nothing more—or less—than ordinary people themselves, who asked the same sorts of questions about Falun Gong as did everyone else. Her conclusion:

I know in my heart that the point of my dealings with the police was to rid me of my attachments . . . of fear and competition [i.e., the idea that she must confront the authorities in the same way as other practitioners, while in fact, a practitioner's responsibility is to the law and not to social pressure]. I required myself to meet the standard of a true cultivator and to maintain a peaceful heart under all circumstances. During the entire experience Master Li's words were always in my heart: "We are not against the government now, nor will we be in the future. Other people may treat us badly, but we do not treat others badly, nor do we treat people as enemies." Looking at my overall experience, sometimes I passed the test fairly well and sometimes I failed. I found that I still have a long way to go compared to those practitioners from other places in China.

Pei was forced to leave China within forty-eight hours of having attempted to lodge her appeal; she did not see her husband again until February 2002, when, as a result of the pressure of the Canadian government and human rights organizations, he was freed from prison in Jiangsu province and allowed to join his wife in Canada.

The problem of how to respond to the Chinese government's campaign against Falun Gong was addressed by many practitioners on a variety of levels. Another practitioner who, like Pei Lihua, was in China at the beginning of the crackdown, spoke of her intense sense of competitiveness vis-à-vis other practitioners who, like her, were seeking the best ways to respond to the campaign. She came to understand that such feelings were unfair to her fellow practitioners and unworthy of true cultivation. As for practitioners outside of China, most expressed disbelief and anger, as well as guilt for being so far from their fellow practitioners in the homeland. Many struggled with feelings of love for their country, and sought to reconcile their patriotic pride with their insistence that this particular policy was dead wrong. This was made all the more difficult by the Chinese government's attempts to label Li Hongzhi and Falun Gong as anti-China and all those who supported them as unpatriotic. One practitioner recounted his anger in the face of China's heavy-handedness and his subsequent decision to join other practitioners in going to Seattle to add the voices of Falun Gong to the antiglobalization movement on the occasion of the World Trade Organization meeting in November 1999 (this was a route many Falun Gong practitioners outside of China came to follow in subsequent months). Another practitioner dealt with his feelings of guilt and ineffectuality by converting himself into a human bulletin board: on his four-hour daily commute to and from work in Toronto, he wore posters on his back and on his stomach with information about Falun Gong and the Chinese government's campaign.

## Conclusion

When Li Hongzhi left China in early 1995, he continued his ministry among a new Chinese diaspora, created since Deng Xiaoping decided to open China to the world. The new Chinese diaspora is made up largely of relatively young, highly educated Chinese who have left the mainland since the mid-1980s and who have been able to integrate themselves readily into the knowledge-based economy, at least in North America, where I have carried out most of my fieldwork. The majority of Falun Gong practitioners outside of China belongs to this group, and Falun Gong in North America—or at least the Chinese members, who make up some 90% of North American practitioners—is thus a bourgeois movement, practitioners being richer and better educated than the average American or Canadian.

In the previous chapter, I sought to read Li Hongzhi in such a way as to reveal why his teachings might be attractive. In the present chapter, I have attempted a similar strategy, seeking in my fieldwork among North American Falun Gong practitioners to understand their view of their practice and its benefits, rather than looking to poke holes in their beliefs. Fieldwork carried out among these practitioners as to the nature of their beliefs revealed a group of people more "normal" than the Chinese government propaganda (which characterized Falun Gong as a "dangerous heterodox sect") might have led one to believe (and more normal as well than one might expect from reading Li Hongzhi's works). Practitioners in North America find in their practice the strength to balance the demands of cultivation, work, family, and politics (since the Chinese state decided to suppress Falun Gong in China). Somehow, their practice enables them to find the moral strength to engage in introspection and self-improvement even as they remain engaged in the world. They have read and reread *Zhuan falun* and other of Li Hongzhi's writings, and are thus aware of his teachings concerning the end of the world, demonic possession, and various supernormal powers associated with cultivation. Many of them believe strongly, as a result of their personal experiences, in the healing power of Falun Gong practice. In the narratives they fashion to share their experiences with one another, practitioners consistently use the language of "tests" or "challenges" which they have to pass or traverse as a part of the teleological obstacle course of life as we know it. Presumably, those for whom Li Hongzhi's teachings are not helpful do not bear witness at experience-sharing conferences nor talk about their failed cultivation with foreign researchers. But I have met, or listened to, many who speak with conviction and quiet, self-reflective dignity of their efforts to live a full, enlightened life.

I would like to be able to compare the results of this fieldwork among Falun Gong practitioners with fieldwork carried out among other members of other redemptive societies, but I know of little comparable research, even among practitioners of other schools of qigong (which would surely reveal interesting similarities and differences). Fieldwork is, of course, impossible in the case of historical examples, and scholars are only beginning to examine redemptive societies in Taiwan or elsewhere in the Chinese diaspora.[34] Perhaps the best I can do at present is to invite future scholars to use my portrait of Falun Gong practitioners as grist for the mill of their comparisons.

# 6

# David Meets Goliath

*The Conflict between Falun Gong and the Chinese State*

This chapter treats the conflict between Falun Gong and the Chinese government. Since the summer of 1999, the suppression of Falun Gong has been a major preoccupation of the Chinese state, which has devoted enormous amounts of time, energy, and money to the destruction of the movement in China and abroad. Within China, literally thousands of books and newspaper articles have been printed denouncing Falun Gong. Chinese television, which is under the complete control of state authorities, has repeated ad infinitum the government's case against the group. Bulldozers have been used to destroy the mountains of Falun Gong paraphernalia confiscated by the police. Foreign anti-cult experts have been invited to China to contribute their "learned analyses" to the study of Falun Gong at international conferences held in major Chinese cities. Outside of China, representatives of the Chinese state have repeated their anti–Falun Gong stump speech on the occasion of important diplomatic meetings, have defended the campaign before various international human rights tribunals, have put pressure on Western political officials (senators, congressional representatives, members of parliament, even mayors of small towns) *not* to support Falun Gong, and have used the power of the Chinese government abroad to spread the campaign against Falun Gong through Chinese-language newspapers and Chinese immigrant associations in North America, Europe, and Australia. Most tragically, the Chinese government has harassed and detained tens of thousands, perhaps hundreds of

thousands, of Falun Gong practitioners in China, has extended this harassment to family members and friends of practitioners, and has imprisoned and
tortured hundreds if not thousands of practitioners. According to Falun Gong
sources, which are generally accepted as accurate by international human
rights agencies such as Amnesty International and Human Rights Watch,
some 3,000 practitioners have died while in police custody or in prison.

The campaign has obviously dominated the lives of Chinese practitioners
in China and around the world as well. Practitioners told me that they long for
the good old days, before the persecution, when they could simply cultivate in
peace without having to worry about how to respond to the crackdown—for
respond they have. Chinese practitioners within China have displayed remarkable (some would say "reckless") courage, demonstrating at Tian'anmen
Square, attempting to appeal the decisions of the Chinese state, and hacking
into cable and satellite broadcasts so as to break the monopoly that Chinese
television has on the representation of the reality of Falun Gong—plus, there
are those who have gone willingly to prison, enduring privation and, on occasion, torture, still holding to their beliefs and spreading the gospel of Falun
Gong to their fellow prisoners and even to prison guards and police officials.
Outside of China, practitioners have set up a number of well-organized Web
sites to allow practitioners around the globe to remain up to date. Others have
translated Li Hongzhi's writings, or gathered evidence on the Chinese state's
campaign against Falun Gong, or written documents making this evidence
available to all interested parties. Others have lobbied political officials in
Washington, Ottawa, Paris, London, and Canberra, hoping to convince Western governments of the need to bring pressure so that the Chinese state will
put an end to its campaign. Others organize locally, distributing flyers,
marching in parades, exercising in public.

Despite the inherent drama of these events, this chapter has not been an
easy one to write. The Chinese government has consistently refused to allow
third-party verification, either of its claims concerning the abuses or "crimes"
allegedly committed by Falun Gong, or of its claims that Falun Gong practitioners who have been incarcerated are well treated. As a result, as a researcher,
I find myself before a mountain of evidence produced by the Chinese state
(much of it extremely repetitive), and a mountain of evidence (equally repetitive) produced by Falun Gong. Both mountains of evidence are full of names,
pictures, and various other "facts," and most Western journalists writing on
Falun Gong have tended to take some "facts" from each pile of evidence in
an attempt to write a "balanced story"—thus producing their own mountain of
"analysis" which, more often than not, is of questionable value (because the
journalist could verify neither the claims of the Chinese state nor the claims of

Falun Gong, which means that the "balanced story" is largely a matter of conjecture or convention).

Although I tend to accept much Falun Gong documentation as trustworthy in its broad outlines, not all of the organization's reports stand up to strict academic scrutiny. Footnotes in such reports, for instance, often cite journalistic accounts which, in turn, cite Falun Gong sources; for Falun Gong practitioners, this is a way to enhance the credibility of their claims by saying, in effect, "Reuters believed us," but the circularity of the chain of evidence remains problematic for the scholar. In addition, such reports often refer to other Falun Gong–affiliated organizations or media without acknowledging that affiliation; a report by the World Organization to Stop the Persecution of Falun Gong, for example, may cite the New Tang Dynasty television network's documentary on the alleged immolation of Falun Gong practitioners at Tian'anmen Square in February 2001, without mentioning that this network was set up largely to propagate the views of Falun Gong among Chinese-speaking audiences throughout the world. In recent years, Falun Gong has multiplied such efforts and is now publishing the *Epoch Times,* a Web- and paper-based newspaper distributed (in limited print runs) freely throughout much of the world, at the same time denying that the newspaper is a "Falun Gong publication" (because the newspaper covers issues other than Falun Gong and employs some non–Falun Gong members). Unfortunately, such denials tend to *diminish* Falun Gong credibility, no matter what the value of the newspaper might otherwise be.

The evidence put forward by Falun Gong concerning the crackdown in China is more convincing than that put forward by the Chinese government. I have spoken personally with practitioners who were mistreated and tortured in China and found their accounts convincing. Moreover, little in Falun Gong documentation suggests outright fabrication of evidence, even if one might quarrel with the organization's handling of that evidence and with the conclusions it draws. And in most of my dealings with Falun Gong practitioners in North America, they have proven themselves to be open and accommodating. This is certainly not true of the Chinese government. If Chinese authorities are telling the truth about the "crimes" Falun Gong committed in China and/or about the conditions of incarceration of Falun Gong practitioners, then all they have to do is open the doors to the prisons and let Amnesty International, or Human Rights Watch, or the independent investigator of their choice find out for themselves. Their consistent refusal to do this strongly suggests that they have something to hide, and this would hardly be the first time.[1]

That being said, there is for the moment no "proof" of the numbers of those tortured and killed in China, or of the means of torture employed, which goes beyond the record produced by Falun Gong practitioners. It is normal and proper that Falun Gong practitioners spearhead the campaign to make known the fate that has befallen their comrades in China. No human rights organization can rival Falun Gong in terms of linguistic skills and contacts on the Chinese mainland. No human rights organization can devote all of its time to a single cause. Falun Gong practitioners can and have done so, and it is to their credit that Western governments and human rights organizations generally accept their work as having been well done, their claims as genuine.[2]

Consequently, this chapter will offer neither a blow-by-blow chronology of the campaign of suppression, nor a case-by-case analysis of the victims of this campaign. Instead, this chapter will examine the events surrounding the Falun Gong demonstration of 25 April 1999, before turning to the question of the state campaign against Falun Gong, focusing particularly on the justification for the campaign—a justification which is less valuable as an analysis of Falun Gong than it is revealing of state attitudes about qigong, religion, and a variety of other topics. A subsequent and much longer section examines Falun Gong responses to the campaign, focusing particularly on Li Hongzhi's statements and on the reactions of diaspora practitioners outside of China.

In terms of the broader arguments developed in this volume, the suppression of Falun Gong is, sadly, precisely the outcome one would have expected; historically, redemptive societies which developed the popularity and visibility to rise to the attention of the state have been targeted for elimination. Part of Falun Gong has survived and has been politicized. We observe in the details of this particular case certain new and interesting wrinkles; the spread of Falun Gong to the Chinese diaspora in the democratic West, for example, has changed—or at least complicated—the relationship between the Chinese state and Chinese redemptive societies, without fundamentally altering state suspicion and hostility. In the activities of Falun Gong practitioners in the diaspora, we note the development of new discourses based on Enlightenment concerns, such as freedom of religion and freedom of speech, and the development of new tools for the advancement of the cause, tools principally connected to the Internet.

Still, the narrative of the denouement has been sadly predictable. As for who was right and who was wrong, Li Hongzhi put his practitioners in danger through his unwise decision to challenge Chinese authorities in late April 1999, and should be held responsible. At the same time, the Chinese state grossly exaggerated the danger Falun Gong represented. Falun Gong was not and is not a "cult" on the order of Aum Shinri kyô or the Solar Temple, and nothing that I have learned about Falun Gong over years of research would lead me to believe that the imprisonment, torture, and death of a single practitioner has been justified. I wish that Falun Gong practitioners and Chinese authorities had been able to read this volume prior to April 1999. Li Hongzhi might have known better than to take on Goliath, and Chinese authorities might have realized that their campaign against David was not worth the effort in terms of time, money, and above all lives. To some extent, it is China's blindness to its own religious history which permitted the qigong boom and its aftermath, the brutal campaign against Falun Gong.

## David Takes on Goliath

It was perhaps inevitable that the strange marriage between the Chinese Communist Party and the qigong movement would end in bitter divorce, for it certainly required exceptional circumstances to bring the two parties together, as chapter 3 illustrated. Yet, even now, it is hard to tell to what extent the campaign against Falun Gong marks the inevitable end of the romance between Chinese authorities and the qigong realm and to what extent Li Hongzhi, as an eccentric qigong master who played his cards badly, brought the campaign on himself and his followers through miscalculation. In any event, a conflict between the authorities and Falun Gong had been brewing for some years, and that conflict is part of a longer history of debate over the place and value of qigong as a whole.

As mentioned in chapter 3, qigong had long had its detractors within China, even during the height of the boom.[3] Some detractors felt that qigong was nothing but an excuse for religious superstition, others argued that qigong masters were no better than gussied-up parlor magicians. Their concerns found their way into local and even national media, but during the height of the qigong movement they were often drowned out by the more vocal enthusiasm of the supportive qigong press, or limited in their circulation and impact by the existence of qigong supporters among high party and government officials. In the late 1980s, however, a number of events came together to strengthen the hand of qigong detractors. In 1988 and 1989, certain well-known qigong masters (including Zhang Baosheng and Yan Xin) proved unable to "emit their qi" in carefully controlled scientific environments (Yan Xin failed in an attempt to destroy a gallstone which had been removed from a patient and placed in a test tube, finally explaining—after two hours—that his powers were only effective on "gallstones which remained inside the body").[4] In early March 1990, Yan gave two qi-enhanced lectures in Shanghai which again proved to be failures; in one of the lectures, a thirty-eight-year-old member of the audience suffered a heart attack while in a trance and died (there is no suggestion that the man was killed by Yan's qi, but there is little doubt that he would have received more-prompt medical attention in a setting where he was *not* surrounded by others who had similarly fallen into trance). Foreshadowing Li Hongzhi's strategy some years later, Yan left for the United States in June of that same year.[5] Zhang Xiangyu, another well-known qigong master, was arrested in 1990 and eventually convicted of "cheating the people."[6] Beginning at roughly the same time, some hospitals (psychiatric and other) reported rising numbers of patients admitted as a result of excessive or improper qigong practice. Nancy Chen, an American anthropologist who did research on psychiatric care institutions in China in the early 1990s, notes that authorities attempted to clamp down on qigong in 1991, checking bookstands for volumes on "unscientific" or "false" qigong and demanding that qigong masters and even practitioners register with authorities.[7]

Despite these developments, efforts by qigong detractors to capitalize on the flagging fortunes of the movement failed to achieve ultimate victory, because high-level supporters of qigong continued to insist that, if there were problems with certain qigong practices and masters, qigong itself remained a recognized national treasure which deserved protection and nurturing, not blind suppression. In March 1994, however, Zhang Zhenhuan, one of the chief defenders of qigong among party and government leaders (see chapter 3) died, removing a major pillar of the high-level qigong establishment. In October of the same year, the Ministry of Civil Affairs ordered the dissolution of the International Federation of Qigong Sciences, an important link in the chain of qigong organizations. The offices of the organization in Xi'an were sealed by the police, and the home of the secretary-general of the organization was searched. This major attack rocked the entire qigong world in China, particularly as it was followed in short order by an internal state council document entitled "Recommendations for Strengthening Our Work in the Popularization of Science," which launched a campaign against "pseudo science." In parallel, Sima Nan, a well-known anti-qigong print and television journalist, argued in books, articles, and documentaries that qigong was nothing more than dime-store magic, and influential intellectuals He Zuoxiu, Zhang Honglin, and Zhang Tongling jointly penned an article published in the *People's Daily* on 2 June 1995, which likened qigong to the feared Aum Shinri kyô sect in Japan. Later that same month, *Southern Weekend*, an important weekly newspaper with a national profile, published the results of the report of the Committee for the Scientific Investigation of Claims of the Paranormal, an American group of scientists and professional magicians who travel the world to verify supposed paranormal phenomena. The group had visited China in 1988 to investigate the claims of qigong masters and had written a highly negative report. Their findings were all the more sensational because they had been suppressed for seven years. In the words of the paper's editorialist: "What have 'superhuman abilities' been able to achieve in the course of sixteen years of research, other than to waste state resources and to introduce chaos into the minds of the people throughout the country?" Yet once again, despite the rising tide of criticism, the remaining supporters of qigong were able to fight a rearguard action and prevent the wholesale condemnation of the movement—though they were forced to concede that magic tricks were hardly the stuff of science (even a highly creative, experimental science like qigong).[8]

Meanwhile, Li Hongzhi emerged in 1992 and scored his first, impressive successes during the same 1992–1994 period, suggesting that more than one trend was afoot. Li sought to finesse the repeated attacks in anti-qigong diatribes on the "magic tricks" of certain qigong masters by characterizing his teachings as qigong "at a higher level." As already mentioned, Li claimed to possess such powers but denigrated them at the same time, rarely—if ever—displaying them during his lectures, and discouraging his followers from pursuing them. In such a manner, he hoped to dodge the bullets fired by Sima Nan and company, as well as to curry favor with high-level supporters of qigong who sought to defend and uphold qigong by agreeing that there were certain "bad apples" in the qigong barrel which needed purging. Li's *Zhuan falun* was on bestseller lists in the spring of 1996.

Still, the anti-qigong criticisms eventually caught up with Li. As early as September 1994, Li told the China Qigong Science Research Society that he would soon end his training sessions and devote his full energies to the study of Buddhism, and he left China in early 1995 out of fear of mounting opposition within some party and government circles. In September 1996, Li had two of his lieutenants in Beijing file for official withdrawal from the CQRS and repeated that Falun Gong would no longer offer training sessions within China. The CQRS accordingly terminated Falun Gong's membership in the umbrella organization in November 1996. Hoping to provide some sort of organizational base for the movement, Li's assistants in Beijing applied for registration as a "social organization," first to the National Minority Affairs Commission, subsequently to the China Buddhist Federation, and finally to the United Front Department. All applications were denied, and Falun Gong was told by the authorities to halt further efforts. In late 1997, Falun Gong wrote to the Ministry of Civil Affairs and the Ministry of Public Security, complying with the regime's wish that it not seek to register as a social organization, and declaring that the Falun Dafa Research Society would immediately cease to exist. The representatives promised to dismantle the Falun Gong organization so that practitioners would henceforth practice only among themselves, as the equivalent of an informal social club.[9] While the full details behind such machinations are lacking, it is nonetheless clear that all was not well between Chinese authorities and Falun Gong.

In addition, Falun Gong fell victim to media attacks during the same period. In June 1996, the influential national newspaper *Guangming Ribao* (Enlightenment Daily) published an article denouncing Falun Gong, condemning *Zhuan falun* as a "pseudo-scientific book propagating feudal superstition," deriding Li himself as a "swindler," and calling on all right-thinking people to join in the arduous fight against superstition.[10] Some twenty major newspapers followed suit, echoing the *Enlightenment Daily*'s criticisms, and on 24 July 1996, the Central Propaganda Department issued an order banning the publication of Li Hongzhi's works.

This was obviously an important challenge, which Falun Gong did not take lying down. Practitioners mounted a letter-writing campaign, flooding the *Enlightenment Daily* and the CQRS with complaints that the media campaign was a violation of the long-standing state policy of toleration of "genuine" qigong. Li Hongzhi added his voice in an Internet commentary dated 28 August, which praised those practitioners who had remained steadfast and chided others who, out of fear, had abandoned the practice or who were tempted to "play politics" with the issue—presumably by lobbying powerful figures or seeking to make alliances with other groups under attack. Foreshadowing the language he would use after the onset of the campaign of suppression, Li called the *Enlightenment Daily* incident a test of practitioners' moral stature.[11]

The results of the practitioners' efforts were mixed. The *Enlightenment Daily* did not back down, nor did the CQRS come to Falun Gong's defense (the two had already parted ways, and the CQRS was willing to sacrifice Falun Gong to try to save the larger movement). At the same time, Chinese authorities did not follow through on the *Enlightenment Daily*'s call for thoroughgoing criticism of Falun Gong, and the ban on Falun Gong publications does not seem to have been enforced consistently. China's leadership thus remained divided on Falun Gong, despite the high-profile attack of June–July 1996, and the movement continued to expand, despite the general anti-qigong mood and the specific attacks on Li Hongzhi and Falun Gong. But the expansion was hardly smooth sailing, and the halcyon days of the qigong boom were clearly over. In January and June 1997, the Ministry of Public Security authorized two nationwide investigations into allegations that Falun Gong was carrying out "illegal religious activities," and then concluded on each occasion that no such problems existed. In July 1998, the same ministry carried out another investigation into charges that Falun Gong was a "heterodox cult," going so far as to authorize the police to infiltrate the Falun Gong network, posing as practitioners so as to gain intelligence, but the outcome again was inconclusive. Moreover, such high-profile figures as Qiao Shi, the former chair of the National People's Congress who had had a long career in public security circles, continued to come to the defense of Falun Gong.

In answer to these repeated investigations and the criticisms they generated in the media, Falun Gong practitioners developed a stance of aggressive response to the media, resulting in some 300 peaceful demonstrations between June 1996 and April 1999. Falun Gong was by no means the only qigong group to protest what it perceived as misrepresentation in the media. The Zhonggong under Zhang Hongbao took some newspapers to court,[12] and Sima Nan told me in a personal conversation that he was careful about going out alone after dark during tense periods of the anti-qigong polemic, as certain qigong masters, stung by Sima's criticisms, were not above hiring thugs to add their fists to their master's qi in an attempt to make Sima see reason. But, to my knowledge, no other group used demonstrations so systematically or so brazenly as did Falun Gong. For example, in late May 1998, the well-known scientist He Zuoxiu appeared on a Beijing television program and denounced Falun Gong as a dangerous practice. According to Falun Gong practitioners who watched the program, the cases that He cited as evidence of the dangers of Falun Gong were erroneous; the people who had been supposedly harmed were not even Falun Gong practitioners, they said. In response, several hundred practitioners proceeded to stage an eight-day sit-in at the Beijing Television station, an act of considerable audacity. The BTV station must be considered the rough equivalent of the *People's Daily* as a mouthpiece for state policy and propaganda.

Any evaluation of the events of 25 April 1999 clearly must take this history of protest into account, and David Palmer argues that the roots of Falun Gong's "militancy" are to be found in this period, protests and demonstrations having become a part of Falun Gong practice, just like reading *Zhuan falun* and doing Falun Gong exercises. My sense is that, while Falun Gong's contentiousness does indeed date to this period, it overstates the case to see protest as having been elevated to a form of cultivation practice; when I was doing fieldwork with practitioners some years later, practitioners (in North America; the situation in China was clearly different) still did not see the two as equivalent and frequently debated the pertinence and even the morality of protests and demonstrations. As is so often the case, we lack sources which would enable us to see past the debates generated by the campaign of suppression. Falun Gong documents addressing the protests prior to 25 April are extremely rare: no practitioner set out to write the history of the movement until after 25 April, and since they were then determined to prove that Falun Gong was not and had never been "political" in its orientation, discussion of dozens or hundreds of sit-ins and demonstrations was clearly inappropriate. Chinese authorities depict the 300 incidents as an organized plot to overthrow the government and replace it with a "theocracy."

It is possible that the practitioners involved in such demonstrations at the time did *not* regard their activities as political, particularly since the word "political," in mainland China, refers narrowly to relations with party authorities and not more broadly to the use of power in the public arena. Falun Gong practitioners, like other qigong enthusiasts, felt that the support they had received from certain high-placed defenders of qigong meant that they had the right to continue to practice and to continue to defend themselves against attacks. Seen in this light, Falun Gong practitioners who demanded the correction or retraction of media reports did not see themselves as engaging in a stark, dangerous fight for "truth" against a unitary state-controlled media. Instead, they felt that the media in question were ill-informed, or under the influence of anti-qigong lobbyists, and practitioners were demanding proper respect for qigong and the policy which defended qigong, rather than demanding a free press. Even the accounts by pro-government critics of Falun Gong fall short of their goal of painting the movement as subversive and dangerously out of control. These accounts invariably strike the tone of the outraged good citizen who can barely contain himself in the face of such reckless behavior, as they recount the names of the newspapers and television stations which have had to endure such assaults.[13] At the same time, and despite the undoubted diligence of the researchers who compiled the list of Falun Gong demonstrations and protests, there is no evidence of broader political intent or of violence; the worst offense that the pro-government critics are able to put forward is that the practitioners "seriously disrupted normal work routines," a charge which hardly seems consistent with the tone of moral outrage. Moreover, even the critics' reports suggest that, in most instances, the newspaper or television station in question relented and either issued a retraction, allowed Falun Gong to present its side of the story, or found another means to address the practitioners' concerns. This is true even in the case of the demonstrations at the television station in Beijing and leads one to believe (or would at least lead practitioners to believe) that media claims concerning Falun Gong were indeed false or exaggerated, that Falun Gong practitioners bargained in good faith, and that the dozens or hundreds of incidents should be understood less as an escalating series of challenges culminating in the Zhongnanhai demonstration, but rather as a series of particular conflicts (reflecting the larger debate on the value of qigong) which were resolved one at a time.

While in hindsight it may appear that Li and his followers were fighting an uphill battle, there had been many twists and turns in the history of qigong and *without* the benefit of hindsight, it was not clear which side was going to win. If Falun Gong managed to stage some 300 protests against media mis-representation over the course of three years with relative impunity, practi-tioners can be forgiven for believing either that such actions had come to be tolerated by the state, or that high-level supporters of the movement continued to exercise considerable influence over Public Security Bureau forces.

The events which immediately preceded 25 April, which constituted the spark which lit the fuse of the larger demonstration, were completely consis-tent with the history of Falun Gong reactions to perceived media misrepre-sentation. He Zuoxiu was once again at the heart of the controversy, having published an article on 11 April 1999 in the Tianjin Normal University's *Young Reader* magazine, in which he argued that young people should not practice qigong, illustrating his case with the same examples he had used in his tele-vision interview in May 1998, which had sparked the important Falun Gong demonstration at the television station. He also compared Falun Gong prac-titioners to the ignorant and superstitious Boxers and denounced Falun Gong for recruiting children in primary school playgrounds.[14] As many as 6,000 Falun Gong practitioners protested the publication of the article and made their discontent known both at the university and at the Tianjin municipal offices. The response of the authorities was to call in the riot police, who reportedly beat an undetermined number of practitioners and arrested 45. When practitioners continued to protest, they were informed that the arrests had been carried out at the request of the central authorities in Beijing and that pressure brought to bear on local authorities in Tianjin would be ineffective.[15]

Li Hongzhi himself arrived in Beijing on 22 April, en route between the United States and Hong Kong, and ultimately Sydney, Australia (where he was to address an experience-sharing conference on 1 and 2 May). Whether Li's stopover was added to his agenda because of the troubles in Tianjin is un-known, but it is impossible to believe that the subject did not come up. Li undoubtedly gave at least tacit consent to the idea of bringing the protest to Beijing, perhaps believing that he still enjoyed enough support from high-level officials—particularly in the national Public Security Bureau—to weather the storm.[16] On the morning of 25 April, some 10,000 Falun Gong practitioners in the capital "spontaneously" gathered outside one of the western gates to Zhongnanhai in an impressive and largely silent demonstration. As in the case of other Falun Gong protests, this one was completely peaceful and nonviolent; the thousands of practitioners collectively limited their consumption of food and drink over the course of the sixteen or so hours of their protest, so as not to overwhelm the capacity of the public toilets, an act of civic conscience rarely witnessed in China—or elsewhere, for that matter.

The practitioners massed around Zhongnanhai were there to lodge an appeal with the highest authorities. This is a "right" with deep roots in Chinese history,[17] which is guaranteed by the Chinese constitution, although the office where such appeals are to be received is *not* at Zhongnanhai—it is hidden, unmarked, on a side street in the south of the city.[18] Many Falun Gong practitioners believe that they were led to Zhongnanhai by public security personnel as part of a plot to incriminate Falun Gong. In any event, most accounts of the events of 25 April acknowledge that Premier Zhu Rongji did emerge from his offices when a sizable crowd began to form, he asked them what they were doing there (and who had sent them), and when informed that they were Falun Dafa practitioners wishing to lodge an appeal, he acquiesced and selected three members of the crowd for extended discussions. According to the account of one of these representatives:

> I arrived at the west entrance of Zhongnanhai at about 7:00 a.m., and I saw several practitioners whom I didn't know arriving one after the other. Everyone remained standing on the sidewalk on the west side of the street, waiting silently to be able to explain the relevant facts concerning Falun Gong to the leading comrades of the Central Committee. At about 8:30 we all suddenly noticed Premier Zhu Rongji, together with some members of his staff, who came out of Zhongnanhai and hurried across the street to the sidewalk where we were standing, and said "What are you doing? Who told you to come here?" Practitioners answered: "We're here about Falun Gong." Zhu replied, "I have already made an official announcement about your problem," to which practitioners responded: "We haven't received it." Premier Zhu then asked for three representatives from among the practitioners to go into Zhongnanhai and explain the situation. Everyone raised his hand, and the Premier himself chose three, of which I was one. We waited in the security area of the west entrance of Zhongnanhai while the Premier arranged for the Deputy Director of the Appeals Office and a high-ranking member of his staff to receive us. I explained the purpose of my coming to Zhongnanhai, which was to demand the liberation of Falun Gong practitioners arrested in Tianjin, the assurance of a proper and lawful environment to pursue Falun Gong cultivation, and the permission to publish Falun Gong literature via normal channels. Having explained these three points, I left.[19]

Despite this report, it seems that the exchange continued until relatively late into the evening (between 9:00 and 11:00 p.m.) and that most of the thousands of Falun Gong practitioners waited patiently and quietly all day long—and much of the evening. The fact that they were allowed to do so—that they were not harassed or dispersed—suggests a cautious response on the part of China's senior leadership, surely reflecting their indecision about what course to take. This indecision was soon to come to an abrupt end.

We can only guess at Li Hongzhi's reasons for authorizing the demonstration outside party headquarters, which must have their roots in some combination of calculation and arrogance. From Li's perspective, his movement had continued to grow in spite of his absence and in spite of sporadic attempts by important forces within China to suppress Falun Gong. Run-of-the-mill practitioners may not have been aware of all 300 Falun Gong demonstrations between 1996 and 1999, but Li surely was, and the fact that Falun Gong seemed to have triumphed more often than not lent his cause, in his eyes, an added air of righteousness and power, understood in both cosmic and earthly terms. As a qigong master and a true believer, Li perhaps could not imagine that China's leaders would turn definitively against qigong. Thus, when Falun Gong practitioners were told that the orders to arrest and imprison the demonstrators in Tianjin had come from Beijing, Li Hongzhi must have decided that the time had come for a showdown. Knowing what we know now, it is clear that this was a deadly miscalculation, but Li must have felt he had the upper hand. He was not the first, nor surely the last, charismatic master of a redemptive society to let his power go to his head.

The events of 25 April mark a turning point in the history of Falun Gong. Up until this date, the history of Falun Gong is part of the broader history of the qigong movement and the relations of this movement with Chinese authorities. As a result of the 25 April demonstration, the Chinese state suppressed first Falun Gong and, eventually, the qigong movement as a whole. Most media and scholarly attention to Falun Gong has focused on the post–April 1999 period, and the campaign of suppression, full of charges and countercharges, violence and brutality, has surely been the most spectacular and most explored part of Falun Gong history. At the same time, much of the discussion generated by the campaign of suppression has been little more than media battles of competing representations, with Falun Gong practitioners and their supporters insisting—rightly, I would say—that their human rights have been violated, and Chinese authorities and their supporters that Falun Gong, as a dangerous "heterodox cult," must be eliminated. For reasons already explained elsewhere, neither of these themes is central to my treatment of Falun Gong. Hence, although I will address human rights and cult issues in passing, I prefer to examine the state discourse condemning Falun Gong, a reassertion of the twentieth-century Chinese state's vision of religion and its place in China which reveals much about the Chinese authorities' recent romance with qigong. A subsequent and much longer section traces the reaction of Li Hongzhi and Falun Gong practitioners to the campaign, a reaction which one must characterize as the inevitable politicization of the movement.

## The Chinese State's Case against Falun Gong

It is hardly surprising that the state reacted precipitously in the wake of the demonstrations of 25 April. The Chinese state is authoritarian, insecure, and concerned about its popular image. Even as they boast about China's economic success story, Chinese authorities cannot ignore the fact that "market socialism" has produced clear winners and losers on the economic front, at the same time eroding many state claims to ideological authority. At the height of the qigong movement, charismatic masters commanded the loyalties of hundreds of millions of Chinese, claiming to work miracles through a combination of traditional Chinese spirituality, upright moral conduct, and manipulation of qi, China's "new science." Although the state sought—with some success and for some years—to co-opt and control the movement, which appeared to stay largely out of politics as traditionally conceived, how could the Chinese state be at ease in the face of a huge, popular movement which considered politics to be largely irrelevant? Insecure authorities can deal with dissent and fear on the part of the population, but being collectively ignored by the people poses a more difficult problem. The pope must feel a similar frustration when compelled to denounce secular humanism.

The Falun Gong demonstration of 25 April catapulted the qigong question to the forefront of state attention *and* strengthened the hand of those who had mistrusted qigong all along. Once Falun Gong (or any school of qigong) came to be viewed in a negative light, it was a *very* slippery slope: the numbers of Falun Gong adherents (whether 60 million or 2 million), the contents of Li Hongzhi's writings, the national (and international) scope of the Falun Gong organization—all were reasons to react and to react quickly.

Between 25 April and 20 July 1999, Chinese authorities put in place the basic pieces of the campaign of suppression, even while suggesting that no such thing was under way. According to James Tong, this delay should be seen less as manipulation and more as an effort by the authorities to accumulate the necessary information about Falun Gong, which had not been a particular focus of Politburo attention prior to the Zhongnanhai demonstration (which would tend to confirm that the 300 Falun Gong demonstrations between 1996 and 1999 had passed largely unnoticed at the highest levels, even if in retrospect they were characterized as an imminent threat to state security).[20] On the evening of 25 April, Jiang Zemin sent a letter to the Politburo expressing his opinion that the Chinese Communist Party would be ridiculed if it could not "defeat" Falun Gong. On 6 June, Jiang gave a "secret" speech in which he labeled Falun Gong the most serious political conflict in China since the student demonstrations of 1989. On 10 June, the first institutional effort in the campaign was taken with the creation (although it remained secret at this point) of what came to be known as the 610 Office (i.e., 10 June), a powerful agency, responsible to no one but Jiang himself, charged with coordination of the campaign against Falun Gong. At the same time, the head of the Party Central Affairs Office and the National Appeals Bureau issued statements on 14 June stating that the people had a right to believe—or not to believe—in qigong and that rumors that an anti–Falun Gong campaign was imminent were false. According to some reports, however, some 3,000 public security personnel spent several weeks between late April and mid-July investigating Falun Gong activities in China and abroad.[21]

On 19 July, however, Jiang announced, at a secret high-level government meeting, his intention to eradicate Falun Gong, and on the following day, arrests of Falun Gong practitioners began, accompanied by confiscation of Falun Gong paraphernalia. The persecution was officially consecrated two days later, on 22 July, when the *People's Daily* published a long article entitled "The Truth about Li Hongzhi," the Ministry of Civil Administration officially banned the Falun Dafa Research Association, and the Ministry of Public Security prohibited Falun Gong practice and the sale or distribution of Falun Gong materials. Chinese Communist Party members were formally forbidden from participating in Falun Gong activities, and 300,000 party members subsequently renounced the practice.[22] In a preemptive strike, Falun Gong leaders in China's armed forces had already been arrested prior to the announcement, and some 5,600 Falun Gong practitioners already had been detained on 20 July.[23] On 28 July, the Chinese Public Security Bureau issued an international arrest warrant for Li Hongzhi and asked for Interpol's assistance in extraditing him and bringing him to justice (Interpol refused). Some attribute Jiang Zemin's determination to crush Falun Gong to his desire not to allow the Falun Gong affair to torpedo his career as the student demonstrations in Tian'anmen Square in 1989 had brought down Zhao Ziyang (a similar fate had befallen Hu Yaobang in early 1987), a determination which prompted his decision to crush Falun Gong rather than to seek a compromise which would not have called for Falun Gong's destruction. In any event, if it is relatively easy in hindsight to imagine alternate courses the Chinese state could have chosen, which might have altered the character of the campaign, the fact that the state did *not* choose those other courses and instead decided to crack down hard is in no way surprising.

Accompanying the policy statements, police directives, and legal strata-gems was a massive propaganda campaign carried out through all of the media at the disposal of Chinese authorities, which produced thousands if not millions of pages of material denouncing Falun Gong. This material tells us less than might be expected about the ultimate motivations of the Chinese authorities in deciding to suppress Falun Gong, but a good deal more about ambivalent elite attitudes concerning qigong, Falun Gong, and popular cul-ture at this juncture in China's development.

The State Discourses

The literature generated by the propaganda campaign against Falun Gong is huge and repetitive; I make no claim to have read everything.[24] The general tone of the campaign was set by publications in leading newspapers and magazines and consisted essentially of evidence of the harm Falun Gong had perpetrated on its followers and a claim that Falun Gong belonged to a category of evil social organizations known the world over as "cults"—which served both to pass judgment on Falun Gong's past activities and to suggest the likely course of future developments were Falun Gong allowed to continue. Although many of the themes set forth by these tone-setting articles are developed more deeply in specialized treatments examined below, it may be helpful to set out the general lines of the state's case against Falun Gong before attempting a more detailed analysis.[25]

Evidence of the harm Falun Gong brought to practitioners consists, in the state discourse, of lists of cultivators who suffered and/or died, either due to failure to treat their medical conditions, as their doctors had asked them to, or due to mental illness brought on by Falun Gong practice. Both types of cases are documented in such books as *The Liar and Cheat Li Hongzhi and His "Falun Gong"*[26] published in September 1999, where the author asserts that 1,404 people had already died as a result of Falun Gong practice, not to mention the thousands who had been physically and mentally handicapped. More specifi-cally, the author provides summary descriptions of 100 presumably repre-sentative cases of those injured or killed by Falun Gong practice.

It is difficult to know what to make of these alleged cases. Many of them are theoretically plausible; a typical plot line concerns an elderly person with, say, high blood pressure, who abandons his medication after taking up Falun Gong cultivation and dies of a stroke as a result. At the same time, the cases raise as many questions as they answer. No information is provided as to how the author amassed his information, and no explanation is provided for why no action had been taken earlier, given that many of the cases pre-date the political problems beginning from the spring of 1999. In addition, certain formulas repeat themselves: "Hu Aiping, a female worker from Taiyuan, Shanxi, once had a happy family. Until, that is, she started practicing Falun Gong with her grandmother in 1996–97, after which she ignored her family, and her health deteriorated."[27] Or:

> Wu Ziming, a peasant living on the outskirts of Bengbu, Anhui, once had a lovely, happy family. His wife Sun Fengling ran a nursery in their home, as their children were already in school. In 1997, Sun went to the Xinhua bookstore to buy books for the children, and while passing the Science Palace, noticed someone practicing qigong and went over to take a look. Someone praised it to her, and from that point forward she became a follower of Falun Gong. Sun Fengling was originally a happy, open person, but once hooked on "Falun Gong" she became less and less talkative. In April 1999 she began to spit up blood, refused treatment and soon died.[28]

The formula here is the happy if naïve person who is hoodwinked by the evil cult. Li Hongzhi and leaders of the Falun Gong organization appear more frequently in these cases than one might have expected, in some cases going to the hospital to convince practitioners that they should not be there. Another puzzling feature is the relatively high number of cases where health problems are said to emerge *during* cultivation activities.

The same book lists 115 cases, drawn from seven medical institutions in Beijing, Tianjin, Hebei, Shandong, and other provinces and municipalities, of Falun Gong practitioners institutionalized because of psychological problems.[29] These cases provide only the bare bones: the patient's surname (the given name is omitted "to protect the rights of the patient"), the number of the medical dossier, sex, age, occupation, educational level, address, institution in which he or she is being treated, date of admission into the institution, chief symptoms, and diagnosis. The patients' symptoms are varied, but include hallucinations, "strange behavior," "confused speech," and insomnia, among many others. The diagnosis is fairly uniform: "psychological problems brought on by cultivation."[30]

The explanation for the evil power of Falun Gong is provided in such articles as the authoritative *People's Daily* editorial of 28 October 1999, entitled " 'Falun Gong' Is Nothing Other than Heterodoxy" (*"Falun Gong" jiushi xiejiao*).[31] The first few sentences set the tone:

Looking back at the past few years, how great Li Hongzhi's "magic powers" have been! In order to achieve objectives which he has been loath to reveal, he has plotted behind the scenes, making all sorts of connections, sending out secret order after secret order, "scripture" after "scripture," so as [to] organize "Falun Gong" practitioners to come together, to surround [media or government buildings], culminating in 10,000 people encircling Zhongnanhai. "Falun Gong" practitioners seem to be possessed by "black magic": they appear when summoned, and disappear with the wave of a hand. Thousands of "Falun Gong" practitioners have suffered family dissolution, mental breakdown, and even death, all the while insisting that they are achieving "consummation of cultivation." Once the truth [i.e., that Falun Gong is a fraud and a cult] was revealed, the "Falun Gong" organization was dissolved, and the vast majority of "Falun Gong" practitioners awoke to their delusion. Yet there remain a minority [of practitioners] who seem possessed by demons, who refuse heartfelt advice, who refuse to see the bloody facts of the matter, and who continue to obey the distant commands of Li Hongzhi, and to sacrifice themselves in order to "protect the Law." What kind of illegal organization can possess this great an evil power [xiejin], this great a power of mind control? The only possible answer is: heterodox cults.

The editorial then goes on to enumerate and discuss the constituent elements of heterodox cults. These include worship of the leader (jiaozhu chongbai), the use of various techniques of mind control (jingshen kongzhi), the creation of heterodox theories (bianzao xieshuo) which include, in the case of Falun Gong, both its theories concerning the end of the world and theories on the health benefits of Falun Gong practice, the making of money (jianqu qiancai), the secrecy of the organization (mimi jieshe), and the intention of damaging society (weihai shehui).

We see in this editorial, as well as in other similar statements, a mixture of traditional Chinese suspicions of unregulated religious or quasi-religious organizations and language and concepts drawn from the anti-cult movement in the modern West. The latter is obvious in such statements as the following:

Since the 1960s and 1970s, many cult organizations have appeared in Western countries, and with their wild activities have created a series of incidents which have shocked the world. Given the social threat they represented, the cries to fight back and suppress the cults have become increasingly insistent. No responsible government will permit cults to injure people's lives, damage social order and stability.

The use of such ideas as "mind control" and "brainwashing" reflects the influence of Western anti-cult literature as well.[32] At the same time, the idea of mind control fits in well with traditional Chinese descriptions of the power of the leaders of "secret sects" to "delude" (*mihuo*) their ignorant followers, although some Chinese commentators on Falun Gong try to make their own contributions to global anti-cult literature, noting for example the use of the Internet to carry out the manipulation of Falun Gong practitioners dispersed throughout the far-flung Chinese diaspora. By contrast, the extreme sensitivity in the Chinese discussion of heterodox cults to the supposed political ambitions of cult organizations seems typically and historically Chinese, although such concerns were brought to the surface anew by the events of 25 April 1999. Chinese authorities are free to cite the cases of Jim Jones and David Koresh, for example, as evidence that cults in general often come in conflict with governmental authorities, but the leap from that assertion to their oft-repeated conclusion that cults the world over "seek to overthrow the government and establish a theocracy" is questionable on empirical grounds and is more a reflection of the imperial *and* modern Chinese state's fear of any unsupervised social mobilization, as well as the state's paranoid tendency to impute political motives to any group it dislikes.

Subdiscourses within the larger anti–Falun Gong propaganda campaign include the following: international comparisons between Falun Gong and cult activities throughout the world; historical comparisons between Falun Gong and similar organizations in China's past; discussions of Falun Gong from the point of view of science and the popularization of science; discussions of Falun Gong from the point of view of religion; and discussions from the point of view of qigong. In terms of the forms in which this literature has been presented, two predominate. One is the propaganda manual, which selects and reprints pertinent documents, including laws, official statements, and right-thinking articles from authoritative newspapers and journals, so that those charged with suppressing Falun Gong will be well-armed. The other form might be called the journalistic exposé. These exposés build on the tradition of *baogao wenxue*, "reportage literature," which rips the veil off Li Hongzhi to reveal the sordid truth—but in this case they seem to possess none of the independence of spirit or vision we often associate with Liu Binyan and other creators of the genre.[33]

This chapter will examine the following subdiscourses, as they are illustrative of contradictions and ambiguities in the state's campaign: criticisms from the point of view of religion; criticisms from the point of view of qigong; and some aspects of the criticisms of the journalistic exposé literature. The discussion will focus on both what is condemned and what, by implication, is affirmed.

Criticisms of Falun Gong from the Point of View of Religion

Authorities in the field of religious studies were called upon to distinguish clearly between cults and religions and, as authorities, to analyze the nature of cults, in particular the nature of Falun Gong. Some articles in this subdiscourse are relatively straightforward. Wei Daoru, for example, contributed a piece entitled " 'Falun Gong' Is Absolutely Not Buddhism," in which he argues that Li Hongzhi invented his "Buddha Law" through cheapening and attacking traditional Buddhism, in order to delude his followers. Li Hongzhi, according to Wei, distorted Buddhist teachings in order to cheat his followers and to deify himself; he has spread the erroneous idea of "karmic retribution" to delude people, to dissuade people from seeking medical help, and to damage society.[34] The author does not appear to be particularly knowledgeable about Buddhism, but rather has simply chosen the stance of indignant anger in the face of Li Hongzhi's slander of Buddhism, which is affirmed by implication. Another, similar article, entitled " A Buddhist commentary on Li Hongzhi's nonsensical statements regarding 'karma'," simply notes that many Buddhists have denied Li Hongzhi's claims to belong to the Buddhist school and then goes on to point out various misuses Li makes of Buddhist terminology.[35] Other articles defend Daoism in the same way and illustrate that Li has deviated from or misinterpreted "orthodox" Daoist theories.

More interesting are articles of a more general nature, such as the dozens with titles like "Cults Are Not Religion," the goals of which are to establish the precise boundaries between the two phenomena. Here, the discussion of cults is not particularly interesting, as it repeats what we find in *People's Daily* editorials and other authoritative statements. What is more interesting is the depiction of religion, the perfectly acceptable social phenomenon from which cults in general and Falun Gong in particular have deviated. For example, Feng Jingyuan, of the Institute of World Religions at CASS, notes in his authoritative paper entitled "Cults Are Not Religion"[36]:

> Religion is a universal social and cultural phenomenon in the history of mankind, the product of the development of the forces of social production to a certain point. Religion has a long history and a broad and deep influence. To speak of the five great religions in our country—not only do they have a history of more than one thousand years, a varied and rich temple architecture, large numbers of believers and religious professionals, but they also possess a complete system of religious beliefs and theories, built out of their writings

and teachings, thus forming a religious cultural system with the religious ideology at its core and as its guiding direction. In such a manner [proper religions] become an important organized aspect of the culture of mankind, serving as a form of identity and practice, carried forward by culture, for the religious believers. This is one of the reasons that these religions have survived for thousands of years down to the present day.[37]

Feng goes on to defend all religions, even new religious movements (*xinxing zongjiao*), which is a new departure, and their right to assume a critical role in modern society:

As a subsystem within a social system, contemporary religions, whether they be traditional religions or new religious movements, are all well adapted to society. In general, they attempt to provide social relief, protect the country, and aid the people, they respect discipline and obey the law, so that their activities can all be carried out within legal boundaries. As a cultural system, they have absorbed much spiritual wealth from the history of mankind, becoming an important organized aspect of traditional culture, and a way of life for many religious believers. These religions serve to harmonize and balance out many social forces, thus serving as a force helping to assure social stability. The positive elements in religious teachings, the moral resources they bring together, have a certain positive significance in the construction of society's material and spiritual civilization. Religious believers, as masters of society, will contribute to the development and progress of society. It is true that as an independent world view, or view of human life, or perspective on society or values, different religions can criticize society from a variety of angles or propose improvements to those who manage society; their goals are to improve society, to help it to progress. Even if some social forces use religion to endanger society, the reason for this lies with those using religion to cause trouble, and not with religion itself.[38]

Another author, Zhao Kuangwei, continues in this vein in his paper "Preaching That the End of the World Is Near Is the Common Feature of all Cults,"[39] arguing that even the millenarian themes found in mainstream religions are perfectly acceptable:

Traditional religions' theories about the end of the world were simply a description and a belief concerning the very end of the world, and all of these had two clear characteristics: 1. all of their theories [*zhuzhang*] about the end of the world were connected to the present day, in the sense that those who had performed well in the present life, those who had been good, would receive a good result, while those whose performance had been bad would be punished; 2. the end of the world was seen to be a distant, future event, and people were unable to predict when it would occur. These millenarian theories were always linked to efforts on the part of these religions to urge people to be good and to oppose evil—it was part of a whole. For this reason, this kind of theory of the end of the world was an organized part of religious teachings designed to encourage good and to punish evil. This had a positive function.[40]

Cults, on the other hand, distort and misuse these otherwise positive orientations in preaching that the end of the world is coming tomorrow. And unlike traditional religions, cult doctrine is nothing but a "hodgepodge" of superstitious elements—and not a "complete system."

The point is not that these scholars are unconvincing as historians of world religions—none of which began as a "complete system" and many of which have suffered schisms and revolts growing out of divergent understandings of end-times and the proper posture of the church toward the end of the world. The point is rather that these scholars appear to be unconvinced Marxists and modernizers. Religion as the "opiate of the masses," part of the ideological superstructure of repression, to be swept away by the modernizing forces of science and revolution has given way to religion as a force for social order. Of course, "proper" religions have had their place in elite visions of modern China since the early twentieth century, as noted earlier in this volume. But the emphasis on religion (and, particularly, certain new religious movements) as a positive force for social stability is new to the reform era.[41]

## Criticisms from the Point of View of Qigong

During the first few months of the anti–Falun Gong campaign, the fate of the rest of the qigong movement was unclear, and it was not until the following summer (2000) that other qigong groups were quietly shut down. The fact that qigong survived this long in the face of the vitriol heaped on Falun Gong, whose roots were unmistakably in the qigong movement, is testimony to the immense popularity qigong had enjoyed among the country's intellectual and political leadership. The critique of Falun Gong from the standpoint of "real" qigong is revealing of the degree to which Chinese authorities invested in this aspect of popular culture during the qigong movement—and after.

One book, *Huashuo liangong zouhuo rumo*, which might be translated as "Let's Talk about Problems of Deviation in Qigong Cultivation," symbolizes the ambivalent attitudes of authorities on this front. The main author is Zhang Tongling, a medical doctor and professor at the Institute of Mental Health at the University of Beijing, who wrote the book with the help of a journalist, Xu Hongzhu, on the basis of her experiences with a clinic she set up to treat qigong deviation in 1989.[42] Since Falun Gong was not in existence in 1989, many of the problems treated have to do with other forms of qigong, and the book is *not* a blanket condemnation of Falun Gong, but rather a discussion of problems with qigong practice in general. The book is folksy and meant to appeal to the general reader; it is part of a series called "Mr. Democracy's Tea House" initiated by the Hunan People's Publishing House to carry forward the spirit of the May Fourth movement in the face of the return of superstition in the reform era. Thus the book also belongs to the category of popularization of science. The table of contents lists the following chapters, providing a general idea of the scope of *Huashuo liangong zouhuo rumo*:

1. Have you seen patients suffering from psychosis as a result of improper qigong practice?
2. Qigong deviation is the same thing as *zouhuo rumo*[43]
3. Science and superstition in qigong practice
4. What is the feeling of qi?
5. Can obsession with exterior qi lead to psychoses?
6. Hallucinations have nothing to do with supernormal powers
7. One should not fast
8. Prevention and treatment of psychoses caused by improper qigong practice

On reading the book, one is struck immediately by the bizarre disconnect between the seriousness of the issues under discussion—the subject matter has to do with psychoses and suicides, for example—and the chatty, occasionally comical (even *intentionally* comical) presentation of the issues. One example of this is the cartoons employed in the book, which are drawn in such a way as to be amusing—someone who didn't read Chinese would immediately assume that these were meant to make one laugh—while the captions are not. One cartoon shows a family—woman, man, and daughter—involved in some sort of struggle, and the captions read:

MOTHER   You're not my husband and daughter, you're just pretending to be [suggesting that they are demons of some sort masquerading as her family].

DAUGHTER   Dad. Mom's lost it [*zouhuo rumo*] and she's biting people![44]

Then one notices that there is blood dripping from all three people and a book on the floor with the title "Fake Qigong." In the text, we find the story of a middle-aged woman, who under the spell of an excessive or incorrect qigong practice, began to dance and sing excitedly, then suddenly grabbed a vegetable knife and started whacking away at family members, wounding her husband's shoulder and her child's hand.

In another example of this anomalous tone, the authors are listing and describing the common symptoms of qigong deviation, and they arrive at number five, "unusual behavior." Under this category, they provide some amazing and grisly cautionary tales. One example is that of a woman who heard a voice telling her she could fly, so she immediately went to the window and prepared to jump; happily, she was restrained by family members. Another example is that of a Falun Gong practitioner who tried to open a hole in her head to let the heavenly eye out. But the authors then conclude the grisly paragraph with what is obviously meant to be a humorous example: that of a practitioner who attempted to stay tuned into his *gong* even during meal times so as to know which strand of noodle to eat first.[45] It is difficult to know why the authors would mix comedy and tragedy so haphazardly unless the goal is, once again, to gloss over the highly ambivalent character of her discussion of qigong and qigong deviations.

Turning now to the contents of the book, the basic argument is that qigong is a good thing, part of ancient wisdom which can heal illness and contribute to general physical and emotional well-being, but which, if misused or abused by the wrong people, can morph into something extremely dangerous—perhaps like nuclear power. The goals of this book and of others like it are to defend proper qigong practice, to provide it with a scientific basis and explanation—but also to provide examples and illustrate the dangers of bad qigong practice. For the purposes of this analysis, what is interesting is less the scientific explanation and defense of qigong—which should eventually be given its due—and more the curious lacunae in the explanation of why bad qigong does such bad things to you.[46] More directly, even a nonbeliever may understand the benefits of qigong in the same way as one understands the benefits of any program of meditation or physical/mental exercise which reduces stress and/or recenters the body and mind.[47] It is less easy to understand the power of bad qigong to make one jump out a window. What is not being said—or emphasized, in any case—in these texts is the notion that superstition is not just the absence of scientific knowledge; superstition is black magic, and it plays the same role in this discourse as the devil did in texts from Puritan New England about witchcraft. The converse of this, that science is white magic, may be equally true—which may help to explain the enthusiasm generated by qigong's scientific claims.

The best way to convey this is to paraphrase the chapter on "Science and superstition in qigong practice," the key chapter for our present purposes.[48] The chapter begins by noting that qigong is good for health and is welcomed by the masses. And yet one should be careful, indeed vigilant, as qigong deviation is everywhere. This means that a practitioner must be scientific in his practice of qigong, just as he is scientific in other aspects of his life. To be scientific, one must first be clear about the conditions under which qigong practice can produce deviations, and avoid improper methods, improper lengths of practice time, and qigong practices which do not fit one's individual psychological or medical needs. Here, the authors go on at some length, in the tone of a personal trainer or nutritionist discussing not only proper nutrition and exercise, but also anabolic steroids and other banned—if potentially useful—substances. Then we arrive at bad qigong:

> No matter what, you must not choose *gongfa* [qigong methods] which
> are full of superstition, because those *gongfa* are suitable for no
> one, and indeed we can call them the dregs of qigong. If we blindly
> believe such things, then there is an extremely great chance that
> there will be deviations and mental problems. Think about it· in the
> qigong process, practitioners are receiving large amounts of feudal
> superstition—gods, devils, fox spirits and the like. With such mes-
> sages repeatedly stimulating your brain, it is very easy for some
> people to lose their minds.[49]

Several frightening examples follow, after which the authors take up their general narrative again:

> One has to pay attention as well to the suitability of qigong practices.
> Some people in their qigong practice overuse their intentionality
> [*yinian*], determined to see results from their practice. They refuse to
> let things develop naturally; and in this way deviation can readily
> occur. This is especially true for those who are intent on going up the

levels, growing their *gongzhu* [literally, gong pillar, a measure of one's success in qigong practice], setting sights on "supernatural powers."[50]

Another study offers a more historical account of qigong and "fake qi-gong," but winds up suggesting that similar powers inhere in superstitious practices:

> Between the 1950s and the 1970s, qigong was basically limited to the medical realm. However, the qigong of the qigong boom was not "real." It went way beyond the medical realm, becoming com-pletely "shamanized" and "deified." Fake qigong became the model of fake science, it was in fact an outpouring of feudal superstitious activity. In the midst of this boom, many qigong masters were out to make their names, to gather followers through preaching qi, and to make money. To achieve these goals, they carelessly exaggerated the function of qigong, and shamanized and mysticized qigong. Some masters even wrapped qigong up in scientific language, saying that they were "human science," and had "supernormal powers." In order to falsely win followers' trust and adoration, they purposely made things out to be mysterious, and talked about religion and theology, recruiting and cheating all over the place, so that many practitioners experienced qigong deviations [*zouhuo rumo*], lost their mental health, in some cases even their bodies were handicapped or injured.[51]

Here again, the curious anomaly is the attribution of nefarious power to something which has been declared to be fraudulent, which from one per-spective looks like overdosing on placebos. One cannot go much further with this line of argument, because I am essentially arguing from the lacunae, from the absence of argument in the texts under examination. But when we turn to the final category of criticism of Falun Gong, we find other evidence suggesting a similarly unexpected ambivalence on the subject of the powers of qigong and qigong masters.

## Criticisms from the Journalistic Exposé Genre

In this literature, what stands out is the excessive—almost *obsessive*—character of the smear campaign against Li Hongzhi himself and the contradictory or ambivalent nature of much of the criticism. The most interesting part of the smear campaign in this regard was that inspired by Li's autobiography, issued as part of his "coming out of the mountains" in the early period of Falun Gong activities. As noted in chapter 4, the autobiography is a remarkable document, recounting Li's supposed spiritual evolution under the guidance of great Daoist and Buddhist masters—and looks very much like similar biographies of spiritually gifted individuals from imperial times. What is interesting is that the anti–Falun Gong campaign did not simply reject this document and its claims out of hand as ridiculous, but decided to investigate—or to at least claim to investigate—apparently tracking down people who knew Li Hongzhi during his youth to find out their impressions of the precocious young master. As already noted, authorities claimed to have interviewed the midwife present at Li Hongzhi's birth, Li's elementary school teachers, and musicians who had played with Li in various ensembles. They also interviewed friends and acquaintances, none of whom reportedly recalled having seen Li Hongzhi practice any sort of cultivation. Investigators also noted that none of his relatives, friends, or classmates had ever heard of the Daoist and Buddhist masters with whom Li's autobiography claims that he studied. ("According to our research, there is no Master Quan Jue, Baji zhenren, or Zhen Daozhi [the names of the masters claimed in Li Hongzhi's autobiography] in Jilin or Inner Mongolia.")[52]

Despite the authors' sneering sarcasm, one cannot help but feel that, in taking seriously Li Hongzhi's claims, in running down the leads suggested by Li's obviously fanciful biography, the authors backhandedly suggest that if Li Hongzhi is not who he claims to be, he could have been, or someone else could be. The very fact of searching for (or claiming to search for) Daoist and Buddhist masters in Jilin and Inner Mongolia suggests that the search is not necessarily pointless—that the claims to have studied with such people are not beyond the realms of credibility. By suggesting that Li Hongzhi was too poorly educated to have produced the great theories he has claimed to produce, they suggest by implication that someone better educated might have been able to do just that. By tracking down the midwife who was present at his birth and by talking to his childhood friends, classmates, and teachers, the smear campaign smacks of pathetically desperate efforts to exorcise this evil from China's midst rather than scientific efforts to expose a fraud. Was it pressure from higher authorities to mount as much evidence as possible against Li Hongzhi which accounts for the tone of the document? Or did the authors perhaps choose to meet qigong practitioners and the "broad mass of superstitious Chinese" on their own-playing field? In any case, the overall tone of this literature suggests an apostate, a disappointed true believer who has now turned against his former master, and the diatribe against him suggests that, although he is not the one, the messiah might still come.

In sum, alongside the predictable reassertion of the modern Chinese state's discourse on religion, we find in the case against Falun Gong many vestiges of the exceptional enthusiasm for qigong, when even state authorities and members of China's elite, unaware of qigong's religious (or superstitious) roots, willingly participated in a genuine mass spiritual movement. The repeated strident denunciations of the movement and its founder seek to erase the complicity between the state and qigong enthusiasts and smack, in part, of denial. The roots of this denial are to be found, once again, in the ignorance of China's ruling elite toward China's own religious heritage. It is ironic that denunciation of Falun Gong may be accompanied by a somewhat warmer embrace of "proper" religion, but this embrace is fully consistent with the religious policy of the modern Chinese state since the early twentieth century and once again postpones a genuine encounter with China's religious reality.

## Li Hongzhi and Falun Gong in the Spotlight

Whatever Li Hongzhi's original intentions may have been in authorizing the 25 April demonstration, and however the practitioners participating in the demonstration may have understood their individual actions, Falun Gong was now destined to be seen as political. No matter how Li Hongzhi backtracked, no matter what spin practitioners brought to their explanations, a demonstration of 10,000 people outside the gates of the central authority translates as a challenge to that authority, and a challenge to authority can only *not* be political if the authority responds adroitly to the challenge and defuses the issue, allowing the challenger to change the nature of his message. This, China's authorities did not do, which in turn politicized Falun Gong practice and practitioners, particularly in China, but to some degree throughout the world. According to some sources, at least some Chinese authorities were open to the idea of allowing Falun Gong practice at home, in secret, but many practitioners seem to have seen this option as tantamount to a renunciation of their faith, and Li Hongzhi called on his followers to withstand the test of persecution. The following section follows the Falun Gong response to the campaign of suppression, tracing the politicization of the movement, a politicization which occurred in fits and starts and even against the will of many practitioners who continued to hope, vainly, to remain both loyal, patriotic Chinese and faithful followers of Li Hongzhi.

In the weeks immediately following the 25 April demonstration, Li Hongzhi attempted to engage in a "dialogue" of sorts with Chinese authorities, a dialogue carried out through his statements to journalists and on Falun Gong Web sites (there were perhaps also more direct exchanges between Li and Chinese authorities, as he had previously enjoyed the support of highly placed officials in the Public Security Bureau, but I am not privy to these). Although this dialogue produced no positive results and Li subsequently disappeared from public view for over a year, it is nonetheless important to examine what Li said during this period, as it is revealing of his motives in launching the 25 April demonstrations, and his statements also set the tone—to some degree—for Falun Gong responses later on.

In fact, it is what Li Hongzhi does *not* say during these few weeks that is most striking: he does not mention that he was himself in Beijing on the eve of the demonstration, having stopped en route between the United States and Australia. He does not say that he was *not* in China, but he repeats several times that he was in transit when the events occurred, and that he first learned about them on arriving in Australia. Especially since, later, even Falun Gong sources admitted that Li was in Beijing on 24 April—without acknowledging or even discussing his role in the organization of the demonstration on the following day—it is difficult to interpret Li's omission as anything other than an effort to deny both personal responsibility and the organized character of the events. It may be true that Li's lieutenants in Beijing had already put all but the finishing touches on preparations for the demonstration before Li arrived. It may be true as well that Li and his advisors decided that it would be more effective to present the demonstrations as a sort of spontaneous outpouring of "practitioner power" instead of as the execution of the will of a charismatic leader. But it is impossible to believe that Li Hongzhi left Beijing on the morning of 25 April unaware that big events were brewing.

Li's explanation of the events underscores the supposedly spontaneous nature of the movement and underplays any strategic intent its organizers might have had. In Li's retelling, practitioners had been provoked by a "small number" of officials in the Public Security Bureau which, he insisted, should be seen as one "arm of the state" among many, and not as the state itself. These officials had abused their powers and had violated state policy concerning the protection of qigong; consequently, Falun Gong practitioners had the right and the responsibility to bring such matters to the attention of the government. Whatever the merits of Li's argument, the reader cannot but be struck, once again, by what is *not* explained: why did the practitioners target Zhongnanhai, and why and how did so many people gather there? Responding to reporters' inquiries, Li was evasive:

Our posture is very clear. We did not oppose the government, we did not organize a demonstration or a march, we were not overzealous in our management of this matter, all we did was report [to state authorities] on the situation. You felt like going [to Zhongnanhai], I felt like going—the numbers started going up. If only 10,000 out of a 100 million went, this hardly even counts, and I would say that if anything, the number was too small! If we had wanted to make a big deal out of it, if we had wanted to be "overzealous," then I think there would have been more than 10,000. But even then, you can't say that just because a lot of people go to express their opinion that this is wrong. Asking questions of the leadership, this is every citizen's duty, his responsibility, his right, am I wrong? No, I'm not wrong. We do not oppose the government, we do not involve ourselves in politics, but at the same time we consciously protect our country's law on this point, am I not right? No matter where we are, we are good people. This is how I see the situation.[53]

In other words, the 10,000 or so practitioners who presented themselves at Zhongnanhai should be seen as a *small percentage* of the total mass of Falun Gong practitioners and not a *large group* of demonstrators. As for the question of the organization of the event, Li simply said that practitioners had learned about it from the Internet (without specifying who put the word on the Internet) or from friends. Again, even if in moments of revolution or social crisis, very large groups can gather seemingly spontaneously, it seems hard to take Li Hongzhi at his word, and his explanations ring false—or at best incomplete.

Li is unconvincing because he is trying to deny the political character of a demonstration which by its very location and object was inevitably destined to be interpreted as political, no matter what the "true" motivations of Li and his followers may have been. It is difficult to gauge Li's sincerity on this question. At some places in his remarks, he strikes a vaguely threatening tone, talking about the vast numbers of Falun Gong practitioners and how it is natural that the government be nervous in the face of such numbers. He explains his own absence from China in similar terms, noting that he had decided to "remove the pressure" from the government by establishing himself abroad (and here, Li had to know that Chinese authorities were aware that he had been in Beijing and would certainly say to themselves "and look what happens when Mr. Li returns"). Elsewhere, he implicitly raises the flag of "people power" in invoking the rights and responsibilities of both leaders and led (even as he categorically denies any connection to the 1989 student movement).In another passage, he suggests, again in a way that seems vaguely threatening, that he has at best limited control over his imperfect followers: "The most frightening thing is to lose the loyalty of the people's hearts. To tell the truth, Falun Gong cultivators are still in the process of cultivating; they are still ordinary people. In the face of injustice, I don't know how long they will be able to endure. This is what worries me the most."[54] This is particularly inflammatory when compared to statements Li made to cultivators during this period, which clearly distinguish them from ordinary people and congratulate them for their achievements.

At the same time, Li often seems more naïve than calculating. He insists over and over that practitioners are good people who obey the law and the government. Their hearts are pure, and they have something to offer:

> People keep asking themselves: how did the practitioners suddenly come out of nowhere and then leave so abruptly? How is it that they were so disciplined? In fact, this is not the right way to look at it. When a person knows how to be a good person, he knows how to handle everything. People in today's society have a hard time understanding this. Leaders throughout the world continually ask themselves: "Why is society so troubled? There are religious problems, racial tensions—how can I manage all this disorder?" Then they pass laws which focus on a particular symptom, without recognizing that even if one symptom is relieved, others will emerge which may be even worse.... In fact, the root cause is that people's hearts are no longer good. If people have a good heart, then everything else will take care of itself. But nowadays, no one seems to recognize this. How could Falun Gong practitioners [present themselves spontaneously and disappear abruptly]? Because their hearts are good. There was no organization. The practitioners all have jobs. Every day, they get up early to do their exercises and they read their books when they have the time. When you try to reproach them, you find that they have done nothing wrong. Genuine practitioners require no organized base.[55]

The following exchanges between Li and reporters reveal the same naïveté; Li has changed character overnight, from a spiritual leader to the leader of a group which the Chinese government can only see as dissident. Li does not seem to have given much thought to the implications of this transformation:

> REPORTER: What are your opinions concerning the practitioners' presentation of the facts to the government and the consequences of such a presentation?

MASTER LI:    The practitioners hadn't considered the consequences. As citizens, they just wanted to present the facts and let the higher authorities know. It was as simple as that....

REPORTER:    You mentioned that today's society is evil. The Chinese government has tried to undermine [Falun Gong]....Is the Chinese government an evil force?

MASTER LI:    I don't think about it that way. I am only saying that the actions taken by the Public Security Bureau were not right; they don't represent the government. It was just a few individuals doing wrong deeds, abusing their position and their power.

REPORTER:    Suppose the good deeds as you see them are in conflict with the laws, morality, or the tolerance level of the Communist Party, then what situation will you face?

MASTER LI:    There is no such problem. This issue doesn't exist.

REPORTER:    Do you mean that the good deeds you refer to and the current Chinese government...

MASTER LI:    The standard of a good person is the same no matter where you go; whatever he does, he thinks of others and for others. I think this kind of person is considered to be good anywhere in the world.

REPORTER:    This is your view. How about the view of the Communist Party? From the viewpoint of officials, for example, to maintain the social order they will kill people, they will imprison people, such as your disciples. What happens if you encounter such a situation?

MASTER LI:    First of all, practitioners will never go against the law. In terms of the scenario you described, I don't think it will happen. The Chinese government will not treat their people like that.

REPORTER:    It depends on how you define "people." My understanding is that Chinese officials judge right or wrong according to their own will, not according to others' wishes, nor according to the will of Falun Gong. As such, what is your attitude and your advice to your followers if your standard of right and wrong conflicts with that of the Chinese government?

MASTER LI:    How the government treats me or Falun Gong is the government's business. We cannot mind the government's business. But I feel that what I have done is worthy of the country, the government and the people. It is all right as long as I am worthy of all the people in the world.[56]

As we all now know, Li Hongzhi's calculations were decidedly wrong, and neither his swagger nor his naïveté won him points with Chinese leaders, who chose to view the events of 25 April as a major challenge to party and state authority. Following a brief period of verbal jousting between Li and the Chinese state in June and July 1999, Li's response to the onset of the suppression campaign in late July was to disappear for more than a year (although he did, as already noted, maintain infrequent "virtual" contact with his followers via the Internet).

## Practitioners Front and Center

The next period in the record of Falun Gong's response to the Chinese state's campaign of suppression is that between July 1999 and October 2000, a period defined necessarily by Li's absence. This period was crucial to the evolution of Falun Gong. Prior to the events of 25 April, Falun Gong had been largely unknown outside of qigong circles, and most Falun Gong practitioners had been unaware of any looming problems between their spiritual movement and the Chinese state. Practitioners' lives prior to 25 April were thus defined largely by their spiritual quest and by their efforts to balance their spiritual practice with the demands of their work and family lives. Most were certainly as shocked by the events of 25 April as were China's party and state leaders. They had no special preparation for the challenges now thrust upon them and had no advance warning that their spirituality was about to take on a political coloration.

Li Hongzhi's absence during this crucial period could have paralyzed the movement, but it did not. Instead, in Li's absence, most practitioners (among those who remained committed to the movement) felt that they must take personal—and collective—responsibility for the defense of the faith and its good name. This was the period in which I carried out my most intensive fieldwork among North American practitioners, and I was constantly impressed by their energy, their sense of commitment, and their eagerness and ability to work together to achieve common goals (something I had *not* often observed in China, despite having spent some four to five years there over the course of the 1980s and 1990s). The largely self-directed, self-motivated initiatives undertaken by practitioners between the summer of 1999 and the fall of 2000 are as much a part of the Falun Gong response to the Chinese state's campaign of suppression as Li Hongzhi's doctrinal statements, even if such initiatives were decentralized, uncoordinated, and dispersed in time and space—and thus more difficult to study and analyze.

Within China, the reality of the new era for practitioners was that their practice had been demonized and declared illegal. While many practitioners responded to this turn of events by discontinuing public practice of Falun Gong, others refused to accept what to them was a manifest injustice and a transparently false depiction of their spiritual practice. Such practitioners chose to protest—or to "appeal," in the language chosen by practitioners—in a manner largely consistent with the tradition of Falun Gong activism, even if state and party hostility to Falun Gong had now changed the larger context in crucial ways. And since the condemnation of Falun Gong, at least from July 1999 onward, was a national policy, many Falun Gong practitioners brought their protests to the symbolic center of the Chinese nation, to Tian'anmen Square, although local appeals and protests were numerous as well.

Without access to the archives of the Public Security Bureau in China, we will never have the final word on these appeals—their numbers, motivations, organization. As is true for so much surrounding Falun Gong, most of our sources come from Falun Gong members who claim to have participated in these appeals and who recorded their experiences to share with other practitioners. Such texts appear in great number as "Eyewitness Accounts" on the Clear Wisdom Web site, under the rubric "The Persecution."[57] Helpfully, the Web site also makes available past postings beginning from January 2000. Although there is no way to verify the accuracy of all of these accounts, I tend to accept them as largely genuine for the following reasons. First, some accounts are more verifiable than others. For example, documents prepared by Montreal practitioners Lin Jinyu and Zhu Xueye appear on the Web site. I have personally interviewed both of these individuals, who returned to China in late 1999 or early 2000 to add their voices to the appeals launched by fellow practitioners in China, and I found their stories both compelling and believable. Nor is my research an isolated case: Ian Johnson's Pulitzer Prize–winning reporting on the fate of Falun Gong practitioners in Weifeng, Shandong, found confirmation in voluminous materials available on the Clear Wisdom Web site. According to Johnson's book, he went to Shandong and interviewed many of the practitioners—and relatives of practitioners—in question.[58] To my mind, this is as close to confirmation as we are likely to come. I have, moreover, spoken with many other practitioners in North America who have either participated themselves in such appeals or who know family members or fellow practitioners who have done so. What I learned in interviews conforms both in broad outline and in detail with the reports available on the Web. We have no way of knowing to what extent the editors of the Web site intervene to impose a common experience on practitioners; the editors are practitioners too, and may well have a greater commitment to the "truth" as understood by a practitioner (or by the movement) than to the integrity of a particular document they might receive. On the other hand, if the reports are fabricated or altered, the editors (as well as practitioners in general) have done a stunning job, for there are thousands of such accounts, which again largely accord with statements one can easily solicit in person from any number of practitioners outside of China. Some may find me naïve, but I have a hard time believing that a conspiracy involving so many people, so widely scattered throughout the world, could achieve such consistent and convincing results. My conclusion is that the accounts found on the Clear Wisdom site are largely credible, even if we have no way of verifying all of the accounts in detail.

These accounts present the appeals "movement" as spontaneous and unorganized, the result of decisions made by individual practitioners, which may well be true or may be the result of efforts not to implicate others (virtually all accounts of appeals also include reports of police interrogations; there are few accounts by those who successfully evaded the police). The following is a typical statement:

> I have been a Falun Dafa practitioner for four years. Through the cultivation practice of these few years, I have come to know the true principles concerning how a person needs to conduct himself and that *Zhen-Shan-Ren* is the sole criterion to discern a good person from a bad one. After setting the standard for myself to be a good person, I am getting healthier and healthier as I cultivate Falun Dafa, and even feel very light in walking. Both my parents have also started practicing Falun Dafa under my influence. Master has removed *futi* [spirit or animal possession] for them, and they have also stayed away from the suffering of many other illnesses, and look younger and younger.
>
> Yet, such a great law of the universe, which brings compassion to people's hearts, helps eliminate their sufferings and illnesses, and has every benefit and not a single drawback, has now been labeled as an evil cult by the Chinese government. We could not understand this. After discussing with my parents, we, as Falun Dafa practitioners and citizens of the People's Republic of China, felt obliged to stand up and say a few words of truth. Although I was pregnant I decided nonetheless to go to Beijing with my parents. As there was no way to appeal to any organization, we went Tian'anmen Square to practice Falun Gong, to help restore the innocence of Falun Dafa.[59]

Another statement sounds similar themes: "I'm an old lady ... of 64 [from Shanghai]. For Falun Dafa and for the sake of all sentient beings, I brought an appeal letter and went to Tian'anmen Square at 9 o'clock on May 11th, 2000."[60] As these specific instances illustrate, such statements are in no way revealing about the events—psychological or organizational—leading up to the decision to go to Beijing. In the narrative structure of the accounts found on the Clear Wisdom Web site, this is the beginning of the practitioner's journey and is presented as a simple moral imperative.

Practitioners' motivations nonetheless shine through more clearly in some of the exchanges between them and the police. To cite further passages from the account of the sixty-four-year-old woman from Shanghai:

> [On arriving at Tian'anmen Square], I saw a strong, young police-man wearing heavy boots kicking a weak young man [who was] wearing glasses.... I said to the policeman: "Young man, resolve problems with words. Don't beat people, beating people is illegal." He yelled back at me, saying: "Who are you?" I said, "I'm a Falun Dafa practitioner." Right away, he twisted my arms behind my back, pushing and beating me, and [led me away].[61]

The practitioner goes on to describe her ordeal while under arrest. She refused to give her name or her address, identifying herself only as a Falun Dafa practitioner who had "descended from heaven." She and other practitioners recited passages from *Zhuan falun* and from master Li's poetry in the face of abuse ("Our voices soared up to the sky. There was someone pouring water and throwing stones at us, but we did not care about these at all"). Still, she and other practitioners were incarcerated, stripped of their money and clothing, photographed, interrogated, beaten, and tortured.

The central element of her narrative, nonetheless, is her rhetorical victory over her interrogators. This passage is worth quoting at some length:

> [The interrogator] asked me: "Why are you here [i.e., incarcerated]?" I answered: "I was looking for the appeals office in the Tian'anmen Square. I saw a strong young policeman beating a young man; it was really terrible. So I went over and nicely asked the policeman to stop beating the young man. That policeman arrested me. So here I am." The interrogator asked: "What were you wanting to appeal?" I replied: "I want to tell the leaders the true situation about Falun Gong based on my own personal experience:
>
> "First, Falun Gong has great effects on healing and keeping fit and is a great exercise, requiring people to become good. I used to be quite ill, confined to my bed. All the big hospitals, specialists and professors of medicine have attempted to treat my illness. According to them, my various body parts were failing one by one; their diag-

nosis was little better than a "death sentence." I lost faith in life and it was very painful. But I was fortunate enough to discover Falun Gong. It has saved my life. All my diseases were cured and I have not spent a penny on medical expenses over the past three years.

"Secondly, Master Li has great virtue. He teaches us to cultivate our moral qualities [*xinxing*], to be a better person than Lei Feng,[62] to obey the law and uphold the law of the universe. He has unconditionally healed my diseases and given me a healthy body. He has told us that we should not be against the government, nor will we in the future. . . .

"Third, this conflict is the fault of the government:

1. Many good party members and good leaders were dismissed from their positions and had their party memberships revoked just because they have practiced Falun Gong. This is turning them into enemies. Is this right?

2. Solely because of my appeal, many people may wind up implicated. Local cadres could be punished, the head of police [where I live] might be demoted . . . the district police might lose their jobs. The responsible people of the local residence committee that I belong to could also lose their positions. . . . Would this be right?

3. All Falun Gong practitioners, man or woman, old or young, are identified as the enemy. Even an old person like myself, who has worked for socialism for 37 years and has always had a close relation with the Communist Party and never committed political errors. I came as a good person to tell the country's leaders the truth about Falun Gong, and I was treated as a bad person, suffering torture and humiliation. This hurts me. My relatives and children might also be implicated. You [i.e., the authorities] have treated a few vicious people, who stirred up the incidents against Falun Gong [i.e., those identified by Li Hongzhi as responsible for the events in Tianjin in mid-April], as good people. Isn't this making good people suffer and rewarding the bad people? I hardly need mention that the constitution also guarantees our freedom of belief. I request that you not further escalate the conflicts and harm more good people."

The interrogator continued: "Why don't you tell us your true name and address?" I said: "Maybe it would make no difference to my children, since they don't live with me and don't cultivate Falun Gong. And my husband is retired. I'm worried about bringing harm to cadres at different levels. Our teacher told us that other people can treat us badly, but we cannot treat others badly. I take responsibility for my actions and bear all the consequences myself." The interrogator was shocked by my answer. Finally, he said: "You are a kind-hearted old lady. I will faithfully report your appeal letter and the situation you have described to my supervisor."[63]

In fact, the practitioner's victory was not assured, and she had to endure more time in jail, more beatings, and more torture before gaining her freedom, but the point of her narrative is to illustrate that righteousness, courageously and tenaciously defended, will triumph over ignorance and brutality.

Other reports sound the same theme. A Mrs. Liu from Jiangxi had traveled to Beijing from Jiangxi in late December 1999 and was arrested on 22 December. When she refused to give her name or her address, police made her lift up her heels and placed a photograph of Li Hongzhi on the floor under her raised heels. She remained on tiptoe until the photograph was removed. Subsequently, she was physically beaten but "smiled at [her interrogator] without any hatred or anger." Her incarceration finally came to the same conclusion as that of the sixty-four-year-old Shanghai practitioner:

> On December 24, as part of the continuing interrogations, the police officer asked, "Why have all of you come to Beijing?" I answered, "Because Falun Dafa was banned and defamed by the central authorities in Beijing." "Where are you going after you are freed tomorrow night?" he asked. I replied, "I take everywhere as my home." "Who beat your face? Was it the police?" The police officer asked me over and over again who had beaten my face. I said, "It's not important. I have no hatred towards anybody." The officer said, "Why can't you tell me where you're from? Don't you want to go home?" I said, "I will never go home before innocence is returned to Falun Dafa. I came here nobly and I will walk out nobly too." In the end, the police officer said, "Your wish has been fulfilled; your goal has been achieved. Now you can go."[64]

Both of these accounts—and there are many, many others—ring slightly false, at least in their narrative reconstruction: the eventual triumph shines forth too clearly even in a moment of sacrifice or martyrdom. Survivors of torture and brutality, particularly survivors who already possessed a strongly teleological world view before their ordeal, may well construct their accounts in such a fashion ("I *knew* the Master would not let me down!"). On the other hand, the editors of the Web site may have shaped the narratives they received as a means of encouraging other practitioners to keep the faith, perhaps to continue to appeal, for it was this naïve hope that authorities, once confronted with the "truth" about Falun Gong, would immediately change their policy, which fueled at least the initial waves of protest by practitioners in China.

The problem was that such triumphs were few and far between (those who were beaten to death were not, after all, able to write their stories), and the protests instead provoked an increasingly violent response on the part of Chinese authorities. Practitioners' accounts on the Clear Wisdom Web site thus rapidly came to reflect another reality: the first negative encounter, on the part of the many Falun Gong practitioners who to that point had been solid, obedient, middle-class Chinese citizens, with the unfeeling brutality of the Chinese state. Although these experiences did not immediately suppress the narrative of triumphant martyrdom, they were at the same time so painful, numerous, and unexpected that the recounting of the atrocities became an important narrative thrust in its own right. The motive was outrage, coupled with the fear that, as Chinese authorities increased their stranglehold on the movement and on the Chinese media, the truth about Falun Gong and about the campaign against Falun Gong would disappear from the public domain.

Such accounts ranged from reports of the deaths of other practitioners, to eyewitness accounts of violence, to personal accounts of brutality and torture. The accounts cover both the experiences of practitioners who brought their appeals to Beijing and those who were harassed and abused by local authorities closer to their homes. Chinese living abroad who returned to lend their voices to the protests wrote in as well. The accounts are very painful to read, despite their repetitive nature, in part because images often accompany the accounts, a result of technological revolutions which have made the transmission of pictures and all sorts of information much easier and cheaper than in the past. The accounts are numerous to the point that they eventually have the unfortunate effect of numbing the reader.

The violence of the Chinese state's campaign against Falun Gong is probably the aspect of the story which has been most treated by others (especially by Falun Gong sources). Although I find Falun Gong's depiction of the violence more credible than the Chinese state's denial of Falun Gong's claims, I question the value of including an extended catalog of the violence suffered by practitioners in the present volume (if the reader is interested in this information, it is widely available). To me, it seems more important to note that the violence had a transformative effect on Falun Gong. The resulting outrage drove practitioners to expand their system of Web sites so as to allow practitioners to communicate with one another and to spread information about what was happening in China both to practitioners and nonpractitioners. The same outrage drove practitioners to seek to influence politicians and public opinion in general to bring pressure on China to stop the campaign. In short, the violence played a major role in transforming Falun Gong from a purely spiritual movement to a spiritual movement with strongly political overtones.[65]

## Falun Gong in Cyberspace

Before politics, however, came the simple desire on the part of persecuted practitioners—and the families and friends of persecuted practitioners—to speak publicly of the indignities they had suffered at the hands of the Chinese authorities. Unjust punishment can be an extremely strong motivating force; when the object of such punishment is not frightened into silent submission, she often feels herself to be charged with a mission to relate the details of her suffering to a larger audience. Such may have been doubly true of Falun Gong practitioners who sought to appeal to the central authorities in the months following the beginning of the campaign of suppression since their initial impulse had been to "speak the truth" to party and government leaders. Finding that such leaders rejected their truth, practitioners sought to speak the truth before the court of world opinion. Speaking the truth also took on re-newed importance in the domestic Chinese context as authorities eliminated all positive messages about Falun Gong (and eventually qigong in general) from the media and attempted to destroy all Falun Gong–related paraphernalia. Under such conditions, speaking the truth came to be a way to tell other practitioners—even practitioners in China—what was going on and to attempt to provide a more balanced picture of events to the general public in China.

The main truth-telling vehicle for Falun Gong practitioners came to be a network of Web sites established—necessarily—outside of China (most of the servers on which these Web sites are housed are presumably located in North America). This virtual network suited Falun Gong for a variety of reasons. First, even in its original Chinese incarnation, Falun Gong had been a relatively decentralized, unstructured movement in which the charismatic leader refused to delegate spiritual power in any meaningful fashion. Web sites are one way to permit the leader to stay in virtual contact with his grassroots followers (so long as the followers wish to do so) without having to build an elaborate organiza-tion. However, the Internet was in its infancy in China in the early 1990s, and it is unclear to what extent Li Hongzhi relied on cybertools to build his original organization between 1992 and 1994.[66] In context of the He Zuoxiu article which set things off, Internet bulletin boards were used to organize Falun Gong's response, but it seems unlikely that the Web had achieved the place it now holds in the movement's life and organization.[67] Still, Li's exit from China in 1995, and the subsequent launch of his global mission among the Chinese diaspora in North America, Europe, and Australia—many members of which possess considerable computer skills—served to underscore the fact that the worldwide Falun Gong community was in the process of becoming all the more dispersed. The onset of the campaign of suppression provided another motivation: Clear Wisdom, the most important Falun Dafa Web site, was launched in Chinese and English on 30 May 1999.

The following discussion of Falun Gong Web sites is incomplete for a number of reasons. First, in marked contrast to their general openness, practitioners have *not* been forthcoming about the organization and management of these Web sites. Most practitioners simply take them for granted and know little about their organization and management, but others who have been involved—at least tangentially—still seem reluctant to answer questions, often citing security reasons. The editors and Web masters of the sites have not responded to my repeated requests (via e-mail, in general) for interviews and information. Consequently, I do not know who the editors are, where the servers are located, or how the work (the volume of which must be staggering) is done. Second, although I consulted the sites from the very onset of my research, and observed their evolution in a general way, I did not think to make the historical evolution of the Web sites a research question.[68] Falun Gong practitioners have now become quite history conscious and are attempting to reconstruct the chronology of their movement—with some attention to important dates in the histories of the Web sites—but this is no substitute for the work I might have done. Consequently, the following discussion of Falun Gong Web sites can do little better than to reproduce the timelessness of the Web sites themselves and will reflect the organization and tone of the Web sites as of this particular moment of writing (May 2005). Should readers of this volume decide to visit the Web sites themselves, it is certain that some things will have changed in the intervening years.

## Clear Wisdom

Clear Wisdom is the most important of the several Falun Gong Web sites, being the one most clearly addressed to veteran Falun Gong practitioners—and especially to Falun Gong practitioners still in China, as the subsequent discussion will illustrate. Launched in late May 1999 in Chinese and English, the site now also boasts German, French, Russian, Japanese, Korean, Spanish, and Vietnamese versions (although not all are identical). The Chinese-language version (available in both simplified and traditional characters) is undoubtedly the richest, and will serve as the basis of my description and analysis.

The home page of www.minghui.net, the Chinese version of Clear Wisdom, contains a horizontal menu across the top, a vertical menu down the left side, a central portion containing the images and information judged by the editors to be the most pressing, and another set of vertical menus descending down the right side. At the bottom of the page are links to related Web sites, many of which are also Falun Gong–run, but some of which are independent sites of recognized human rights organizations. As a researcher, one is immediately struck by the sheer volume of information made available, which is overwhelming. Although it may be tiresome, it is nonetheless useful and illustrative to describe in some detail what is offered simply by the first set of horizontal menus at the top of the home page:

1. The first menu, entitled "About Falun Gong," provides a simple introduction to the practice, advice on how to start cultivation, and a brief discussion of Falun Gong's origins. The music to be listened to while doing Falun Gong exercises is provided (and can be downloaded onto one's personal computer). There is a photo essay on the historical development of Falun Gong (i.e., from the time Li Hongzhi began giving conferences in China in the early 1990s), accompanied once again by music. There are reports from 1999 through 2003 documenting the health benefits of practicing Falun Gong.

2. The second menu, "News from the Mainland" is focused on the persecution of Falun Gong in China. There are comprehensive reports of the persecution, timely news bulletins, photographs of cultivation activities *before* the onset of the campaign of suppression (presumably to help practitioners remember how things used to be), letters urging practitioners to remain loyal to the cause, and letters from practitioners renouncing their forced denunciation of Falun Gong before Chinese authorities. To give the reader an idea of the volume of material available, there are 1,346 letters urging practitioners to remain loyal, stretching back to June 1999, and 1,604 documents renouncing the writers' former denunciation, extending back to June 2000.

3. The third menu is concerned more generally with current affairs, where we find readers' comments on the affairs of the day; a subsequent submenu entitled "Our World and How We Live It" (*shidao renqing*, 796 entries) which contains many readers' comments on how bad things are in China at present, how corrupt the Chinese Communist Party has become; and a final section containing reflections

from outside of China (although in Chinese, and thus often from diaspora practitioners) on the state of affairs within China (605 entries, including "The True Story of China's Inflation" and "China CCTV: The Planet's Most Corrupt Medium").

4. The fourth menu, entitled "News from Abroad" (meaning, "news from outside China," even if Minghui is itself organized from outside of China), includes information on the activities of Falun Gong practitioners elsewhere in the world, including both their cultivation activities (5,663 entries) and their efforts to come to the aid of their brethren in China (1,897 entries). There are also many reports on the campaign of persecution, including comprehensive reports (1,324 entries), reports from other media (5,690 entries), legal cases brought against Chinese officials (285 entries), and cases of persecution of practitioners outside of China (565 entries); 387 pictures of Falun Gong activities abroad (illustrating that the practitioners are still active, so that their Chinese counterparts do not give up hope); and snippets of information (1,213 of them) enabling practitioners to know what is happening with Falun Gong in a general way around the world ("Publication of a New French Translation of *Zhuan falun*"; "Formal Establishment of the Turkish Falun Gong Association").

5. The fifth menu—and one of the richest—is entitled "The World of Cultivation."

   a. The first submenu, "Individual Cultivation," includes four sub-submenus: "Returning to the Great Law" (316 entries), "Improving Morality" (218 entries), "Health" (813 entries), and "Understanding of the Law Principle" (15 entries).

   b. A second submenu, "Cultivating the Righteous Way," contains three sub-submenus: "Essays with Li Hongzhi's Comments" (13 entries), "Polishing the Principles of the Law" (4,378 entries), and "Cultivation Experiences," this latter further subdivided into "The True Salvation of the People of the World" (3,293 entries), "Using Righteous Thoughts to Transform the Persecution" (2,951 entries), and "Using Words and Actions to Realize the Great Law" (1,005 entries). A fourth sub-submenu, "Special Suggestions," includes comments from practitioners on the topics of cultivating the righteous law (277 entries), emitting righteous thoughts (260 entries), and cleaving to proper beliefs and proper actions (473 entries). A fifth sub-submenu addresses the subject of elevating one's *xinxing* (morality as manifested through cultivation; 188 entries). A sixth sub-submenu, entitled "Cultivating Once Again," contains 469

texts written by those who had abandoned Falun Gong cultivation only to return to it later ("After My Mistake: The Frightening
Perspective from Another World"; "I'm Once Again Back by Teacher's Side"). A seventh sub-submenu provides for the exchange of
experiences in spreading the law (1,286 entries). A final sub-submenu is devoted to "Miscellaneous" (91 entries).

c. A third submenu is devoted to accounts of miracles in cultivation
(612 entries; "The Hot Water Heater Stopped Leaking"; "Dafa
Wakes Up a Patient in a Vegetative State").

d. A fourth submenu is entitled "Cultivation of Young Disciples,"
further subdivided into "Stories of Small Children's Cultivation"
(403 entries), fairy tales (4 entries), and "Adolescents Cultivating
the Law" (44 entries).

e. A fifth submenu is devoted to the world of those just beginning
cultivation (496 entries): "From a New American Practitioner: My
Story of Quitting Smoking"; "A Leukemia Patient Returns to Life").

f. A sixth and final submenu contains 47 ancient stories of cultivation,
drawn from Chinese history.

6. A sixth menu, "Support from Society," includes mentions of awards
and prizes Li Hongzhi has received (1,330 entries), examples of
virtuous conduct by nonpractitioners (i.e., tales of those who should be
involved in the suppression of Falun Gong, but who refuse; 514
entries), expressions of support for Falun Gong, often by political
bodies (2,142 entries), written declarations of assistance for Falun
Gong from around the world (189 entries), and a rubric entitled
"People Are Gradually Coming to Understand" (1,346 entries; "The
Awakening of a Party Secretary"; "Having Understood the Truth, the
Boss of a Television Station Refuses to Broadcast Slanderous
Propaganda").

7. The seventh menu is entitled "Between Heaven and Earth [*tianren
zhi ji*]" and concerns the interconnection between human behavior and
the response of the universe. The first submenu, entitled "Reward
and Retribution for Good and Evil" is appropriately divided into
"Rewards for Good" (670 entries) and "Punishments for Evil" (1,386
entries, the majority of which recount the awful fates which have
befallen those participating in the campaign of suppression against
Falun Gong). The second submenu consists of 44 prophecies drawn
from daily life and from Chinese and Western sources (such as the
Book of Revelation). The third submenu is entitled "Mysteries of Life"
("Scientists Discover That Plants Can Think"; "Results of Experiments

on Practitioners' Blood Surprise Scientific Experts"; 319 entries). A fourth submenu is entitled "My Views of Science" and takes issue with the Communist Party's representation of Falun Gong as "superstition"; 123 entries include such topics as "How the Communist Party Uses 'Atheism' to Harm Freedom of Belief," "Man Did Not Evolve from Monkeys," and "Nobel Prize Winner Discovers That God and Science Can Coexist." A fifth submenu on "The Universe and Space" discusses strange astronomical phenomena (239 entries). A sixth submenu focuses on historical examples of the interaction between human behavior and the natural world, largely through traditional stories which emphasize positive rewards for virtuous behavior (extracts from the *Twenty-Four Stories of Filial Piety*, for example; 288 entries). A final "Miscellaneous" submenu contains many stories of natural disasters in China, presumably the result of the anti–Falun Gong campaign.

8. The eighth menu is entitled "Technical Reference" and is of considerable interest. The first submenu, entitled "Breaking through the Web," contains 251 fairly technical entries on IP addresses, proxies, proxy switches—everything a practitioner would need to know to get around the anti–Falun Gong firewalls and filters installed by the Chinese authorities policing the Internet. A second submenu continues on the same theme with a greater focus on personal computers ("Which Is Safer: Accessing the Web via a Wireless Network or via a Cellular Phone?" "How to Further Compress MP3 Files"; "Do Not Use Anti-Virus Software Produced in China"; 218 entries). A third submenu deals with printers and printing ("A Good Way to Reuse Old Ink Cartridges"; "The Problem of Overly Dark Printing by the Canon 1210"). A fourth submenu contains 73 entries on the preparation of printed materials for distribution and circulation ("How to Reduce the Size of the Image in Microsoft Word"; "Providing a Printable Cover of *Zhuan falun* for Mainland Practitioners"). A fifth submenu contains 231 entries on making VCDs (as well as DVDs). Representative contributions include "Basic Information on Burning VCDs," "My Experience Transforming RA Files to MPG Files," and "Making VCD Covers Using Fireworks and Acrobat." A sixth submenu contains 64 entries on making scrolls and banners. A seventh submenu contains 41 entries on cellular phone security ("Please, Mainland Practitioners, Be Careful when Using Text Messaging on Your Cellular Phones to Tell the Truth about Falun Gong"; "An Effective Method to Avoid Surveillance when

Talking on Your Cellular Phone"). An eighth submenu contains 38 entries on making cassettes (audio and video): "How to Record Downloaded Music onto Tapes"; "Two [Ready-to-Print] Covers for Cassettes Revealing the Truth about Falun Gong." A ninth submenu, entitled "Broadcasting and Television Techniques," contains 34 entries on a variety of topics, including short-range broadcasting within China, the development of underground television stations, how to receive New Tang Dynasty broadcasts via satellite, how to make a loudspeaker which works on a timer, and broadcasting Falun Gong messages. A tenth submenu contains 17 entries on pictures, photographs, and their manipulation through such computer programs as Photoshop and PowerPoint. A final "Miscellaneous" submenu contains 63 entries ranging from "A Simple Method to Stick Posters to the Wall" to "How to Distribute Flyers"[69] and "How to Make a Life-Protecting Talisman."

9. The final menu, "Material Portraying the True Situation," is meant to provide practitioners with material they can use, among other things, to sway others to adopt the cause. The first submenu, "Articles Depicting the True Situation," is divided into "Overviews" (1,387), regional reports (1,301), and topical reports (168). The second submenu, entitled "Pictures of the World," contains 630 video clips on predictable themes concerning the persecution, the "true situation," lawsuits brought against Jiang Zemin, and 9 animated video clips (or cartoons), a number of sets of slides for PowerPoint, and 52 flashing images (*shanhua*).

I suspect that most readers have been skimming for some paragraphs already, and I will stop my inventory here, but I will point out yet again that this is only a portion of the totality of the information available via the site (particularly since archived materials going back to 1999 or 2000 are now available as well, in compressed form, so that the site comes close to representing the whole of the "virtual" Falun Gong experience since 1999 as seen by practitioners and, actually, since the inception of the movement, as many historical documents are made available as well). It is clear that practitioners can and do turn to this site for information, for inspiration, for consolation, and for guidance. But the encyclopedic nature of the site and the professionalism with which it is designed and maintained suggest that participation in the site, both in the form of sending in letters or articles and in the form of editorial, technical, or translation work are in themselves important forms of devotion to the cause. In other words, practitioners outside of

China devote themselves to the site because they cannot demonstrate, or lobby, or serve legal papers to visiting Chinese officials every day, and in the absence of other outlets to express their frustration or their devotion, site maintenance, originally a means, has become, in addition, an end in itself.

## FalunDafa.org

While Clear Wisdom is the most important Falun Gong site, it is hardly the only one. Probably the second most important site is www.falundafa.org, which is designed to help those newly interested in practicing Falun Gong to locate the scriptures they will need and the groups of veteran practitioners with whom they can practice the exercises. At one time, the home page showed four practitioners—two Caucasian, two Asian—seated in the lotus position; now it shows a drawing of the Buddha and asks the user to click on his language of choice (including English, Spanish, French, Chinese—regular and simplified characters—Portuguese, Polish, Russian, Bulgarian, Dutch, Finnish, Vietnamese, Swedish, Czech, Japanese, Korean, Burmese, Hebrew, Persian, Greek, Indonesian, Thai, Bosnian, Danish, German, Croatian, Hindi, Italian, Norwegian, Romanian, Albanian, Slovak, Tibetan, and "Other"— Amharic, Hungarian, Telugu, Sinhalese, and Turkish, which are in various states of preparation). The first paragraph of the English-language Web (as of the summer of 2005) site sets the tone of friendly helpfulness:

> Welcome to FalunDafa.org, a Web Site designed and hosted entirely by Falun Dafa practitioners. We hope that you will find this Web Site a good place to start learning about the practice of Falun Dafa. All of the content in this site—excepting the founder's writings— represents the ideas and opinions of Falun Dafa practitioners, and should not be taken as representative of Falun Dafa itself. We merely hope to introduce this wonderful practice to you, and we hope you take some time to explore it for yourself!

The main rubrics are the following: "Falun Dafa: A Brief Introduction," "Getting Started in the Practice," "The Falun Dafa Books," "The Exercises of Falun Dafa," "Answers to Common Questions," "Falun Dafa in Your Area," "Audio and Video Materials," "Searching for Articles," and "Ordering Books and Videos." The most important of these is undoubtedly "The Falun Dafa Books," which makes available freely, in downloadable, printable format, the principal writings of Li Hongzhi: *Zhuan falun* (three different translations provided), *Falun Gong* (often cited as *China Falun Gong*), *Essentials for Further Advancement*, and several others, including his most recent pronouncements. (More texts are available on the Chinese-language Web sites, and some sites are clearly "under construction": only the introduction to *Zhuan falun* is provided on the Tibetan-language Web site, for example, and a major effort of practitioners has been to make this central work available in all possible languages.) Another important link is to "Falun Dafa in Your Area," which includes a list of Falun Gong Web sites throughout the world (Asia, Canada, Europe, Oceania, Central America, South America, USA), including sites from Iran and Israel, Belize and Brazil. These sites provide information about where and when group practice sessions are held (six sites in Paris, for example, eight on the Isle de France, thirteen outside of the capital area). Phone numbers, e-mail addresses, and occasionally the names of the practitioners leading the sessions are provided as well. The sites are not uniform, and some are much more sophisticated than others (compare, for example, the rather primitive French site with the much more state-of-the-art British version). In other words, these local sites are quite visibly the work of local practitioners and not the result of a coordinated central strategy. Indeed, they are often out of date, as I discovered during my fieldwork when I tried to use them to find out, for instance, when an experience-sharing conference was to be held in Boston, New York, or Toronto. It turned out that local practitioners were often too busy with the organization of the events to publicize them on their Web sites, waiting instead until the events were over to communicate the happy results to other interested practitioners.

Other Sites

A third important site is the Falun Dafa Information Center (www.faluninfo .net), a site dedicated to providing "news and information about Falun Gong around the world" so as to raise public awareness of the ongoing campaign of suppression in China. Following the link entitled "About InfoCenter," we learn that this is a volunteer organization whose mission is to "compile, cross-check, organize and publish" documents coming out of China on the subject of the anti–Falun Gong campaign:

> Utilizing emails, websites, faxes, payphones, and other means, individuals throughout China have courageously reported on a wide range of stories. They've collected facts on large-scale police actions, on secret government orders, on police who have tortured and killed, and even on local authorities in some regions who have come to understand Falun Gong and no longer carry out persecution orders.

This information is then "provided to government officials, international media, human rights organizations, and the general public . . . through email alerts, weekly newsletters, press briefings, print publications and our official website." The Falun Dafa Information Center is registered in the state of New York and maintains an office on West 57th Street in Manhattan. The names of volunteer spokespersons—in the United States, Canada, Hong Kong, Europe, and Australia—are provided on the Web site, together with their contact numbers. There are links to other pages in Chinese, Dutch, French, German, Hebrew, Japanese, Korean, Russian, Bulgarian, Spanish, Swedish, and Vietnamese, although these are quite varied in terms of their organization and the information they provide.

The English-language version begins with a weekly bulletin of the most important events relating to Falun Gong, events which are explored in greater detail in links to related stories. A set of menus across the top of the home page includes links to

1. InfoCenter news (feature stories, news stories, press statements, editorials, and media advisories).
2. world news related to Falun Gong.
3. lead stories, which in fact are the major themes repeated in all Falun Gong publications: bringing Jiang Zemin to justice, freeing those still in prison, etc.
4. a newsletter, which reprises the weekly bulletin that figures prominently on the home page.
5. family rescue, which highlights individual cases of relatives of practitioners outside of China who remain incarcerated inside China.
6. an "activity center," which allows those who wish to do so to "send a beautiful on-line postcard to spread the word about the persecution of Falun Gong";[70] it also provides the e-mail addresses of American senators, representatives, and the president plus letter-writing guidelines—including sample letters—for those wanting to write a letter to Chinese leaders such as the Chinese ambassador to the United States. These are actually quite balanced and moving. Another "activity" is signing a petition to be presented to President George W. Bush to bring Jiang Zemin to justice, or another petition to demand the release of all Falun Gong prisoners.
7. a "media center" designed to help journalists properly do their jobs in reporting on Falun Gong–related issues. Headings include "Looking for a Story?" although some of the suggestions go back to 2002,

suggesting that this strategy of pointing media attention in certain directions may not have brought the hoped-for results. Other sections provide "resources for the media," "recent InfoCenter press statements," and a fact file.

Also on the home page are links to photo galleries, to a discussion of the Tian'anmen self-immolation, to torture methods, to the online newspaper *Falun Gong Today*, to the online magazine *Compassion*, and to eight online videos. Further links take the reader to the introductory site (www.falundafa .org), to a site explaining why practitioners are tortured and murdered in China, to a site which catalogs and documents the torture methods used in China, to Clear Wisdom, to a site dealing with lawsuits against the genocide in China (www.flgjustice.org), to the home page of the Falun Gong Human Rights Working Group (www.flghrwg.net), to another site investigating Falun Gong genocide (www.upholdjustice.org), to the site of Friends of Falun Gong (www.fofg.org), and to the home page of Global Mission to Rescue Persecuted Falun Gong Practitioners (www.globalrescue.net). These last five sites represent a multiplication of Falun Gong efforts over the past years. They have a more specific vocation than the more general sites and follow, for example, the persecution of practitioners, or perhaps legal efforts to bring Chinese officials to justice, and provide a wealth of information (see below for more details).

The importance of these cybertools is amply illustrated by the fact that the Chinese government accords them a fundamental importance as well. I do not have the documentation to write a full history of the cyberwars between Falun Gong and the Chinese state, but practitioners have told me fascinating stories on this front. The Chinese government—particularly but not exclusively at important moments in the ritual calendar of Falun Gong, such as Li Hongzhi's birthday or the anniversary of the 25 April demonstrations—has attempted to hack into or otherwise crash the main Falun Gong Web sites even in North America. Happily for Falun Gong, many of its members are experienced computer programmers and technicians, and they have been able to respond in kind, rebuilding firewalls, replacing servers, frustrating the hackers. It is difficult not to be reminded of the cosmic battles of Sun Wukong, the Monkey King in the traditional Chinese novel *Journey to the West*, this time carried out in cyberspace.

Within China, as is well known, the Chinese state has made massive investments in state-of-the-art technology in an attempt to control the information available to Chinese users of the Internet.[71] In essence, the Chinese state (or the companies chosen by the Chinese state) has set itself up as the sole service provider, and just as AOL or any other similar company could, technically, maintain records of sites visited and e-mail received by any or all of its clients, the Chinese state can and does. Although the amount of information is staggering, the Chinese state can and does search for and/or filter out references to Falun Gong and Li Hongzhi in private e-mail correspondence and it has constructed firewalls in such a way as to prevent clients from visiting Falun Gong–related Web sites in China or elsewhere. Information available on Falun Gong Web sites tells practitioners how to get around state-imposed firewalls (obviously such information must be exchanged otherwise than via the web). Although we are perhaps far from the barricades of the Paris Commune, the battle of democracy against dictatorship (or vice versa) is just as vital in cyberspace as on the streets.

## Li Comes Back

Li Hongzhi resumed his role as the active, or at least visibly active, spiritual leader of Falun Gong in the fall of 2000, giving speeches in San Francisco and in Ann Arbor, Michigan, before returning to a fuller schedule of lectures in 2001. The battle lines were already well drawn at the moment of his return: the Chinese state's campaign had been ongoing for more than a year and was becoming increasingly brutal; and Falun Gong practitioners in China and in the diaspora were fighting back as best they could, mounting protests in Tian'anmen Square and buttonholing congressional representatives on Capitol Hill. Li's lectures, it must be said, did little to make a difficult situation easier. Li fanned the flames of what was already a fiery confrontation, in words that could easily be taken as an encouragement to martyrdom.

In Li's defense, it is not obvious what he should have said after a silence of more than a year. Having presented himself as omniscient and omnipotent, having claimed to be able to protect his followers wherever they might be in the world, he could hardly admit that the demonstration of 25 April had been a colossal blunder, nor could he apologize to those followers who had been beaten, tortured, or killed. To maintain any sort of consistency, Li had to claim that everything that had happened was part of a plan and that he could foresee the final outcome, which would necessarily be positive from the point of view of Falun Dafa.

I should preface my analysis of Li's interpretation by noting that I find his speeches during this period to be largely incomprehensible. None of Li's writings are rigorously logical or even particularly well written, and most contain passages which I "bracket out" and do not submit to careful analysis, but *Zhuan falun*, to take the most prominent example of Li's work, possesses a global vision—despite its structural flaws and esoteric references—and I feel confident in saying that I understand most of it, even if I do not view it as universal truth. Li's speeches from the fall and winter of 2000, by contrast, are dense, contradictory, frustratingly vague.[72] Practitioners with whom I spoke at the time admitted that they, too, found these speeches difficult, and they organized informal meetings to discuss their meaning (something practitioners *never* do with texts such as *Zhuan falun*). Among other things, the difficulty of these speeches means that my summary interpretation, which leaves out a great deal of what Li talked about (for example, that aliens were the original inhabitants of the earth), may make more sense, at least from a lay perspective, than do Li's talks.

As far as I can tell, Li's explanation for the Chinese state's campaign against Falun Gong is as follows: unbeknown to most of the forces of the universe, Li's mission to preach the Fa to humanity coincided with a major Fa rectification of the universe itself—because the Fa of Falun Gong was a particularly imposing Fa. The idea of the "Fa rectification of the universe" seems to be another way to refer to the end of a *kalpa*, the vastly long periods of time into which the history of the world—and its renewal—are divided according to certain Buddhist schools. In other words, the Fa rectification of the universe seems to be roughly parallel to the apocalypse, although Li's discussion only hints at the massive destruction and reconstruction presumably associated with this event, and seeks more to explain how the conjunction of the Fa rectification of the universe with Li's own teaching of the Fa to his followers resulted in the Chinese state's campaign of suppression against Falun Gong.

Li's explanation seems to be that the other gods and great beings of the universe, existing at numerous levels too complex for human understanding, were unaware of the coincidence of Li's mission among his followers and the larger Fa rectification. Consequently, they arranged a persecution of Li and Falun Gong similar to that which befell Jesus Christ and other spiritual figures in history, which had in the past constituted a test for both the spiritual leader and his followers, using, for their purposes, the evil forces of authority in China:

> The things that are happening today were arranged long ago in history. At no point has anything gone astray. Of course, this arrangement was made by those high-level beings in the old cosmos.... Their purpose was also to save this cosmos. They think that they've given their all in trying to do these things well and consummate this matter—which includes today's Dafa and even Dafa disciples.... Originally they wanted to treat us the way religions were treated in the past. Their warped notions have made them think that the persecution of Gods in history was rightful. Incidents such as Jesus

being nailed to the cross have become the precedent for high-level beings who come down to save people. How could this be acceptable? This itself is degenerate! A God comes down to save people, yet humans nail him to a cross—what a huge sin people have committed![73]

Li permitted this to happen because it allowed him—as the ultimate authority in the universe—to gauge the spiritual quality of the various gods and powers so as to better prepare the postapocalyptic universe, even though the test was huge because the Fa in question was great as well: "This evil drama in ordinary human society today is also part of what was arranged by the high-level beings. This is, at the same time, the biggest display of their *xinxing* not meeting the requirements of the Fa, and it has fully shown the different-level participants' standards for *xinxing* and beings."[74] As for the innocent Falun Gong followers who suffered and died as a result of this cosmic coincidence, Li suggests that instant "consummation" (i.e., enlightenment) will be theirs:

> In the past, a person had to go through a lifetime of cultivation or even several lifetimes, yet today we're having people reach Consummation in as little as a few years. The process of enduring is but a brief moment, and besides, time has been accelerated. In the future when you look back—if you can reach Consummation, that is—you'll find that it was nothing and was just like a dream.[75]

What Li clearly does *not* say to his followers is that their personal safety might be more important than the larger cause:

> On the other hand, those who haven't stepped forward, have hidden themselves, and have sided in their understanding with the evil beings—how could they still be Dafa disciples? Are those whose notions have sided with the evil that persecutes Dafa and who are doing bad things still Dafa disciples? Do they have the mighty virtue necessary for Consummation as the others do? Moreover, Gods are not like humans. For example, some students were arrested and imprisoned. When they couldn't endure the severe torture, they wrote repentance statements. But in their minds they were thinking: "This is to fool them. I'll still practice after I get out. I'll still go out to validate the Fa and I'll still go to Tiananmen." But this is unacceptable. It's because this kind of notion is something developed in the human world after humans have become degenerate. But Gods aren't like that. They don't have thoughts like these. Once they've decided on a certain path they'll definitely stick with it.[76]

The confrontation between the Chinese state and Falun Gong reached a symbolic climax in the early winter of 2001, when Li in his New Year's Day message called on practitioners to "go beyond the limits of forbearance,"[77] and in February, alleged Falun Gong practitioners set themselves on fire in Tian'anmen Square, supposedly to protest the ongoing campaign of suppression. Although questions remain as to master Li's intent and as to the true identities of the victims of the self-immolation, these events mark a major turning point in the battle of images waged by Chinese authorities and Falun Gong since the summer of 1999. My impression is that the Chinese state won the battle, as public opinion in China, which had been divided on Falun Gong (and on the campaign against Falun Gong) up to that point, turned against the group, now perceived as dangerous and unstable. Most foreign journalists seem to have followed Beijing's general interpretation of the events, and if they did not necessarily turn against Falun Gong as did much of the Chinese general public, a certain media fatigue began to set in over the spring and summer of 2001.

## Li's New Year's Day Message

Unlike Li's lengthy addresses to his followers over the course of the fall, his 2001 New Year's Day message was brief—although still difficult to interpret. On the surface, Li's message seems to be a call to arms, as he clearly states that forbearance, one of the cardinal virtues of Falun Gong practice and one of the basic principles of the universe, does not apply in all circumstances. The forces persecuting Falun Gong, Li insists, are "evil beings who no longer have any human nature or righteous thoughts.... Such evil's persecution of the Fa can thus no longer be tolerated."[78] But does this mean that his followers are henceforth to practice "an eye for an eye" rather than turning the other cheek?

Falun Gong followers in North America with whom I spoke at the time understood the message to mean that they should not have qualms about resisting the suppressive measures employed by the Chinese state. They should not feel guilty; they should not feel that they are violating the dictum to not be involved in politics. Li had given them the permission to stop "acting like sheep" (in the words of one practitioner with whom I spoke) and simply surrendering to the police at the first moment of a confrontation. They could run away, they could organize, they were, in a word, free of whatever constraints the necessity to "forbear" had previously placed upon them—because after all, an attachment to the idea of forbearance is still an attachment, and all such are to be eschewed. At the same time, no one to whom I talked interpreted Li's message as a green light for the use of violence. Violence of any sort is so alien to Falun Gong principles that no one with whom I spoke at the time associated Li's message with the idea of an eye for an eye. The understanding of most North American practitioners seems to have been that Li had called for an end to meek submission; henceforth they could insist that Falun Gong was good and that the campaign of suppression was bad without having to worry about violating the cardinal tenet of forbearance. I recall discussing this question with a very intense Falun Gong practitioner who was delighted that Li Hongzhi had pointed out that there were limits to forbearance. When I asked her how she intended to modify her personal behavior as a result of Li's remarks, she replied that the next time she dropped off Falun Gong literature at the local 7-11 convenience store and the clerk made disparaging remarks, she was going to tell him directly that Falun Gong was a good thing and that he shouldn't ridicule her, her practice, or her master.

What Li himself actually meant is not at all clear. On one hand, he seems to be saying that an attachment to the principle of forbearance is like any other attachment which can get in the way of enlightenment. On the other, he seems to say that forbearance can only become an attachment during a period of Fa rectification, like the one which had created the great havoc of which he spoke over the course of the fall. In any event, he assures his followers that they are right to want to eradicate the evil forces and that this evil will indeed be eradicated—although the form taken by such apparent militancy, beginning later in the spring of 2001, was that of sitting in a meditative posture and "emitting righteous thoughts." Once again, what Li most assuredly does *not* say, at least not directly, is that those followers who might choose *not* to go "beyond the limits of forbearance" and confront a powerful Chinese state determined to destroy Falun Gong by whatever means necessary, remain nonetheless worthy followers in the eyes of the master. This was one question that many practitioners in China were surely asking themselves, and the deeper meanings that we might read into Li's message may well have seemed less compelling than Li's failure to provide reassurance for practitioners who must have been utterly terrified and lacking in direction.

## Fire in the Square

In the midafternoon of 22 January, the eve of the Chinese New Year, five alleged Falun Gong practitioners doused themselves in gasoline and set themselves ablaze in Tian'anmen. One man, Wang Jingdong, aged fifty-one, sat down in a posture resembling the lotus position employed by Falun Gong practitioners (and other groups as well) and remained seated as the flames consumed him. The other four, Liu Chunling, thirty-six, and her daughter Liu Siying, twelve, and another mother-daughter pair, Hao Huichun (in her fifties) and Chen Guo (nineteen), remained erect after setting themselves on fire, running across the square with their hands raised in a manner that recalls part of the basic Falun Gong repertoire of exercises. Security officials extinguished the flames as rapidly as possible, and only one of the four, Liu Chunling, died on the square. The others were taken by ambulance to area hospitals. A CNN camera crew was on the square at the time, but their film was confiscated by security officials and not returned.[79]

Xinhua offered a brief report of the events that very evening—but only to foreign reporters and news outlets. Nothing was revealed of the self-immolation within China proper until more than a week later, on 31 January, when a thirty-minute special edition of *Forum*, which follows the nightly news on CCTV, revealed the grisly details to the Chinese public. These details included the fact that there were two other alleged Falun Gong practitioners who were in (or in the vicinity of) Tian'anmen Square who had intended to set themselves alight with their fellow practitioners, but who had had second thoughts at the last minute. All of the practitioners were from Kaifeng, Henan, and had been "hoodwinked," in the language of the news report, by Li Hongzhi and Falun Gong, imagining that they would ascend immediately to heaven. Unsurprisingly, the feature focused on the youngest members, particularly twelve-year-old Liu Siying, whose charred body could hardly fail to solicit a reaction. Liu was filmed crying out for her mother and for her uncle (Chinese often refer to any older male as an "uncle," regardless of the existence of a blood relationship), and she explained, in interviews conducted in the hospital, that she had believed that there would be no pain and that she would be ushered quickly into paradise, "a wonderful world with gold everywhere." Others who burned themselves spoke of betrayal at the hands of the master (although Wang Jingdong apparently remained faithful, talking about a "final test" to be organized by Li Hongzhi). The report also included interviews with shocked relatives and repeated the general and specific themes of the anti–Falun Gong campaign well known to most Chinese.

Falun Gong representatives from outside of China immediately contested the accuracy of the reports coming from the mainland. Over and over again, they insisted—correctly—that there is no sanction for violence in Li Hongzhi's writings or in Falun Gong practice, whether it be violence directed at someone else or at oneself. In addition, these diaspora practitioners—together with a certain number of skeptical foreign journalists—began to point out a number of anomalies which might lead one to wonder if the events were as straightforward as Xinhua had portrayed them. For instance, why were the police officers patrolling the area equipped with fire extinguishers, allowing them to put out the flames relatively quickly? Fire extinguishers are not standard equipment for most police officers on the beat, in China or elsewhere. And how did Xinhua manage to produce a report (for foreign consumption) so quickly, communicating the events to the outside world only a few hours after they occurred? Normally, the process of vetting and authorization takes considerably longer. These very basic questions suggested to some that Chinese authorities were ready for the events that transpired on the afternoon of 22 January.

Over the succeeding weeks, other questions were added. Philip Pan, a journalist for the *Washington Post*, traveled to Kaifeng, found where Liu Chunling and Liu Siying had lived, and talked with neighbors to learn that no one was aware that they were Falun Gong practitioners and that Liu Chunling had a troubled past and present; apparently, she had struck her elderly mother and her daughter, and worked as an escort in a local nightclub.[80] Perhaps she turned—secretly—to Falun Gong as a result of her personal difficulties, but this is hardly a typical profile of a practitioner. Foreign journalists were not allowed to interview those recovering in hospitals, and neither were their relatives. Xinhua's and other official accounts of the events mentioned suicide notes left by certain practitioners (which rather strangely survived the fire), but were reticent about publishing more than a few sentences from documents which, they said, sometimes ran to a length of several pages.

A later Falun Gong analysis of the film of the incident broadcast by Chinese authorities pointed out other questions or inconsistencies.[81] Wang Jingdong, for example, appeared on close analysis to be holding a plastic bottle which remained intact in spite of the conflagration. Falun Gong's reconstruction of the footage seems to reveal as well that Liu Chunling was killed not by the flames, but by a heavy object striking her head. The group's analysis points out also that the interview with the twelve-year-old Liu Siying supposedly occurred on the heels of a tracheotomy, which would have made it very difficult for Liu to talk (she spoke clearly and even sang in the report). In short, Falun Gong's analysis suggests that the event was staged from beginning to end: those who supposedly set themselves on fire were not Falun Gong practitioners, they did not perhaps set themselves on fire (or did so imagining that the flames would be put out immediately), and the voices heard in the supposed interviews from the hospitals were perhaps not those of the injured.

Although the arguments of Falun Gong practitioners seem cogent, it is very difficult to arrive at a final judgment about the self-immolation. If those who set themselves on fire were not practitioners, then who were they? Where would Chinese authorities have found "actors" (including children) willing to play such roles? What would have been their motivation? I suppose that it is possible that there are desperate people in China (and elsewhere) who will do *anything* for money (which would go to their families in this case, one supposes, unless the authorities had promised to rescue them before the flames could do harm). Or the entire event could have been staged. But it seems just as possible that those who set themselves on fire might have been new or unschooled Falun Gong practitioners, had discovered and practiced Falun Gong on their own (and badly) in the post-suppression period, and, for whatever reason, decided to make the ultimate sacrifice.

Whatever the final truth about the incident, it was a crucial moment in the public relations battle between the Chinese state and Falun Gong. The war between the two has been waged on many battlefields: at the local level in China,[82] at central places in China like Tian'anmen Square, at various international venues (such as the United Nations and the World Court), and in the pages of the Chinese and international media. It is difficult to overestimate the importance of this last battlefield, for it was largely through the media outside of China that Falun Gong practitioners succeeded in bringing pressure to bear on the Chinese state, and it was largely through the media that the Chinese state spread the image of Falun Gong as a dangerous heterodox sect (at least within China). Up until the self-immolation incident, many Chinese within China seem to have reserved judgment on Falun Gong, and outside of China, diligent Falun Gong practitioners had managed to wrestle the Chinese state to a standstill, having succeeded in keeping at least part of their message in the public eye. After the self-immolation incident, however, Chinese within China increasingly came to see Falun Gong as dangerous and untrustworthy, and media outside of China slowly began to disengage as well.

This media fatigue was a major blow to the efforts of Falun Gong practitioners outside of China. In North America, the group is not particularly numerous and does not constitute an important voting bloc (even in areas with large concentrations of Chinese such as New York, San Francisco, or Toronto, Falun Gong cannot claim to represent the Chinese community, which remains very divided about Falun Gong). When the media began to lose interest, Falun Gong practitioners lost their most important tool to gain the attention of legislators and government servants; there was no more pressure from "public opinion" and less chance for a politician to make headlines by nobly responding to a humanitarian cause. Consequently, Falun Gong practitioners have had to develop other means to try to make known their truth and to seek justice, and the means they have chosen have once again contributed to the politicization of the movement as a whole.

Within China, practitioners continue to try to tell their truth about Falun Gong in a variety of ways. Practitioners burn CDs of Falun Gong–related materials (including their interpretation of the self-immolation incident and much else) and leave them in bicycle baskets, mailboxes, anywhere that might lead the recipient to wonder what the CD might be and to insert it into his computer. According to Falun Gong Web sites, practitioners continue to hold experience-sharing conferences secretly in China and to publish information about such conferences post facto on Falun Gong Web sites. More spectacularly, as already mentioned above, practitioners within China have successfully hacked into cable and even television transmissions inside China so as to broadcast Falun Gong's versions of reality to a public denied access to more than one version of the "truth."

Outside of China, many practitioners have decided to try to bring China and China's leaders to justice through the courts. They accuse China's leaders of torture, of genocide, and of trafficking in the organs of Falun Gong practitioners held prisoner in China. They do the legal paperwork and legwork necessary to get their concerns onto the agenda of the World Court, or UNESCO, or the United Nations, and accompany such gestures with peaceful demonstrations at those venues, particularly when Falun Gong motions are being heard. Other practitioners follow similar strategies within national borders, bringing suit in the United States, Canada, Australia, and New Zealand, and attempting to serve papers on Chinese officials when they visit those countries. An excellent window into these activities is the Web site at www.flgjustice.org, which provides details (including the legal documents filed) on some sixty-one legal actions undertaken by the group. The home page of the site[83] notes,

On May 1st, 2006, International Advocates for Justice (IAFJ) published . . . statistics which show that Falun Gong group has filed as many as 54 civil and criminal lawsuits in 33 different countries on . . . five continents against Jiang Zemin . . . , Luo Gan and 30 other high-level officials of the Chinese Communist Party that have been playing the most active roles in the persecution of Falun Gong. According to IAFJ, Falun Gong has filed the largest number of human rights lawsuits in the 21st century and the charges are among the most severe international crimes defined by international criminal laws.

Other groups of practitioners do the investigative work necessary for the legal groups to function. See, for example, the sites at www.upholdjustice.com and www.flghrwg.net. The former, whose mission is "to investigate the criminal conduct of all institutions, organizations, and individuals involved in the per-secution of Falun Gong," provides a wealth of information on a wide variety of topics under the rubrics "Hot Cases," "Organ Harvesting, Torture and Mur-der," "Government and 610," "State-run Media," "Labor Camps, Psychiatric Facilities, Brainwashing," "Culture and Education," "Economics," "Overseas/ Embassy," "Internet Blockade," and "Other." The latter (the Falun Gong Hu-man Rights Working Group) focuses on the abuse of the human rights of Falun Gong practitioners and provides a great many publications free of charge. The site www.globalrescue.net is yet another with a very similar orientation. It is clear that the sites themselves, as well as the work they represent, have come to be important axes of devotion for Falun Gong practitioners devastated by the ongoing campaign in China and frustrated by media fatigue in the West.

## The *Epoch Times*

Truth telling remains an important aspect of Falun Gong activities as well. All of the sites just mentioned (and numerous others) seek to inform the public about the fate of Falun Gong practitioners in China. Web sites, however, are limited, in the sense that one must type an address into a Web browser, or follow a link from another site, in order to consult the information provided. To some extent, then, Web sites preach only to the converted and cannot accomplish the goal Falun Gong practitioners have set for themselves from the very beginning of the campaign of suppression. Consequently, Falun Gong practitioners founded a newspaper, the *Epoch Times*, which has been available electronically and in a print version since its inception in 2000. According to the testimony of Stephen Gregory, one of the newspaper's English-language publishers,

> The Chinese-language edition has grown rapidly and now has a cir-culation of 1,179,100 copies in 28 countries, making it the most widely distributed Chinese-language newspaper in the world. The Chinese-language website receives 700,00 page views a day with 80,000 original visitors . . . [including] 137,000 page views per day and 30,000 original visitors from inside mainland China. In August of 2004 the English-language edition of *The Epoch Times* began publishing in Manhattan. In less than one year, the English-language edition has grown very fast. It is now published in eight US cities, three Canadian cities, Australia and the UK. English-language edi-tions are expected to begin publishing soon in New Zealand, Ireland, and northern Europe. *The Epoch Times* has also expanded this past

year into other languages, and is now published in: French, Spanish, German, Russian, Korean, and Japanese.[84]

To my mind, the *Epoch Times* is representative of the evolution of Falun Gong over the past few years. First, the undertaking speaks to the ambition and the organizational acumen of diaspora practitioners. In an age when major print newspapers are losing advertising and readership to the Internet and podcasting, Falun Gong practitioners decide to launch a worldwide newspaper, with both Web and print editions, and they make it work—at least for the moment. The *Epoch Times* is a newspaper with a mission, that of reporting on issues bearing on human rights throughout the world, which allows for considerable focus on China and Falun Gong. My impression of the newspaper is that articles are well written and interesting, if occasionally idiosyncratic in their coverage (when compared to a mainstream newspaper dedicated to publishing "all the news that's fit to print"). It is sometimes difficult to determine who the *Epoch Times* journalists are and where they get their information, but in an age when so much of journalism is shaped by blogs commenting on the primary research carried out by the *New York Times*, the *Washington Post*, and other major media with the means to underwrite investigative journalism, the *Epoch Times* would be hardly the only newspaper to recycle information (even major players do this when they use wire service reports).

Second, the *Epoch Times* is clearly political. Again, Falun Gong had no choice but to become political once the campaign of suppression began, even though this was not its choice and even though it tried very hard to frame the issues otherwise, as most practitioners consider themselves Chinese patriots and did not see their practice of Falun Gong as a challenge to Communist Party leadership. As for the *Epoch Times*, the newspaper's focus on human rights is both humanitarian and political, but the paper's editorial stance, particularly its publication of the "Nine Commentaries on the Communist Party" and its appeal to Chinese Communist Party members to renounce their membership, constitutes a direct attack on the legitimacy of China's government and very nearly a call for its overthrow—if by peaceful means. The Nine Commentaries are a blanket condemnation of Communism in general and of Chinese Communism in particular. Although there is undoubtedly some truth in the commentaries, they lack balance and nuance, and read like anti-Communist propaganda written in Taiwan in the 1950s, or perhaps like McCarthyite boilerplate from 1950s America. I can readily understand the anger of Falun Gong practitioners toward Chinese authorities and toward Chinese Communism, and I accept the idea that the Communist party has, over time, inflicted extreme, unnecessary violence on the Chinese people, but as a professional historian I cannot sanction such one-sided depictions, which ultimately reveal much more about the authors of the texts than about their subjects. As for the newspaper's claims to chronicle the dissolution of the party from within (as of 14 July 2006, some 11,747,309 former Communist party members have renounced their membership, according to the *Epoch Times* home page, www.theepochtimes.com), what can one say? I know of no way to verify such claims independently, and find it difficult to believe that a Falun Gong newspaper could have such an impact within China, even if it is true that some party members have found the campaign against Falun Gong exaggerated and ultimately fruitless. On my recent trips to China, however, I must say that the fall of the party did not seem imminent.

Finally, the *Epoch Times* illustrates certain tensions that seem to have beset Falun Gong activists, or the posture of Falun Gong in general, as their fight against the Chinese state has dragged on. For example, neither practitioners in general nor those who work for the *Epoch Times* like to call it a "Falun Gong newspaper," even though it was founded by Falun Gong practitioners, most if not all of its publishers are Falun Gong practitioners, many of its journalists are Falun Gong practitioners, and at least part of its staff is made up volunteer workers, many of whom are Falun Gong practitioners. They don't like to be called a "Falun Gong newspaper" in part because they fear they will not be taken seriously and thus will have difficulty reaching the readers they hope to reach. "Would you call the *New York Times* a Jewish newspaper?" asked one *Epoch Times* publisher whom I interviewed by telephone, pointing out that the *Epoch Times* covers more than just Falun Gong issues. I understand the publisher's point, but the parallel is hardly exact. I *would* call the *Christian Science Monitor* a Christian Science newspaper.

In addition, in the hopes of avoiding the appellation "Falun Gong newspaper," the *Epoch Times* has adopted a wary, almost paranoid stance toward the outside world. A former student of mine—a Falun Gong practitioner—is a journalist for the French-language Montreal edition of the *Epoch Times*, *La Grande Époque*. I wrote to him via e-mail, asking if I could interview him about his work and offering to visit the Montreal offices of the newspaper. After several days, I received a terse reply to the effect that he was too busy and that a visit to the newspaper offices would not be possible. In a telephone interview with a North American publisher, I had great difficulty getting straight answers to basic questions about the organization and financing of the newspaper, even though I am known to be sympathetic to Falun Gong. The publisher told me that non-Chinese-language editions are for the moment subsidized by the Chinese-language edition and that she had put some of her own money into her edition of the paper. But she claimed not to know how many of her staff were volunteers or how many were Falun Gong practitioners, while admitting that there were "a significant number." Unfortunately, this kind of reticence creates the impression that there is something to hide, which naturally feeds suspicions that the *Epoch Times* is in fact Falun Gong–financed and Falun Gong–run—precisely the suspicion they are trying to avoid. And since Falun Gong has never quite won the battle of images in the public arena and shed the "cult" or "sect" label, anything less than total honesty and total transparence feeds the lingering suspicion that there might be something not quite legitimate about the whole story.

At the same time, it is not difficult to understand the publisher's frustrations. Falun Gong has—justifiably—become quite cynical about mainstream Western journalism. Practitioners see themselves as the equivalent of battered women whose stories appear in the pages of the Western press alongside the denials of their "abusive partners" (i.e., the Chinese state) to the effect that no abuse has occurred, or if it has, it was justified—this because Western journalists insist on giving equal weight to both "sides" of the story. When practitioners decided to set up the *Epoch Times*, their goal was to break through this frustration, to get their message out without having to go through standard Western media. They want to be read for their content and respected for their intentions, not questioned about their financing and organization.

Sadly, this probably will not work, because only a series of half-truths allows the newspaper, or practitioners, to deny that the *Epoch Times* is a Falun Gong newspaper. True, it may not receive a monthly check from Li Hongzhi, and Falun Gong may not even be a financial entity, but the *Epoch Times* was set up by Falun Gong practitioners with their own money, and if Falun Gong practitioners ceased their work—paid or voluntary—for the newspaper, the *Epoch Times* would fold. Similarly, while the newspaper covers more than Falun Gong issues, it would not have been founded in the absence of the conflict between Falun Gong and the Chinese state, and were this conflict to be resolved, it is not clear that the newspaper would continue to exist. Ultimately, one might think of the *Epoch Times* as a political arm of Falun Gong, and in denying that the newspaper is Falun Gong–financed and –run, practitioners get to preserve the psychologically reassuring fiction that the movement itself and individual practitioners remain apolitical. This comes very close to dishonesty (or at least a Clintonian sleight of hand) and discredits to some degree the integrity of practitioners and the movement—in addition to working at cross-purposes with the goals they hope to achieve.

Falun Gong's allegations concerning the organ harvesting of Falun Gong prisoners in China provide an excellent example of the dilemma in which the group finds itself. China has long been accused of trafficking in organs harvested from executed—and sometimes still living—prisoners. In hearings before the Subcommittee on International Operations and Human Rights of the House International Relations Committee, Michael E. Parmly, principal deputy assistant secretary of state, Bureau of Democracy, Human Rights, and Labor, testified on 27 June 2001 that the Hong Kong and British media had reported such allegations as early as the mid-1980s and that U.S. officials had repeatedly raised such concerns in meetings with high-level Chinese officials throughout the 1990s. The point of his testimony was to note that such practices had continued and were perhaps even expanding, with Americans traveling to China to take advantage of organ availability whereas earlier the practice had largely been confined to neighboring countries in Asia.[85] Harry Wu (Wu Hongda), a Chinese dissident who spent some fifteen years in Chinese jails and who maintains the China Information Center, has reported on prison conditions in China for some years, and in February 2006 he completed a report about the harvesting of organs of death-row prisoners at a hospital in Chengdu in Sichuan province, which he shared with certain Falun Gong media, which went on to publicize the information.

On 10 March 2006, the *Epoch Times* published a front-page story entitled "Shocking Inside News: Shenyang Concentration Camp Has Body Crematorium," alleging a similar operation on a much larger scale in Sujiatun, some fifteen kilometers outside of Shenyang city: 6,000 practitioners were being held and thousands of organs had been extracted since 2001; in the story, comparisons were made to Nazi concentration camps. Shocked by the allegations but puzzled by certain aspects of the *Epoch Times* story, Harry Wu carried out his own investigations, sending people to the Sujiatun facility and finding no trace of a "concentration camp." Wu brought his findings to the attention of Falun Gong—as well as to members of the U.S. Congress—and Falun Gong spokespeople reacted with anger, calling Wu a "butcher" and a "spy" and alleging that he was on the side of the Communists. On 13 April, Falun Gong announced, "The world cannot wait until all the evidence becomes available because the crimes will worsen. Even if there is a one percent probability that this is true, it is worth the whole world to carefully and fully investigate the matter and deal with it."[86]

In March 2006, the Coalition to Investigate the Persecution of Falun Gong, a Washington-based Falun Gong advocacy group, contacted David Matas and David Kilgour, well-known Canadian lawyers, human rights activists, and politicians (Kilgour having served in Parliament), asking them to investigate charges of mass organ harvesting from Falun Gong prisoners in China and offering to pay their expenses. Matas and Kilgour, deeply disturbed by the allegations, volunteered their services free of charge and released their report to the media on 6 July 2006. The report seems hastily prepared, but then again, Chinese authorities refused the lawyers' request to visit China and investigate the charges, so the data available to them were limited to existing information about Chinese practices in organ harvesting and trafficking, to third-party accounts about such practices as they relate to Falun Gong, and to broader information about the conflict between China and the movement. Inevitably, since they were working on a topic treating the persecution of Falun Gong, Matas and Kilgour made extensive—though not exclusive—use of material from Falun Gong sources. Among these sources were the most damning: a number of phone calls, placed "on behalf of Falun Gong community" or by the Coalition to Investigate the Persecution of Falun Gong, to hospitals and transplant centers in China. The callers posed as concerned family members and inquired as to the availability of certain organs and to the identities of their "donors"; the responses made it quite clear that young, often male Falun Gong practitioners were available to provide the desired organs. Matas and/or Kilgour listened to tapes of these conversations, which were provided to them by the Falun Gong advocacy group, with a certified Chinese-English translator, but did not attempt to reproduce the exercise independently. The transcripts of these conversations are chilling, as is the interview with the ex-wife of a doctor who, according to the interview subject, had performed some 2,000 cornea-removal operations on Falun Gong practitioners in the Sujiatun hospital. The practitioners had been injected, she claimed, with a drug which caused cardiac arrest, but some were not yet dead when their corneas and other organs were removed.

Matas and Kilgour concluded, in lawyerly fashion, that while definitive proof of the allegations was lacking, the preponderance of evidence led them to accept the allegations as true:

> We have concluded that the government of China and its agencies
> in numerous parts of the country, in particular hospitals but also
> detention centres and "people's courts," since 1999 have put to death
> a large but unknown number of Falun Gong prisoners of consci-
> ence. Their vital organs, including hearts, kidneys, livers and corneas,
> were virtually simultaneously seized involuntarily for sale at high
> prices, sometimes to foreigners, who normally face long waits for
> voluntary donations of such organs in their home countries.

Matas and Kilgour subsequently released an updated version of their report, in January 2007, reiterating their conclusions and adding further evidence to bolster their claims, although the new evidence remains third-party hearsay.[87]

Chinese authorities have denied specific charges related to Falun Gong prisoners, but in July 2005, Vice Minister of Health Huang Jinfu had already admitted that the practice of organ harvesting existed and had promised to draft new regulations on organ harvesting, which came into force in July 2006.[88] In November 2006, a Chinese doctor admitted publicly that harvesting of and trafficking in the organs of executed prisoners did take place, but that this was the work of "rogue doctors" who must be more closely supervised.[89] An undercover investigation carried out by the BBC and made public in September 2006 found that the market in harvested organs from Chinese prisoners was flourishing.[90] The European Commission, while insisting that evidence concerning "concentration camps" and thousands of murders is lacking, has promised to continue its investigations, and other organizations have expressed similar concerns.[91]

In sum, while evidence of the harvesting of Chinese prisoners' organs seems to be beyond dispute, the scale of the practice is not known. There appears to be little evidence that imprisoned Falun Gong practitioners have been a particular target of the practice or that concentration camps have been set up to facilitate the harvesting of practitioners' organs. On the other hand, it seems likely that Falun Gong practitioners who are part of the prison population would be candidates for harvesting, in part because at least some practitioners are young and healthy, in part because the movement has been vilified within China. In other words, it does not stretch the bounds of credibility to imagine that some imprisoned Falun Gong practitioners have been targets for organ harvesting, and accounts of such are found in Falun Gong sources as early as 1999.[92]

But Falun Gong spokespeople clearly overplayed their hand when they talked about concentration camps (or even a network of some thirty-six concentration camps)[93] and the huge numbers of prisoners who have been victims of the practice. I understand that Falun Gong is desperate to get its cause back into the news and that the lesson it has learned over the years is that sensationalism works. Hence, the choice of words such as "concentration camp" or "genocide," which have a shock value demanding a response on the part of the international community. Sadly, when the evidence is not forthcoming to substantiate the charges, Falun Gong inevitably loses credibility, and third-party observers come to doubt *all* information provided by Falun Gong sources—and not just the sensational claims. This is unfortunate, for even if concentration camps do not exist, the persecution of Falun Gong has been real, and even if the group has stretched the truth to try to win media points, this does not make it a cult. It is too easy to dismiss all Falun Gong claims of suffering and victimization on the basis of their leaders' desperate attempts to call attention to the plight of their fellow practitioners.

## Conclusion

Although the campaign of suppression against Falun Gong has been a major news event in the history of reform era China, I have argued that it was the preceding period of liberalization and the qigong boom that were unusual, and not the campaign against Falun Gong. The fortunes of qigong had been declining for some time before 1999, and to some extent Li Hongzhi's failed gamble in late April 1999 pushed events toward what may well have been an inevitable rupture. But Li's bold decision to authorize the mass protest challenged the regime in particularly galling ways, raising questions of rights, loyalty, and legitimacy which had been implicit in the qigong movement before but had rarely come to the surface. Li's gesture surely conjured up in China's leaders' minds the fears associated with historical examples of redemptive societies. It is in no way surprising that the Chinese state fought back, and fought back hard.

The tenacity of the response of Falun Gong practitioners has surprised many, including Chinese authorities. China's rulers did not foresee the difference that a committed group of activists located outside of China, in the Chinese diaspora, could make. Nor did they foresee the stubbornness of many Falun Gong practitioners within China, who were motivated by incomprehension of the government's actions and by Li Hongzhi's calls for continued sacrifice. To my mind, the only explanation for this stubbornness is the outrage born out of the conviction that theirs is a good cultivation practice which has been wrongly vilified. This conviction has, over time, led to an inevitable politicization of the movement and to tactics which, unfortunately, will not gain Falun Gong many new friends. I hope that the practitioners can maintain their commitment to truth, goodness, and forbearance even as they swim in the muddy water of politics.

# Conclusion

*Unpacking Contexts*

The qualified sympathy which greeted Falun Gong at the beginning of the campaign of suppression in 1999 and 2000 has largely evaporated over the years, and the group seems to receive scant attention and less support from mainstream media in the West. In part, this is a result of the aggressive lobbying tactics employed by certain Falun Gong spokespeople, the paranoia exhibited by Falun Gong media such as the *Epoch Times*, and exaggerated claims such as those concerning the alleged widespread organ harvesting of Falun Gong prisoners discussed in chapter 6—all of which strain the patience of many who might have maintained a neutral attitude about the group. In part, it is also because most of us have a limited capacity for sympathy for distant groups with little direct connection to us; Falun Gong has been pushed off the front page by the disaster of the week, to become yesterday's news. In part, it is because the label "cult," applied to Falun Gong by the Chinese authorities, has never really gone away, and a visceral distaste for—even fear of—cults is common in our society. Indeed, even many of my colleagues in Chinese studies seem to shun Falun Gong for the same reason my teenagers don't eat their vegetables—it just doesn't look like something they want to get close to.

But the fact that some Falun Gong representatives are insistent, or even annoying, is not a sufficient reason to ignore or dismiss the group, as there is considerable evidence that the group has been subjected to an extensive campaign of persecution, even if the Falun

Gong media may exaggerate the extent of that persecution. Similarly, that Falun Gong founder and leader Li Hongzhi has made bizarre statements, has made money from his publications, and has presented himself as the greatest god in the universe are not reasons to deny the basic humanity of Falun Gong practitioners, who seem to have found in Li's teachings a fulfilling guide for living. Too often, discussions of Falun Gong have echoed the accusations and rejoinders of the debate between Chinese authorities and Falun Gong over the supposed cult status of the group, as if the discovery that Li Hongzhi lied about his birthday, or that his handlers removed some of his more incendiary writings from the Web site, give credence to Chinese authorities and, therefore, Falun Gong is indeed a cult, which means that we can dismiss it from our concerns. This book has, I hope, illustrated that, however we may personally react to Li Hongzhi's writings and whatever political course the Falun Gong movement may have taken since 1999, large numbers of perfectly normal people have been able to find spiritual significance in the scriptures and corporal technologies offered by Falun Dafa. We can decide that Falun Gong is not for us, but refusal to respect the beliefs of others is at best disinterest—callous disinterest when the beliefs are used to justify persecution—and at worst bigotry.

Dismissing Falun Gong as a strange anomaly obscures as well its importance in Chinese history, which has been a major focus of this study. Indeed, much of this book has been devoted to unpacking a series of contexts, enabling us to see Falun Gong and indeed the qigong movement as a whole not as bizarre eruptions from out of nowhere, equivalents perhaps of the hula hoop craze of 1950s America, but rather as social and cultural phenomena linked to specific, identifiable aspects of China's history and popular religious culture. Unpacking these contexts enables us to connect Falun Gong both to China's past and to China's future, for this volume has illustrated that the discourses underlying qigong and Falun Gong are neither antiquarian relics nor momentary fads, but instead continue to exercise a genuine appeal for Chinese—even well-educated Chinese in China and in the Chinese diaspora—at the beginning of the twenty-first century.

Having unpacked these contexts, it is clear that Falun Gong and especially the larger qigong boom mark important moments in the religious history of modern China. Properly understood, the experiences of qigong and Falun Gong bring into very different focus large territories of modern Chinese history. If, for example, my linkage of Falun Gong and, more broadly, qigong to the longer history of redemptive societies is sustained in future research, this will go a long way toward explaining the appeal of such groups even in a traditional, rural context. Charismatic masters in late imperial Qing times may have preached the healing power of moral practice in ways broadly similar to what we have found in our reading of Li Hongzhi, which might explain why believers would risk censure, arrest, and even punishment: like Falun Gong practitioners, their aches and pains felt better, they saw nothing out of the ordinary in the message purveyed by their master (except, of course, that it eased their aches and pains), and they found popular cultural sanction for chanting mantras, practicing meditation, consulting scriptures, and sharing vegetarian meals.

If such were the case, it is easy to imagine that such groups were quite widespread in Ming and Qing times as, viewed from below, they were simply a modified form of lay Buddhism, one of the foundation stones of Chinese popular culture since medieval times. If these groups were numerous and generally unexceptional, this would in turn explain the seemingly explosive emergence of redemptive societies under the republic. For although Communist historians have sought to label such groups *huidaomen*, a pejorative term with little content but whose political intent is to link the groups with bogeymen such as secret societies and heterodox religions, even a cursory examination of the reality surrounding these redemptive societies illustrates the limits, the shallowness of the association Communist historians have sought to make.

What is most obvious about these redemptive societies under the republic (and one could say much the same about similar groups in Taiwan today) is that they were not *marginal*, neither socially, nor ideologically, nor in terms of sheer numbers. Quite apart from the numbers of adherents, their charity work, and their connections to highly placed political and military figures, the profiles of the leaders of at least some redemptive societies provide ample illustration of this point. David Palmer has written a preliminary biography of Li Yujie, founder of the Tiandijiao (the Heavenly Lord Teachings), in which Li's life can be read as an embodiment of the modern Chinese experience.[1] Educated as a young boy in the Confucian village school, he became an enthusiastic proponent of modernity during the May Fourth period (having studied under Hu Shi). He subsequently became a well-known journalist and served as well in the Finance Ministry of the Nanjing government under Song Ziwen. His health suffered, and he took up meditation, even though his modernist friends and colleagues scorned him for his choice, and in the early 1930s he began an involvement with redemptive societies. In 1937, Li moved with his family to Huashan, one of China's sacred mountains, where he lived in a series of caves with his wife and four sons—for six years. It was during this period that he composed the scriptures that would eventually become the basis of his teachings; part of these teachings appeared as divinely transmitted characters on a yellow cloth Li had hung in one of his caves, and his son was ordered to transcribe the characters as quickly as they appeared. At the end of China's civil war, Li followed the Nationalists to Taiwan, where he once again became a well-known journalist and university professor (and a rather unsuccessful businessman). He founded his religion in 1979, his son succeeded him, and the religion is alive and well today.

The point is not that Li Yujie was not eccentric, whatever that might mean—clearly he was. The point is rather that his eccentricity was one that was accepted and understood (and perhaps shared) by a substantial portion of the elite of his generation, including many prominent Nationalist and Communist figures with whom Li was familiar over the course of his life. In other words, twentieth-century (pre-Communist) Chinese culture—even at the elite, educated level, to say nothing of middle- and lowbrow culture—*permitted* Li Yujie to engage in the sort of religious activities I just described, without demanding that he marginalize himself or that he sacrifice his right to speak to "normal" Chinese.

This cultural space occupied by Li Yujie and by the redemptive societies in general was closed down on the mainland in the early 1950s, but clearly reopened—if partially and under different circumstances—in the 1980s and 1990s to permit the qigong boom and Falun Gong. The hundreds of millions of Chinese who embraced qigong did so *not* because it was a novelty, *not* because it was strange and exciting, but because the notion of finding health, happiness, and power through moral practice and corporal technologies spoke to something deeply embedded in Chinese popular religious culture—or, more accurately, in Chinese popular culture *tout court*, for if people had realized the "religious" dimensions of what they were doing, they likely would have shunned it. The appeal of qigong and Falun Gong in Taiwan and elsewhere in the Chinese diaspora illustrates that we must look past the spiritual vacuum created by the failure of Mao's revolution to explain the rise and expansion of qigong. Indeed, I suspect that the history of redemptive societies might be relevant to much of the modern history of popular religion in Taiwan and in the Chinese communities of Southeast Asia—or perhaps even more broadly, to the modern history of Asian popular religion in general.

But what is equally remarkable about this important moment in the modern history of Chinese religion is that no one in China (and few outside of China) seems to have recognized it as such. For complex reasons, China is largely blind to its own religious history, having adopted an overly restrictive definition of religion in the early twentieth century and having attempted ever since to make reality fit the mold rather than the other way around, even if the only way to do that is to wear blinders (in these "blindered" Chinese eyes, Li

Yujie may have been comprehensible, but he was not "religious"). Indeed, one can interpret the rise of qigong and even the conflict between the Chinese state and Falun Gong as a sort of ironic vengeance exacted by popular religion and popular culture on the Chinese elite, for it was the fiction, created by the Communist establishment, that the healing powers of traditional spiritual discourses were real, but could be "tamed" by socialist science and revolutionary politics, that opened the door to the qigong mass movement.

But Western students of China have not been much better. Until very recently, Chinese religion has been seen as an epiphenomenon, its study marginal to the metanarrative of modern Chinese history, a subject for antiquarian sinologists, perhaps, but not for those interested in the reality of modern China. To my knowledge, there is, for example, no book entitled *History of Religion under the Chinese Republic*, and redemptive societies are not even mentioned in most standard textbook treatments of China's modern experience. Why might this be?

In the preface to this book, I wrote that the Chinese immigrant to Canada, practicing Falun Gong, working as an accountant, and living in a Toronto suburb in the early twenty-first century, is as important to China's past and future as the North China peasant who supported Mao Zedong and the Red Army in the 1940s. To some degree, this was but a rhetorical flourish penned by an author finishing his book on Falun Gong, but there is more than a little truth in the statement as well, and I would like to finish my conclusion by exploring that truth.

The North China peasant, poor, long-suffering, and passive until transformed through the efforts of Mao Zedong and the Chinese Communist Party, has long been at ground zero in our historical narrative of the modern Chinese experience, a narrative most succinctly and elegantly expounded in Lucien Bianco's classic *Origins of the Chinese Revolution, 1915–1949,*[2] long the most popular textbook on modern Chinese history in North American universities. The reasons for this are obvious and profound: the North China peasant of the Communist liberated areas of the 1930s and 1940s has personified the social basis of the revolution which remade China, a revolution long taken by historians, both Chinese and Western, as the end point of what one might call the teleological unfolding of Chinese history since the early nineteenth century. Had Mao not found the North China peasant, or had the North China peasant not found Mao, Chinese history would have continued on its collision course with disaster (think Africa). Having found one another, China was regenerated, reborn in an event of cataclysmic, world-shaking importance. Hence, the iconic status of the North China peasant. Hence, the tendency to recount all of Chinese modern history with reference to this primordial event.

Explanations thus begin from this central moment, this crucial meeting. The tragic drama of imperial China's long decline and fall and the manifest and tragicomic failures of the Republican period—up until Yan'an and the marriage of Mao and the North China peasant—are seen through the lens of peasant misery, peasant isolation, and the lack of a peasant voice, of peasant representation—all of which was remedied at Yan'an and then applied to China as a whole. Similarly, the history of the People's Republic since 1949 is often told with reference to loyalty to, or betrayal of, the contract with the North China peasant authored by Mao and the CCP at Yan'an. I exaggerate the paradigm, of course, but only slightly. Anyone who has ever taken (or taught) a modern Chinese history course will immediately recognize the centrality of this *problématique* to the history and historiography of modern China. Anyone who has ever read a modern Western textbook history of the modern Chinese experience can probably recall chapter titles which divide Chinese historical time in this manner.

Of course, not everyone has bought into this paradigm. Chinese historians in Taiwan have always told a somewhat different story, and scholars such as Chalmers Johnson long ago pointed out the importance of the nationalistic reaction to the Japanese invasion of China as an explanation of peasant support for Mao.[3] More recently, China's abandonment of Maoist revolution in favor of market-driven economic development in the post-Mao period has led to a wholesale reappraisal of the history of the Communist revolution, a reappraisal fueled in part by the highly critical attitude toward Mao Zedong adopted even by Western scholars of the Left who identify themselves as sympathetic to the Chinese people. Indeed, the North China peasant paradigm has been crumbling for some time, although a new one has not yet risen to take its place. How can one read Kathleen Hartford and Steven Goldstein's *Single Sparks*,[4] Chen Yung-fa's *Making Revolution*,[5] or Edward Friedman, Paul Pickowicz, and Mark Selden's *Chinese Village, Socialist State*[6] and still see "the peasant" as a conscious subject of the revolutionary experience? Similarly, how can one read such works as the (seriously flawed) *Mao: The Unknown Story* by Jung Chang and Jon Halliday[7] and continue to see Mao as a "friend" to anyone or anything except his immense ego? The most exciting task before historians of China at the present moment is precisely that of rethinking what has been taken as the basic narrative of modern Chinese history, reevaluating for instance the historical importance of the Republican period (instead of seeing it as a "necessary failure" paving the way for the "inevitable" Communist revolution), or reexamining the similarities between the histories of the PRC and the Republic of China on Taiwan (instead of seeing Taiwan as, at best, a footnote to the greater history of the "real" China). It is impossible to know what shape this rethinking will finally assume, but it stands to reason that even if the Chinese revolution remains a central element in the historical narrative of modern China, the North China peasant may well lose his iconic status.[8]

At the very least, this rethinking of the narrative structure of modern Chinese history will put revolution in its place by illustrating that, however important the political and social restructuring engineered by the revolution, this restructuring was less all-encompassing than we have often tended to imagine. The year 1949 marked perhaps less of a rupture than we have believed; at the level of popular culture, especially, continuity may have been as important as change. Beliefs about health, the body, health care practices, and medicine, to take examples central to the concerns of this volume, surely survived the revolution largely intact, to be incorporated in unchanged or unpredictable ways into the new Chinese socialist culture, as the history of qigong so richly illustrates. As the revolutionary motif fades from China's current reality, and from our recounting of China's modern history, the history of the revolution will ultimately be both *more* and *less* than the revolution proper. This will of course enrich immensely our understanding of China's history (and of China's revolution), in the same way, say, that research in the field of diaspora studies has enriched our understanding of the history of immigration.

This volume argues that Chinese religion needs to figure prominently in our rethinking and rewriting of China's modern history, as well as in our reflections on China's future, as the qigong boom and the rise and fall of Falun Gong leave little doubt as to religion's power to heal, to motivate, to mobilize, and to unsettle China's rulers.

# Appendix 1

*Chinese Emigration to North America, 1951–2002*

The U.S. Immigration and Naturalization Service (and its successor, the Department of Homeland Security) provides a bewildering wealth of data on immigrants to America. Historically, U.S. immigration authorities sorted immigrants according to their "country of last residence," which provides an accurate picture so long as the majority of immigrants arrive directly from that country. Any attempt to trace a comprehensive portrait of Chinese migration, however, must take into account Hong Kong and, to a lesser extent, Taiwan, as many mainland Chinese left China for Taiwan (in the period around the revolution of 1949) and Hong Kong (in a series of waves of emigration) from the mid-1940s through the present. Unfortunately, figures for emigration from Taiwan have been blended into the figures for China since 1957, and it is thus impossible to distinguish between the two; this is not terribly important because there has been little emigration from the mainland to Taiwan since the early 1950s—and thus little "chain migration" from China to Taiwan to the United States—and also because Canadian figures (see discussion below) suggest that Taiwan has not been a particularly important source of Chinese immigration to North America until very recently. Immigration authorities in the United States have kept separate data for immigrants from Hong Kong since 1952, and in 1992 began to record immigrants according to their country of birth as well as their country of last residence. Figures on immigration by country of last residence clearly indicate a significant increase in those coming directly from China beginning in the 1971–1980 period (presumably from the end of the period), while a certain percentage of immigrants from Hong Kong were Chinese who had transited through the former British colony.

Immigrants to the United States by Country of Last Residence[1]

| Period | From China | From Hong Kong |
|---|---|---|
| 1951–1960 | 9,657 | 15,541 |
| 1961–1970 | 34,764 | 75,007 |
| 1971–1980 | 124,326 | 113,467 |
| 1981–1990 | 346,747 | 98,215 |
| 1991–2000 | 419,799 | 109,779 |

More-recent annualized figures illustrate that immigration from China continues at a rapid pace:

Immigrants to the United States by Country of Last Residence

| Year | From China | From Hong Kong |
|---|---|---|
| 1998 | 41,034 | 7,397 |
| 1999 | 29,579 | 6,533 |
| 2000 | 41,801 | 7,299 |
| 2001 | 50,821 | 10,307 |
| 2002 | 55,974 | 7,952 |

The Canadian picture is similar to that in the United States, although the data have been compiled and presented somewhat differently, and, more important for the future of Canada (or more precisely, the future of Canadian cities, for Chinese immigrants choose overwhelmingly to live in Toronto, Vancouver, or Montreal), Chinese immigration to Canada is proportionally much more important than Chinese immigration to the United States. In recent years, Canada has received roughly half as many Chinese immigrants as has the United States, but Canada's population is barely more than a tenth of the American population.

Between 1966 and 1970, figures for China, Hong Kong, and Taiwan were grouped together as "From China," giving the following totals:

Immigrants to Canada by Country of Last Residence[2]

| Year | From China |
|---|---|
| 1966 | 4,097 |
| 1967 | 6,409 |
| 1968 | 8,382 |
| 1969 | 8,272 |
| 1970 | 5,972 |

Beginning in 1971, Immigration Canada began to record separately immigrants from China, Hong Kong, and Taiwan, again by country of last residence:

Immigrants to Canada by Country of Last Residence

| Year | China | Hong Kong | Taiwan | China + HK | China + HK + Taiwan |
|---|---|---|---|---|---|
| 1971 | 47 | 5,009 | 761 | 5,056 | 5,817 |
| 1972 | 25 | 6,297 | 859 | 6,322 | 7,181 |
| 1973 | 60 | 14,662 | 1,372 | 14,722 | 16,094 |
| 1974 | 379 | 12,704 | 1,882 | 13,083 | 14,965 |
| 1975 | 903 | 11,132 | 1,131 | 12,035 | 13,166 |
| 1976 | 833 | 10,725 | 1,178 | 11,558 | 12,736 |
| 1977 | 798 | 6,371 | 899 | 7,169 | 8,068 |
| 1978 | 644 | 4,740 | 637 | 5,384 | 6,021 |
| 1979 | 2,058 | 5,966 | 707 | 8,024 | 8,731 |
| 1980 | 4,936 | 6,309 | 827 | 11,245 | 12,072 |
| 1981 | 6,551 | 6,451 | 834 | 13,002 | 13,836 |
| 1982 | 6,295 | 4,952 | 600 | 11,247 | 11,847 |
| 1983 | 2,217 | 6,710 | 570 | 8,927 | 9,497 |

From 1984, Immigration Canada began to record immigrants according to their country of birth and their country of last residence, which allows for slightly more precision in understanding the origins of the immigrants in question:

Immigrants to Canada by Country of Last Residence/Country of Birth

| Year | From China | From Hong Kong | From Taiwan |
|---|---|---|---|
| 1984 | 2,214/5,796 | 7,696/5,013 | 421/420 |
| 1985 | 1,883/5,121 | 7,380/5,121 | 536/611 |
| 1986 | 1,902/4,178 | 5,893/4,318 | 695/650 |
| 1987 | 2,625/6,611 | 16,170/12,618 | 1,467/1,424 |
| 1988 | 2,778/7,903 | 23,281/18,355 | 2,187/2,066 |
| 1989 | 4,430/9,001 | 19,908/15,694 | 3,388/3,185 |
| 1990 | 7,989/14,193 | 29,261/23,134 | 3,681/3,549 |
| 1991 | 13,915/20,261 | 22,340/16,425 | 4,488/4,244 |
| 1992 | 10,429/22,160 | 38,910/27,927 | 7,456/7,021 |
| 1993 | 9,466/19,692 | 36,576/27,246 | 9,867/9,362 |
| 1994 | 12,486/23,313 | 44,196/33,676 | 7,411/7,003 |
| 1995 | 13,291/20,950 | 31,746/24,870 | 7,691/7,425 |
| 1996 | 17,516/24,959 | 29,966/24,129 | 13,207/12,741 |

After 1996, the only data available on Chinese immigration to Canada are the "Facts and Figures" reports, which are produced by Citizenship and Immigration as a preliminary step in the preparation of the more comprehensive

"Immigration Statistics" Reports compiled every five years following the completion of the census. The "Facts and Figures" reports record only the top ten sources of immigration and only in terms of country of last residence:

Immigrants to Canada by Country of Last Residence

| Year | From China | From Hong Kong | From Taiwan |
| --- | --- | --- | --- |
| 1997 | 18,520 | 22,280 | 13,320 |
| 1998 | 19,764 | 8,087 | 7,191 |
| 1999 | 29,095 | 3,663 | 5,464 |
| 2000 | 36,716 | 2,857 | 3,511 |
| 2001 | 40,315 | —[a] | 3,111 |
| 2002 | 33,231 | — | — |

a. The dashes indicate that no data are available.

# Appendix 2

*Falun Dafa Practitioners Questionnaire*

Falun Dafa Practitioners Questionnaire    May 2000

Distributed also in Chinese.

Dear Practitioners,
This is a questionnaire composed by university researchers at the University of Montreal and Dawson College, interested in Falun Gong. We would appreciate your donating your time to fill out and return this questionnaire. The data we gather will be confidential and private, and used for academic purposes only. This project is independent of the Falun Dafa volunteers and contact persons, and it is up to you to decide if you wish to participate. You can fill this questionnaire out during the conference, or send it later in the self-addressed envelope. Thank you for contributing your valuable time to our research.

Professor David Ownby (University of Montreal) and Dr. Susan Palmer (Dawson College)

Have you ever paid a membership fee to Falun Gong, or signed a membership form?

    Yes __    No __

Sex:    Male - 1    Female - 2

What is your current age? _____
Where were you born? _____
If immigrant, when did you arrive in Canada/USA? _____
If immigrant, where was the last place you lived before coming to Canada/
USA? (please provide country and city) _____

What is your educational background? (give highest degree)

High school diploma or equivalent  - 1
Some university courses            - 2
Undergraduate degree               - 3
Graduate degree, master's          - 4
Ph.D.                              - 5
Technical training                 - 6
Medical school                     - 7
Law school                         - 8

Where did you receive your education? (country and institution) _____
_____

What is your current marital status?

Single - 1   Married - 2   Divorced - 3   Separated - 4   Other – 5

Which term best describes your current household living arrangements?

1. Live alone
2. Husband and wife only
3. Husband, wife, and children
4. Husband, wife, children, parents
5. Husband, wife, children, other relatives
6. Other (please describe)

What is your occupation?

What was your household income (before taxes) in 1999?

1. less than $10,000
2. between $10,000 and $20,000
3. between $20,000 and $40,000
4. between $40,000 and $60,000

5. between $60,000 and $80,000
6. between $80,000 and $100,000
7. more than $100,000

In China, would you describe your standard of living as:

1. Middle class
2. Below middle class
3. Higher than middle class

Please compare your standard of living in China and in Canada/USA:

1. My standard of living is higher in Canada/USA
2. My standard of living was higher in China
3. My standard of living is roughly the same in Canada/USA as it was in China

Did you experiment with other forms of qigong before discovering Falun Gong?

Have you previously belonged to a church or other religious group before discovering Falun Gong? If yes, which?

What are/were the professions of your parents?

Mother_____    Father_____

Do your parents practice Falun Gong?

Mother_____    Father_____

Have your parents experimented with other forms of qigong before discovering Falun Gong?

Mother_____    Father_____

Did your parents previously belong to a church or another religious group before discovering Falun Gong? If yes, which?

Mother_____    Father_____

What year did you begin the cultivation practice? _____

Where did you begin practicing?

1. China   2. Canada   3. USA   4. Other

How did you first hear of it?

1. Internet
2. Relative
3. Friend
4. Work colleague
5. Book (*Zhuan falun*)
6. Observing the practice outdoors
7. Other (explain)

What first attracted you to the practice? (you can select more than one)

1. the ideas
2. the exercises
3. Master Li
4. the community
5. the health benefits
6. the spiritual growth/elevation
7. other things (explain)

If you practiced in China, please list the activities in which you engaged (you may select more than one):

1. attended Master Li's lectures
2. attended group cultivation sessions
3. purchased books and videos
4. practiced on my own or with friends/family

If you practiced in China, please estimate how many hours a week you devoted to Falun Gong on average _____

In your current Falun Gong practice, please estimate how many hours a week you devote to Falun Gong on average _____

What percentage of this time goes to:

1. individual cultivation____
2. group cultivation____
3. efforts to publicize Falun Gong_____

Which of the following activities have you engaged in?

1. circulated petitions
2. written letters to Chinese/Canadian/US embassy
3. returned to China to appeal to Chinese authorities

Has your heavenly eye opened?    1. Yes        2. No

Have you ever experienced spirit possession?    1. Yes        2. No

Please add any other comments which you feel would be helpful to us.

# Notes

CHAPTER I

1. Although Falun Gong founder Li Hongzhi denounced many other forms of qigong almost from the beginning of his career as a qigong master, Falun Gong in fact arose out of the qigong milieu and, in its early years, belonged to the national qigong association, the China Qigong Science Research Society. Whatever its later differences with more mainstream qigong, Falun Gong could not have emerged had the qigong boom not preceded it, and virtually everyone considered Falun Gong a kind of qigong in the early 1990s.

2. See "Fact File," http://www.faluninfo.net (accessed 4 June 2007).

3. Faison, "Beijing Journal: If It's a Comic Book, Why Is Nobody Laughing?"

4. See Browne, "China Jails U.S.–based Falun Gong Member."

5. See, for example, the essays in the journal *Nova Religio* 6.2 (April 2003), all of which treat Falun Gong.

6. On this revival, see Miller, ed., *Chinese Religions in Contemporary Societies*; MacInnis, *Religion in China Today: Policy and Practice*; and Kipnis, "The Flourishing of Religion in Post-Mao China and the Anthropological Category of Religion," 32–46.

7. Ian Johnson surveys this culture of contention in his *Wild Grass: Three Stories of Change in Modern China*. For more scholarly perspectives, see Perry and Selden, eds., *Chinese Society: Change, Conflict, and Resistance*.

8. There is as yet no single-volume history of China's rebellions. On the Taipings, see Spence, *God's Chinese Son: The Taiping Heavenly Kingdom of Hong Xiuquan*. I discuss the White Lotus extensively below; for an overview

of rebellions in early Chinese history, see Schipper, "Millénarismes et messianismes dans la Chine ancienne," 31–49.

9. I use the terms "religion" and "popular religion" largely interchangeably in this volume and argue that the modern Chinese state's construction of the category of religion has rendered discussion of such issues extremely difficult. Although there is a large literature debating the proper definition of religion and attempting to establish the boundaries between religion and popular religion, I do not choose to engage that literature here.

10. On religion under Mao, see Luo Zhufeng, ed., *Religion under Socialism in China*; MacInnis, *Religious Policy and Practice in Communist China: A Documentary History*; and Welch, *Buddhism under Mao*.

11. By "local cult," I refer to popular religious groups organized around deified individuals, forces, or even animals, which were found in great number throughout much of Chinese history. Although sometimes overlapping, these were sometimes separate from the ancestral cult and from the "bureaucratic" gods who policed Chinese villages and households. Local cults often merged syncretically with larger traditions such as Buddhism and Daoism and were often managed by the local elite, who used them to enhance their status and control. On bureaucratic gods, see Wolf, "Gods, Ghosts, and Ancestors," 131–182. On local cults, see Weller and Shahar, *Unruly Gods: Divinity and Society in China*; Szonyi, *Practicing Kinship: Lineage and Descent in Late Imperial China*; and Dean, *Taoist Ritual and Popular Cults of Southeast China*.

12. Asad, *Genealogies of the Secular: Discipline and Reasons of Power in Christianity and Islam*.

13. See Goossaert, "1898"; Goossaert, "Le destin de la religion chinoise"; and Nedostup, "Religion, Superstition, and Governing Society in Nationalist China."

14. "Three-self" is a shorthand reference to the three basic principles of religious organization in China—self-governance, self-support, and self-propagation—emphasizing the independence of China's religious establishment from outside missionary influence (particularly in the Christian context). This movement had its roots in the Republican period and was appropriated by Communist authorities for the purposes of nationalism and control. See Wickeri, *Seeking Common Ground: Protestant Christianity, the Three-Self Movement, and China's United Front*.

15. See Ownby, "A History for Falun Gong."

16. Vincent Goossaert provides much more detailed analysis of this transition in his fascinating article "1898," demonstrating, among other things, that while Confucian fundamentalism and anticlericalism had characterized much of late imperial discourse on religion, the element of anti-superstition came to be added in the early twentieth century. See also Chen Hsi-Yuan, "Confucianism Encounters Religion: The Formation of Religious Discourse and the Confucian Movement in Modern China."

17. David Palmer, *La fièvre du qigong: Guérison, religion et politique en Chine, 1949–1999*, and the English-language version, *Qigong Fever: Body, Science, and Utopia in China, 1949–1999*, constitute the essential starting point for any serious study of qigong.

18. These themes are developed more fully in chapter 3.

19. Among book-length studies examining the popular search for meaning in post-Mao China, one might well consult Ye, *China Candid: The People on the People's Republic*; Barmé, *In the Red: On Contemporary Chinese Culture*; Munro, "Syncretic Sects and Secret Societies: Revival in the 1980s"; Davis, ed., *The Consumer Revolution in Urban China*; Link, Madsen, and Pickowicz, *Popular China: Unofficial Culture in a Globalizing Society*; Liu, *Jumping into the Sea: From Academics to Entrepreneurs in South China*; Solinger, *Contesting Citizenship in Urban China: Peasant Migrants, the State, and the Logic of the Market*; and Overmyer, ed., *Religion in China Today*.

20. Among book-length studies of Chinese politics since the rise of Deng Xiaoping, one might profitably consult Saich, *Governance and Politics of China*; and Fewsmith, *China since Tian'anmen: The Politics of Transition*.

21. See "Fact File," http://www.faluninfo.net (accessed 17 July 2006). I will discuss the accuracy of Falun Gong estimates in more detail in chapter 6, but will note here that most human rights organizations take Falun Gong claims seriously even if they sometimes question their figures.

22. See Keith and Lin, "The 'Falun Gong Problem': Politics and the Struggle for the Rule of Law in China," 623–642.

23. See Hsu, *The Transmission of Chinese Medicine*.

24. Micollier's ideas are most fully developed in her Ph.D. thesis, "Un aspect de la pluralité médicale en Chine populaire: Les pratiques de Qi Gong—Dimension thérapeutique/dimension sociale." A capsule introduction to her work is in Micollier, "Control and Release of Emotions in Qigong Health Practices," *China Perspectives* 24: 22–30. See also her "Entre science et religion, modernité et tradition: Le discours pluriel des pratiquants du *qigong*," 205–223.

25. Nancy N. Chen, "Urban Spaces and Experiences of *Qigong*," 347–361; Chen, "Healing Sects and Anti-Cult Campaigns," 505–520; Chen, *Breathing Spaces: Qigong, Psychiatry, and Healing in China*; Ots, "The Silenced Body —The Expressive Leib. On the Dialectic of Mind and Life in Chinese Cathartic Healing," in *Embodiment and Experience: The Existential Ground of Culture and Self*, ed. Thomas Csordas (Cambridge: Cambridge University Press, 1999), 116–136. For a brief account of the importance of this line of investigation, see the review of Csordas's volume by Adeline Masquelier in *American Ethnologist* 24.4 (November 1997): 940–941.

26. Xu, "Body, Discourse, and the Cultural Politics of Contemporary Chinese Qigong," 961–991.

27. Palmer, *Qigong Fever*.

28. Click on the link "Religions and Movements" (case studies) under the heading "Texts and Documents" and scroll down to find Falun Gong.

29. Madsen, "Understanding Falun Gong," 243–247.

30. Chan, "Falun Gong in China: A Sociological Perspective," 665–683.

31. Tong, "An Organizational Analysis of Falun Gong Structure, Communications, Financing," 636–660.

32. Penny, "The Life and Times of Li Hongzhi: Falun Gong and Religious Biography," 643–661; and Penny, "The Body of Master Li."

33. Wessinger, "Falun Gong Symposium: Introduction and Glossary," 215–222; Ownby, "A History for Falun Gong," 223–243; Irons, "Falun Gong and the Sectarian Religion Paradigm," 244–262; Lowe, "Chinese and International Contexts for the Rise of Falun Gong," 263–276; Bell and Boas, "Falun Gong and the Internet: Evangelism, Community, and Struggle for Survival," 277–293; Fisher, "Resistance and Salvation in Falun Gong: The Promise and Peril of Forbearance," 294–311; Edelman and Richardson, "Falun Gong and the Law: Development of Legal Social Control in China," 312–331; Burgdoff, "How Falun Gong Practice Undermines Li Hongzhi's Totalistic Rhetoric," 332–347; and Palmer, "From Healing to Protest: Conversion Patterns among the Practitioners of Falun Gong," 348–364.

34. See, for example, Blackburn, "Movements of Power and Acts of Resistance: Falun Gong and the Politics of Everyday Life"; Bruseker, "Falun Gong: A Modern Chinese Folk Buddhist Movement in Crisis"; Dalby, "Between Discipline and Dignity: An Examination of the Appropriation and Reproduction of Falun Gong Cultivation in Western Spaces"; Li Junpeng, "New Religious Movements and the State: The Case of Falun Gong"; Munekage, "China's New Religious Movement: Falun Gong's Cultural Resistance and Political Confrontation"; Yao, "A Rhetorical Analysis of Falun Gong in China: Inheritance of Tradition, Contemporary Appeals, and Challenge to the Social Order."

35. Perry, "Challenging the Mandate of Heaven," 163–180.

36. Shue, "Global Imaginings, the State's Quest for Hegemony and the Pursuit of Phantom Freedom in China: From *Heshang* to Falun Gong," 210–229.

37. Munro, "Judicial Psychiatry in China and Its Political Abuses," 106–120.

38. Keith and Lin, "The 'Falun Gong Problem.'"

39. Chang, *Falun Gong: The End of Days*.

40. Porter, "Falun Gong in the United States: An Ethnographic Study." The volume is available via www.amazon.com. See also his "Professional Practitioners and Contact Persons Explicating Special Types of Falun Gong Practitioners," 62–83.

41. John Wong and William T. Liu, *The Mystery of China's Falun Gong: Its Rise and Its Sociological Implications*.

42. Schechter, *Falun Gong's Challenge to China: Spiritual Practice or "Evil Cult"?* and Adams, Adams, and Galati, *Power of the Wheel: Falun Gong Revolution*. Galati is a lawyer who has defended Falun Gong causes in Canada.

43. See, for example, Ji Shi, *Qishi hairen de Li Hongzhi jiqi "Falun Gong"*; Tan, Qin, and Kong, eds., *Falun Gong yu minjian mimi jieshe: Xiejiao Falun Gong neimu dajiemi*, 4–20; *Huoguo yangmin "Falun Gong."*

44. See, for example, Hua and Zhong, *Falungong Fengbao*; Kang, *Falungong shijian quan toushi*; Pan, *Falun dafa zhi xianfan bianzheng*.

45. See Palmer, *Qigong Fever*, ch. 8; David A. Palmer, "Falun Gong: La tentation du politique," 36–43; Palmer, "Le qigong au carrefour des 'discours anti,'" 153–166; Palmer, "La doctrine de Li Hongzhi: Le Falun Gong, entre sectarisme et salut universel," 14–24; Palmer, "Modernity and Millennialism in China: Qigong and the

Birth of Falun Gong," 79–109; Palmer, "Le qigong et la tradition sectaire chinoise," 471–480.


CHAPTER 2

1. The terms Falun Gong and Falun Dafa are interchangeable in that they refer to the same beliefs and practices. Practitioners often prefer "Falun Dafa" ("the great way of the revolving wheel") to "Falun Gong" ("the discipline of the revolving wheel") because they believe that their practice is at a higher level than ordinary qigong, and using the term "dafa" rather than "gong" underscores the distance between Falun Dafa and qigong.

2. "'Cultivation' refers to the improvement of one's heart and mind through the careful study of universal principles based on truthfulness, benevolence, and forbearance; 'practice' means doing exercises and meditation to energize the body." See the home page of Falun Dafa at www.falundafa.org (accessed 4 June 2006).

3. See, for example, the recent literature on Melanesian cargo cults: Hermann, "The Yali Movement in Retrospect: Rewriting History, Redefining 'Cargo Cult,'" 55–71; Kaplan, *Neither Cargo nor Cult: Ritual Politics and the Colonial Imagination in Fiji*; Lindstrom, *Cargo Cult: Strange Stories of Desire from Melanesia and Beyond*; and Whitehouse, *Inside the Cult: Religious Innovation and Transmission in Papua New Guinea*.

4. See, for example, Buruma, "The Sect That Became the Enemy of the State," *New York Times*, 15 July 1999; Perry, "Challenging the Mandate of Heaven"; Chang, *Falun Gong: The End of Days*; Chen and Dai, eds., *"Falun Gong" yu xiejiao*.

5. Basic English-language treatments of the White Lotus include De Groot, *Sectarianism and Religious Persecution in China*; Naquin, *Millenarian Rebellion in China: The Eight Trigrams Uprising of 1813*; Naquin, "The Transmission of White Lotus Sectarianism in Late Imperial China," in Johnson, Nathan, and Rawski, *Popular Culture in Late Imperial China*, 255–291; Overmyer, *Folk Buddhist Religion: Dissenting Sects in Late Traditional China*; Overmyer, "Values in Chinese Sectarian Literature: Ming and Ch'ing Pao-chüan," in Johnson, Nathan, and Rawski, *Popular Culture in Late Imperial China*, 219–254; Overmyer, *Precious Volumes: An Introduction to Chinese Sectarian Scriptures from the Sixteenth and Seventeenth Centuries*; Ter Haar, *The White Lotus Teachings in Chinese Religious History*; Hubert Seiwert, with Ma Xisha, *Popular Religious Movements and Heterodox Sects in Chinese History*. The scholarly literature in Chinese and Japanese is extensive. For an introduction to some of this literature in Chinese, see Ownby, "Recent Chinese Scholarship on the History of Secret Societies," 139–158.

6. Ter Haar, *The White Lotus Teachings in Chinese Religious History*.

7. See particularly Overmyer, *Precious Volumes*; and Seiwert and Ma, *Popular Religious Movements and Heterodox Sects*.

8. See, for example, Richard Shek and Tetsuro Noguchi, "Eternal Mother Religion: Its History and Ethics," in Liu and Shek, *Heterodoxy in Late Imperial China*, 241–280.

9. Prasenjit Duara discusses this historiography in his *Sovereignty and Authenticity: Manchukuo and the East Asian Modern*, 103–105.

10. Dubois, *The Sacred Village: Social Change and Religious Life in Rural North China*.

11. On syncretism in Chinese religion in general, see Brook, "Rethinking Syncretism: The Unity of the Three Teachings and Their Joint Worship in Late-Imperial China," 13–44; and Bokenkamp, "The Silkworm and the Bodhi Tree: The Lingbao Attempt to Replace Buddhism in China and Our Attempt to Place Lingbao Taoism," 341–384.

12. The following section draws on Ownby, "Imperial Fantasies: The Chinese Communist and Peasant Rebellions," 65–91; and Ownby and Qiao, trans. and eds., "Scriptures of the Way of the Temple of the Heavenly Immortals," 1–101.

13. Representative examples of these scriptures are translated in Ownby and Qiao, "Scriptures of the Way of the Temple of the Heavenly Immortals."

14. Dubois, *Sacred Village*, 111–112, recounts another case and there are undoubtedly more, but in general, researchers have examined either police documents or society-generated scriptures, without necessarily bringing the two together.

15. Analysis of the scriptures of redemptive societies can help to correct the biases of police records, but they present their own problems as sources, revealing more about the master, his influences, and his literary skills than about the followers. See Dubois, *Sacred Village*, 3. My interpretation of Falun Gong would have been very different if I had relied solely on Li Hongzhi's writings, without doing fieldwork with practitioners.

16. Dubois, *Sacred Village*, uses the term "sectarian," which I have changed to "redemptive society" without, I hope, doing violence to his excellent research.

17. Dubois could not do fieldwork on the Way of Penetrating Unity, since it had been suppressed. Consequently, the tone of the chapter treating this group is quite different from other chapters of his book, which reinforces the importance of sources to our understanding of such societies.

18. Dubois, *Sacred Village*, 1.

19. Ibid., 155–156.

20. Ibid., 107.

21. Ibid., 166.

22. See Duara, *Sovereignty and Authenticity*, 111–122.

23. Zhongguo huidaomen shiliao jicheng bianzuan weiyuanhui, ed., *Zhongguo huidaomen shiliao jicheng*, 2, lists 4,542 names of *huidaomen* during the Republican period.

24. Duara, "Pan-Asianism and the Discourse of Civilization," 118–119.

25. Ibid., 117.

26. David Palmer and I, together with scholars from Taiwan, China, and Europe, are undertaking a major research project on Republican period redemptive societies.

27. The president of the society, the famous intellectual Kang Youwei, believed that the true importance of the nation grew out of its "self-transcendence in

the universalist utopia of Datong (Great Unity), an ideal that meshed well with Manchukuo's rhetoric of civilization." See Duara, *Sovereignty and Authenticity*, 112–113.

28. Ibid., 110.

29. Jones, "Religion in Taiwan at the End of the Japanese Colonial Period," 23–24.

30. Duara, *Rescuing History from the Nation: Questioning Narratives of Modern China*, 97.

31. Ibid., 95–98.

32. Goossaert, "Le destin de la religion chinoise," 436.

33. Sheridan, *Chinese Warlord: The Career of Feng Yü-hsiang*, 116. More generally, see Bastid-Bruguière, "La campagne antireligieuse de 1922," 77–93.

34. Welch, *The Buddhist Revival in China*, 148.

35. Duara, *Rescuing History from the Nation*, 99.

36. Duara, *Sovereignty and Authenticity*, 109.

37. Ibid., 110.

38. Ibid., 103.

39. Shao, *Zhongguo huidaomen*, 452–456.

40. Welch, *Buddhism under Mao*, 123.

41. Dubois, *Sacred Village*, chs. 5 and 7.

42. Chau, *Miraculous Response: Doing Popular Religion in Contemporary China*.

43. Potter, "Belief in Control: Regulation of Religion in China," 319.

44. Tang, *The Cultural Revolution and Post-Mao Reforms: A Historical Perspective*, 18.

45. Duara, *Sovereignty and Authenticity*, 109.

46. Shao, *Zhongguo huidaomen*, 3.

47. This is beginning to occur with redemptive societies in Taiwan. See, for example, Tiandijiao Jiyuan jiaoshi weiyuanhui, ed., *Tiandijiao jianshi*.

48. For a brief introduction to such topics, see Ownby, "Chinese Millenarian Traditions."

49. See, in particular, Overmyer, *Precious Volumes*; and Seiwert and Ma, *Popular Religious Movements and Heterodox Sects*.

CHAPTER 3

This chapter draws heavily on the work of David Palmer, who has produced an excellent historical overview of the rise and fall of qigong in his *Qigong Fever*. Although I footnote Palmer repeatedly throughout this chapter, my debt to him is such that I want to acknowledge it explicitly here, for this chapter could not have been written without Palmer's work, and the narrative I recount largely follows Palmer's. I use his research with his express permission.

1. Translated in Teng and Fairbank, *China's Response to the West: A Documentary Survey 1839–1923*, 51–52.

2. See ibid., 50.

3. Schwarcz, *The Chinese Enlightenment: Intellectuals and the Legacy of the May Fourth Movement of 1919*; Keenan, *The Dewey Experiment in China: Educational Reform and Political Power in the Early Republic.*

4. Kwok, *Scientism in Chinese Thought, 1900–1950.*

5. Unschuld, *Medical Ethics in Imperial China: A Study in Historical Anthropology*, 118.

6. Scheid, *Chinese Medicine in Contemporary China: Plurality and Synthesis*, 10–11.

7. Croizier, *Traditional Medicine in Modern China: Science, Nationalism, and the Tensions of Cultural Change*, 73–74, 129–130; Lampton, *The Politics of Medicine in China: The Policy Press, 1949–1977*, 9–17.

8. See Lei, "When Chinese Medicine Encountered the State: 1910–1949," ch. 2.

9. Although Traditional Chinese Medicine, like many modern Western doctors, does preach the gospel of good diet and healthy living as the best way to avoid disease.

10. See Lei, "When Chinese Medicine Encountered the State," ch. 3.

11. Terminological issues are complex here. Traditional Chinese Medicine would not have been recognized as either "traditional" or even necessarily "Chinese" in pre-twentieth-century China. The term "Traditional Chinese Medicine," often abbreviated as TCM, is in fact a Western term (although employed by Chinese when addressing Western audiences) used to describe a branch of "alternative medicine" which is, in fact, not "traditional" at all: TCM theory and practice are the result of considerable "modernization" carried out under the dictates of biomedicine since the 1950s. When traditional practitioners reacted to the threat of extinction in the late 1920s, they referred to "national medicine" or "Chinese medicine" and did not always consciously evoke tradition, as "tradition" was unscientific and hence problematic. See Scheid, *Chinese Medicine in Contemporary China*, ch. 3; Taylor, "'Improving' Chinese Medicine: The Role of Traditional Medicine in Newly Communist China, 1949–1953," in Chan, Clancey, and Loy, *Historical Perspectives on East Asian Science, Technology and Medicine*, 251–263.

12. See Scheid, *Chinese Medicine in Contemporary China*, ch. 2.

13. Despeux, "Le *qigong*, une expression de la modernité chinoise," 267–281.

14. The following section draws on Palmer, *Qigong Fever*, ch. 1.

15. On Neiyanggong, see Wang and Zhou, *Zhongguo qigong xueshu fazhanshi*, 511.

16. Lampton, *The Politics of Medicine in China*, 14.

17. Cited in Croizier, *Traditional Medicine in Modern China*, 160–161.

18. Ibid., 171–172.

19. Palmer, *Qigong Fever*, 35–36.

20. Indeed, qigong is mentioned rarely if at all in many studies of Chinese medicine in the People's Republic, even those, like Scheid's, that were researched during and written after the qigong boom. Scheid, *Chinese Medicine in Contemporary China*, 18, lists "the flowering of *qigong* movements" as one example among many of the "visible reemergence of unofficial healing practices" and in a footnote (296n30)

adds, "The encounter between the state and the popular *Falungong* movement that was ongoing while I was completing the manuscript for this book will provide valuable insights into articulations between the religious, medical, and scientific domains in contemporary China," but does not elaborate further.

21. Palmer, *Qigong Fever*, ch. 1.

22. Hsu, *The Transmission of Chinese Medicine*, 23.

23. Lampton, *The Politics of Medicine in China*, 62–65.

24. The following section is based on Palmer, *Qigong Fever*, ch. 1.

25. Ibid., 43. Chinese medicine in general was attacked on the same grounds, but at the same time, the emphasis in public health during the Cultural Revolution period was on "service to the masses," in whose names large numbers of barefoot doctors were sent to (or recruited from) the countryside—in addition to well-trained urban doctors who underwent rustification for political reasons. To the extent that Chinese medicine was part of a barefoot doctor's toolkit or could otherwise be made to serve the masses, it was endorsed, but Scheid, *Chinese Medicine in Contemporary China*, 76–81, argues that Chinese medicine suffered greater losses than did Western medicine during this period.

26. Palmer, *Qigong Fever*, ch. 1.

27. The following draws principally on ibid., ch. 2.

28. On the Lingnan school, see Croizier, *Art and Revolution in Modern China: The Lingnan (Cantonese) School of Painting, 1906–51*.

29. Additional information on Guo Lin can be found on Web sites devoted to her. See, for example, http://alternativehealing.org/guo_lin_qigong.htm (accessed 14 March 2006), and http://www.zhanzhuanggong.bizland.com/qigongetcancer/anecdotes/bioguolin.htm (accessed 14 March 2006).

30. The following section draws on Palmer, *Qigong Fever*, ch. 2.

31. Translated in ibid., 51–52.

32. Translated in ibid., 52–53.

33. Ibid., ch. 2.

34. Ibid., 31.

35. Ibid., 32.

36. Ibid., ch. 2.

37. Ibid.

38. For an intelligent discussion of Chinese journalism under Mao, see Cheek, *Propaganda and Culture in Mao's China: Deng Tuo and the Intelligentsia*.

39. See the entire volume of *Journalism Studies* 1.4 (November 2000), entitled "Chinese Journalism Today: Of the Party and in the Market," which contains a number of excellent articles on the theme; see also Huang, Davies, and Wright, "Beyond Party Propaganda: A Case Study of China's Rising Commercialised Press"; and Cheek, "Redefining Propaganda: Debates on the Role of Journalism in Post-Mao China," in Chang, *Mainland China after the Thirteenth Party Congress*, 133–158.

40. Karchmer, "Magic, Science, and *Qigong* in Contemporary China," 311–322.

41. See Palmer, *Qigong Fever*, ch. 2.

42. Ibid., 60.

43. Ibid., ch. 2.

44. Ibid.

45. See ibid. Wu was a protégé of Wang Zhen, having served as his secretary in the 1970s, was trained as a nuclear physicist, and is playing a leading role in the organization of the 2008 Beijing Olympic games.

46. Ibid., 68.

47. Ibid., 82–85.

48. The following section draws on ibid., ch. 4.

49. David Palmer, personal communication, estimates that there were tens of thousands, if we include those who did not attempt to establish their own schools.

50. See Palmer, *Qigong Fever*, ch. 4, as well the Web sites http://www.chinaqigong.net/english/qgsk/ymj.htm (accessed 15 March 2006); http://www.qimagazine.co.uk/qigong.htm (accessed 15 March 2006); and http://www.qimagazine.co.uk/55_4article.htm (accessed 15 March 2006). Michael Tse, a well-known qigong master in England, was Yang's student. See http://www.qimagazine.com/main.html (accessed 15 July 2006).

51. Translated in Palmer, *Qigong Fever*, 88–89.

52. See Palmer, *La fièvre du qigong*, 107–108. Hsu, *The Transmission of Chinese Medicine*, 22, notes:

> Present day *qigong* practices are in general new versions—often complete transmutations—of former Daoist meditation traditions, sometimes including elements of Buddhist meditation practices. Since *wushu* [i.e., martial arts] . . . masters were least affected by efforts at modernisation, the meditative practices widespread today under the name of *qigong*, are mainly derived from *wushu* traditions. Formerly, I was told, all "Chinese doctors" engaged in meditative practices for self-cultivation, engaged in what a modern *qigong* healer would call "soft *qigong*" . . . as opposed to the *wushu* masters' "hard *qigong*." . . . The former practice strengthened one's Inner *qi* . . . , the latter one's Outer *qi*.

Statistical evidence to this effect is provided in Palmer, *Qigong Fever*, 93, where he notes that 47.5% of masters initiated before the qigong boom claimed a martial arts affiliation.

53. Cinnabar was one of the products produced by Daoist alchemy in traditional China, and should be seen as an elixir.

54. See Palmer, *Qigong Fever*, ch. 4.

55. Ibid.

56. See ibid. Although Yan Xin was a major phenomenon in China, there is very little information about him available outside of Palmer's treatment. Some information about Yan's teachings and powers can be found in books such as Lu, *Scientific Qigong Exploration: The Wonders and Mysteries of Qi*; and Lin et al., eds., *Secrets and Benefits of Internal Qigong Cultivation: Lectures by Qigong Master Dr. Yan*

*Xin.* Yan Xin's own Web site, www.yanxinqigong.net (accessed 20 July 2006), provides little useful information.

57. The following section draws on Palmer, *Qigong Fever,* 146–150, 208–218. There is even less information available on Zhang than on Yan Xin. Like Yan, Zhang has his own Web site, http://www.tianhuaculture.net/eng (accessed 20 July 2006), which is much richer than Yan Xin's. Zhang's movement was ultimately suppressed by Chinese authorities, and he fled to Guam in 2000 before finally relocating to the United States. On his Web site, he expressed support for Falun Gong and attacked the Chinese Communist Party much as Falun Gong has done. Zhang died in an automobile accident in the United States on 31 July 2006.

58. Palmer, *La fièvre du qigong,* 317–18.

59. Ibid., 295–96.

CHAPTER 4

1. The following draws on such sources as "Li Hongzhi qiren qishi"; and Tan et al., eds., *Falun Gong yu minjian mimi jieshe,* 4–20. These are obviously state propaganda, produced in the context of the campaign against Falun Gong, but they nonetheless provide essential details of Li's life. With the exception of Li Hongzhi's biography, discussed below, Falun Gong sources are not revealing about Li's life prior to his becoming a master, and Li himself insists that his "human life" is not particularly important to his teachings.

2. Some online sources give Li's date of birth as 7 July rather than 27 July. See for example http://www.britannica.com/eb/question-338603/49/Li-Hongzhi-born.

3. Falun Gong Research Society, "A Short Biography of Mr. Li Hongzhi, the Founder of China Falun Gong and Chairman of Falun Gong Research Society," was originally published as an appendix to the Chinese version of *Zhuan falun* (Hong Kong. Falun Fofa, October 1997). This document is no longer available on Falun Gong Web sites, but can be found in "Brief Biography of Li Hongzhi, Founder of Falun Gong and President of Falun Gong Research Society," *Chinese Law and Government* 32.6 (2000): 14–23, and on the Web at http://web.archive.org/web/20001024123353 and http://www.compapp.dcu.ie/~dongxue/biography.html (accessed 21 July 2006).

4. One cannot help but wonder how these earlier masters escaped political censure.

5. Tan et al., eds., *Falun Gong yu minjian mimi jieshe,* 7–8. Falun Gong practitioners have since replied that oxytocin was not available until after 1953; see the article on the Clear Wisdom Web site, available at http://clearwisdom.net/emh/articles/2001/2/2/4853.html (accessed 21 July 2006).

6. Tan et al., eds., *Falun Gong yu minjian mimi jieshe,* 9. Li was born in 1951 or 1952 and would have begun elementary school in 1957 or 1958. If his third-grade teacher, to take a hypothetical example, had been forty years old in 1960, she would

have been seventy-nine in 1999, when the campaign against Falun Gong began. One cannot but marvel at the "supernormal powers" of the elementary school teacher who recalls the mediocre writing skills of an unexceptional student forty years earlier.

7. Tan et al., eds., *Falun Gong yu minjian mimi jieshe*, 9.

8. Ibid., 10.

9. Ibid., 9.

10. Ibid., 27.

11. Ibid., 8.

12. Chan is better known in the West by its Japanese name, Zen. The terms "nine palaces" and "eight trigrams" are both drawn from traditional popular religious traditions. See, for example, Naquin, *Millenarian Rebellion*.

13. Tan et al., eds., *Falun Gong yu minjian mimi jieshe*, 10–11.

14. See Pure Insight Net, "A Chronicle of Major Events of Falun Dafa, Part 1 (Revised Edition)," available at http://www.pureinsight.org/pi/index.php?news=2097 (accessed 21 July 2006).

15. Palmer, *Qigong Fever*, 221.

16. See, for example, http://clearwisdom.net/emh/articles/2004/11/14/54527.html (accessed 20 July 2006).

17. See Yi Pi Falun Gong Xueyuan, *Jielu Changchun jishaoshu ren de yinmou*; also http://fr.clearharmony.net/articles/200411/17037.html (accessed 20 July 2006).

18. I arrived at the figure of 60,000 by adding together the attendance figures for individual events given in "A Chronicle of Major Events of Falun Dafa," on the Pure Insight Web site. The precise sum for the period through the beginning of 1995 comes to 60,240, but there are several venues where no attendance figures are given. In any event, the 60,000 figure greatly exceeds previous estimates of 20,000 for the total of those who attended Li's lectures during this period, which is found in a variety of sources. The only possible way to verify these competing figures would be to have access to the records of ticket sales, which should have been kept by the sponsoring agency and perhaps by Falun Gong. Calculations based on the lower estimate of 20,000 give an average attendance of some 370 per event, which seems rather low. Using the 60,000 figure gives an average of 1,111, which is credible. In any event, had the practitioners who compiled these figures wished to exaggerate Li's influence during this period, they could have inflated the figures considerably more before reaching the threshold of unbelievability.

19. Palmer, *Qigong Fever*, 223.

20. Gong'anbu xuanchuanju, ed., *Li Hongzhi: Qiren qishi*, 33.

21. Authorities had apparently paid little attention to Falun Gong prior to the demonstration of 25 April 1999. James Tong persuasively argues that the three-month delay between the demonstration and the formal launch of the campaign against Falun Gong in late July is best explained by the felt need on the part of China's high-level authorities to gather information about the group. See Tong, "Anatomy of Re-

gime Repression in China: Timing, Enforcement Institutions, and Target Selection in Banning the Falungong, July 1999," 795–820.

22. Tong, "An Organizational Analysis."

23. See Pure Insight Net, "A Chronicle of Major Events of Falun Dafa."

24. See ibid.

25. See "The Truth behind the April 25th Incident," at http://www.faluninfo.net/ SpecialTopics/april25abridged.doc (accessed 21 July 2006).

26. *Time Asia*, available at http://cnn.com/ASIANOW/time/asia/magazine/ 1999/990510/interview3.html (accessed 20 October 2002).

27. Most of Li Hongzhi's writings are available both in printed form and on the Internet. However, most libraries, including major research libraries, only purchase Li's most important works, such as *Zhuan falun* and *China Falun Gong*. A comprehensive study of Li's writings would have to use the printed versions rather than the Internet versions, which obscure the constant editing of Li's works, including the complete removal of texts which have come to be considered controversial. However, for the reader who prefers to consult Li's work in English, Falun Gong Internet Web sites have the advantage of providing a large selection of Li's writings in their most recent translations. This is important, as the translations have improved considerably over time. Unless otherwise noted, my footnotes to Li's works will thus be to the www.falundafa.org Web site, where Li's works can be found, and to the most recent translation (I am writing in June 2007) available on that page. The site offers Li's works in html, PDF, and Word formats. My notes will be to the Word documents, because, unlike the html documents, these are paginated, and they are easier to search and to manipulate than PDF documents. The reference to the "small fluorescent screen like a television" will thus be found in Li Hongzhi, *Zhuan falun*, 26, which is an abbreviation for Li Hongzhi, *Zhuan falun*, 2003 translation, Internet Microsoft Word edition, available at http://www.falundafa.org/book/eng/doc/zfl_new.doc (accessed 24 July 2006), 26.

28. Li Hongzhi, *Zhuan falun*, 57–62; Li Hongzhi, *Zhuan falun fajie*, 64.

29. Li Hongzhi, *Falun Dafa: Lecture in Sydney*, 34.

30. See *Time Asia*, available at http://cnn.com/ASIANOW/time/asia/magazine/ 1999/990510/interview3.html (accessed 4 May 2003).

31. See http://www.falundafa.org/book/chigb.htm.

32. See http://www.falundafa.org/eng/books.htm.

33. See http://www.falundafa.org/media/indexgb.html.

34. There is no "critical edition" of Li's writings, and if the Web sites provide convenient access, they also permit the editors of the Web sites to remove writings which come to seem problematic (such as Li's biography), or to edit Li's speeches before they are transcribed—the Web sites being the "transcription of record." I was present at an impromptu speech given by Li at an experience-sharing conference in Ottawa in May 2001. Li used very strong language in attacking the Communist Party, language which was softened by the editors of the Web site before Li's speech was posted.

35. Although I devised my own approach over the course of this research project, I was delighted to find a more elaborate version presented by Barker, "Presidential Address: The Scientific Study of Religion? You Must Be Kidding!" 287–310.

36. Li Hongzhi, *Zhuan falun*, 18.

37. Ibid., 32–33.

38. Ibid., 37–38, seems to confirm the idea of immortality; ibid., 53, seems to question it.

39. Ibid., 182.

40. Li Hongzhi, *Falun Buddha Fa: Lectures in the United States*, 34–35.

41. Indeed, at the beginning of my research, I had hypothesized that diaspora practitioners might have found in Falun Gong a way to remain "Chinese" even while leaving China and settling in Canada or the United States. However, as my research progressed, I found that relatively few practitioners seemed to suffer from a cultural identity crisis. Some worried about their children growing up relatively unexposed to Chinese culture and education, but adult immigrants seemed quite secure in their Chineseness despite having immigrated to North America.

42. Li Hongzhi, *Falun Buddha Fa: Lectures in the United States*, 28.

43. Li Hongzhi, *Guiding the Voyage*, 17.

44. Li Hongzhi, *Falun Buddha Fa: Lecture at the First Conference in North America*, 6.

45. Many claim that Li's reflections on science *guide* important work in theoretical physics throughout the world. Another well-respected Chinese scientist and practitioner compared Li's views to those of the novelist Michael Crichton in his book *Timeline*.

46. Li Hongzhi, *Zhuan falun*, 34–35.

47. Li Hongzhi, *Falun fofa: Jingjin yaozhi*, 21–22.

48. Li Hongzhi, *Falun Buddha Fa: Lectures in the United States*, 11–12.

49. Ibid., 28.

50. Ibid., 26.

51. Ibid., 25.

52. Ibid., 46.

53. Li Hongzhi, *Zhuan falun*, 1.

54. Li Hongzhi, *Zhuan falun fajie*, 87. Translation corrected.

55. Li Hongzhi, *Falun fofa: Jingjin yaozhi*, 38–39.

56. Li Hongzhi, *Zhuan falun fajie*, 102. Translation corrected.

57. Ibid., 101. Translation corrected.

58. Li Hongzhi, *Falun Dafa: Lecture in Sydney*, 9.

59. Ibid., 17.

60. Li Hongzhi, *Falun Buddha Fa: Lectures in the United States*, 32.

61. Li Hongzhi, *Falun Dafa: Lecture in Sydney*, 17.

62. Li Hongzhi, *Falun Buddha Fa: Lectures in the United States*, 38.

63. Ibid., 32.

64. Li Hongzhi, *Falun Buddha Fa: Lectures in the United States*, 14.

65. Li Hongzhi, *Zhuan falun*, 50.

66. Li Hongzhi, *Falun Buddha Fa: Lectures in the United States*, 32.

67. See, for example, Li Hongzhi, *Falun Dafa: Lecture in Sydney*, 17–19.

68. Li Hongzhi, *Falun Buddha Fa: Lectures in the United States*, 3–4.

69. Li Hongzhi, *Falun fofa: Jingjin yaozhi*, 104.

70. Li Hongzhi, *Zhuan falun*, 7. Translation corrected.

71. Li Hongzhi, *Falun Dafa: Lecture in Sydney*, 29.

72. Li Hongzhi, *Falun fofa: Jingjin yaozhi*, 33. On the fox spirits and others mentioned by Li, see Dorfman, "The Spirit of Reform: The Power of Belief in Northern China," 253–289; and Kang, *The Cult of the Fox: Power, Gender, and Popular Religion in Late Imperial and Modern China*.

73. See, among other passages, Li Hongzhi, *Zhuan falun*, 40–46.

74. See, among other passages, ibid., 57–62.

75. Li Hongzhi, *Explaining the Content of Falun Dafa*, 35.

76. Li Hongzhi, *Falun fofa: Jingjin yaozhi*, 99.

77. Li Hongzhi, "Mojie shi de renlei," in *Zhuan falun II*. This text, published in November 1995, was available on Falun Dafa Web sites in the 1990s, but was removed early in the twenty-first century.

78. Li Hongzhi, *Falun Buddha Fa: Lecture at the First Conference in North America*, 50.

79. Li Hongzhi, *Falun Dafa: Lecture in Sydney*, 22.

80. Li Hongzhi, *Zhuan falun*, 121.

81. Li Hongzhi, *Falun fofa: Jingjin yaozhi*, 48.

82. Li Hongzhi, *Zhuan falun*, 43.

83. Ibid., 121.

84. Li Hongzhi, *Falun Dafa: Lecture in Sydney*, 22–23.

85. Li Hongzhi, *Falun fofa: Jingjin yaozhi*, 75.

86. Ch'en, *Buddhism: The Light of Asia*, 35–36.

87. Li Hongzhi, *Zhuan falun*, 7–8.

88. Ibid., 144.

89. Ibid., 141.

90. Ibid., 136–137.

91. Ibid., 116.

92. Ibid., 114.

93. Ibid., 115. Translation slightly modified.

94. Ibid., 80.

95. Li Hongzhi, *Falun fofa: Jingjin yaozhi*, 36–38.

96. Ibid.

97. Ibid.

98. Li Hongzhi, *Zhuan falun*, 129.

99. Ibid., 17.

100. Palmer, *Qigong Fever*, 139–143.

101. See, for example, Bill Moyers' documentary "The Mystery of Chi [Qi]," part of his series *Healing and the Mind* (1993), which can be purchased at http://www.documentary-video.com/displayitem.cfm?vid=376 (24 July 2006). Moyers

authored a book on the same subject: Bill D. Moyers, *Healing and the Mind* (Garden City, NY: Doubleday, 1993). Qigong is discussed on 257–314.

102. Falun Gong Research Society, "A Short Biography of Master Li Hongzhi."

103. Li Hongzhi, *Zhuan falun*, 17–18.

104. Ibid., 37–38.

105. Ibid., 187.

106. Ibid., 21.

107. Ibid., 67.

108. Ibid., 24–25.

109. Ibid., 29.

CHAPTER 5

1. See Pure Insight Net, "A Chronicle of Major Events of Falun Dafa."

2. Li moved to the United States in 1996 but did not receive his green card until 1998.

3. On transnational Chinese religion in general, see Julia C. Huang, *Wings of Belief: Modern Chinese Religious Transnationalism*.

4. Falun Gong diaspora practitioners outside of North America are of course worthy of study as well. See Ackerman, "Falun Dafa and the New Age Movement in Malaysia: Signs of Health, Symbols of Salvation," 495–511.

5. See Pure Insight Net, "A Chronicle of Major Events of Falun Dafa."

6. Li never lectured in Shanghai, for example, because he was not invited early enough during the 1992–1994 period, when he was lecturing extensively in China. See Li Hongzhi, *Falun Buddha Fa: Lectures in the United States*, 42.

7. There is an extensive if uneven literature on the new Chinese diaspora. Some of the better book-length studies include Benton, *Chinese in Europe*; Ma and Cartier, eds., *The Chinese Diaspora: Space, Place, Mobility, and Identity*; Nyiri and Savel'ev, eds., *Globalizing Chinese Migration: Trends in Europe and Asia*; Louie, *Chineseness across Borders: Renegotiating Chinese Identities in China and the United States*; and Thuno, *Beyond Chinatown: New Chinese Migration and the Global Expansion of China*.

8. See, for example, the article by Alexander V. Lomanov on the problems of counting the Chinese in Russia, "On the Periphery of the 'Clash of Civilizations': Discourse and Geopolitics in Russian-Chinese Relations."

9. See Citizenship and Immigration Canada, "Facts and Figures" and "Immigration Overview," available at http://www.cic.gc.ca (accessed 22 July 2006).

10. The English-language version of the questionnaire is reproduced in appendix 2.

11. See http://www.ruf.rice.edu/~tnchina/commentary/ownby1000.html (25 June 2001).

12. Ownby, "China's Inner War," reprinted as "Why China's Falun Gong Shakes Communist Rule."

13. The judgment of the court is available at http://www.math.mcgill.ca/triples/infocult/ZhangcChau2002.txt (accessed 24 July 2006).

14. Such concerns were apparently unjustified. I returned to China in 2004 and 2005, had no trouble obtaining a visa either time, and was not harassed while in China.

15. Falun Gong Web sites repeatedly report on abuses carried out by Chinese embassies and consulates outside of China. I have no reason to believe that these reports are exaggerated.

16. Noah Porter has done similar work; see his "Falun Gong in the United States: An Ethnographic Study," available at http://www.dissertation.com. The results from his fieldwork in South Florida largely accord with what I recount below. On 113–116, Porter helpfully brings together social science survey work done on Falun Gong in China and elsewhere, displayed in a table titled "Falun Gong Demographics Worldwide." Palmer, *Qigong Fever*, 257–259, reproduces some of these survey data as well. The data reveal, however, that little valuable social science work has been done and that while the data enable us to ask better questions, they do not permit us to draw definite conclusions.

17. See Dollelaere, *Soka Gakkai: From Lay Movement to Religion*; Hammond, *Soka Gakkai in America: Accommodation and Conversion*.

18. Not all respondents answered every question on the survey form, and I cannot guarantee that none of these Chinese came from Hong Kong or Taiwan, but there is no doubt that the vast majority of practitioners surveyed were originally from mainland China and had left there by the late 1980s.

19. Survey data from China seem to indicate that the average practitioner there would have been some ten years older. See Porter, "Falun Gong in the United States," 113–116; while Palmer, *Qigong Fever*, 258, notes, "According to Falun Gong sources based on surveys of practitioners made in various cities in 1998, almost three quarters . . . were women and almost two-thirds were over 50 yrs of age. . . . However, over one-fifth (two-fifths in Beijing) . . . were college graduates."

20. The first survey, in Montreal, did not include "medical school" among the choices on the questionnaire. This was added in subsequent surveys.

21. See http://www.census.gov (accessed 25 October 2005).

22. See http://www.statcan.ca (accessed 25 October 2005).

23. See http://ceps.statcan.ca/english/profil (accessed 25 October 2005).

24. See http://www.census.gov/prod/2003pubs/p60–221.pdf (accessed 25 October 2005), 9.

25. This is based on the Toronto and Boston surveys. These questions were not asked in the first survey, circulated in Montreal.

26. Follow the links from http://faluncanada.net (accessed 25 February 2001).

27. These are composite figures, the result of combining all three surveys. For this question, respondents were allowed to select more than one response, but were asked to number them in order of importance.

28. See, for example, the witness statement of a Quebec practitioner, given at an experience-sharing conference:

In August 1997 [my husband] Pierre found the site of Falun Dafa on the Web, and printed out the first three chapters of the French translation of *Zhuan*

*falun.* As soon as I started to read, it was obvious that this was an extraordinary writing. I couldn't put it down, even if I had to read slowly because its
vocabulary was quite singular, as if the translator had had to make a special
effort to faithfully translate the work. My own reading went beyond the
words on the page, and I immediately found answers to my questions as well
as a purity, an innocence and a simplicity which drew me in from the beginning.... From the moment I began to read, I had to go to the bathroom,
where I vomited and had diarrhea. I closed my eyes while vomiting and while
emptying my bowels, and saw white snakes, white weasels, and little black,
gray and white animals coming out of my mouth and my guts. I open my
eyes and close them again, but see the same thing. What is this? What is
going on? I thought that it must be some sort of purge, but a purge occurring
at a different level from what I had experienced before. But I saw no connection with what I was reading, given how lost I felt. I went to bed and
continued my reading, but had to return to the bathroom repeatedly.

She subsequently recounts finding in *Zhuan falun* Li Hongzhi's references to the
physical effects of a first reading of the text, including explicit mentions of vomiting,
diarrhea, snakes, weasels, and other animals.

29. The following pages are based on witness statements presented at experience-sharing conferences I attended in Montreal, Toronto, Ottawa, Boston, and New
York between 2000 and 2002. In addition to the notes I took while practitioners
delivered their statements, conference organizers were also often kind enough to
provide me with the written versions of the witness statements which practitioners
had provided to them—so that the statements could be translated to or from Chinese,
English, and/or French. These translations were often rather haphazard, and I have
allowed myself to correct the English of written statements, in the interests of accurately representing what practitioners meant to say. Many similar statements can
be found on the Clear Wisdom Web site, at http://www.clearwisdom.net/emh/
index.html (accessed 13 May 2002), particularly under the rubrics "Personal Cultivation" and "Practitioners' Insights." While I believe the statements on the Web site to
be genuine reflections of practitioners' opinions, and find in general that the same
narrative structure informs both the statements which I personally witnessed and
those appearing on the Web site, it is nonetheless true that statements on the Web site
have been selected in accordance with the Web masters' points of emphasis and have
probably been edited as well, if only for space considerations.

30. Yao Ming's rise to stardom with the Houston Rockets only consolidated the
hold of the NBA on the imaginations of China's youth. Michael Jordan (*Qiaodun*) and
the Chicago Bulls (*Niudui*) were wildly popular in China throughout the 1990s.

31. This is less dramatic in Canada than it might well be in America, as health
care is provided by the state. Benefits might include employer-paid private insurance
to cover dental care or some medical procedures not covered by the basic policy.

32. Angela could have found similar sanction in fundamentalist Christianity or
any variety of faiths. Elsewhere in her testimony, she speaks of having tired of
Christianity—she attended Christian schools in Hong Kong—because of its emphasis

on hierarchy and its concern with money. She also speaks of visions she experienced while meditating, perhaps suggesting an affinity for mysticism which, as a Chinese, she might seek to satisfy in Chinese religious practices.

33. The main objective of public security authorities in Beijing, at least at this stage of the campaign, was to keep practitioners out of the capital. Representatives of provincial Public Security Bureaus set up offices in Beijing to "repatriate" practitioners to their homes.

34. Jordan and Overmyer's *The Flying Phoenix: Aspects of Chinese Sectarianism in Taiwan* might be one place to begin.

CHAPTER 6

1. For an introduction to China's "dark side," see Wu, *Troublemaker: One Man's Crusade against China's Cruelty*, and his Web site, http://www.laogai.org (accessed 25 July 2006).

2. This is my impression from having spoken personally with researchers who work for human rights organizations. Mickey Spiegel of Human Rights Watch, for instance, confirmed to me in a conversation in 2004 that she had not found factually incorrect information concerning torture and abuse in a Falun Gong document (obviously, claims about the "evil" of the Communist Party are of another order), although she wonders on occasion whether Falun Gong might exaggerate certain punishments. Most reports on human rights problems in China which address the campaign against Falun Gong, such as those prepared by Human Rights Watch, Amnesty International, or the Department of State, use Falun Gong–provided information, without necessarily insisting on its absolute veracity.

3. The following draws chiefly on Palmer, *Qigong Fever*, ch. 6.

4. Ibid., 162.

5. Ibid., 165.

6. See http://www.csicop.org/sb/9503/china.html (accessed 26 July 2006).

7. Nancy N. Chen, "Healing Sects."

8. Palmer, *Qigong Fever*, 211.

9. Tong, "An Organizational Analysis," 640–641.

10. Palmer, *Qigong Fever*, 249.

11. Li Hongzhi, *Essentials for Further Advancement*, 31.

12. Palmer, *Qigong Fever*, 215–216.

13. See, for example, Tan et al., eds., *Falun Gong yu minjian mimi jieshe*, 62–65.

14. Palmer, *Qigong Fever*, 266. On the Boxers, see Cohen, *History in Three Keys: The Boxers as Event, Experience, and Myth*; and Esherick, *The Origins of the Boxer Uprising*.

15. See Palmer, *Qigong Fever*, 267; and http://www.faluninfo.net/SpecialTopics/april25abridged.html (accessed 25 July 2006).

16. Palmer, *Qigong Fever*, 267:

According to Kang Xiaoguang, a researcher in the Chinese intelligence agency, whose sources are not specified and cannot be verified, Li Hongzhi had been given a full report of the Tianjin developments upon his arrival in Beijing. According to this account, in the evening of the 23rd, Li Hongzhi and the key Falun Gong organizers in China—Li Chang and Ji Liewu—decided to move the demonstration to Beijing.

17. See, for example, Ocko, "I'll Take It All the Way to Beijing: Capital Appeals in the Qing," 291–315.

18. See Johnson, *Wild Grass*, 268.

19. *Lishi huigu*, transcription of a radio transmission in China. Cited in Palmer, *La fièvre du qigong*, 397–398.

20. Tong, "Anatomy of Regime Repression in China."

21. Ibid., 804.

22. Ibid., 796.

23. Ibid., 814–815.

24. For a sample of the literature, see special issues of *Chinese Law and Government*, edited by Shiping Hua and Ming Xia under the titles "The Battle between the Chinese Government and Falun Gong" and "Falun Gong: Qigong, Code of Ethics and Religion."

25. According to Tong, "Anatomy of Regime Repression in China," 799, Jiang Zemin was himself responsible for the general structure of the attack on Falun Gong, proposing in a Politburo meeting held on 7 June 1999 a "strategy of gathering intelligence, exposing Li Hongzhi's political motives, systematically critiquing superstition, and publicizing cases where the practice of Falungong caused deaths, suicides or schizophrenia."

26. Ji, *Qishi hairen de Li Hongzhi*.

27. Ibid., 19.

28. Ibid., 20.

29. On the question of the participation of the psychiatric profession in China in the persecution of Falun Gong practitioners, see Munro, "Judicial Psychiatry in China and Its Political Abuses," 106-120; and the response to Munro by Lee and Kleinman, "Psychiatry in Its Political and Professional Contexts: A Response to Robin Munro," 21–25.

30. Ji, *Qishi hairen de Li Hongzhi*, 101–130.

31. Reprinted in *Chajin quti xiejiao zuzhi: Falü fagui*, 102–111.

32. Although, ironically, the very idea of brainwashing came to the anti-cultists through Robert Lifton and the American condemnation of the practices of the Chinese People's Liberation Army against American prisoners of war during the Korean War.

33. I might also note that this exposé genre also builds on the supposedly journalistic accounts of the exploits of qigong masters, which helped to build their followings during the qigong boom of the 1980s and 1990s. Most, if not all, of the masters either encouraged or allowed a journalist to record the story of their "coming out of the mountains," and, interestingly, two of the journalists, Ke Yunlu and Ji Yi, went on to become qigong masters of a sort themselves. The anti-qigong literature,

spearheaded by such people as Sima Nan, also took the form of *baogao wenxue* exposés.

34. Wei Daoru, "'Falun dafa' juefei Fofa," in Chen and Dai, *"Falun Gong" yu xiejiao*, 83.

35. Huang, "Fojiao dui Li Hongzhi de 'yeli' shuoxia," in Chen and Dai, *"Falun Gong" yu xiejiao*, 91. Both Wei's and Huang's arguments presumably grew out of a more general Buddhist opposition to the rise of Falun Gong, discussed in Palmer, *Qigong Fever*, 262–263.

36. Feng Jingyuan, "Xiejiao bushi zongjiao", presented at the International Symposium on Destructive Cults, Beijing, 9–11 November 2000, and reprinted in Wei Zhihong, ed., *Lun xiejiao: Shoujie xiejiao wenti guoji yantaohui lunji*, 18–25.

37. Ibid., 20.

38. Ibid., 23.

39. Zhao Kuangwei, "Xuanyang moshi lailin shi yiqie xiejiao de gongtong tezheng," presented at the International Symposium on Destructive Cults, Beijing, 9–11 November 2000, and reprinted in Wei Zhihong, ed., *Lun xiejiao: Shoujie xiejiao wenti guoji yantaohui lunji*, 90–97.

40. Ibid., 95.

41. See, for example, "Opium Can Be Benign," *Economist*, 21 February 2007.

42. Zhang Tongling and Xu Hongzhu, *Huashuo liangong zouhuo rumo*.

43. A literal translation of these characters is "to walk through fire [i.e., to court disaster] and to frequent devils."

44. Zhang and Xu, *Huashuo liangong*, 16.

45. Ibid., 18.

46. Nancy Chen, *Breathing Spaces*, 77–106, addresses the question of qigong deviation.

47. See, for example, Benson, *Timeless Healing: The Power and Biology of Belief.*

48. Zhang and Xu, *Huashuo liangong*, 22–25.

49. Ibid., 23.

50. Ibid., 24.

51. Tan et al., eds., *Falun Gong yu minjian mimi jieshe*, 153.

52. Ibid., 9.

53. Li Hongzhi, "Falun fofa: Zai Xinxilan Fahui shang jianghua." To my knowledge, this text has not been translated into English.

54. Li Hongzhi, *Falun fofa: Jingjin yaozhi*, 89–90.

55. "Master Li Hongzhi Met with Chinese Media in Sydney," 10–11. This is a translation of a transcription of a press conference given to Chinese media in Sydney on 2 May 1999. I have corrected the English.

56. Ibid., 28–30. I have corrected the English.

57. See www.clearwisdom.net for the English-language version and www .minghui.org for the Chinese-language version.

58. See Johnson, *Wild Grass*. The story of Chen Zixiu and her mother—a central narrative thread in Johnson's account—is found in the "Persecution" section of the Clear Wisdom site.

59. "Story of a Pregnant Practitioner Who Went to Appeal."

60. "A 64-Year-Old Female Shanghai Practitioner Brutally Tortured in Dong-cheng Detention Center, Beijing."

61. Ibid.

62. A famous model soldier from pre–Cultural Revolution China.

63. "A 64-Year-Old Female Shanghai Practitioner."

64. "Enduring Tribulations with No Hatred or Anger: Experience of a Practitioner from Jiangxi in Tiananmen Square Police Station."

65. As I write this sentence in early May 2005, one main thrust of Falun Gong activism is the elaboration of the Nine Commentaries on the Chinese Communist Party, accompanied by an effort to persuade party members to renounce their membership. Even if Falun Gong does not see itself as a possible replacement for the Communist Party, it is hard to see such initiatives as anything other than "political."

66. Chinese authorities claim to have shut down some eighty Falun Gong Web sites in the early days of the crackdown, but the sites' role in the Falun Gong organization seems to have been secondary at best. See Tong, "Anatomy of Regime Repression in China," 795; and Tong, "An Organizational Analysis."

67. Palmer, *Qigong Fever*, 266–277.

68. It is supposedly possible to access previous editions of Web sites via the site http://www.archive.org/index.php, but the previous versions do not seem to be fully functional, at least in the case of Falun Gong sites I have consulted.

69. "1. seek out a place where many people circulate, and distribute the flyers from above. 2. design a container (using lighted incense and string) which will come open some time later, thus allowing the practitioner to leave the area in security."

70. This did not work when I tried to send one to myself.

71. Among the many studies of this topic, see http://www.opennetinitiative.net/studies/china (accessed 28 July 2006); Human Rights Watch, "Freedom of Expression and the Internet in China"; and Walton, "China's Golden Shield: Corporations and the Development of Surveillance Technology in the People's Republic of China."

72. These speeches are available at http://www.falundafa.org/book/eng/daohang.htm under the title "Guiding the Voyage."

73. Li Hongzhi, "Teaching the Fa at the Great Lakes Conference in North America."

74. Ibid., 7.

75. Ibid., 9.

76. Ibid.

77. See http://www.clearwisdom.net/eng/2001/jan/02/jingwen010201.html (accessed 28 July 2006).

78. Ibid.

79. CESNUR provides access to journalistic reports on the self-immolation in major (and minor) newspapers throughout the world at www.cesnur.org (accessed 28 July 2006). Falun Gong provides a detailed analysis of the event on most if not all of its Web sites. See, for example, www.upholdjustice.org/English.2/s_i_investigation .pdf (accessed 28 July 2006).

80. Pan's reports can be found on the CESNUR site; see, for example, http://www.cesnur.org/2001/falun_jan07.htm#Anchor-3800 and http://www.cesnur.org/2001/falun_feb03.htm#Anchor-14210 (both accessed 28 July 2006).

81. Available at http://faluninfo.net/tiananmen/immolation.asp (accessed 28 July 2006).

82. Ian Johnson's *Wild Grass* provides a sobering account of the anti–Falun Gong campaign in Shandong.

83. Accessed 13 July 2006.

84. Stephen Gregory, "Testimony before the House Committee on International Relations Subcommittee on Africa, Global Human Rights, and International Operations, July 21, 2005."

85. See http://www.state.gov/g/drl/rls/rm/2001/3792.htm (accessed 23 March 2007).

86. See http://www.observechina.net/info/artshow.asp?ID=39862 (accessed 4 April 2007) for the Chinese version. An English-language translation is available at http://www.zonaeuropa.com/20060806_1.htm (accessed 4 April 2007).

87. Both reports, in addition to much other information, are available at http://OrganHarvestInvestigation.net (accessed 4 April 2007). I wrote to the address provided on the Web site, hoping to ask Matas and Kilgour questions about their investigation, but received no reply.

88. See http://www.forbes.com/business/forbes/2007/0129/072a.html?_requestid=2669 (accessed 8 April 2007).

89. See http://www.asianews.it/view.php?l=enandart=7771# (accessed 8 April 2007).

90. See http://www.laogai.org/news and http://news.bbc.co.uk/go/pr/fr/-/2/hi/asia-pacific/5386720.stm (accessed 8 April 2007).

91. See http://www.laogai.org/news/newsdetail.php?id=2679 (accessed 8 April 2007).

92. See http://www.clearwisdom.net/emh/articles/2000/12/28/9170.html (accessed 8 April 2007).

93. See http://www.faluninfo.net/displayAnArticle.asp?ID=9375 (accessed 12 April 2007).

CONCLUSION

1. Palmer, "Tao and Nation."

2. Bianco, *Origins of the Chinese Revolution.*

3. Johnson, *Peasant Nationalism and Communist Power: The Emergence of Revolutionary China, 1937–1945.*

4. Hartford and Goldstein, *Single Sparks: China's Rural Revolutions.*

5. Chen Yung-fa, *Making Revolution: The Communist Movement in Eastern and Central China, 1937–1945.*

6. Friedman, Pickowicz, Selden, with Johnson, *Chinese Village, Socialist State.*

7. Jung and Halliday, *Mao: The Unknown Story.*

8. I do not mean to suggest that I am the only one to have reflected on such questions. See, for example, *Modern China* 21.1 (January 1995), which is given over entirely to an excellent set of essays on the theme of "Rethinking the Chinese Revolution: Paradigmatic Issues in Chinese Studies."

## APPENDIX I

1. All of the tables treating Chinese immigration to the United States have been compiled from data taken from the Web sites of the U.S. Immigration and Naturalization Service and its successor, the Department of Homeland Security.

2. All of the tables treating Chinese immigration to Canada have been compiled from data taken from the Web sites of Citizenship and Immigration Canada.

# Bibliography

Ackerman, S. E. "Falun Dafa and the New Age Movement in Malaysia: Signs of Health, Symbols of Salvation." *Social Compass* 52.4 (2005): 495–511.

Adams, Ian, Riley Adams, and Rocco Galati. *Power of the Wheel: Falun Gong Revolution*. Toronto: Stoddard, 2000.

Asad, Talal. *Genealogies of the Secular: Discipline and Reasons of Power in Christianity and Islam*. Stanford, CA: Stanford University Press, 2003.

Barker, Eileen. "Presidential Address: The Scientific Study of Religion? You Must Be Kidding!" *Journal for the Scientific Study of Religion* 34.3 (1995): 287–310.

Barmé, Geremie R. *In the Red: On Contemporary Chinese Culture*. New York: Columbia University Press, 1999.

Bastid-Bruguière, Marianne. "La campagne antireligieuse de 1922" [The 1922 antireligion campaign]. *Extrême-Orient Extrême-Occident* 24 (2002) : 77–93.

Bell, Mark R., and Taylor C. Boas "Falun Gong and the Internet: Evangelism, Community, and Struggle for Survival." *Nova Religio* 6.2 (April 2003): 277–293.

Benson, Herbert. *Timeless Healing: The Power and Biology of Belief*. New York: Simon and Shuster, 1996.

Benton, Gregor. *Chinese in Europe*. New York: St. Martin's, 1998.

Bianco, Lucien. *Origins of the Chinese Revolution*. Stanford, CA: Stanford University Press, 1971.

Blackburn, Michael Lewis. "Movements of Power and Acts of Resistance: Falun Gong and the Politics of Everyday Life." M.A. thesis, University of Victoria (Canada), 2000.

Bokenkamp, Stephen R. "The Silkworm and the Bodhi Tree: The Lingbao Attempt to Replace Buddhism in China and Our Attempt to Place Lingbao Taoism." In *Religion and Chinese Society*: vol. 1, *Ancient and Medieval China*, ed. John Lagerwey, 341–384. Hong Kong: Chinese University Press, 2004.

"Brief Biography of Li Hongzhi, Founder of Falun Gong and President of Falun Gong Research Society." *Chinese Law and Government* 32.6 (2000): 14–23; also available online at http://web.archive.org/web/20001024123353; and http://www.compapp.dcu.ie/~dongxue/biography.html (accessed 21 July 2006).

Brook, Timothy. "Rethinking Syncretism: The Unity of the Three Teachings and Their Joint Worship in Late-Imperial China." *Journal of Chinese Religions* 21 (1993): 13–44.

Browne, Andrew. "China Jails U.S.–based Falun Gong Member," Reuters, 12 December 2000, available online at http://www.cesnur.org/testi/falun_077 .htm#Anchor-49575 (accessed 19 January 2007).

Bruseker, Gregor. "Falun Gong: A Modern Chinese Folk Buddhist Movement in Crisis." M.A. thesis, Department of Chinese Studies, Leiden University, The Netherlands, 2000.

Bruun, Ole. *Fengshui in China: Geomantic Divination between State Orthodoxy and Popular Religion*. Copenhagen: NIAS Press, 2003.

Burgdoff, Craig A. "How Falun Gong Practice Undermines Li Hongzhi's Totalistic Rhetoric." *Nova Religio* 6.2 (April 2003): 332–347.

Buruma, Ian. "The Sect That Became the Enemy of the State." *New York Times*, 15 July 1999.

*Chajin quti xiejiao zuzhi: Falü fagui* [Laws and regulations concerning the interdiction and elimination of heterodox organizations]. Beijing: Chunzhong chubanshi, 1999.

Chan, Cheris Shun-Ching. "Falun Gong in China: A Sociological Perspective." *China Quarterly* 179 (2004): 665–683.

Chang, Maria Hsia. *Falun Gong: The End of Days*. New Haven, CT: Yale University Press, 2004.

Chau, Adam Yuet. *Miraculous Response: Doing Popular Religion in Contemporary China*. Stanford, CA: Stanford University Press, 2006.

Cheek, Timothy C. "Redefining Propaganda: Debates on the Role of Journalism in Post-Mao China." In *Mainland China after the Thirteenth Party Congress*, ed. King-yuh Chang, 133–158. Boulder, CO: Westview, 1990.

———. *Propaganda and Culture in Mao's China: Deng Tuo and the Intelligentsia*. Oxford: Clarendon, 1997.

Ch'en, Kenneth K. S. *Buddhism: The Light of Asia*. Woodbury, NY: Barron's Educational Series, 1968.

Chen Hongxing and Dai Zhenjing, eds. *"Falun Gong" yu xiejiao* ["Falun Gong" and cults]. Beijing: Zhongjiao wenhua chubanshe, 1999.

Chen Hsi-Yuan. "Confucianism Encounters Religion: The Formation of Religious Discourse and the Confucian Movement in Modern China." Ph.D. diss., Harvard University, 1999.

Chen, Nancy N. *Breathing Spaces: Qigong, Psychiatry, and Healing in China.* New York: Columbia University Press, 2003.

———. "Healing Sects and Anti-Cult Campaigns." *China Quarterly* 174 (2003): 505–520.

———. "Urban Spaces and Experiences of Qigong." In *Urban Spaces in Contemporary China,* ed. Deborah Davis, 347–361. Washington, DC: Woodrow Wilson Center Press, 1995.

Chen Yung-fa. *Making Revolution: The Communist Movement in Eastern and Central China, 1937–1945.* Berkeley: University of California Press, 1986.

"Chinese Journalism Today: 'Of the Party and in the Market.'" *Journalism Studies* 1.4 (November 2000), special issue.

Ching, Julia. "Falun Gong: Religious and Political Implications." *American Asian Review* 19.4 (2001): 1–18.

Cohen, Paul A. *History in Three Keys: The Boxers as Event, Experience, and Myth.* New York: Columbia University Press, 1996.

Croizier, Ralph C. *Art and Revolution in Modern China: The Lingnan (Cantonese) School of Painting, 1906–51.* Berkeley: University of California Press, 1988.

———. *Traditional Medicine in Modern China: Science, Nationalism, and the Tensions of Cultural Change.* Cambridge, MA: Harvard University Press, 1968.

Dalby, Scott. "Between Discipline and Dignity: An Examination of the Appropriation and Reproduction of Falun Gong Cultivation in Western Spaces." M.Sc. thesis, Vrije University, Amsterdam, 2005.

Davis, Deborah, ed. *The Consumer Revolution in Urban China.* Berkeley: University of California Press, 1999.

Dean, Kenneth. *Taoist Ritual and Popular Cults of Southeast China.* Princeton, NJ: Princeton University Press, 1993.

De Groot, J. J. M. *Sectarianism and Religious Persecution in China.* Shannon: Irish University Press, 1974.

Deng, Zixian, and Fang Shimin. "The Two Tales of Falun Gong: Radicalism in a Traditional Form," 2000, available online at www.xys.org/xys/netters/Fang-Zhoiuzi/religion/2tales.doc (accessed 14 November 2003).

Despeux, Catherine. "Le *qigong*, une expression de la modernité chinoise" [*Qigong*: An expression of Chinese modernity]. In *En suivant la Voie Royale: Mélanges en hommage à Léon Vandermeersch* [Following the royal way: Mixtures in honor of Léon Vandermeersch], ed. Jacques Gernet and Marc Kalinowski, 267–281. Paris: Ecole française d'extrême-orient, 1997.

Dollelaere, Karel. *Soka Gakkai: From Lay Movement to Religion.* Salt Lake City, UT: Signature, 2001.

Dorfman, Diane. "The Spirit of Reform: The Power of Belief in Northern China." *Positions: East Asia Cultures Critique* 4.2 (1996): 253–289.

Duara, Prasenjit. "Pan-Asianism and the Discourse of Civilization." *Journal of World History* 12.1 (2001):99–130.

———. *Rescuing History from the Nation: Questioning Narratives of Modern China.* Chicago: University of Chicago Press, 1995.

————. *Sovereignty and Authenticity: Manchukuo and the East Asian Modern.* Lanham, MD: Rowman and Littlefield, 2003.

Dubois, Thomas David. *The Sacred Village: Social Change and Religious Life in Rural North China.* Honolulu: University of Hawaii Press, 2005.

Edelman, Bryan, and James T. Richardson. "Falun Gong and the Law: Development of Legal Social Control in China." *Nova Religio* 6.2 (April 2003): 312–331.

Eisenberg, David. *Encounters with Qi: Exploring Chinese Medicine.* New York: Norton, 1985.

"Enduring Tribulations with No Hatred or Anger: Experience of a Practitioner from Jiangxi in Tiananmen Square Police Station," 10 January 2000, available online at http://www.clearwisdom.net/emh/articles/2000/1/10/10675 (accessed 25 May 2005).

Esherick, Joseph W. *The Origins of the Boxer Uprising.* Berkeley: University of California Press, 1987.

Faison, Seth. "Beijing Journal: If It's a Comic Book, Why Is Nobody Laughing?" *New York Times*, 17 August 1999.

Falun Dafa Information Center, "Fact File," available online at http://www.faluninfo.net (accessed 17 July 2006).

Feng Jingyuan. "Xiejiao bushi zongjiao" [Cults are not religion]. In *Lun xiejiao: Shoujie xiejiao wenti guoji yantaohui lunji* [On cults: Essays from the First International Symposium on the Question of Cults], ed. Wei Zhihong, 18–25. Nanning: Guangxi renmin chubanshe, 2000.

Feuchtwang, Stephan, and Wang Mingming. "The Politics of Culture or a Contest of Histories: Representations of Chinese Popular Religion." *Dialectical Anthropology* 16 (1991): 251–272.

Fewsmith, Joseph. *China since Tian'anmen: The Politics of Transition.* New York: Cambridge University Press, 2001.

Fisher, Gareth. "Resistance and Salvation in Falun Gong: The Promise and Peril of Forbearance." *Nova Religio* 6.2 (April 2003): 294–311.

Friedman, Edward, Paul G. Pickowicz, Mark Selden, with Kay Ann Johnson. *Chinese Village, Socialist State.* New Haven, CT: Yale University Press, 1991.

Fullton, Bent. "Freedom of Religion in China: the Emerging Civic Discourse." In *Civic Discourse, Civil Society, and Chinese Communities*, ed. Randy Kluver, 53–66. Stamford, CT: Ablex, 1999.

Gong'anbu xuanchuanju [Propaganda Bureau of the Public Security Agency], ed. *Li Hongzhi: Qiren qishi* [Li Hongzhi: The man and his life]. Beijing: Chunzhong chubanshe, 1999.

Goossaert, Vincent. "Le destin de la religion chinoise au 20ème siècle" [The fate of Chinese religion in the twentieth century]. *Social Compass* 50.4 (2003): 429–440.

————. "1898: The Beginning of the End for Chinese Religion?" *Journal of Asian Studies* 65.2 (May 2006): 307–336.

Gregory, Stephen. "Testimony before the House Committee on International Relations Subcommittee on Africa, Global Human Rights, and International

Operations, July 21, 2005," available online at http://wwwa.house.gov/ international_relations/109/gre072105.pdf (accessed 28 July 2006).

Hammond, Phillip E. *Soka Gakkai in America: Accommodation and Conversion.* New York: Oxford University Press, 1999.

Hartford, Kathleen, and Steven Goldstein. *Single Sparks: China's Rural Revolutions.* Armonk, NY: Sharpe, 1989.

Hermann, Elfriede. "The Yali Movement in Retrospect: Rewriting History, Redefining 'Cargo Cult.'" *Oceania* 63.1 (1992): 55–71.

Hsu, Elisabeth. *The Transmission of Chinese Medicine.* Cambridge: Cambridge University Press, 1999.

Hua Chu and Zhong Han. *Falungong Fengbao* [The storm of Falun Gong]. Hong Kong: Pacific Century, 1999.

Huang, Chengju, Chris Lawe Davies, and Alan Wright. "Beyond Party Propaganda: A Case Study of China's Rising Commercialised Press," 2002, available online at http://www.ejournalism.au.com/ejournalist/propaganda.pdf (accessed 17 April 2004).

Huang, Julia C. *Wings of Belief: Modern Chinese Religious Transnationalism.* Leiden: Brill, 2003.

Huang Xianian. "Fojiao dui Li Hongzhi de 'yeli' shuoxia" [A Buddhist commentary on Li Hongzhi's nonsensical statements regarding "karma"]. In *"Falun Gong" yu xiejiao* [Falun Gong and cults], ed. Chen Hongxing and Dai Zhenjing, 87–99. Beijing: Zhongjiao wenhua chubanshe, 1999.

Human Rights Watch. *China: State Control of Religion.* New York: Human Rights Watch, 1997.

———. "Freedom of Expression and the Internet in China," available online at http://www.hrw.org/backgrounder/asia/china-bck-0701.htm (accessed 28 July 2006).

Hunter, Alan, and Don Rimmington, eds. *All under Heaven. Chinese Tradition and Christian Life in the People's Republic of China.* Kampen: Uitgeversmaatschappij J. H. Kok, 1992.

http://alternativchealing.org/guo_lin_qigong.htm

http://ceps.statcan.ca

http://fr.clearharmony.net

http://www.census.gov

http://www.cesnur.org

http://www.chinaqigong.net

http://www.clearwisdom.net

http://www.csicop.org/sb/9503/china.html

http://www.faluncanada.net

http://www.falunDafa.org

http://www.faluninfo.net

http://www.flghrwg.net

http://www.flgjustice.org

http://www.fofg.org

http://www.globalrescue.net
http://www.laogai.org
http://www.minghui.org
http://www.opennetinitiative.net/studies/china
http://www.OrganHarvestInvestigation.net
http://www.qimagazine.com
http://www.ruf.rice.edu/tnchina/commentary/ownby1000.htl
http://www.statcan.ca
http://www.tianhuaculture.net
http://www.upholdjustice.org
http://www.yanxinqingong.net

Irons, Edward. "Falun Gong and the Sectarian Religion Paradigm." *Nova Religio* 6.2 (April 2003): 244–262.

Ji Shi. *Qishi hairen de Li Hongzhi jiqi "Falun Gong"* [The cheat and criminal Li Hongzhi and his "Falun Gong"]. Beijing: Xinxing chubanshe, 1999.

Johnson, Chalmers A. *Peasant Nationalism and Communist Power: The Emergence of Revolutionary China, 1937–1945.* Stanford, CA: Stanford University Press, 1962.

Johnson, Ian. *Wild Grass: Three Stories of Change in Modern China.* New York: Pantheon, 2004.

Jones, Charles B. "Religion in Taiwan at the End of the Japanese Colonial Period," in *Religion in Modern Taiwan: Tradition and Innovation in a Changing Society,* ed. Philip Clart and Charles B. Jones (Honolulu: University of Hawaii Press, 2003), 10–35.

Jordan, David K., and Daniel L. Overmyer. *The Flying Phoenix: Aspects of Chinese Sectarianism in Taiwan.* Princeton, NJ: Princeton University Press, 1986.

Jung Chang and Jon Halliday. *Mao: The Unknown Story.* New York: Knopf, 2005.

Kang Xiaofei. *The Cult of the Fox: Power, Gender, and Popular Religion in Late Imperial and Modern China.* New York: Columbia University Press, 2006.

Kang Xiaoguang. *Falungong shijian quan toushi* [The complete story of the Falun Gong affair]. Hong Kong: Mingbao chubanshe, 2000.

Kaplan, Martha. *Neither Cargo nor Cult: Ritual Politics and the Colonial Imagination in Fiji.* Durham, NC: Duke University Press, 1995.

Karchmer, Eric. "Magic, Science, and *Qigong* in Contemporary China." In *China Off Center: Mapping the Margins of the Middle Kingdom,* ed. Susan D. Blum and Lionel M. Jensen, 311–322. Honolulu: University of Hawaii Press, 2002.

Keenan, Barry. *The Dewey Experiment in China: Educational Reform and Political Power in the Early Republic.* Cambridge, MA: Council on East Asian Studies, Harvard University Press, 1977.

Keith, Ronald, and Zhiqiu Lin. "The 'Falun Gong Problem': Politics and the Struggle for the Rule of Law in China." *China Quarterly* 175 (2003): 623–642.

Kipnis, Andrew B. "The Flourishing of Religion in Post-Mao China and the Anthropological Category of Religion." *Australian Journal of Anthropology* 12.1 (2001): 32–46.

Kohn, Livia. "Quiet Sitting with Master Yinshi: The Beginnings of Qigong in Modern China." In *Living with the Dao: Conceptual Issues in Daoist Practice* Cambridge, MA: Three Pines, E-Dao series, 2002.

Kunio, Miura. "The Revival of *Qi: Qigong* in Contemporary China." In *Daoist Meditation and Longevity Techniques*, ed. Livia Kohn, 331–358. Ann Arbor: University of Michigan, 1989.

Kwok, D. W. Y. *Scientism in Chinese Thought, 1900–1950*. New Haven, CT: Yale University Press, 1965.

Lampton, David M. *The Politics of Medicine in China: The Policy Press, 1949–1977*. Folkestone, Kent, England: Dawson and Sons, 1977.

Lee, Sing. "Chinese Hypnosis Can Cause Qigong-Induced Mental Disorders." *British Medical Journal* 320 (2000): 803.

Lee, Sing, and Arthur Kleinman. "Psychiatry in Its Political and Professional Contexts: A Response to Robin Munro." *Journal of the American Academy of Psychiatry and the Law* 30.1 (2002): 21–25.

Lei, Sean Hsiang-lin. "When Chinese Medicine Encountered the State: 1910–1949." Ph.D. diss., University of Chicago, 1999.

Li Hongzhi. *Essentials for Further Advancement*, available online at www.falundafa .org.

———. *Explaining the Content of Falun Dafa*, available online at www.falundafa.org.

———. *Falun Buddha Fa: Lecture at the First Conference in North America* (1998), available online at www.falundafa.org.

———. *Falun Buddha Fa: Lectures in the United States* (1997), available online at www.falundafa.org.

———. *Falun Dafa: Lecture in Sydney*, available online at www.falundafa.org.

———. *Falun fofa: Jingjin yaozhi* [The Falun Buddhist way: Essentials to further advancement], available online at http://www.falunDafa.org/book/chigb/ jjyz.htm.

———. "Falun fofa: Zai Xinxilan Fahui shang Jianghua" [The Falun Buddhist Way: A talk at the New Zealand Experience-Sharing Conference], 8 May 1999, available online at http://www.falundafa.org/book/chigb/newzland.htm.

———. *Guiding the Voyage* (n.d.), available online at www.falundafa.org.

———. "Mojie shi de renlei" [Humankind at the end of times]. In *Zhuan falun II*. This text, published in November 1995, was available on Falun Dafa Web sites in the early period, but was removed early in the twenty-first century.

———. "Teaching the Fa at the Great Lakes Conference in North America," 9 December 2000, available online at http://www.falundafa.org/book/eng/ daohang.htm.

———. *Zhuan falun*, available online at www.falundafa.org.

———. *Zhuan falun fajie* [Zhuan falun explained], available online at www .falundafa.org.

"Li Hongzhi qiren qishi" [Li Hongzhi: The man and his life]. In *Huoguo yangmin "Falun Gong"* ["Falun Gong": Calamity for the nation and for the people], 1:1–11. Beijing: Zhongguo renmin gong'an daxue chubanshe, 2002.

Li Junpeng. "New Religious Movements and the State: The Case of Falun Gong." M.A. thesis, Department of Sociology, University of North Carolina at Chapel Hill, 2006.

Lin, Hui, et al., eds. *Secrets and Benefits of Internal Qigong Cultivation: Lectures by Qigong Master Dr. Yan Xin*. Malvern, PA: Amber Leaf, 1997.

Lindstrom, Lamont. *Cargo Cult: Strange Stories of Desire from Melanesia and Beyond*. Honolulu: University of Hawaii Press, 1993.

Link, Perry, Richard Madsen, and Paul Pickowicz. *Popular China: Unofficial Culture in a Globalizing Society*. Lanham, MD: Rowman and Littlefield, 2001.

Liu, Xiuwu. *Jumping into the Sea: From Academics to Entrepreneurs in South China*. Lanham, MD: Rowman and Littlefield, 2001.

Lomanov, Alexander V. "On the Periphery of the 'Clash of Civilizations': Discourse and Geopolitics in Russian-Chinese Relations." In *The "New Migrant": State and Market Constructions of Modernity and Patriotism*, ed. Pal Nyiri, available online at http://cio.ceu.hu/courses/CIO/modules/Modul01Nyiri/pn1_index.html.

Louie, Andrea. *Chineseness across Borders: Renegotiating Chinese Identities in China and the United States*. Durham, NC: Duke University Press, 2004.

Lowe, Scott. "Chinese and International Contexts for the Rise of Falun Gong." *Nova Religio* 6.2 (April 2003): 263–276.

Lu, Zuyin. *Scientific Qigong Exploration: The Wonders and Mysteries of Qi*. Malvern, PA: Amber Leaf, 1997.

Luo Zhufeng, ed. *Religion under Socialism in China*. Armonk, NY: Sharpe, 1991.

Ma, Laurence J. C., and Carolyn L. Cartier, eds. *The Chinese Diaspora: Space, Place, Mobility, and Identity*. Lanham, MD: Rowman and Littlefield, 2003.

MacInnis, Donald E. *Religion in China Today: Policy and Practice*. Maryknoll, NY: Orbis, 1989.

———. *Religious Policy and Practice in Communist China: A Documentary History*. London: Hodder and Stoughton, 1967.

Madsen, Richard. "Understanding Falun Gong." *Current History* 99.638 (2000): 243–247.

"Master Li Hongzhi Met with Chinese Media in Sydney," 2 May 1999, available online at www.zhuichaguoji.org/en/upload/docs/ThirdPartyDoc/G_3.doc.

Micollier, Evelyne. "Un aspect de la pluralité médicale en Chine populaire: Les pratiques de Qi Gong—Dimension thérapeutique/dimension sociale" [An aspect of medical pluralism in the People's Republic of China: Qigong practices— therapeutic and social dimensions]. Ph.D. thesis, University of Provence (Aix-Marseille I), 1995.

———. "Control and Release of Emotions in Qigong Health Practices. " *China Perspectives* 24 (1999) : 22–30.

———. "Entre science et religion, modernité et tradition: Le discours pluriel des pratiquants du *qigong*" [Between science and religion, modernity and tradition: The plural discourse of *qigong* practitioners]. In *Soigner au pluriel: Essais sur le pluralisme médical* [Plural healings: Essays on medical pluralism], ed. Jean Benoît, 205–223. Paris: Karthala, 1996.

Miller, James, ed. *Chinese Religions in Contemporary Societies*. Santa Barbara, CA: ABC-CLIO, 2006.

Moyers, Bill D. *Healing and the Mind*. Garden City, NY: Doubleday, 1993.

Munekage, Natsuko. "China's New Religious Movement: Falun Gong's Cultural Resistance and Political Confrontation." M.A. thesis, University of Oregon, 2001.

Munro, Robin. "Judicial Psychiatry in China and Its Political Abuses." *Columbia Journal of Asian Law* 14.1 (2000): 106–120.

———. "Syncretic Sects and Secret Societies: Revival in the 1980s." *Chinese Sociology and Anthropology* 21.4 (1989): 1–111.

Naquin, Susan. *Millenarian Rebellion in China: The Eight Trigrams Uprising of 1813*. New Haven, CT: Yale University Press, 1976.

———. "The Transmission of White Lotus Sectarianism in Late Imperial China." In *Popular Culture in Late Imperial China*, ed. David Johnson, Andrew Nathan, and Evelyn Rawski, 255–291. Berkeley: University of California Press, 1985.

Nedostup, Rebecca. "Religion, Superstition, and Governing Society in Nationalist China." Ph.D. diss., Columbia University, New York, 2001.

Nyiri, Pal, and I. R. Savel'ev, eds. *Globalizing Chinese Migration: Trends in Europe and Asia*. Aldershot, England: Ashgate, 2002.

Ocko, Jonathan. "I'll Take It All the Way to Beijing: Capital Appeals in the Qing." *Journal of Asian Studies* 47.2 (1988): 291–315.

"Opium Can Be Benign." *Economist*, 21 February 2007.

Ots, Thomas. "The Silenced Body—The Expressive Leib: On the Dialectic of Mind and Life in Chinese Cathartic Healing." In *Embodiment and Experience: The Existential Ground of Culture and Self*, ed. Thomas Csordas, 116–136. Cambridge: Cambridge University Press, 1999.

Overmyer, Daniel L. *Folk Buddhist Religion: Dissenting Sects in Late Traditional China*. Cambridge, MA: Harvard University Press, 1976

———. *Precious Volumes: An Introduction to Chinese Sectarian Scriptures from the Sixteenth and Seventeenth Centuries*. Cambridge, MA: Harvard University Press, 1999.

———. "Values in Chinese Sectarian Literature: Ming and Ch'ing Pao-chüan." In *Popular Culture in Late Imperial China*, ed. David Johnson, Andrew Nathan, and Evelyn Rawski, 219–254. Berkeley: University of California Press, 1985.

Overmyer, Daniel L., ed. *Religion in China Today*. New York: Cambridge University Press, 2003.

Ownby, David. "China's Inner War." *New York Times*, op-ed, 15 February 2001. Reprinted as "Why China's Falun Gong Shakes Communist Rule." *International Herald Tribune*, op-ed, 16 February 2001, available online at http://www.cesnur.org/2001/falun_feb12.htm#Anchor-5185.

———. "Chinese Millenarian Traditions: The Formative Age." *American Historical Review* 104.5 (December 1999): 1513–1530.

———. "A History for Falun Gong: Popular Religion and the Chinese State since the Ming Dynasty." *Nova Religio* 6.2 (April 2003): 223–243.

———. "Imperial Fantasies: The Chinese Communist and Peasant Rebellions."
*Comparative Studies in Society and History* 43 (2001): 65–91.

———. "Recent Chinese Scholarship on the History of Secret Societies." *Late Imperial
China* 22.1 (June 2001): 139–158.

Ownby, David, and Qiao Peihua, trans. and eds. "Scriptures of the Way of the
Temple of the Heavenly Immortals." *Chinese Studies in History* 29.3 (1996):
1–101.

Palmer, David A. "La doctrine de Li Hongzhi: Le Falun Gong, entre sectarisme et salut
universel" [The doctrine of Li Hongzhi: The Falun Gong between sectarianism
and universal salvation]. *Perspectives chinoises* 64 (2001): 14–24.

———. "Falun Gong: La tentation du politique" [Falun Gong and the temptation of
politics]. *Critique internationale* 2 (2001): 36–43.

———. *La fièvre du qigong: Guérison, religion et politique en Chine, 1949–1999* [Qigong
fever: Healing, religion and politics in China, 1949–1999]. Paris: Editions de
l'Ecole des Hautes Etudes en Sciences Sociales, 2005.

"La fièvre du qigong. Guérison, religion et politique en Chine, 1949-1999" [Qinggong
fever: Healing, religion and politics in China, 1949-1999], PhD diss., École
Pratique des Hautes Études, 2002.

———. "Modernity and Millennialism in China: Qigong and the Birth of Falun
Gong." *Asian Anthropology* 2 (2003): 79–109.

———. "Le qigong au carrefour des 'discours anti': De l'anticléricalisme communiste
au fondamentalisme du Falungong" [Qigong at the crossroads of the "anti-
discourse": From Communist anticlericalism to Falun Gong fundamentalism].
*Extrême-Orient Extrême-Occident* 24 (2002): 153–166.

———. *Qigong Fever: Body, Science, and Utopia in China, 1949–1999.* New York:
Columbia University Press, 2007.

———. "Le qigong et la tradition sectaire chinoise" [Qigong and the Chinese sectarian
tradition]. *Social Compass* 50.4 (2003): 471–480.

———. "Tao and Nation: Li Yujie's Appropriation of Huashan Taoism." In *Taoism in
the Twentieth Century: Between Eternity and Modernity*, ed. David A. Palmer and
Liu Xun, forthcoming.

Palmer, Susan J. "From Healing to Protest: Conversion Patterns among the
Practitioners of Falun Gong." *Nova Religio* 6.2 (April 2003): 348–364.

Pan Peiqing. *Falun dafa zhi xianfan bianzheng* [Separating immortal from ordinary in
the Falun Dafa]. Taibei: Jinxing chuban, 2004.

Penny, Benjamin. "The Body of Master Li." *Australian Religious Studies Association*,
available online at http://users.senet.com.au/~nhabel/Lectures/penny.pdf.

———. "The Life and Times of Li Hongzhi: Falun Gong and Religious Biography."
*China Quarterly* 175 (2003): 643–661.

Perry, Elizabeth J. "Challenging the Mandate of Heaven." *Critical Asian Studies* 33.2
(2001): 163–180.

Perry, Elizabeth J., and Stevan Harrell, eds. "Syncretic Sects in Chinese Society."
*Modern China* 8.3 and 8.4 (1982).

Perry, Elizabeth J., and Mark Selden, eds. *Chinese Society: Change, Conflict, and Resistance.* New York: Routledge, 2003.

Porter, Noah. "Falun Gong in the United States: An Ethnographic Study." M.A. thesis, Department of Anthropology, University of South Florida, 2003.

———. "Professional Practitioners and Contact Persons: Explicating Special Types of Falun Gong Practitioners." *Nova Religio* 9.2 (2005): 62–83.

Potter, Pitman B. "Belief in Control: Regulation of Religion in China." *China Quarterly* 179 (2003): 319.

Powers, John, and Meg Y. M. Lee. "Dueling Media: Symbolic Conflict in China's Falun Gong Suppression Campaign." In *Chinese Conflict Management and Resolution,* ed. Guo-Ming Chen and Ringo Ma, 259–274. Westport, CT: Ablex, 2002.

Pure Insight Net. "A Chronicle of Major Events of Falun Dafa, Part 1 (Revised Edition)," available online at http://www.pureinsight.org/pi/index.php?news=2097.

Rahn, Patsy. "The Chemistry of a Conflict: The Chinese Government and Falun Gong." *Terrorism and Political Violence* 14.4 (2002): 41–65.

———. "Falun Gong: Beyond the Headlines." *Cultic Studies Journal* 7 (2000): 166–186.

Saich, Tony. *Governance and Politics of China.* New York: Palgrave Macmillan, 2004.

Schechter, Danny. *Falun Gong's Challenge to China: Spiritual Practice or "Evil Cult"?* New York: Akashic, 2000.

Scheid, Volker. *Chinese Medicine in Contemporary China: Plurality and Synthesis.* Durham, NC: Duke University Press, 2002.

Schipper, K. M. "Millénarismes et messianismes dans la Chine ancienne" [Millenarian and messianic movements in ancient China]. In *Actes of the XXVIth Conference of Chinese Studies,* 31–49 (Rome: IsMeo 1978).

Schwarcz, Vera. *The Chinese Enlightenment: Intellectuals and the Legacy of the May Fourth Movement of 1919.* Berkeley: University of California Press, 1986.

Seiwert, Hubert, in collaboration with Ma Xisha. *Popular Religious Movements and Heterodox Sects in Chinese History.* Leiden: Brill, 2003.

Shao Yong. *Zhongguo huidaomen* [Chinese heterodox sects]. Shanghai: Shanghai renmin chubanshe, 1997.

Shek, Richard, and Tetsuro Noguchi. "Eternal Mother Religion: Its History and Ethics." In *Heterodoxy in Late Imperial China,* ed. Kwang-Ching Liu and Richard Shek. Honolulu: University of Hawaii Press, 2004, 241–280.

Sheridan, James. *Chinese Warlord: The Career of Feng Yü-hsiang.* Stanford, CA: Stanford University Press, 1966.

Shiping Hua and Ming Xia, eds. "The Battle between the Chinese Government and Falun Gong." *Chinese Law and Government* 32.5 (September–October 1999).

———. "Falun Gong: Qigong, Code of Ethics and Religion." *Chinese Law and Government* 32.6 (November–December 1999).

Shue, Vivienne. "Global Imaginings, the State's Quest for Hegemony and the Pursuit of Phantom Freedom in China: From *Heshang* to Falun Gong." In *Globalisation and Democratisation in Asia*, ed. Catarina Kinnvall and Kristina Jönsson, 210–229. London: Routledge, 2002.

"A 64-Year-Old Female Shanghai Practitioner Brutally Tortured in Dongcheng Detention Center, Beijing," 18 July 2000, available online at http://www .clearwisdom.net/emh/articles/2000/7/18/7653.html.

Solinger, Dorothy. *Contesting Citizenship in Urban China: Peasant Migrants, the State, and the Logic of the Market*. Berkeley: University of California Press, 1999.

Spence, Jonathan D. *God's Chinese Son: The Taiping Heavenly Kingdom of Hong Xiuquan*. New York: Norton, 1996.

"Story of a Pregnant Practitioner Who Went to Appeal," 7 April 2000, available online at http://www.clearwisdom.net/emh/articles/2000/4/7/8511.html.

Szonyi, Michael. *Practicing Kinship: Lineage and Descent in Late Imperial China*. Stanford, CA: Stanford University Press, 2002.

Tan Songqiu, Qin Baoqi, and Kong Xiangtao, eds. *Falun Gong yu minjian mimi jieshe: Xiejiao Falun Gong neimu dajiemi* [Falun Gong and popular secret societies: The inside story of the heterodox cult Falun Gong]. Fuzhou: Fujian renmin chubanshe, 1999.

Tang Tsou. *The Cultural Revolution and Post-Mao Reforms: A Historical Perspective*. Chicago: University of Chicago Press, 1986.

Taylor, Kim. "'Improving' Chinese Medicine: The Role of Traditional Medicine in Newly Communist China, 1949–1953." In *Historical Perspectives on East Asian Science, Technology and Medicine*, ed. A. K. L. Chan, G. K. Clancey, and H. C. Loy, 251–263. Singapore: Singapore University Press, 2002.

Teng Ssu-yu and John K. Fairbank. *China's Response to the West: A Documentary Survey 1839–1923*. Cambridge, MA: Harvard University Press, 1954.

Ter Haar, Barend J. *The White Lotus Teachings in Chinese Religious History*. Leiden: Brill, 1992.

Thomas, Kelly A. "Falun Gong: An Analysis of China's National Security Concerns." *Pacific Rim Law & Policy Journal* 10.2 (March 2001): 471–496.

Thornton, Patricia M. "Framing Dissent in Contemporary China: Irony, Ambiguity and Metonymy." *China Quarterly* 171 (2002): 661–681.

Thuno, Mette. *Beyond Chinatown: New Chinese Migration and the Global Expansion of China*. Honolulu: University of Hawaii Press, 2006.

Tiandijiao Jiyuan jiaoshi weiyuanhui [The History Committee of the Ji Temple of the Tiandijiao], ed. *Tiandijiao jianshi* [A brief history of the Tiandijiao]. Taibei: Tiandijiao, 2005.

*Time Asia*, available online at http://cnn.com/ASIANOW/time/asia/magazine/1999/990510/interview3.html (accessed 20 October 2002).

Tong, James. "Anatomy of Regime Repression in China: Timing, Enforcement Institutions, and Target Selection in Banning the Falungong, July 1999." *Asian Survey* 42.6 (November–December 2002): 795–820.

———. "An Organizational Analysis of Falun Gong Structure, Communications, Financing." *China Quarterly* 171 (2002): 636–660.

"The Truth behind the April 25th Incident," available online at http://www.faluninfo
    .net/SpecialTopics/april25abridged.doc.
Unschuld, Paul U. *Medical Ethics in Imperial China: A Study in Historical Anthropology.*
    Berkeley: University of California Press, 1979.
Walton, Greg. "China's Golden Shield: Corporations and the Development of
    Surveillance Technology in the People's Republic of China," available online
    at http://www.ichrdd.ca/english/commdoc/publications/globalization/
    goldenShieldEng.html.
Wang Buxiong and Zhou Zhirong. *Zhongguo qigong xueshu fazhanshi* [The academic
    history of the evolution of qigong]. Changsha: Hunan kexue jishu chubanshe,
    1989.
Wei Daoru. " 'Falun dafa' juefei Fofa" ["Falun Gong" is absolutely not Buddhism]. In
    *"Falun Gong" yu xiejiao* ["Falun Gong" and cults], ed. Chen Hongxing and Dai
    Zhenjing, 83–96. Beijing: Zhongjiao wenhua chubanshe, 1999.
Welch, Holmes. *Buddhism under Mao.* Cambridge, MA: Harvard University Press,
    1972.
———. *The Buddhist Revival in China.* Cambridge, MA: Harvard University Press,
    1968.
Weller, Robert, and Meier Shahar. *Unruly Gods: Divinity and Society in China.*
    Honolulu: University of Hawaii Press, 1996.
Wessinger, Catherine. "Falun Gong Symposium: Introduction and Glossary." *Nova
    Religio* 6.2 (April 2003): 215–222.
Whitehouse, Harvey. *Inside the Cult: Religious Innovation and Transmission in Papua
    New Guinea.* Oxford: Clarendon, 1995.
Wickeri, Philip Lauri. *Seeking Common Ground: Protestant Christianity, the Three-Self
    Movement, and China's United Front.* Maryknoll, NY: Orbis, 1988.
Wolf, Arthur. "Gods, Ghosts, and Ancestors." In *Religion and Ritual in Chinese Society*,
    ed. Arthur Wolf, 131–182. Stanford, CA: Stanford University Press, 1974.
Wong, John, and William T. Liu. *The Mystery of China's Falun Gong: Its Rise and Its
    Sociological Implications.* Singapore: World Scientific Publishing and Singapore
    University Press, 1999.
Wu, Harry [Hongda]. *Troublemaker: One Man's Crusade against China's Cruelty.*
    London: Vintage 1997.
Xu, Jian. "Body, Discourse, and the Cultural Politics of Contemporary Chinese
    Qigong." *Journal of Asian Studies* 58.4 (1999): 961–991.
Yao, Weiming D. "A Rhetorical Analysis of Falun Gong in China: Inheritance of
    Tradition, Contemporary Appeals, and Challenge to the Social Order." Ph.D.
    diss., University of Pittsburgh, 2004.
Ye, Sang. *China Candid: The People on the People's Republic.* Berkeley: University of
    California Press, 2006.
Yi Pi Falun Gong Xueyuan [A group of Falun Gong practitioners]. *Jielu Changchun
    jishaoshu ren de yinmou* [Revealing the plot of a small group of people in
    Changchun]. Internal document, Falun Gong, 1999.

Zhang Tongling and Xu Hongzhu. *Huashuo liangong zouhuo rumo* [Let's talk about problems of deviation in qigong cultivation]. Changsha: Hunan renmin chubanshe, 1999.

Zhao Kuangwei. "Xuanyang moshi lailin shi yiqie xiejiao de gongtong tezheng" [Preaching that the end of the world is near is the common feature of all cults]. In *Lun xiejiao: Shoujie xiejiao wenti guoji yantaohui lunji* [On cults: Essays from the First International Symposium on the Question of Cults], ed. Wei Zhihong, 90–97. Nanning: Guangxi renmin chubanshe, 2000.

Zhongguo huidaomen shiliao jicheng bianzuan weiyuanhui, ed. *Zhongguo huidaomen shiliao jicheng* [Collection of historical materials on Chinese sects]. Beijing: Zhongguo shehui kexue chubanshe, 2004.

# Index